# The Multiracial Promise

D1237078

# THE MULTIRACIAL PROMISE

HAROLD WASHINGTON'S CHICAGO
AND THE DEMOCRATIC STRUGGLE
IN REAGAN'S AMERICA

## Gordon K. Mantler

THE UNIVERSITY OF NORTH CAROLINA PRESS | CHAPEL HILL

*This book was published with the assistance
of the Thornton H. Brooks Fund of the
University of North Carolina Press.*

Designed by April Leidig
Set in Kepler by Copperline Book Services, Inc.

Manufactured in the United States of America

Cover illustration courtesy of Chicago Public Library.

Library of Congress Cataloging-in-Publication Data
    Names: Mantler, Gordon Keith, 1972– author.
Title: The multiracial promise : Harold Washington's Chicago and the
    democratic struggle in Reagan's America / Gordon K. Mantler.
Other titles: Harold Washington's Chicago and the democratic struggle
    in Reagan's America | Justice, power, and politics.
Description: Chapel Hill : The University of North Carolina Press, [2023] |
    Series: Justice, power, and politics | Includes bibliographical references
    and index.
Identifiers: LCCN 2022036024 | ISBN 9781469673851 (cloth ; alk. paper) |
    ISBN 9781469673868 (paperback ; alk. paper) | ISBN 9781469673875 (ebook)
Subjects: LCSH: Washington, Harold, 1922–1987. | African American mayors—
    Illinois—Chicago. | Mayors—Illinois—Chicago. | Chicago (Ill.)—Politics
    and government—1951– | Chicago (Ill.)—Race relations. | United States—
    Politics and government—20th century.
Classification: LCC F548.54.W36 M36 2023 | DDC 977.3/11043—dc23/eng/20220817
LC record available at https://lccn.loc.gov/2022036024

**To Zella and Dashiell**

# Contents

List of Illustrations  ix

Introduction  1

1  From Politics to Protest  13

2  Shifting Alliances  39

3  Winning by Losing?  63

4  We Were Invisible  89

5  The Grassroots Challenge  117

6  Race and a New Democratic Coalition  147

7  Fighting Wars of All Kinds  163

8  Latinos and a Governing Majority  195

9  The Fragility of Coalitions  225

Epilogue. Legacies and the New Machine  253

Acknowledgments  265

Notes  269

Bibliography  315

Index  337

# Illustrations

**Figures**

Earl Dickerson and Brenetta Howell Barrett  27

Martin Luther King Jr. and Al Raby  31

Bobby Rush speaks to the press  51

Ralph Metcalfe and Mayor Daley  55

Cha-Cha Jiménez  76

Rudy Lozano at CASA meeting  95

*Keep Strong* cover of Helen Shiller  102

Jane Byrne and Tim Black  109

Lu Palmer and Harold Washington  119

Washington and Lozano at rally  139

Marion Stamps and Washington  141

Bernard Epton among supporters  153

Washington and Ed Vrdolyak chat  165

Women's Commission meeting  173

Nancy Jefferson and Washington  181

Chuy García and Washington in parade  197

Washington and Luis Gutiérrez campaign  211

Latino Commission meets with mayor  220

Tim Evans, Eugene Sawyer, and Jesse Jackson  241

Commission on Gay and Lesbian Issues gathers  243

Mayor Daley remembers Washington  255

**Map**

Chicago wards and neighborhoods  10

# The Multiracial Promise

You're sure not gonna liberate Black people
through electoral politics.—Gus Savage interview,
HistoryMakers Digital Archive

"**W**hen we started this campaign, we all said, 'We can win,'" an exuberant Harold Washington told supporters just days before the Chicago mayoral primary in February 1983. "About ten days ago, I woke up and said, 'We have won!'" The crowd of 200 Black, white, and Latino supporters packed into a South Side campaign office roared in response as the one-time machine politician now expressed confidence that his campaign's vast grassroots effort would beat the city's legendary Democratic political organization. It would take longer than expected to secure the victory; another month and a half passed, marked by vicious white race-baiting during a surprisingly competitive general election. But in the end, Washington made history. He would become the city's first African American mayor.[1]

But who was the "we" Washington referred to? Who won exactly? The multiracial crowd of boisterous supporters at Washington's February rally suggested that a diverse electoral coalition of many races, classes, and experiences were the clear winners. Those who had triumphed included not only the city's African Americans, who had long played an essential yet subservient role in its political machinery, but also Chicagoans of all races who were interested in reform and a sharp rejection of the status quo. Strikingly, many Americans across the nation—hungry for an alternative to the conservative federal policies of President Ronald Reagan—also felt encouraged by the news from Chicago.

Who actually won and lost that winter, however, proves more complicated. Despite the emergence of electoral politics as the most prominent vehicle of Black and Latino empowerment in the 1970s and 1980s, elections alone too often fell short in bringing about the democratic reforms needed to fulfill the citizenship rights of those most marginalized in Chicago and the nation. Harold Washington's 1983 victory surely demonstrated the importance of multiracial coalition-building and activism to the era's progressive mostly Democratic urban politics. Long-term development of neighborhood coalitions around issues such as worker and immigrant rights, affordable housing, community-police relations, public health, and economic development suggested something other than a linear march toward federal Reaganesque austerity. Rather, the Washington moment and movement showed how Black, Latino, and progressive white activists, when working together, could reshape politics and policy in U.S. cities and, of equal importance, provide a clear playbook for national politics.

But Chicago also underscored the obvious, unmistakable limits to electoral politics. Despite the campaign's incredible energy and organization, the Washington administration struggled to overcome a vast array of structural barriers to govern effectively, especially in ways that helped its most fervent, most marginalized, working-class supporters. White supremacy, deindustrialization, dysfunctional and corrupt institutions, as well as voters' own unrealistic and contradictory expectations at both the local and national levels slowed or thwarted many of the administration's most far-reaching reforms. Only when grassroots activism by neighborhood-based organizations and coalitions sustained political pressure on officials did genuine reform take place. And even in those cases, the progress was painstaking, with uncertain long-term results. Winning elections matters, of course. But ultimately, the story of Harold Washington's election and mayoralty is both a qualified triumph of the kind of grassroots multiracial activism that would become a cornerstone of the modern Democratic Party *and* a cautionary tale about placing too much weight—too many resources, too much emotional and physical energy, just too much attention—on electoral victories above all other civic action. The lessons of this history remain powerful for the present.

HAROLD WASHINGTON continues to be a legendary figure in Chicago. He served as mayor for just four and a half years, his service cut short by a massive heart attack the day before Thanksgiving in 1987. But more than a generation later, Chicagoans still refer to him by his first name and speak of him as if he had just left the room. His presence in the city continues to loom large, from the mammoth downtown library bearing his name to the diverse stamp his administration left on city policies, jobs, and contracts. Many of his allies remain active in politics, and periodically, memories of Washington's tenure and coalition flood back. In recent mayoral races, for instance, Washington's name continues to be invoked; in 2015, protégé Jesús "Chuy" García tried to recreate the Washington coalition and pushed incumbent and former Obama White House chief of staff Rahm Emanuel into a runoff. Four years later, Lori

Lightfoot became the first Black woman elected mayor, beating another Washington protégé, Toni Preckwinkle. What if "Harold" had lived, and how can we recreate that magic, his magic, people ask. Yet, in many ways, a clear understanding of this era remains obscured—particularly how Washington's election and administration reflect the nation's political and cultural priorities in the 1970s and 1980s, as well as the overall promise and limits of elections alone.

Historically, scholars, journalists, and the public have focused narrowly on Washington himself. "Harold" was a gifted, charismatic politician who could disarm the greatest skeptic with his oratory, intellect, and willingness to talk to anyone, eat anything, or dance to any music, especially on the campaign trail. In a classic example of great man theory, Washington's rise has been told as the triumphant tale of a one-time machine politician who showed his true colors by running as a reformer and freeing himself from the shackles of party bosses. As one biographer suggests, "It was the man more than the plan."[2] Both a more recent biography and powerful documentary—not to mention other accounts of the Washington era from the 1980s—largely embrace this view, characterizing Washington's advocacy of progressive reform as real and underscore that any lasting success relied heavily upon his personality and political skills.[3]

Other interpretations place more emphasis on African Americans collectively. "Above all, it was the massive, unprecedented, and crusade-like folk movement led by charismatics and 'race' men that swept Washington into office," conclude political scientists Melvin Holli and Paul Green. "The base for Washington's victory was simply the overwhelming Black vote."[4] Indeed, by registering and voting in record numbers, African Americans bucked the local regular Democratic Party organization—generally referred to as the "machine"—in a way that had not been seen since its advent in 1931. Black Chicagoans long had been taken for granted by an efficient, white-led machine that showered a few community leaders with patronage and money in exchange for votes—as well as silence on civil rights. But in 1983, African Americans rallied around Washington in such profound and personal ways that his election can be considered the pinnacle of independent Black political power in the city—even more so than the election of Chicago's adopted son Barack Obama as president a generation later.[5]

If African Americans were the clear winners in this interpretation, the losers were the members of the mostly conservative white Democratic machine, which experienced a steep decline in its influence and power after the death of longtime mayor, party chairman, and boss Richard J. Daley in 1976. In less than ten years beginning in 1979, the machine lost three straight mayoral elections, first to upstart former official Jane Byrne and twice to Harold Washington, as well as scores of other races in congressional, legislative, and ward districts across the city. By 1986, the regular Democratic organization had lost the city council majority as well. These three interpretive threads—related to each other and yet distinct—still dominate the extensive writing and commentary about Harold Washington's election.[6]

While valid, these interpretations fall short of fully explaining why Washington's triumph is so significant to understanding how urban politics in the nation changed in the 1970s and 1980s. Washington's coalition was not simply Black and white but also Latino and Asian, elite and working class, men and women, native Chicagoan and transplant, straight and gay. And Chicago reflected the shifting demographics of American cities, as African Americans became a plurality there (and the majority in other cities), Latinos achieved a critical mass outside of the Southwest, and gay men and lesbians made deeper commitments to urban living outside of the closet. As I and others have argued, multiracial coalitions, electoral or otherwise, were inherently situational, contingent, and fragile—full of real differences over ideology, strategy, and personality.[7] Sometimes these could be overcome. Alliances to elect local officials, form unions, and oppose state violence proved productive, something activists achieved as early as the 1930s and 1940s. But coalitions cannot easily be generalized or categorized as success or failure, in terms of winners or losers. Even at the peak of Washington's coalition, Chicago's multiracial politics reflected these contingencies as well, with implications for the nation as a whole.[8]

Chicago in the 1980s also demonstrated the ongoing influence of the social movements of a generation before. Undoubtedly, the Black freedom struggle—including Dr. Martin Luther King Jr.'s Chicago Freedom Movement in 1966 and the local Black Panther Party of Fred Hampton two years later—made Black electoral victories more possible. Through the long-term development of African American community organizations and networks and the rising expectations of what was possible in the city in terms of minority access to first-class jobs, education, and dignity, activists in labor unions to street gangs to everything in between created an institutional foundation necessary to win elections on their own terms.[9] This work included the clear articulation of community control by Hampton and Black Power advocates in the city, as well as calls for a Rainbow Coalition with people of other races by the Black Panthers and later Jesse Jackson's organization and national presidential campaigns. "Insurgent demands for Black indigenous control," writes political scientist Cedric Johnson of the 1970s, "converged with liberal reform initiatives to produce a moderate Black political regime and incorporate radical dissent into conventional political channels."[10] This political convergence was witnessed in major American cities from Philadelphia to Los Angeles and prominently signaled by the National Black Political Convention in 1972, held in Gary, Indiana, a majority-Black steel town that had elected Richard Hatcher as its first Black mayor five years before. The convention, convened by Hatcher, Detroit congressman Charles Diggs, and Black Power poet and Newark activist Amiri Baraka, brought together Blacks across the ideological spectrum and, despite those sharp differences, under-scored activists' belief that winning elective offices had become a, if not *the*, primary vehicle of African American empowerment in the 1970s.[11]

Movements by women, gay men and lesbians, Latinos, poor whites, and pro-gressive workers played roles similar to that of the Black freedom struggle in shaping both city and national politics. These movements staked out clear iden-tities and built networks with other communities around common goals such as opposition to police violence and workplace discrimination. Whether it was the Chicago Black United Communities, Chicanos' Center for Autonomous So-cial Action, the Chicago Women's Liberation Union, the Chicago Gay Alliance, the Black Panthers and Young Lords, or the Young Patriots and Intercommunal Survival Committee (ISC), the street protests, marches, boycotts, and other ac-tivism for basic human rights in the 1970s evolved slowly but steadily toward the pursuit of formal levers of power in the 1980s. The result was a modest re-shaping of political power in the city and the possibility of such around the nation.[12]

One of the most important legacies of the Washington era was the empower-ment of Latinos and other historically marginalized groups, including Asians, women, and gay men and lesbians, in electoral politics and policy. Not only did the mayor and his allies give Latinos critical support in redrawing council district maps, but they also helped Latino communities evade the worst of tra-ditional gentrification and urban renewal efforts. In turn, Latinos maintained and rebuilt these communities, which then became strongholds for Mexican American and Puerto Rican politicians, reflecting a trend in cities such as Hous-ton, San Antonio, and Los Angeles. With some irony, Latinos emerged from the Washington era stronger and more politically empowered in Chicago than even Blacks; a generation after Washington, Latinos remained a more central, sought-after component of the city's governing coalition, a reality increasingly reflected as national parties fought over the so-called "Latino vote."[13]

Yet Washington and his Black and Latino counterparts in mayor's offices across the country struggled to address the grinding poverty, police violence, cultural isolation, and other inequalities of urban America. They may have largely kept the cities from burning as they did in the 1960s, but it was primar-ily by what historian Michael Katz calls "managing marginalization" through "selective incorporation" and "mimetic reform." More often than not, Black and Latino mayors such as Washington received the benefit of the doubt from constituents, even if they only achieved symbolic policy changes. For instance, many scholars of the carceral state have demonstrated that not only has police violence toward and state-sponsored terror of Black and Latino communities been endemic to modern U.S. history, but such brutality also continued no matter who was in charge.[14] Thus, the turn to electoral politics—especially during what could be called the Age of Reagan—revealed serious questions about how much the attainment of traditional political power, ironically, could fulfill minorities' citizenship rights. Chicago already boasted a long tradition of some modicum of formal Black political life, back to the 1920s. But, at mid-century, Chicago's one Black congressman and six Black aldermen remained largely self-serving and ineffective in helping the greater community. By the 1970s, some candidates for office were bona fide freedom movement activists. But they struggled with the transition from the street protests of the 1960s to more inside-the-system electoral work, although for different reasons than their predecessors. While drawing on their earlier efforts both practically and ideologically, activists' commitment to traditional politics ended up representing a break from the more radical impulses of the movement, even "community control"—more so than those scholars who fully embrace the language and framing of a "long civil rights movement" usually acknowledge.[15]

The emphasis on a handful of representatives walking the halls of power, be it City Hall, the courthouse, the state legislature, or Congress, quietly, perhaps inadvertently, risked diluting the rich protest culture and potential for grassroots revolutionary change emitted by the freedom struggle. Of course, some organizing tactics worked in electing candidates. The supposed halcyon days of King, the Student Nonviolent Coordinating Committee (SNCC), and others in the nonviolent struggle should not be romanticized for eschewing their own compromises; they made plenty of them, as did their Black Power counterparts.[16] Nor does it seem entirely accurate to label the era's emerging Black political class as inherently "neocolonial," as political theorist Adolph Reed suggested, for instance.[17] But something changed as communities stressed the concentration of political power in a relative handful of Black and Latino individuals—even if one of them was the celebrated Harold Washington.

This reality becomes even clearer amid the broader national context of resurgent political conservatism, deindustrialization, stagnant wages, and a federal retreat from the social safety net and social contract promised since the New Deal. On its face, the emergence of Washington's coalition in Chicago undermines the common interpretation of the 1980s as simply an Age of Reagan, in which political conservatism vanquished liberalism.[18] Clearly, a progressive, grassroots alternative emerged during this period—as suggested by the historic presidential campaigns of Jesse Jackson in 1984 and 1988, and the movements for sanctuary, a nuclear freeze, environmental justice, and AIDS awareness and funding.[19] Washington supporters—even the mayor himself—were engaged in several of these movements. Much of this "front porch politics," to quote Michael Foley, was driven by people's personal experiences, at times emotional impulses "to defend their home, hearth, and livelihood in circumstances where government failed to do so."[20] But rather than reject a role for government, as the dominant narratives of the 1980s—really many common narratives of American history—often contend, citizens sought state remedies to protect themselves. Perhaps the level of social intervention seen during the New Deal would not return, but a thread of what historian Lizabeth Cohen called "moral capitalism," in which citizens expected a "fair share" in an otherwise capitalist society, persisted in the nation's politics. Predictions that the "era of big government" was over were premature. In fact, the state remained essential. And Americans—conservative and liberal, Democratic and Republican—despite their rhetoric to the contrary, embraced state solutions, big and small. Even Ronald Reagan himself, as both president and governor of California, championed the state—albeit the more punitive side of it more times than not.[21]

In the case of Chicago, including many who supported Harold Washington and others against the local political machine, these politics often translated into demands for City Hall to do more, not less, in response to federal cutbacks and cultural cues by the Reagan administration. Those demands ranged from protection from market-driven gentrification, local and federal police violence, and pandemics to affirmative efforts at job creation, more genuine representation, and education. Thus, the Reagan moniker for the era remains appropriate to some extent, given how much federal policies and attitudes toward race, class, gender, and sexual orientation influenced the local debate—not just economically but socially and culturally as well. To build a winning progressive coalition against a conservative machine from his own Democratic Party, Washington consistently campaigned against the president and the GOP's policies. First as a freshman congressman and then as a big-city mayor, Washington remained one of Reagan's fiercest critics—from demonstrating how the administration's social spending cuts hurt the city to condemning the impact an expanded Cold War in Central America, South Africa, and elsewhere had on the city's immigrant communities. Moreover, conservatives in the nation's capital hamstrung the city's efforts to address, in humane ways, AIDS, drug-related violence, deindustrialization, and scores of other urban challenges. Thus, the conservatism espoused by Ronald Reagan and his allies in both parties loomed large during this era, but in a way that was more complex and more nuanced than normally thought.

WASHINGTON PREDICTED during his first term that he would be mayor for twenty years—a tenure that would have rivaled Richard J. Daley's twenty-one-year reign.[22] Instead, Washington died seven months into his second term, plunging city politics into disarray and his supporters into despair. Much of what Washington and his followers wanted to accomplish—as messy and contradictory as these policies could be—had just started, often coming to fruition by pressure from below and outside the administration. And, thus, what reforms did occur proved quite fragile in application and, at the very least, needed more time to make a real impact. This was particularly the case with Washington's broad efforts to make the government more transparent and more inclusive of all Chicagoans. But his successor, Eugene Sawyer, turned out to be primarily a caretaker mayor who lost to a retooled and resurgent Democratic machine under Richard M. Daley, the state's attorney and boss's son, in 1989. With some irony, it would be the younger Daley who became the longest-serving mayor in Chicago history instead. It was an extraordinary turnaround for a political organization counted out just two years before. While not inevitable by any means, as some scholars contend, this result surprised few longtime observers of Chicago politics. The machine, after all, was arguably the city's most durable institution in the twentieth century, in part because it was malleable enough for Daley to fully embrace the neoliberal policies that had become the norm for both national political parties by the 1990s.[23]

In Chicago, some of Washington's policies endured into the twenty-first century, but more often than not they reflected rhetorical and symbolic action rather than substantive long-term policy shifts. The younger Daley—and his successor, Rahm Emanuel, fresh out of the Obama White House—did not return to the exact ways of Daley's father but instead relied increasingly on a corporate network of advisers and financial supporters, infused with "pinstripe patronage," that transformed the once-industrial city into a neoliberal icon marked by remarkable inequality. Meanwhile, the hollowing out of working-class communities of all colors, whom Washington had tried to represent, instead accelerated, as they found themselves battling rampant gang violence, closed schools and firehouses, public health crises, and a political class—white, Black, and Latino—too often out of touch with its constituents. The surprising rise of former federal prosecutor and political outsider Lori Lightfoot, the city's first Black woman and lesbian to be elected mayor, sadly seems to have led to more of the same. Police killings of Black and Latino citizens, economic and neighborhood inequalities, and other twenty-first-century urban challenges have persisted apace, compounded by the COVID-19 pandemic and highlighted by the protests sparked by George Floyd's death. Lightfoot's infamous decision to raise the bridges over the Chicago River to isolate mostly Black South Siders from the predominantly white North Side during the 2020 protests epitomized her perspective on public safety for many Chicagoans as well as reflected a seeming inability for even liberal politicians to combat basic assumptions about race, criminality, and inequality.[24]

One might be tempted to interpret the brevity of Washington's term and the ultimate resilience of the machine as persuasive evidence of the city's exceptionalism politically. Where else can the kinds of political drama Chicago is known for, and glimpsed in these pages, really occur? Without a doubt, Chicago *is* exceptional in many ways—its culture, its industriousness, its gruff charm, its weather, its occasional inferiority complex. But the city's politics are less exceptional than meets the eye. As the Harold Washington movement and moment suggests, Chicago's politics resemble those of other cities in many ways—perhaps with different political labels—and, thus, do offer an instructive window into how much we really should rely primarily on electoral politics, in contrast to other kinds of organizing, to achieve a more just society, then and now.

Who won on that chilly Chicago night in 1983? The answer, as we will see, may be "nobody," or no one entirely.

## A Note about Terminology

This book uses *African American* and *Black* as generally interchangeable terms for people of African descent in the United States—a decision consistent with the use of the historical actors in these pages, who embraced both terms during their lifetimes. That includes the capitalization of *Black* as an affirmation of a distinctive cultural and political experience, including remarkable levels and kinds of discrimination. In contrast, I have left *white* lower-cased—not to suggest that whites are somehow not raced; of course they are—but more to reflect that people who call themselves white do not share the same history and culture or face the same sort of discrimination as Black Americans, although I recognize some will disagree with this decision. Moreover, the terms used to identify Spanish-speaking people (and their descendants) are even more contested. In these pages, I use *Latino* to describe Spanish-speaking people of

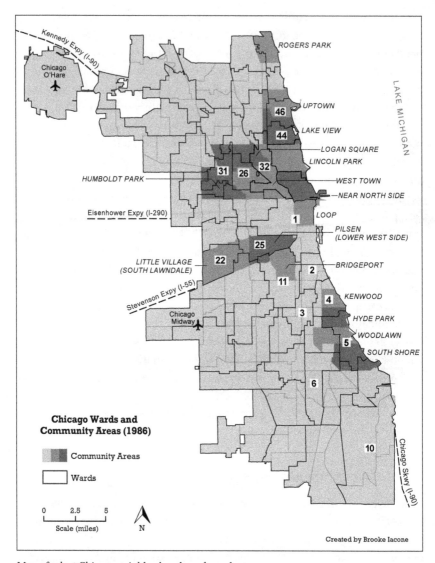

Map of select Chicago neighborhoods and wards.

different ancestral nationalities in the United States, including Mexican Americans, Puerto Ricans, and Cuban Americans. This contrasts with *Hispanic*, a term still popular today that nonetheless privileges European heritage over Indigenous and African influences in the Americas, or *Latinx*, an important recognition of gender inclusion that the historical actors in this book, however, would not recognize or use themselves. While I suspect that not all readers will agree with that decision either—especially a younger generation of readers—I have erred on the side of my informants who came of age in the 1970s and 1980s and, for those still with us, prefer the term *Latino* to identify themselves now as they did then. Lastly, when referring to people of Mexican descent, I use *Mexican American* unless specifically referring to recent immigrants from Mexico (*Mexican immigrant*) or to a person of Mexican descent who identified as part of the Chicano movement of the late 1960s and 1970s (*Chicano*). This discussion is all a reminder about how language is dynamic, not static. If I was writing in 1950 or 2000 or 2050—and not in 2022—my choices would surely be different.[25]

Also, while Chicago's racial and ethnic map has long been dynamic, for the purposes of this book, understanding the city's social geography alongside its physical geography is helpful. I identify neighborhoods generally as on the North, West, South, Northwest, or Southwest Side of Chicago. These references might be intuitive for Chicagoans, but for those unfamiliar, they refer to a neighborhood's relationship to the Loop, Chicago's downtown business district. The additional "Near" suggests anything generally within a few miles in that direction from the Loop. There is no east side of Chicago, of course, because that would be in Lake Michigan.

## CHAPTER 1

# From Politics to Protest

We were able to get some people interested in what we
were talking about, which was to not denigrate marches
and demonstrations but saying that there should be another
element, and that was heading toward the ballot box.
—Brenetta Howell Barrett interview

"The future of the Negro struggle," wrote Bayard Rustin in February 1965, "depends on whether the contradictions of this society can be resolved by a coalition of progressive forces which becomes the effective political majority in the United States." In his now famous treatise, "From Protest to Politics," the veteran civil rights organizer, peace movement leader, and confidante of Dr. Martin Luther King Jr. went on to cite as models the coalitions assembled in support of the 1963 March on Washington, the Civil Rights Act of 1964, and, perhaps most strikingly, the landslide election of President Lyndon Baines Johnson later that year. It would be Black Americans—along with trade unionists, white liberals, and socially conscious people of faith—who could bring about "the reorganization of American political life" by proposing "alternatives to technological unemployment, urban decay, and the rest." What would not work, according to Rustin, was a go-it-alone, "no win" strategy of Black isolation that routinely condemned white liberals as enemies; conservative Republicans and racist southern Democrats were the real foes. "There is a limit to what Negroes can do alone," he concluded, in a not-so-subtle swipe at Black nationalist critics, such as Malcolm X and, increasingly, members of SNCC.[1]

At the time, many activists viewed Rustin's move toward more traditional politics as "disquieting," to quote his biographer. Despite his success in organizing the 1963 march, Rustin's criticism of Black nationalism, support for Johnson's "guns and butter" policies that implicitly accepted the Vietnam War, and his openly gay identity made him increasingly anathema to a shifting civil rights constituency. Moreover, the "classical" period of the civil rights struggle, as he acknowledged, already incorporated a heavy dose of politics. This was not simply about integrating lunch counters and other public accommodations. The inclusion of jobs and housing in activist demands in 1963 Birmingham were, for instance, "a conscious bid for political power," wrote Rustin. "Direct-action techniques are being subordinated to a strategy calling for the building of community institutions or power bases." Of course, he downplayed the dispiriting experience of Mississippi activists who for years had pursued voter registration and the development of the interracial Mississippi Freedom Democratic Party, only to be denied seats in favor of white supremacists at the 1964 Democratic National Convention. "We left Atlantic City with the knowledge that the movement had turned into something else," recalled activist Cleveland Sellers. "Our struggle was not for civil rights, but for liberation."[2]

Despite such realities, Rustin's emphasis on political power proved prescient in key ways. Just months after publishing his essay in *Commentary*, a vast protest movement prompted the events of Selma and the rapid passage of the Voting Rights Act, toppling most of the legal suffrage obstacles that Blacks had faced in the Deep South. More and more African Americans—and Latinos—including those who had been activists, began running for political office and winning inside and outside of the South. Some were quixotic candidacies such as Eldridge Cleaver's presidential run on the Peace and Freedom Party ticket or Chicano land grant rights leader Reies López Tijerina's bid for governor of New Mexico, both in 1968.[3] Most, however, were more serious bids for real political power inside the structure—from former Congress of Racial Equality president James Farmer, who lost his 1968 run for Congress in New York City, to the Lowndes County Freedom Organization's John Hulett, whose election as sheriff in 1966 made him the most important official in that rural Alabama county.

More than any individual race or candidate, the National Black Political Convention, held in 1972 in Gary, Indiana, signaled the emergence of electoral politics as central to the ongoing movement, as well as the shortsightedness of Rustin's views on Black Power and the relationship between politics and community control. An "intriguing troika" of Gary mayor Richard Hatcher, Congressman Charles Diggs of Detroit, and Black Power poet and activist Amiri Baraka of Newark, New Jersey, organized the convention, at which about 3,000 official delegates gathered and another 4,000 attended as observers. Nearly every Black constituency was present, from Democrats and Republicans to nationalists, integrationists, and everything in between. The delegates flirted with the founding of an all-Black third political party—"It's Nation Time," as Jesse Jackson declared—but the convention ultimately embraced a clear commitment to electoral politics through the Democratic and Republican Parties as the best way to improve material conditions for Black America. Parallel to African American efforts, Chicano movement activists briefly pursued a third party called La Raza Unida in the early 1970s, mostly in the Southwest, only to abandon it after years of factionalism in favor of running as major-party candidates. All of this meant that African Americans and Latinos increasingly sought out the political allies Rustin had predicted years before.[4]

In one sense, the rapid rise of Black and Latino participation in electoral politics across the nation, North and South, West and East, was nothing less than remarkable. Few could have predicted just a few years earlier that by 1973 there would be more than 2,600 Black elected officials—including 1,200 in the South—and several hundred Latinos, mainly in the Southwest. In contrast, in 1941, there had been only 33 Black officials, just 2 in the South. And while the increase had slowed by the mid-1970s, African Americans continued to win elected office in increasingly prominent places north and south, such as mayoral contests in Detroit and Oakland and congressional races in Houston and Atlanta. African Americans even occasionally won seats in places where they remained a numerical minority, such as Tom Bradley's mayoral victory in Los Angeles. Each of these victories featured its own peculiarities and factors specific to that city and candidate. But, more times than not, these politicians saw themselves as continuing the freedom struggles of the 1960s and the "pursuit of first-class citizenship," writes one scholar. They had an obligation to advance the interests of their constituents.[5]

In Chicago, a similar phenomenon played out. While Black Chicagoans had not lost their voting rights in the same way as their southern counterparts during the Gilded Age, they had witnessed sharp limits on the efficacy of those rights. Chicago produced the nation's first Black Democratic congressman and a genuine Black political boss, but white ethnic dominance of the machine kept African American power under increasingly tight constraints. When Richard J. Daley became mayor and the undisputed party boss in 1955, he stripped Black submachine boss William Dawson of much of his power. By the late 1950s, and accelerating throughout the next decade, protests by African Americans, Mexican Americans, Puerto Ricans, and poor whites against housing and school segregation, police brutality, and welfare limits began to change the city's political landscape, as similar coalitions did in other cities.

Thus, the progressive electoral coalition Rustin envisioned slowly began to form in Chicago, in fits and starts, as activists of many stripes attempted to translate their protests against the existing biracial political elite into a more representative form of electoral politics. A venue once seen as dominated by "hardheaded realists who are willing to trade political positions and favorable legislation for votes," according to scholars St. Clair Drake and Horace Cayton, gradually became more attractive to those who had dedicated themselves to civil rights.[6] By 1968, African Americans and a few of their independent allies who explicitly identified with the freedom struggle, including the city school boycotts of 1963 and the Chicago Freedom Movement three years later, ran for office; a handful even won. But the relationship between Black Power, civil rights, and electoral politics turned out to be far more intertwined, far more complex than Rustin and most scholars have suggested. The road "from protest to politics" was a far windier one, full of potholes and other obstacles municipal politicians often encounter, than traditional narratives of Black and Latino politics in the 1960s normally allow. In fact, in Chicago and the nation writ large, the process could be more accurately described as "from politics to protest" and back again.

THEY CALLED IT the promised land. The warmth of other suns. The Black Metropolis. For at least four generations, African Americans flocked to Chicago to escape the living hell of the South's Jim Crow racial caste system and to seek out greater opportunity for themselves and their families. They went far from home, braved far worse weather, into a far more urban area in the hopes of finding better jobs, schools, and lives than they had in the South. Sometimes they followed a father, an aunt, or some other relative to the city. Sometimes they simply jumped on the Illinois Central or another railroad line to see where it would take them. They went to other cities, too, such as Detroit, Baltimore, and Los Angeles. But more than any place, the destination was Chicago. On the other side, they often found themselves working in the industries that made the city famous—meatpacking, steel, and the railroad. Or they worked in the defense industry sparked by war in the 1910s and again in the 1940s. They also found conditions that were better—but not much better—than those they left behind in Mississippi, Alabama, Louisiana, and elsewhere in the Deep South. Housing in the city's Black Belt, even for middle-class African Americans, was usually crowded and cramped, prone to fires and rats. Petty crime and worse, sometimes spilling from Black neighborhoods' lucrative and illegal numbers rackets, plagued the streets, as did trash and grime. The public schools were better than those in the South but strikingly segregated and increasingly crowded and underresourced. And while many Blacks lived just a short train ride away from the downtown Loop, most businesses there refused to serve them.[7]

The 1919 race riots were particularly eye-opening and unnerving for African

Americans, revealing how violence reinforced the city's inequalities. Sparked by the stoning death of Black swimmer Eugene Williams, who crossed an invisible Black-white demarcation line at the Twenty-Third Street beach on Lake Michigan, the violence lasted more than a week. Thirty-eight people died, 23 of them Black, and another 537 were injured, two-thirds of them Black, as white mobs indiscriminately attacked them in their own neighborhoods. Blacks, many of them veterans of World War I, fought back, preventing worse carnage. But despite Blacks' clear signal that they would valiantly protect themselves and their communities with guns and fists, whites' message to African Americans, new arrivals and longtime residents alike, remained crystal clear: Do not linger outside of your neighborhood. Do not take our jobs, or our daughters and sisters. Do not think about moving outside of where we say you can live. Among the leaders of the rioting whites were members of the Hamburg Athletic Club, an Irish American youth gang to which future mayor Richard J. Daley belonged and which he eventually led. Because the white youths were never prosecuted or even investigated for their role in the riots, it is not clear if Daley participated, but many historians reasonably suspect that he did, given how important the gang was to his youth and eventual rise in local politics.[8]

The violence by such gangs, in coordination with the police, masked the other organizations behind the solidification of the city's color line. Alarmed by the seemingly never-ending influx of Black migrants to the South and West Sides, the Chicago Real Estate Board in 1917 established a strategy of "block-by-block segregation," in which blocks were to be filled with African Americans before another block could be touched; four years later, the board reinforced this rule by calling for the "immediate expulsion from the Chicago Real Estate Board . . . any member who sells a Negro property in a block where there are only white owners." Banks, even the Black-owned Binga Bank, the city's first, made sure to lend only to African Americans buying in areas deemed Black-friendly. The bank's founder, Jesse Binga, had made a fortune, among other things, by gouging Black renters for subpar housing—illustrating the uncomfortable truth that a significant portion of the Black middle class in Chicago and other American cities may have been unethical landlords themselves. The Board of Education established neighborhood schools as policy. The local Roman Catholic Church established Saint Monica's Parish as reserved for Blacks only. And the Republican Party organization of Mayor William "Big Bill" Thompson, which increasingly depended on African American votes in the city, viewed a concentrated Black electorate as to its advantage in voter organization and turnout. The color line became firmer and firmer even as more and more Blacks flocked to the city.[9]

Despite the disappointment new arrivals sometimes felt, Chicago offered genuine opportunities for African Americans, often reinforced by the encroaching segregation they encountered. Notwithstanding the romance surrounding the Harlem Renaissance, the Black community of Bronzeville in the decades after World War I rivaled Black New York in its rich culture of debate, commerce, music, dance, food, literature, and religion. And, as Adam Green argues convincingly, this culture represented more than just an oppositional one, which it was, of course, in part. The culture of Bronzeville, and Black Chicago more generally, helped transform all of Chicago and what it meant to be a modern city in the twentieth century. From the flourishing of Black publishing and insurance to the innovation of Black jazz and dance clubs along South State Street, Black Chicago represented a striking complement to white-dominated business districts and a model for Black ones in the rest of the country. One of the more famous passages from St. Clair Drake and Horace Cayton's magisterial study of Black Chicago, *Black Metropolis*, captures a little of this: "In the nearby drugstore colored clerks are bustling about (they are seldom seen in other neighborhoods). In most of the other stores, too, there are colored salespeople, although a white proprietor or manager looms in the offing. In the offices around you, colored doctors, dentists, and lawyers go about their duties. And a brown-skinned policeman saunters along swinging his club and glaring sternly at the urchins who dodge in and out among the shoppers." As this passage suggests, African Americans could be police officers, street car operators, and other members of the public workforce. They could be entrepreneurs and newspaper staffers, teachers and bankers. They could be criminals, too, both small-time crooks and gangsters with outsized influence over the lucrative policy trade, as the numbers racket was called.[10]

And, more than any other place in the country at the time, they could be elected politicians. In 1915, Oscar DePriest became the city's first Black alderman, representing Bronzeville and the Second Ward, as part of the Republican machine. Before there was a Democratic machine, Mayor "Big Bill" Thompson had his own, one that relied in part on African American voters' loyalty to the party of Lincoln fifty years after abolition. While he made no effort to enforce Blacks' civil rights, especially during the 1919 riots, Thompson in his three terms as mayor oversaw the appointment of more than 2,000 Blacks to city positions and generally protected Black businesses, from the most elite to the seediest. Although more symbolic than anything else, DePriest's victory set a precedent. Black Chicagoans enjoyed nominal representation locally, with the number of Black aldermen expanding to five by 1928, and nationally, when that same year DePriest became the first Black member of Congress since 1901. DePriest was succeeded by Black Democrat Arthur Mitchell and then William Dawson, who switched from Republican to Democrat just as the majority of Blacks in the city did so to support President Franklin Roosevelt's federal New Deal program. It would be Dawson who built a durable submachine in the Black South Side wards as part of the Democratic organization started by Mayor Anton Cermak, continued by Mayor Ed Kelly and Cook County party chair Pat Nash, and perfected by Richard J. Daley.[11]

William Dawson's political career epitomized the contradictions of African American opportunities in Chicago. Born in Georgia, he was one of the many members of the city's Black elite who migrated from the South, could relate and speak to new arrivals, and yet not fully represent them.[12] He first entered the arena in the 1920s through protest politics, challenging the Black Republican establishment of Oscar DePriest. Dawson eventually won an aldermanic seat in the Second Ward in 1933 as a Black independent Republican and, for a short time, partnered with community activists to fight high rents and evictions. Often downplayed by scholars of Chicago politics, Dawson's initial political work was, in fact, instrumental "in the construction of a vibrant and diverse political scene in 1930s and 1940s Black Chicago," including the weakening of the DePriest machine.[13]

But Dawson also cultivated a working alliance with Democratic mayor Ed Kelly, who, despite being considered one of the most corrupt mayors in Chicago's history, supported open housing for Blacks and skillfully guided New Deal spending in the city. After Dawson switched parties, Kelly endorsed him for the powerful role of Democratic committeeman in the Second Ward, a position considered to make one "the absolute master of the ward organization," according to political scientist Milton Rakove—even more than that of alderman. Wielding "aldermanic privilege," an alderman could initiate or block any project in his ward, each of which had anywhere from 50,000 to 65,000 residents. But "once a man is elected committeeman, it is almost impossible to dislodge him from his position unless the party leadership decrees that he step down," writes Rakove in his analysis of the modern machine. To challenge a committeeman, a candidate needed the signatures of 10 percent of registered party members in the ward, which was five times more than an aldermanic candidate needed. This was quite difficult given a ward committeeman's remarkable power:

All party electoral funds are channeled directly through him, to be distributed by him at his pleasure. All patronage positions distributed by the county central committee to the ward organizations are funneled through him. All

precinct captains are appointed by him and are subject to summary dismissal without recourse. . . . All favors dispensed by the party hierarchy and
by city and county officials connected with the party require his approval. . . .
No person from his ward can be hired in any patronage position at the city
and county level without his sponsorship. And people who have been hired
might be fired on his request from positions they hold. . . . In other words, he
holds in his hands the destinies and livelihoods of all members of his ward
organization.[14]

This positioned Dawson perfectly to win the Democratic machine's endorsement to succeed Arthur Mitchell, who stepped down from Congress in 1942.
Dawson won easily and represented the First Congressional District until his
death in 1970. Rather than champion Black Chicagoans' civil rights in housing,
schools, and the streets, Dawson accumulated power by doling out city jobs,
services, and other small favors in exchange for loyalty, to the point that he was
seen as the second-most powerful elected figure—albeit a distant second—in
the machine behind the mayor. To Dawson, Black Chicagoans, especially recent
and mostly poor migrants moving into the rapidly changing West Side, were
"good people, but they were excitable. What these people need is help in the
little things . . . that are big things to them. There are very few issues that concern them or interest them."[15]

Such paternalism worked for some would-be voters. Dawson's personal success, proximity to the mayor, and ability to provide basic material needs to loyal
followers were enough to persuade many Blacks that Chicago indeed represented the opportunity they sought and that Dawson's politics were sufficient.
But he also operated with impunity to protect his own power, leaving political
casualties in his wake. One casualty was Roy Washington, the future mayor's
father, who had been a loyal precinct captain and corporation counsel in the
Third Ward since the 1930s and hoped to become an alderman and committeeman himself. Instead, Dawson blocked Washington's rise, which prompted
Washington to advise his son to work with Ralph Metcalfe, a Black Olympic
gold medalist and rising political star in the machine. The facade of Dawson's
political power began to show cracks in the 1950s after Richard J. Daley became
mayor.[16]

Of course, there always had been community-level protest politics challenging Dawson, the machine, and their cronies. From the Negro Labor Relations
League, which Dawson actually helped start in the 1930s, to the Chicago chapter of the National Negro Congress, Black labor and civil rights activists, often
women, did not accept Dawson's unwillingness to challenge the racial status

quo. Through information campaigns, economic boycotts, strikes, and other pressure tactics, many of these organizations pushed to win greater power for workers and residents—often through not radical solutions but a moderate liberalism that called for open housing and the hiring and retention of Blacks in private-sector jobs. The politics of Earl Dickerson, a lawyer and president of the Chicago Urban League who served as Second Ward alderman from 1939 to 1943, reflected another path but one ultimately not taken by most African American officials. Having beaten Dawson in the Democratic primary in 1939, Dickerson allied with radical trade unionists in backing an antidiscrimination clause for city employment against machine wishes. Dickerson's efforts stalled and, having bitten the hand that fed him, he was ousted after one term. After Dickerson's brief interregnum, such protest stayed largely outside of the realm of electoral politics—until the 1950s.[17]

Ironically, as Dawson appeared from the outside to wield ever more power, the opposite in fact was happening. In 1955, Dawson helped engineer the Democratic machine's dumping of incumbent mayor Martin Kennelly, not over civil rights but rather the reform-minded mayor's belated promise to crack down on vice and gambling on the South Side. Daley, then chairman of the Cook County Democratic Party, embraced Dawson, who made sure the five Black-majority wards under his control voted for Daley by wide margins. After Daley won the primary by nearly 100,000 votes, the Black-owned *Defender* newspaper declared, "The Negro voter has become enormously powerful and politically mature. He has learned to reward friends and punish enemies." Yes, African American votes represented 60 percent of Daley's totals, but the victory for Black Chicagoans was short-lived. Daley won the general election easily and quickly began to consolidate his power, in several key ways that altered African American influence within the machine. For the first time in Chicago history, the mayor retained the chairmanship of the Cook County party, where he had enormous say over who could run and not run for local offices. He also turned the City Council into a rubber stamp by stripping it of what he called "administrative and technical duties." These included the influential tasks of preparing the city budget and approving any city contracts above $2,500. Shifted to the fifth floor of City Hall, these duties gave the mayor even more power over patronage. At the same time, Daley diluted Dawson's power by dealing directly with Ralph Metcalfe and the other Black South Side aldermen known as the "Silent Six" for their unwillingness to challenge the machine's racism. Even as urban machines in New York and other big cities across the country faced tougher electoral times, Daley maneuvered to become the most powerful boss in the city's history. All of a sudden, "boss" Dawson looked weak.[18]

As Dawson's influence in Chicago declined, Black mobility and opportunity through the machine seemed less possible, which opened up space for independent electoral challenges. The first of those came with the establishment of the Chicago League of Negro Voters in 1958. Founded in preparation for the 1959 municipal primaries, the bipartisan league featured Black sponsors from both parties tired of "boss rule," such as independent publisher Bennett Johnson, journalist Gus Savage, acclaimed novelist and union organizer Frank London Brown, and surgeon and civil rights giant T. R. M. Howard. Also behind the scenes was young Democratic Party operative Harold Washington, who had attended Roosevelt University with Johnson and Savage; by many accounts, Roosevelt, where sociologist St. Clair Drake taught, had been an early incubator for coalition politics, including when Washington became student body president. T. R. M. Howard, best known for his civil rights leadership in Mississippi's Regional Council of Negro Leadership (RCNL) and the all-Black town of Mound Bayou, moved to Chicago permanently in 1956 after persistent death threats stemming from his high-profile condemnations of the Emmett Till lynching. Howard had invited Congressman Dawson to Mississippi just a few years earlier to speak at the first annual RCNL conference, the first time a Black congressman had spoken in the state since Reconstruction. But after moving north, Howard challenged Dawson for Congress as a moderate Republican, and then after losing helped establish the voters league. There was nothing radical about the league, at least on its face. It was dominated by middle-class Black men and assured supporters that "it was not a rejection of integration or white support; rather it will promote both by building the confidence, increasing the power, and releasing the full militancy of Negroes." With independents, Republicans, and Democrats as founders, the league challenged the two major parties to take civil rights seriously. "Democrats have been called the party of war, and Republicans the party of depression, but neither can be called the party of equality," wrote executive director Albert Janney. "All Americans will benefit from our unity."[19] Moreover, the league played a certain level of practical politics. Not only did its members see voting as the best way to improve Black living conditions in the city but the league also made sure to praise Dawson for submitting a civil rights bill in Congress. "To us this suggests that you realize the time has come when respected voices must speak out in support of principle without partisan consideration," league president and attorney Lemuel Bentley wrote Dawson.[20]

Despite such praise, the league's creation symbolized real change. Lemuel Bentley vied for city clerk in the Democratic primary, the first time an African American had run for citywide office, with the league's endorsement. "The political well-being of the nation and . . . human principles can be enhanced in America by the intelligent, organized use of Negro votes," the Alabama native told the *Chicago Tribune*. Bennett Johnson and businessman Carter Jones also ran for alderman under the league's banner. In what organizers saw as a victory, Bentley polled more than 10 percent overall—nearly 59,000 votes—outpacing the admittedly weak Republican in Black wards and even some white wards. In an analysis of the 1959 elections, the league concluded that the promotion of "racial togetherness" could make a genuine difference for Blacks politically, and in turn lead to improvements of their neighborhoods. It took credit, perhaps too much, for helping liberal white attorney and independent alderman Leon Despres win reelection in the Fifth Ward, which was roughly 40 percent Black. The league's voter turnout was also indirectly credited for the appointment of a Black alderman to the City Council's powerful Rules Committee and the elevation of an African American to Superior Court judge soon after the election. Ultimately, the league demonstrated a long overdue independent voice in the city's electoral politics, one that only grew stronger as the civil rights struggle reached new heights of urgency and protest in Chicago and the rest of the nation.[21]

INCREASINGLY, historians now point to the massive school boycotts of 1963 and 1964 as a key turning point in the city's civil rights history—a reminder that the quality of schools animated many movements in the North.[22] Frustration over continued poor conditions in Black, Latino, and migrant communities, especially over Chicago's crowded schools, had reached a boiling point. Black and Latino students attended schools using double shifts and portable classrooms dubbed "Willis wagons" after schools superintendent Benjamin Willis, while nearby whites attended underutilized, sometimes half-empty facilities. Adhering to so-called colorblind policy, school officials including Willis claimed that such measures were necessary and that any disparities reflected de facto residential segregation. Three years earlier, the U.S. Civil Rights Commission infamously had called Chicago the "most residentially segregated city" in the United States, but African Americans knew that the city's segregation was not simply voluntary but also the product of state-sanctioned discrimination in federal and local housing policies, enforced violently by the police. Carefully crafted school attendance policies perpetuated the segregation. According to a 1962 Chicago Urban League report, class sizes in predominantly African American schools were 25 percent bigger, while per-pupil expenditures were 33 percent lower than those for whites.[23]

Convinced that Willis, Daley, and their allies on the school board would not act unless pressured, African Americans and other activists turned up the heat. In the summer of 1961, the local chapter of the National Association for the Advancement of Colored People (NAACP) sued the school board over its discriminatory policies of denying transfers to Black students. And less than a year later, both middle- and working-class African Americans staged sit-ins and other demonstrations in South Side and West Side neighborhoods. Emerging out of these protests was the Coordinating Council of Community Organizations (CCCO), made up of organizations ranging from local Parent Teacher Associations (PTAs) to more militant community groups such as The Woodlawn Organization (TWO). Formally led by former teacher Al Raby and pastor Arthur Brazier of TWO, the CCCO joined a constellation of other efforts in the city challenging everything from employment discrimination by the city and private sector to persistent prejudice within Roman Catholic institutions. In the 1940s and 1950s, despite declining union influence from deindustrialization and rising anticommunism, radical labor organizers remained active in Chicago, especially in the United Steel Workers and the United Packinghouse Workers. Chicago also became a target city for the Economic Research and Action Project of the Students for a Democratic Society, in which mostly white college students aimed to organize poor whites, Puerto Ricans, and American Indians in the Uptown community around issues of unemployment, welfare, high rent, and police brutality. The Chicago chapters of the American Friends Service Committee and Women for Peace pushed locally against the growing militarization of the Cold War. And those fighting urban renewal and the displacement of poor people, most prominently veteran activist Saul Alinsky, whose Back of the Yards Neighborhood Council inspired activists to form TWO, had been effectively using direct action against gentrification efforts by the city and the University of Chicago on the South Side.[24]

But quality education remained the most galvanizing issue in the city in 1963. Protests spearheaded by Black mothers and students such as Rosie Simpson magnified in response to a particularly egregious use of trailers to build a new "school" for students of color on vacant land. Protesters literally lay in front of bulldozers to stop it. Under increasing pressure by the school board and the public over integration, Superintendent Benjamin Willis resigned in October—only to see the board rescind his resignation after overwhelmingly white supporters threatened to march themselves in protest. This in turn triggered a boycott of nearly 225,000 students, mostly Black and Latino, later in the month, with another 175,000 walking out in February 1964. The Chicago boycotts were part of a wave of civil disobedience for quality education and foreshadowed the better documented but numerically smaller "blowouts" by Chicano students in California and the Southwest in 1968. Thousands of marchers led by the CCCO kept the heat on Daley and his allies, periodically tying up schools and downtown streets. When the protests failed to move machine politicians, Al Raby, coconvener of the CCCO, filed a formal complaint with the U.S. Office of Education, charging the school board with operating a segregated public-school system—a move that threatened $32 million in federal funds. Raby also helped persuade Dr. Martin Luther King Jr. to come to Chicago and launch the Chicago Freedom Movement.[25]

Amid the street protests, and often overshadowed by them in scholarship, was another potent electoral challenge to the machine by Black and white independents in 1963.[26] Despite its defeat four years earlier, the Chicago League of Negro Voters continued to empower Black political independence in the city in small but significant ways. It led sympathy protests against the Mississippi lynching of Mack Charles Parker, contributed to an emergency fund for displaced African Americans in Tennessee, hosted a regional meeting of Black voters—addressed by Alabama civil rights icon Fred Shuttlesworth—and continued to endorse select independent candidates, no matter what race or party. In 1963, even after the league itself disappeared in name, several of its members ran for office, including the first African American woman to run for alderman, Clory Lee Bryant, a forty-year-old hairdresser and mother of five in the Forty-Second Ward. Carter Jones ran again in the Twenty-Seventh Ward on the West Side, this time challenging the ward's white machine "outsiders" with an explicitly diverse coalition of Puerto Ricans, Mexican Americans, Blacks, and poor whites. In the Seventeenth Ward, Charles Chew took on an aging white machine alderman in a ward that had transitioned to majority Black. And teacher and labor and civil rights activist Timuel "Tim" Black took on entrenched Black machine alderman Claude Holman, declaring that "we consider as an insult to all Negroes the offering of two loaves of bread or a dozen eggs by some of your precinct captains as a bribe for a Negro vote for any candidate." Instead, Black ran on a progressive platform for "civil rights, for better housing, for better schools, for your welfare." Only Chew succeeded, taking advantage of the ward's dramatic demographic shifts and the incumbent's absenteeism, to become the first independent Black alderman on the council. But he did not stay long; rather than face reelection, he made his peace with the machine, accepted its support, and ran and won a state Senate seat in 1967. Chew, as one observer cynically put it, "became known for his string of Cadillacs."[27]

In contrast, Carter Jones's unsuccessful run turned out to be more significant in its challenge to what Tim Black famously called "plantation politics." Unlike on the South Side, where African Americans had some modicum of influence inside the Black-majority wards and a fading but still recognized kingmaker of the submachine in congressman Dawson, Black West Side politicians were genuine puppets. Poor Black and Latino migrants had transformed the West Side into what Arnold Hirsch dubbed "the second ghetto" after World War II. But even though the previous white ethnic residents had streamed steadily into the suburbs, leaving ever larger Black and Latino majorities, white committeemen, aldermen, and patronage chiefs remained, often living in the suburbs themselves or along the city's toney North Side lakefront. The West Side's Twenty-Ninth Ward, for instance, had "the classic absentee ward boss" in Bernie Neistein, whom one reporter described as "a violin-playing reputed Mafia front man [who] ruled the ward from his Gold Coast condominium." Izzy Horwitz had the same arrangement in the Twenty-Fourth Ward. If a Black puppet challenged the status quo in any way, as Alderman Ben Lewis appeared to do in the Twenty-Fourth Ward, he could be eliminated. In the case of Lewis, the first Black alderman elected on the West Side, this was not just figurative; after demanding more power—and perhaps a larger share of the ward's illegal gambling—the dapper Lewis was found murdered in "classic gangland fashion." Lewis's murder remained unsolved decades later because informants were still afraid to talk. Remarkably, white absentees' political dominance of the West Side survived well into the 1980s.[28]

Despite his loss, Carter Jones's efforts suggested a rising discontent with the lack of real representation, one which led to the Protest at the Polls campaign that fall and into 1964. Founded by many of the people involved in the Chicago League of Negro Voters, such as publishers Bennett Johnson and Gus Savage, Protest at the Polls fielded Black candidates in several committeeman, state, and congressional races, including William Dawson's seat. The group's stated goal was to "provide a political action arm of the Freedom Movement" and "to achieve progress in jobs, housing and education by increasing the quality and quantity of Negro representation." Brenetta Howell Barrett, a local NAACP official, PTA mother, and recording secretary of the new organization, ran against incumbent Democrat Thomas O'Brien in the Sixth congressional district. A South Side native who moved to the West Side to work, among other things, as a cub reporter for Savage's *Lawndale Booster*, Barrett recalled years later that they were trying "to fight, if anything, the bartering of votes—in exchange for turkeys, hosiery, etc." Barrett, along with fellow congressional hopefuls Clory Lee Bryant and mortician A. A. "Sammy" Rayner, wholeheartedly endorsed the school protests. "We intend to translate the school boycott into a vehement

Former congressman Earl Dickerson, *second from left*, talks with Brenetta Howell Bar-
rett, *far right standing*, in a meeting of two generations of Black independents at the
State of the Black Economy Symposium in Chicago in 1972. Nixon administration official
Arthur Fletcher (*far left*), Fania Davis (scholar-activist Angela Davis's sister), and an
unidentified man are also pictured. Brenetta Howell Barrett Papers, box 87, photo 214,
Vivian G. Harsh Research Collection of Afro-American History and Literature, Chicago
Public Library.

protest at the polls," they declared in a letter to the *Chicago Defender*. "We call
upon an aroused citizenry to remove from public every official who opposes
either obliquely or frontally the improvement of Chicago's educational system."
They managed to register some voters, win endorsements from a handful of
progressive unions and churches, and, perhaps most important, strike a bit of
fear in the Black and white establishment. Barrett recalled a friend receiving at
least one bomb threat for hosting a coffee for her candidacy. Meanwhile, Black
machine aldermen and committeemen abruptly established the Assembly to
End Prejudice-Injustice-Poverty, what civil rights activists concluded was a
sham group dedicated to undermining the school protests and activism relating to them. Welfare recipients and public housing residents also received
threats if they voted the wrong way. In the end, Protest at the Polls candidates
lost their elections handily. But in the electoral aftermath, the group's activists
maintained their antiestablishment stance by continuing their protests against
Ben Willis and, more provocatively, questioning the overwhelming whiteness

of the Independent Voters of Illinois, the traditional alternative to the machine made up of both Democrats and Republicans.[29]

Indeed, the rising Black independence movement in the early 1960s also co-incided with the most serious electoral challenge Richard J. Daley faced after his hard-fought victory against incumbent Mayor Kennelly in 1955. Taking on Daley was "Polish renegade" and former Republican state's attorney Benjamin Adamowski. A one-time machine politician and friend of Daley's in the 1920s and 1930s, Adamowski had grown increasingly critical of machine politics, first as a legislator and then as Mayor Kennelly's corporation counsel. In 1955, he ran for mayor as a Democratic reformer but lost in a three-way race with Daley and Kennelly. The following year, having burned his bridges with the machine, Adamowski ran for Cook County state's attorney as a Republican and won narrowly. From this perch, he probed several Democratic scandals, including a notorious police burglary ring run out of the Summerdale precinct and exposed by the "babbling burglar." Adamowski's aggressive pursuit of corruption made him anathema to the Daley machine, which defeated him in his 1960 reelection bid.[30]

But Adamowski remained a dangerous opponent for Daley three years later. As a highly intelligent, seemingly fearless politician with a successful citywide run under his belt, his background and heritage gave him inherent credibility with the city's large Polish population, one of the machine's most prominent white ethnic constituencies. It was often said, with considerable exaggeration, that Chicago boasted the most Polish-speaking people outside of Warsaw. Framing his candidacy as a good-government reformer, Adamowski hammered Daley for the city's profligate spending, taxes, and waste. Violence and high taxes were driving "good" Chicagoans out of the city, replaced by "indigent, illiterate and lazy people," Adamowski argued. "Aid to dependent children has increased from 1.9 million dollars in one month in 1955 to 9 million in January this year." As his racial dog-whistling suggested, Adamowski did not champion civil rights. Interested in siphoning off a significant amount of the Polish vote from the machine, Adamowski explicitly opposed calls for open housing and integration. Of course, Daley did not support them either. But he was able to downplay this position enough to avoid losing Black votes to the more vocal Adamowski. Accordingly, even William Dawson's weakened submachine was able to run up overwhelming numbers for Daley, who won with about 56 percent of the overall vote; in the predominantly Black Twenty-Fourth Ward, for instance, Daley's ratio over Adamowski was nearly eighteen to one. The 1963 victory would, however, be the last time that Daley won such significant numbers of votes from

African Americans, as activists were increasingly able to highlight Daley's opposition to civil rights, sending some of his most loyal supporters looking for
political alternatives.[31]

WHILE CCCO PROTESTS over school segregation may have peaked in 1964,
activists kept the heat on along a series of fronts—against the city's top-down
approach to the War on Poverty, the expanding U.S. presence in Southeast Asia,
and the ways both perpetuated racial inequality in the city's schools, workplaces, and streets. The effectiveness of Daley's strategy of waiting activists
out, offering bits of empty rhetoric and symbolism in support of a vague but
unrealized equality, seemed to have waned. Chicago's version of the War on
Poverty, declared by President Lyndon Johnson in 1964, was potentially worth
millions in federal dollars for Chicago alone. But despite the Economic Opportunity Act's clause that called for the "maximum feasible participation" of the
poor in local antipoverty agencies' decision-making and implementation, Chicago's plan sidelined them. In fact, Daley, a close ally of Johnson, with whom he
spoke regularly, found the prospect bewildering. "It would be like telling the
fellow who cleans up to be the city editor of a newspaper," reasoned Daley, who
communicated his displeasure with Johnson. "What in the hell are you people
doing?" Johnson aide Bill Moyers recalled the mayor saying. "Does the President
know he's putting money in the hands of subversives?" Of course, Daley had
no problem with millions in federal spending for the city, as long as he and the
machine controlled it. Thus, Daley formed the Chicago Committee on Urban
Opportunity, whose board the mayor chaired and which was comprised mostly
of loyalists, city bureaucrats, and other members of the mayor's coalition. Only
seven board members came from poor communities, and Daley chose Deton
Brooks, a sociologist, former Cook County official, and Black machine loyalist,
as the executive director. Brooks tapped directors for twelve service centers,
who then chose local residents for advisory panels. The result was a thin veneer
of participation by the poor; Daley and his allies remained in firm control.[32]

Critics called it more of the same, linking the new agency to a generation
or more of political elites and machine partisans enriching themselves in the
name of poor people. Moreover, activists connected the antipoverty program's
deficiencies to the unresponsiveness of school district and urban renewal officials. Chicago's antipoverty initiative "is only more of the ancient, galling war
against the poor," argued the Reverend Lynward Stevenson, a Kentucky-born
pastor and new leader of The Woodlawn Organization, which had applied for

modest funding to no avail. "We want the federal law on maximum feasible local participation enforced in Chicago," Stevenson told members of Congress, adding that "grass roots organizations" are the best hope for the poor, not "men who drive Cadillacs, eat 3-inch steaks and sip champagne at luncheon meetings." Critics' suspicions were correct. Federal investigators determined that more than 70 percent of the city's antipoverty funds went to pay the salaries of machine-connected bureaucrats. More than a quarter of those students in Head Start, a key antipoverty program, came from families over the income limit. And when pressed by members of Congress, Brooks could not name one board member who could be considered poor.[33]

In protest, activists took to the streets again, with charismatic Black comedian and organizer Dick Gregory leading near-daily marches throughout the summer of 1965, including in Daley's own Bridgeport. As historian Erik Gellman points out, Daley long characterized his neighborhood as representative of the city and protesters agreed; Bridgeport, they charged, reflected Chicago's suffocating segregation and belligerent white hostility to any kind of civil rights advances. As activists expected, counterdemonstrators came out in force, jeering Gregory's marchers and holding up homemade signs that made their racial loyalties clear: "Nig, You Have Every Thing. What Else You Want?" While the back and forth over the War on Poverty garnered the most attention, some Chicago activists began to focus on Vietnam, where President Johnson had recently committed up to 500,000 U.S. troops to prop up teetering ally South Vietnam in its civil war with the North. Reflecting the arguments made by the Students for a Democratic Society, who drew 25,000 marchers to the first of many antiwar rallies on the National Mall in April 1965, their Chicago counterparts explicitly linked the war with the Black freedom struggle and the War on Poverty. As Chicago's leftist W. E. B. Du Bois Club posed in leaflets at a downtown demonstration that July, "Why Are American Troops in South Viet Nam and Not in Mississippi?" Such questions only multiplied as the decade wore on.[34]

It was in this context that Dr. Martin Luther King Jr. came to Chicago and launched the Chicago Freedom Movement (CFM). Hoping to give the city's grassroots campaign more publicity, Al Raby and others invited King to bring his national profile to the freedom struggle in Chicago. King had been interested in going north, but despite a lengthy negotiation over how the partnership between the Southern Christian Leadership Conference (SCLC) and the CCCO would work, no other city's local people were as excited about an SCLC campaign. Philadelphia civil rights activists, for instance, believed King's coming to town might bring more complexity than it was worth. In contrast, "the Southern Christian Leadership Conference," declared Raby, "will always be welcome

Dr. Martin Luther King Jr., flanked by SCLC aide Andrew Young and Chicago activist Al Raby, walk up Independence Boulevard to apartments at 3808 West Fillmore Street in North Lawndale as part of King's Chicago Freedom Movement in 1966. Raby later tried unsuccessfully to use his friendship with national civil rights leaders such as King and Young to win an aldermanic seat. ST-40000567–0003, *Chicago Sun-Times* collection, Chicago History Museum.

here in Chicago." After all, most Blacks in Chicago had Deep South roots. As King aide Bernard Lafayette recalled, "Something like forty-two percent of the Blacks in Chicago were either first or second generation from Mississippi . . . so there was a good deal of appreciation for what we were doing." Added King, "Chicago is a symbol of *de facto* desegregation. I feel there is a very critical situation here that could grow more serious and ominous unless the city's leaders are eternally vigilant." But some observers worried that King, underestimating Daley's conservative power base, mistakenly believed that the mayor could be persuaded to embrace nondiscrimination and institute it through the machine.[35]

Despite identifying the real risk of violence—Chicago saw its share of uprisings during the next several summers—King and the SCLC misjudged many other dynamics at work in Chicago, from the intensity of white ethnic hostility to civil rights to the influence of preexisting Black resistance networks amid a waning Black submachine. King and his aides deserve some credit for recognizing the organizing potential of the city's youth gangs, including the West Side's Conservative Vice Lords and the South Side's Blackstone Rangers and Black Disciples; the same could be said for the SCLC's tentative entreaties to Puerto Ricans, who staged the 1966 Division Street uprising in and around Humboldt Park on the city's Near Northwest Side after a police shooting that summer. But in both cases, campaign leaders did not follow through completely, in part because they would not engage with rampant skepticism of nonviolent strategy. Other scholars have exhaustively offered King-centric accounts of the CFM, including its ambitious goals to "end the slums" through open housing, the fierce opposition and even violence these efforts faced, the success of the SCLC's selective-buying campaign Operation Breadbasket led by young aide Jesse Jackson, and the ultimate deficiencies of the Summit Agreement of August 1966.[36] That agreement ended controversial—many said risky— freedom marches in residential areas including lily-white Gage Park and Cicero in exchange for a vague set of official promises to combat housing discrimination, including the establishment of an organization, the Leadership Council for Metropolitan Open Communities, to monitor fair housing progress. The Leadership Council did prove effective in certain ways over the years, as did Operation Breadbasket, in securing better housing and jobs for Black Chicagoans.[37] But neither effort remade the city as Black activists and their allies had hoped. When King held up the Summit Agreement as a victory, many characterized it as "a bunch of empty promises" and the "most unkind cut of all." Labor activist and longtime machine critic Tim Black expressed the angry feeling of betrayal held by many: "With his Negro and white Judas Iscariots, the Mayor had taken on the great Dr. Martin Luther King and . . . won."[38]

Indeed, the opposition to King by the city's Black politicians was striking, and consistent. When announcing yet another machine-backed "civil rights coalition" to blunt real reform, alderman and Dawson protégé Ralph Metcalfe stated, "This is no hick town. We have a lot of intellect and can take care of these situations ourselves." Dawson, sounding a lot like a white southern sheriff, called King "an outside agent." Despite such attacks, King was careful not to challenge the machine in a partisan way, especially its Black representatives. While Raby announced a nonpartisan voter registration campaign to bolster nonwhite voters on the South and West Sides, King expressed private concerns to aide Stanley Levison that a focus on electoral politics could taint the campaign as one of short-term ambition. King endorsed issues, not candidates, especially in the rough-and-tumble world of Chicago politics. He did meet with several independent candidates, including Charles Chew and Richard Newhouse, as well as with Fred Hubbard, after the latter was shot. This was King's "way of endorsing him without actually endorsing him," according to independent political strategist Don Rose. But King made a point to tell the press that he "was not leading any campaign against Mayor Daley" or the city's Black politicians. Perhaps they could be allies one day. And besides, in 1966, the extent of Black political power in Chicago remained impressive when compared to the fledgling electoral efforts in the post–Voting Rights Act South with which King was most familiar.[39]

For Harold Washington, a first-term state legislator backed by the machine at the time, King's campaign placed Black politicians like him in a bind. A charismatic and dynamic organizer considered central to the Third Ward organization, Washington had built the strongest Young Democrats arm in the city, which had proven instrumental in the ward, producing the most votes for Daley in 1963. The ward's alderman, Ralph Metcalfe, viewed Washington as essential to his success, if a headache at times. Recalled one former precinct captain, "Washington was indispensable to Metcalfe, so he got away with a whole lot." Indeed, Washington was not the traditional machine politician in Springfield. Many of his closest friends, such as Bennett Johnson and Gus Savage, were political independents who actively participated in the Chicago League of Negro Voters, Protest at the Polls, and the Chicago Freedom Movement. Washington's colleagues noticed how skeptically he considered the "idiot card," the party machine's explicit instructions on how legislators were to vote on each bill in Springfield. That skepticism included his critique of police brutality and stop-and-frisk policies, as well as his calls for a civilian review board to investigate police misconduct. Officer Renault Robinson, who cofounded the Black Power–oriented Afro-American Patrolmen's League, was surprised when a Black machine legislator—not a white liberal or independent—agreed to sponsor legislation to create such a review board. The bill went nowhere, and Washington nearly lost the machine's endorsement. But the issue, at least, received some necessary attention—something biographer Gary Rivlin believed was Washington's primary objective. And yet not even Washington could endorse King's efforts openly. Instead, Washington attended the first meeting of Metcalfe's civil rights coalition designed to counter the CFM. Later that night, an upset Washington went out for drinks with friend and future state Supreme Court justice Charles Freeman. "We just sat there in the car for a while, maybe fifteen or twenty minutes," Freeman recalled. "Just sat. I don't remember if Harold said a single word." As Rivlin pointed out, Washington "blew off subsequent meetings" of Metcalfe's group, "but by showing up that one time he had taken part."[40]

Despite the CFM's general avoidance of partisan politics, it had an immediate electoral impact—one that cut both ways. Just two years after President

Lyndon Johnson and national Democrats won a landslide victory against Barry Goldwater, the 1966 midterm elections saw liberals swamped by conservatives in both parties. In Illinois, the senior U.S. senator and a key Daley ally, Paul Douglas, lost to Republican businessman Charles Percy, while the GOP won the race for Cook County sheriff and an additional U.S. House seat. Both Douglas and Daley blamed Democratic losses on the CFM protests and marches, the "white backlash." "It was a very strong force, beyond question," Douglas said a month after the election. "Democrats were identified with the fight for free residence. I suffered the consequences." But it proved more complex than that. While the gubernatorial campaigns of Ronald Reagan in California and Lester Maddox in Georgia that year suggested an uptick in racialized law-and-order rhetoric designed for white audiences, 1966 did not represent a sudden shift in response to Black Power rhetoric or renewed civil rights marches. Nationally, as other scholars have demonstrated, white voters already had begun to support more conservative candidates on race in both parties in the 1950s and 1960s. Growing opposition to the Vietnam War—not to mention Douglas's age, seventy-four, and the violent death of Percy's daughter during the campaign—likely contributed to the defeat of a senator known as a war hawk.[41]

African Americans also abandoned many Democrats, and not because they were too progressive on civil rights. Rather, Black opposition to police brutality and discrimination in schools and housing pushed them to either stay home or vote for independents or select Republicans with moderate civil rights records and rhetoric such as Percy, the telegenic president of Bell & Howell. African American activist and humorist Dick Gregory endorsed Percy on the eve of the election because, while he liked Douglas personally, the senator was part of the "Democratic machine here that has been strangling my people." African Americans also bucked the machine by electing two Black independents to the state Senate. Concluded the *Daily Defender* a day after the election, "What must be weighed . . . is that what backlash existed in Chicago was augmented by a substantial number of Negro voters who did not go to the polls. It was their way of expressing their resentment of the local machine."[42]

The complicated politics of state violence threatened to spill into 1967, prompting consternation among Democratic Party regulars as they looked toward city elections that spring. Some began to ask if Daley could lose. The day after the fall election, the *Tribune* described a "post-election gloom" in City Hall; the tireless Daley did not even go to the office that day, only saying tersely that his candidacy "does not hinge on the outcome of this race or any other race." But without an opponent as credible on white law-and-order issues as former state's attorney Adamowski was, Daley coasted to victory. In contrast to past elections, however, all but one Black-majority ward produced lower vote totals for Daley. Moreover, "the bulk of the Black wards no longer ranked among the machine's most productive units," pointed out political scientist William Grimshaw. "This was the first firm indication that race was replacing class as the city's main political divide." While a bit simplistic in its race-class analysis, it was true that white ethnic wards increasingly began replacing Blacks in Daley's coalition, giving him larger and larger numbers on law and order—a position bolstered by his showdowns with civil rights and peace activists before and during the 1968 Democratic National Convention in Chicago.[43]

Instead of concentrating on the mayor's election race, political independents in Chicago turned their attention to a handful of Black, disproportionately middle-class wards and highlighted how law and order and state violence played out differently for many African Americans. Independents managed to elect mortician A. A. "Sammy" Rayner and lawyer William Cousins to the Sixth and Eighth Wards, respectively, that spring. While personality may have played a role, both emphasized issues of police and machine corruption, too. Despite the importance of schools, open housing, and jobs, as Beryl Satter has noted, "it was the job of the police within this system . . . to keep the Blacks in line." From uniformed officers on the beat to the infamous Subversive Unit, or Red Squad, Daley's police department kept Black citizens in check, through surveillance, intimidation, and physical violence. "This system has made us so politically feeble that we have accepted crumbs in return for the large contributions which we have given," remarked Cousins during the campaign. "The ballot is the best equalizer of opportunities which has ever been made available to a people. We must use it wisely." It was this realization—that continued racial discrimination in housing, schools, and workplaces relied on state, or police, violence—that became one of the most important products of the CFM and other activism of the time, and yet so rarely mentioned by scholars.[44] It clearly demonstrated how Daley, Dawson, Metcalfe, and the rest of the machine regulars simply were not reliable advocates for Black civil rights, especially regarding how Chicago's "finest" treated Black citizens. Those interested in bettering their communities beyond a few municipal jobs or some free gifts at the holidays would have to build their own citywide political coalition.[45]

IF NOT ALREADY APPARENT, the reality that grassroots activists needed to challenge the machine even more aggressively became acute in 1968, a year in which the city's police suddenly had the whole world watching them, literally. Violence during the first several months left an indelible mark on the nation's psyche—from ongoing carnage in Vietnam, epitomized by the Tet Offensive, to the assassinations of King and Senator Robert F. Kennedy. The response to King's death was sharp and immediate, as more than 150 cities burst into flames in a spasm of sorrow and rage over the violent death of a nonviolent man. Chicago's West Side was one of the hardest hit. Over two days, 9 African Americans died, more than 500 people were injured, and 2,900 were arrested; much of the business corridor along West Madison Street was destroyed, with upward of $10 million in overall property damage to an area of twenty-eight square blocks. Police responded to the uprisings with more restraint than expected, but just days later Mayor Daley infamously endorsed policies to "shoot to kill" arsonists and "shoot to maim" looters. Condemned by Black leaders, clergy members, and even the conservative City Club of Chicago, Daley refused to apologize. Later that month, in a harbinger of the more infamous police riot outside of the Democratic National Convention, officers clubbed antiwar protesters organized by the Chicago Peace Council, as well as some bystanders, in downtown's Grant Park. "By making a non-violent protest impossible," stated march organizer Clark Kissinger, "they made a violent one inevitable."[46]

Few Black politicians other than Alderman Sammy Rayner condemned the police actions; instead, it was some Black police officers who felt most compelled to reject police excess. That spring, officers Edward "Buzz" Palmer and Renault Robinson founded the Afro-American Patrolmen's League (AAPL) and called for the equitable treatment of African Americans on both sides of the badge, officer and citizen. "The police were just absolutely abusive in every way you can think," recalled Robinson, who had dropped out of college and joined the force two years earlier. "I mean they had no respect for Black people whatsoever. . . . We couldn't participate in it." African Americans made up about 15 percent of the force, despite being about 35 percent of the city's population. And among the nation's largest cities, Chicago's department held the dubious honor of killing the most Black civilians, both by raw number and by rate. After months of hushed conversation and informal meetings, Palmer, Robinson, and others started an organization remarkable in its approach. Challenging the popular understanding of groups like the Black Panthers, the AAPL blended notions of Black Power with police work and routinely sought better conditions for Black officers as well as an end to the corrosive relationship between the department and the poor communities it routinely harassed. During the next decade, AAPL activism, including lawsuits, rid the department of some of its worst racist behavior. But its activism also prompted harassment from members' fellow officers and politicians. Daley himself angrily demanded the firing of Palmer, who eventually left after years of abuse. Robinson faced no less than 100 suspensions for minor, often made-up infractions, in his many years on the force. In its first months and years, the AAPL faced considerable resistance, making it difficult to recruit even those most sympathetic to the cause. Unlike most employment available to African Americans, police jobs were relatively well-paying and secure. Robinson recalled lobbying Black officers' wives to implore their husbands to join the AAPL. Many would, eventually, but not in time to prevent the police riot that made that year's Democratic National Convention so infamous.[47]

The police riot of 1968 did not surprise Black and Latino Chicagoans, many of whom had seen the blunt end of a billy club, if not worse. Thus, it was really "not a critical moment in the history of police and state violence" in the city, historian Simon Balto reminds us. Instead, what came to be known as the "Battle of Michigan Avenue" was a "critical moment in America's political history," namely because its brazenness was caught on film for all to see, especially sheltered white Americans sitting in their living rooms. Taunted by peace activists hoping to embarrass Daley and his pro–Vietnam War allies, the police seemingly went berserk and, for twenty minutes, beat hundreds of people, including protesters, journalists, clergy members, medics, and other bystanders—to the point that at least twenty members of the media required hospitalization, people found themselves pushed with such force that they broke plate-glass windows, and all by officers who had either covered up or taken off their badges. An estimated 100 people were injured, and about 180 arrested, by night's end. As police rampaged, scores of witnesses began to chant, "The whole world is watching!" And they were, including from the Democratic convention floor. There, cameras clearly captured Mayor Daley cursing at Connecticut senator Abraham Ribicoff, who condemned the police's "Gestapo tactics" from the podium. In the days that followed, Daley, yet again, remained unapologetic, knowing that his base of white ethnic supporters expected this perverted version of "law and order" in their city. So did the Republican presidential nominee Richard Nixon, who rode similar racial dog whistles into the White House that November.[48]

But at least for Chicago's independents—and a small but growing number of whites—the need for a citywide political coalition was even more dire. Because of the city's demographics, such an alliance would have to include more than African Americans and a handful of well-meaning whites. It would take truly multiracial efforts, and several did develop in the streets and communities of Chicago in the next few years, the best-known being the nascent Rainbow

Coalition of Fred Hampton, Bobby Lee, and a small cohort of Black Panthers. This particular collaboration was not explicitly about electoral politics. And yet the violent response by the police to such coalition-building, including Hampton's brazen assassination, did not have the intended effect of pacifying or intimidating people. Instead, it galvanized enough Black voters to revolt at the ballot box.

## CHAPTER 2

# Shifting Alliances

Mayor Daley is not God.—Ralph Metcalfe,
"Metcalfe: Daley Is Not God," *Chicago Defender*,
June 1, 1972

They filed past Fred Hampton's apartment in the days and weeks after December 4, 1969. Men, women, and children, most in heavy coats to protect from the wintry chill, wanted to see for themselves what the police had done this time. Before the authorities belatedly sealed the crime scene with yellow tape, hundreds of people walked through the shot-up apartment on Monroe Street in the West Side's East Garfield Park community, paying their respects and taking in the aftermath of the carnage that had occurred there. In the predawn hours of December 4, Hampton and Mark Clark, a member of the Peoria chapter of the Black Panther Party, were murdered in a hail of gunfire by police working for the state's attorney. Ostensibly there with a warrant to search for illegal guns, the deputized officers instead fired more than 100 shots into the apartment compared with 1 shot from inside, later determined to have been errantly fired by Clark after taking a bullet in the chest. Clark died immediately, but according to surviving witnesses, Hampton was still breathing after the barrage, only to be shot in the head point blank by one of the officers after they entered. After a long delay, the state's attorney's office claimed that the officers shot in self-defense, a narrative that the physical evidence of the apartment demolished. In its subsequent report by an independent inquiry, a commission cochaired by NAACP president Roy Wilkins and former U.S. attorney general Ramsey Clark concluded that "systems of justice—federal, state, and local—failed to do their duty to protect the lives and rights of citizens." The commission all but said that Hampton and Clark were murdered.[1]

Black and brown Chicagoans had grown accustomed to state violence disrupting their lives, families, and communities. One would be hard-pressed to find a resident of color in the city who did not have at least one friend or family member who had a physical run-in with a Chicago police officer. In the two years after the riots outside the Democratic National Convention, the Chicago police killed at least fifty-eight Black people, and injured hundreds, perhaps thousands, more. Stop-and-frisk policies had become standard police procedure in the 1960s and inherently invited conflict. And yet, despite citizen complaints, most African American officials believed they could not speak up without risking the wrath of Mayor Daley. Instead, William Dawson, Ralph Metcalfe, and others deflected criticism of the police to other targets, often to individuals themselves or a larger culture of pathology and crime. But the Panther deaths exposed cracks in this wall of silence. State representative Harold Washington, who occasionally challenged the machine's marching orders while in Springfield in the 1960s, was one of the first to speak out in the weeks after Hampton's murder, reflecting the shock that politicians like himself and their constituents felt over its brazenness. "Based on my examination of the house, there is no doubt that there are conflicts between the explanation of the state's attorney's office and the physical facts," Washington declared. "The only way to resolve this conflict is to have an independent investigation." Others, including fellow Black state representatives Lewis Caldwell and Raymond Ewell and state senator Charles Chew, agreed.[2]

They were shocked not just by the retrograde actions of the police, but also by their target. Fred Hampton was not just any Black Chicagoan. He had emerged as one of the most eloquent voices of his generation, a twenty-one-year-old activist with the NAACP Youth Council and then the Panthers whose oratory and raw leadership skills projected someone much older and more experienced. As one of the founders of Chicago's original, multiracial Rainbow Coalition with other young activists, Hampton was, in the words of one scholar, "trying to re-imagine the social contract." While as critical of the police as their counterparts in California and elsewhere, the Hampton-led Illinois Panthers prominently embraced alliances with other oppressed peoples, and not just rhetorically. "We say you don't fight racism with racism," Hampton said in 1969. "We're gonna fight racism with solidarity." In 1968 and 1969, Hampton collaborated with one-time street gangs and youth organizations of every hue, including the North Side's Young Lords Organization, a primarily Puerto Rican street gang, and the Young Patriots, a white group representing mostly Appalachian transplants. While such organizing was difficult and very much in its beginning stages, the coalition's potential terrified the police, according to internal communication by the police department's anticommunist Red Squad, which infiltrated each group. The result was a year in which Hampton and the small Panther cadre found themselves increasingly under siege—the year ending with his death, several other members severely wounded, and the practical end of the Panther chapter. While others courageously kept the rainbow rhetoric alive, the murders did take their toll, and the coalition ceased to exist for all intents and purposes less than a year later.[3]

But while the Rainbow Coalition itself faded, the murder of two Panthers sparked productive organizing around police reform that eventually transformed the relationship between the machine and many Black politicians—most prominently Ralph Metcalfe. This happened at the same time that more and more Latinos were arriving in the city, solidifying the Near Southwest Side communities of Pilsen and Little Village as Latino strongholds, and as Puerto Ricans specifically were responding to police violence and harassment with activism and even rebellion, as illustrated in the 1966 Division Street uprising after police shot and killed a youth near Humboldt Park. Accordingly, between the late 1960s and the mid-1970s, a number of diverse coalitions that followed the Rainbow Coalition—from Citizens Alert and the Alliance to End Repression to the Black Crime Commission, the Afro-American Policeman's League, and Metcalfe's own Concerned Citizens for Police Reform—worked to change the culture of the police, from both outside and inside the department. While this activism was painstaking, it arguably had a more profound impact on electoral politics than it did even on police practices. After all, 1972 was the same year that notorious police commander Jon Burge began his systematic torture of Black police suspects on the South Side. By the end of that year, when thousands of delegates had descended on next-door Gary, Indiana, to attend the National Black Political Convention, African Americans in Chicago took a huge step toward electoral independence. Metcalfe finally broke with party bosses over police brutality—this time over the beating of two personal friends—and Black voters rejected the architect of Hampton's 1969 assassination, Democratic state's attorney Edward Hanrahan. Activists and political independents across the racial spectrum saw this transformation as quite possibly the golden opportunity to finally change the political calculus in the city, rein in the party machine, and perhaps even defeat Mayor Daley in 1975.

WHILE AFRICAN AMERICANS were at the heart of the city's activism against police brutality and harassment, strides would not have been made without significant contributions and sacrifices by whites and Latinos, especially Puerto Ricans. Despite facing such prejudice in their everyday living and working conditions, Puerto Ricans—in contrast to Blacks—had played only a small role in the city's electoral politics. While U.S. citizens, Puerto Ricans had only begun to arrive in the city in sizable numbers during and immediately after World War II, as part of Operation Bootstrap and other programs to fill labor needs on the mainland and combat unemployment on the island. By 1953, officials estimated that nearly 20,000 Puerto Ricans lived in Chicago, with thousands more coming by the end of the decade, and about 78,000 living in the city by 1970—mostly on the North and Northwest Sides. Puerto Ricans, however, remained a minority among Spanish-speaking people in the city—although because they often moved to the edges of predominantly white working-class neighborhoods, such as the North Side's Lincoln Park, their conspicuousness belied their relatively small numbers.[4]

Since the beginning of the twentieth century, "El Norte" had been an increasingly desired destination for Latinos of all kinds. Mexican Americans, the largest subgroup, sought to escape the Mexican Revolution in the 1910s and to seek stability, work, relative prosperity—even adventure—in the United States.[5] While first men and then their families began their new lives in the agricultural fields of the Southwest and Midwest, Chicago's industries attracted more and more migrants, primarily to steel, railroads, and meatpacking on the city's South Side. For a while, at least, before the Depression, Mexican Americans even outnumbered African Americans in the steel industry. And their numbers increased each year, with the brief exception of the 1930s, when Depression-era unemployment and repatriation campaigns drove many Mexican Americans south of the border. "Arguably the most popular Midwestern destination during much of the interwar period for Mexicans looking for work and a chance to prosper, the Chicago area provided employment, hope, and socioeconomic advancement for Mexicans," writes historian Michael Innis-Jiménez, "just as it had previously done for tens of thousands of European immigrants and African American migrants from the South." The same was true for other Latinos. In her study of Mexicans in Chicago, Gabriela Arrendondo observes that, while Mexicans "predominated in the Latin American population" of the city, a sizable number of Central and South Americans came seeking work and escaping instability and war back home. During and immediately after World War II, the number of Mexican and Puerto Rican migrants throughout the country skyrocketed as formalized labor importation programs brought hundreds of thousands of contract workers to the country. By 1945, at least 15,000 Mexicans came to work in Chicago-area railroads as part of the largest of these government labor initiatives, the Bracero program. Thousands more came in the years afterward.[6]

Similar to African Americans' experiences, Latinos found that opportunity in Chicago too often came with low pay, poor working and living conditions, and remarkable discrimination in housing, education, and city services. Many Mexican and Central Americans were "othered" in the United States by both law and custom because of language, class, and immigration status. Polish landowners in South Chicago, for instance, limited where Mexican Americans could rent, packing them into areas with other Latinos and African Americans, while Irish and Polish street gangs extrajudicially patrolled their communities to waylay outsiders. As we saw in the first chapter, one of those gangs, the Hamburgs, was run by a young Richard J. Daley. Thus, Mexican Americans often clustered into several close-knit enclaves near the industries in which they worked. Steelworkers tended to live in South Chicago, while those in meat-packing, tortilla factories, railroads, and related industries lived on the Near West Side or in the Back of the Yards neighborhood on the South Side. One result of this concentration, especially in the wake of the 1930s repatriation campaigns throughout the country, was the solidifying of a clear Mexican American identity, one that was not simply another kind of "white."[7]

If anything, urban renewal of the Near West Side reinforced this identity. Long an entry point to the city by new immigrants and symbolized by Jane Addams's Hull House, this area by 1950 "faced increasing physical decay, dramatic population changes, massive federal highway construction, and the rapid expansion of public housing," writes historian Lilia Fernández. "Earlier generations of European transplants had exhausted the life span of worn housing structures. Once new migrants arrived in the mid-twentieth century amid severe housing shortages, many buildings were beyond repair." Moreover, city officials and the white business community had grown increasingly alarmed at having a large, heterogeneous working-class population—increasingly dominated by poor, Spanish-speaking immigrants—on the edge of the downtown business Loop. Thus, not unlike Los Angeles's destruction of Chavez Ravine to build Dodger Stadium or New York City's razing of Lincoln Square to construct the Lincoln Center for the Performing Arts, Mayor Daley and his business allies in Chicago displaced a sizable working-class community through the construction of the University of Illinois Circle campus in 1963–64. While a small number of Italian Americans remained in the area, Mexican Americans largely went south to the Lower West Side, or Pilsen. Along with neighboring Little Village—the former South Lawndale renamed by realtors trying desperately, and in vain, to stanch white flight—Pilsen became the heart of the city's Mexican American community, one that has been defended politically and culturally from encroachment ever since. At the same time, displaced Puerto Ricans joined an existing enclave on the Near North Side, but, despite having citizenship, they remained marginalized because of language, culture, and the heterogeneity of their skin color, and just a decade later faced more displacement from their North Side homes in Lincoln Park and Lake View. By the 1970s, many had moved yet again to Humboldt Park, Logan Square, and West Town on the Near Northwest Side. As Young Lords leader Cha-Cha Jiménez described, the constant movement to find adequate housing impacted every aspect of their lives, including education and police-community relations and in ways that were not that much different than African Americans.[8]

Unlike African Americans, however, neither Puerto Ricans nor Mexican Americans were much involved in electoral politics, because of their still small numbers. While most likely an undercount, Latinos officially made up only 3 percent of Chicagoans in the 1970 census, and they made up an even smaller percentage of the electorate, prevented from voting by immigration status and discouraged by the machine's general inattention to them, save in a handful of ward operations. The city's few Latino political organizations had limited clout and served primarily as brokers. For instance, the Amigos for Daley was made up mainly of a small Mexican American contingent of moderate to conservative business and homeowners, lending the Daley machine some symbolic diversity while supporting the mayor on a range of issues from law-and-order policing to a Roman Catholic–infused cultural conservatism. But Latinos had not elected one of their own to a prominent position since William Emilio Rodriguez, a Mexican American lawyer who won two city council races between 1915 and 1918 as a member of the Socialist Party in the Fifteenth Ward, in what is current-day West Town. Instead, most Latino groups in the city remained service-oriented, from the church-affiliated Caballeros de San Juan to the Spanish Civic Committee, not to mention the "fighting" youth gangs like the Spartans, Marquis, and Young Lords, all of which formed to protect neighborhood turf amid shifting racial boundaries. Such narrow emphases began to shift, however, when Chicago police officer Thomas Munyon shot twenty-year-old Puerto Rican Arcelis Cruz on June 12, 1966, sparking three nights of unrest.[9]

The Division Street uprising does not receive as much historical attention as African American rebellions in Watts, Harlem, Detroit, or even on Chicago's West Side later that summer.[10] No one was killed, and injuries and building damage were minimal, as opposed to the scores of deaths and millions of dollars in property damage in the better-known rebellions of the mid-1960s, including those in other parts of Chicago. But not only was the Division Street uprising the first of its kind by mainland Puerto Ricans, this "solidarity experience," as activist José Acevedo called it, also helped transform Latino activism and coalition-building in Chicago—changes that reverberated throughout the city's politics for a generation. Bad police shootings and other forms of police violence for years had been the norm in the Puerto Rican enclave of Humboldt Park, and the source of persistent community complaints. As one scholar of Puerto Rican Chicago concluded, "Residents of the Division Street area shared a pervasive belief that policemen were physically brutal, harsh, and discourteous to them because they were Puerto Ricans." And it was not just perception; because of their color, Puerto Ricans were far more likely to be stopped by the police than white Chicagoans. Police brutality, coupled with chronic concerns over poor housing, education, health care, and employment opportunities, made the community a powder keg. Ironically, Cruz's shooting and the subsequent unrest came at the end of the newly city-sanctioned "Puerto Rican Week" festival, which many community leaders had celebrated as a genuine gesture of inclusion by Mayor Daley. Instead, the city's inherent and often violent exclusion of Puerto Ricans was put on display. City officials and conservative opinion makers such as the *Tribune* responded by blaming the violence on outsiders such as Dr. Martin Luther King Jr., communists, and general "apologists for the riots . . . looking for reasons to blame unemployment, interracial friction, and 'the ghetto,'" as perceived by the *Tribune* editorial page. The editors went on to assert, ludicrously, that "the evidence has been overwhelming that the police in northern cities bend over backward to be gentle with members of minority groups."[11] For his part, King and the SCLC did try to use the uprising as another way to reach out to Latinos. "You suffer from the pressures and pains of prejudice because you are darker," SCLC aide James Orange told a group of Puerto Ricans the next week. "We're dark, too." Such efforts were often awkward and unsuccessful, especially in the short term; few Puerto Ricans ultimately rallied behind the Chicago Freedom Movement, for instance.[12]

Instead, Puerto Ricans and Latinos of all backgrounds stepped up their own organizing against the structural disadvantages they faced, and almost always in coalition with other grassroots organizations in Chicago. Hundreds of Puerto Ricans marched five miles to City Hall a few days after the uprising and made formal demands about police brutality and a general lack of services in their neighborhoods. Daley responded with hearings by the Commission on Human Relations into Puerto Rican concerns, and appointed Claudio Flores, the publisher of the local newspaper *El Puertorriqueño* and a Daley supporter, to the commission. More substantively, Latinos formed several new organizations that were explicitly political and what could be called panethnic—the beginning of what scholar Felix Padilla calls a "Latino or Hispanic ethnic consciousness in Chicago," and parallel to national efforts at creating a sustainable

Latino coalition. Obed López Zacarías, a Mexican American initially active in the Chicago Freedom Movement, started the Latin American Defense Organization (LADO) to advocate for welfare rights, while other activists founded the Spanish Action Committee of Chicago. In the years that followed, a number of Latino issue-oriented organizations emerged, such as the Spanish Coalition for Jobs, the Spanish Coalition for Housing, the Association for Workers Rights, and eventually the Latino Institute.[13]

Perhaps most striking was the transformation of several youth gangs, especially the Young Lords, into explicitly political groups. Started in West Lincoln Park in 1959 by Orlando Dávila, a dark-skinned Mexican American, the Young Lords had formed as most street gangs do—created by young men seeking friendship and protection in a hostile environment, in this case, working class white ethnics who resented the changing nature of their neighborhood. After years of escalating experimentation with violence, drug use, and petty crime as teenagers, the gang slowly developed a consciousness about inequality and poverty under the leadership of José "Cha-Cha" Jiménez, a founding member from age eleven whose family had moved to the neighborhood's "La Clark" (Clark Street) when he was an infant. Instead of simply protecting community turf from other gangs—a time-honored tradition in Chicago—what became the Young Lords Organization in 1966 attempted to protect the community from the authorities, and while predominantly Puerto Rican, the organization included a handful of Mexican American, Black, and even white members. "We saw a common enemy and we used that to unite the community," Jiménez said years later. "The common enemy . . . was the urban renewal and the police that was attacking us every day." Indeed, just like Mexican Americans and Puerto Ricans on the Near West Side, poor migrants who had initially settled in the Near North Side communities of Lincoln Park and Old Town faced tremendous pressure to move north and west to create a middle-class buffer for the downtown Loop. The police, more than anyone else, were charged with enforcing these shifting boundaries. Fueled by several short prison stints in Illinois and Puerto Rico for drug possession, the red-haired Jiménez developed both a broader political consciousness about the colonization of Puerto Ricans and the commonalities they held with African Americans, and even poor whites. He read Thomas Merton, Malcolm X, and the *Black Panther* newspaper, and saw clear application to the lives of poor people around them. As Lilia Fernández points out, "The Young Lords distinguished themselves from other Latino gangs in other neighborhoods in that they found themselves more deeply immersed in a radical political environment in Lincoln Park."[14]

The Young Lords became known for their spirited opposition to urban renewal in the neighborhood. Asked by leftist white activist Pat Devine-Reed to bring people to critique a proposed housing plan, Jiménez coaxed sixty people, many of them skeptical, to attend and showed them, "'Look, that is your house and they are going to knock it down'—real simple urban renewal analysis." After telling those gathered that the process should stop until Black and Latino representatives were consulted, Jiménez recalled, "to make the point clearer, somebody started throwing chairs." From then, the Young Lords remained committed to fighting urban renewal, even more so after an off-duty police officer killed Puerto Rican teenager Manuel Ramos during an argument. In a particularly daring move under the auspices of the multiracial Poor People's Coalition of Lincoln Park in May 1969, the Young Lords spearheaded the symbolic takeover of the Presbyterian-affiliated McCormick Theological Seminary's administration building for five days to protest what they called the institution's complicity in pushing poor people out of the neighborhood and its unwillingness to disburse promised funds for community projects. Nearly 300 people participated and, after initial stonewalling, the seminary agreed to pursue funds from the United Presbyterian Church for many of the activists' demands, including low-income housing, two free health clinics, a community legal aid office, and a Puerto Rican cultural center. Concluded seminary president Arthur McKay, in a speech to unconvinced businessmen, "There is a need." While that was more than apparent, most of the occupiers' demands, in the end, went unmet, stymied by city officials uninterested in an alternative community vision. But the McCormick takeover became just the first of many increasingly influential Latino church occupations across the country.[15]

The Young Lords also spawned several chapters, most prominently one in New York City, but of all the efforts made by the group, the most captivating and, at times, romanticized was the Rainbow Coalition.[16] Not to be confused with Jesse Jackson's presidential campaigns of the 1980s, the first Rainbow Coalition was the brainchild of Chicago Black Panthers Fred Hampton and Robert E. "Bobby" Lee. After serving as president of the NAACP Youth Council in the West Side suburb of Maywood, the twenty-one-year-old Hampton joined and quickly became chairman of the Illinois chapter of the Panthers in 1968. After Dr. Martin Luther King Jr.'s assassination, the charismatic Hampton mesmerized a conference of Black youth in Chicago, including Bobby Rush. Impressed by the young man's poise, oration, and articulate questioning of nonviolent strategy, Rush worked with Hampton and several other young men from East Garfield Park to turn a defunct SNCC chapter into a viable local Black Panther organization. The Chicago chapter established the traditional community survival programs for which the Panthers became known, such as free breakfasts and later a free health clinic. But the chapter, more than others across the country, also embraced rhetorical and material alliances with other oppressed peoples—in Lee's words, "All power to the people."[17]

For a time, they followed through with this objective. Together with the Young Lords, Hampton's Panthers allied with another former street gang, the Young Patriots. Poor white Appalachian migrants from Uptown and Lincoln Park on the Near North Side similarly had started off by simply protecting their turf from perceived outsiders, which over time translated into political activism addressing urban renewal, police brutality, and unemployment. Facilitated by Bobby Lee, the Patriots became a vocal partner in the Rainbow Coalition thanks to a handful of young white Appalachian transplants, Hy Thurman, Jack "Junebug" Boykin, and the Patriots' titular spokesman, Bill "Preacherman" Fesperman, a charismatic local seminary student who had grown up poor in a North Carolina mill town. By mid-1969, more than a dozen Panther sites on the West and South sides fed nearly 4,000 children daily, with hundreds more served through sites run by the Patriots and Lords. A number of other groups operated in the orbit of the Rainbow Coalition, too, including LADO, a multiracial antipoverty organization that emerged after the Division Street uprisings, and Rising Up Angry, a group of radical white working-class youths in Logan Square on the Northwest Side. Both ran free health clinics, and Rising Up Angry published a respected community newspaper of the same name that focused much of its reporting on multiracial grassroots activism against police harassment and other state oppression. Indeed, the critique of the police state stitched together this loosely organized alliance of youth better than any other issue, even urban renewal.[18]

At first glance, it might seem odd that none of these organizations were engaged with electoral politics directly. After all, the Daley machine was the power structure that maintained a regime of urban renewal predicated on racial segregation, deep pockets of poverty, unemployment, and underresourced schools, and a local police state designed to keep the system in place and the people in line. And yet, at least initially, the organizations in the Rainbow Coalition did not endorse specific candidates for mayor, alderman, or any other elected position. For most of them, the revolution simply would not arrive through the ballot box. Analysis of radical newspapers such as the *Black Panther* and *Rising Up Angry* in the late 1960s reveals little explicit discussion of local elections; this system was part of the problem, not the solution. More practically, in 1969, city elections were not for another two years, the presidential and gubernatorial elections for another three. But the police murder of Fred Hampton and Mark Clark changed that reality dramatically.

IN A CITY DUBBED the "national capital of police repression," Daley and the Democratic machine viewed a viable Rainbow Coalition as a serious threat. Not unlike the Federal Bureau of Investigation under J. Edgar Hoover and its extensive counterintelligence program (COINTELPRO), the Chicago Police Department responded accordingly. The police's subversion unit, known as the Red Squad, long had targeted the Left, from moderate organizations such as the Southern Christian Leadership Conference and Chicago Peace Council to more radical ones, such as the Panthers and Young Lords. As documented by the city's underground press, activists were convinced that coalition work among these organizations made them even more vulnerable to what could only be called state-sponsored terrorism. Throughout 1969, the Panthers and their allies weathered constant harassment by Red Squad agents, from dubious charges, assault, and entrapment to unannounced raids in which offices were ransacked, posters ripped down, breakfast program food ruined, and files and office equipment stolen. Several gun battles had broken out, leaving two Panthers dead. By the fall of 1969, the Panthers had spent considerable energy combating state violence, including a November shootout that killed three people, including two officers. The Illinois chapter of the Panthers, exhausted and isolated, entered the next winter with only a few dozen active members.[19]

None of this harassment, however, prepared the Panthers or their allies for the assault on the morning of December 4. The brazen attack went beyond what even the Red Squad normally did, and the evidence left behind flew in the face of the state's official narrative. Thus, not surprisingly, the murders initially appeared to unify a rainbow of opposition to Mayor Daley and his police department. In the days after the killings, at least a thousand people walked by the site patiently to pay their respects; thousands more attended memorial services across the city. Calling for investigations by a grand jury, Congress, and the Justice Department, even Harold Washington—in a rare rebuke by a Black elected official in the city—assailed the police in the aftermath of Hampton's death. "It would be an excellent idea and healthy for police associations . . . to take an investigative attitude toward this matter, rather than an accusatory attitude toward the Black Panthers," he stated. "They more than anyone else should want to know the truth."[20]

Ralph Abernathy, Jesse Jackson, and other national civil rights leaders joined more than 4,000 people at Hampton's official funeral. While most onlookers and attendees were African American, whites, Puerto Ricans, and Mexican Americans also participated, as Hampton's survivors vowed to continue the Rainbow Coalition. In the months afterward, that seemed possible. By the summer of 1970, coalition partners had shared resources and opened free health clinics, the Panthers naming theirs after another martyred local Panther, Spurgeon Jake Winters. Greater efforts against police brutality emerged in other quarters as well, most notably the Alliance to End Repression, a more middle-class multiracial coalition of organizations that spearheaded several lawsuits against the police department. Perhaps most boldly, the Panthers led by Bobby Rush announced a bold new effort in 1972 for "community control of the police." But Hampton's murder diminished the city's organizing in other, equally significant ways, routinely isolating younger, radical, and often working-class leaders by fomenting an intense atmosphere of fear. Tipped that the police would target him next, Rush briefly went into hiding before reemerging under the care of Jesse Jackson's Operation Breadbasket and the Afro-American Patrolmen's League. Cha-Cha Jiménez went underground, but for much longer—more than a year—to avoid a trumped-up charge of stealing $23 worth of lumber. Also facing questionable charges, Bill Fesperman left for New York City, while Bobby Lee went home to his native Texas. None of their organizations or their multiracial efforts fully recovered after the assassination.[21]

Moreover, the initial outrage over Hampton's death did not translate into anything more than token electoral opposition to Richard J. Daley's reelection in 1971. Despite initial predictions to the contrary, Daley coasted to his fifth straight term when no credible opponent chose to challenge him. Jesse Jackson, arguably the most charismatic African American leader in the city after Hampton died, flirted with running for mayor. "No more pieces, no more tokens, no buy-offs," declared Jackson in February 1971. "We want to run our own lives, to plan our own future and to reap the rewards of our efforts. We want to assume the power and exercise the power that controls our existence and our destinies." But despite Operation Breadbasket's success in obtaining what Martin Deppe estimates were 4,500 jobs and $57 million in annual economic gains for Black businesses and workers over six years, Jackson failed to get the number of signatures required to run for mayor—instead challenging the constitutionality of the requirement, and then, after losing that battle, briefly pursuing a quixotic write-in quest. On the eve of the election, he implored African Americans to vote for white liberal independent Richard Friedman; many observers wondered, as with many other Jackson efforts before, whether he really had wanted to run in the first place or if he simply sought free publicity. Jackson's failure to get a relatively small number of signatures underscored the limits of

Black Panther leader Bobby Rush, at a press conference in 1972, announces that a special investigator has been appointed to probe the police murders of Black Panthers Fred Hampton (*shown in the poster behind Rush*) and Mark Clark. Rush made his first run for alderman in 1975. ST-19020331–0005, *Chicago Sun-Times* collection, Chicago History Museum.

his activism; while certainly charismatic, Jackson and his more consumerist approach often placed him on the wrong side of more radical activists, such as the Coalition for United Community Action led by former King aide C. T. Vivian, which sought greater economic power through the building trades. In the summer of 1969, the coalition shut down dozens of construction sites, demanding more job opportunities, especially for young Black men, whose employment rate had hit 31 percent. While Jackson backed the coalition rhetorically, it was its allied Black gangs—the Lords, Disciples, and Rangers—that proved decisive in holding the industry accountable and getting it to admit its discrimination. Jobs came slowly, but in the end, it was not because of Jackson. To his critics, the pattern repeated itself two years later.[22]

Ultimately, Daley won by an overwhelming 400,000-plus votes out of 1 million cast. Some Chicagoans had decided years before that police violence could be acceptable to combat rising crime and gang violence; even some African Americans had drawn that conclusion, at least before the Hampton raid. But now clear warning signs had grown bigger as once-reliable Black support for the Daley machine steadily eroded. For the first time in the Daley era, predominantly African American wards backed the machine by smaller majorities than their white ethnic counterparts, while two more independents joined the City Council. Black lawyer and civil rights activist Anna Langford, who lost a close (some said stolen) race in 1967 won a rematch in the Sixteenth Ward, while thirty-year-old white political scientist Dick Simpson triumphed in the Forty-Fourth Ward on the Northwest Side. They joined a few other independent voices, including Leon Despres in what turned out to be his last term as the council's conscience, to create a small but dedicated and vocal antimachine bloc.[23]

NATIONALLY, law-and-order politics, white racial resentment, and a rejection of a counterculture that questioned many traditional U.S. values served President Richard Nixon well, helping the Republican win reelection in a landslide in November 1972, even in Illinois. But just a year after Daley's win, the excesses of local law enforcement played out differently in a city where African Americans and Latinos now made up more than 40 percent of the city's population. It was the product of years of grassroots frustration with the Chicago police and political elites who either turned a blind eye toward or actively supported such repression. Despite Daley's resounding reelection, a series of events in 1972 revealed the issue's potency to shift local politics in unexpected ways and culminated in the shocking defeat of machine-backed state's attorney Edward Hanrahan to Republican Bernard Carey that fall.

Founded quietly in the wake of the Hampton-Clark murders, the Alliance to End Repression emerged in 1970 as an important middle-class force in addressing inequalities in the local criminal justice system. Bringing with it a certain moral authority, the multiracial, multifaith coalition represented more than sixty organizations, ranging from the Amalgamated Meat Cutters and the Mattachine Society to a range of small Black and Latino community groups, and championed greater accountability of the police through a series of criminal justice reforms. The Alliance absorbed Citizens Alert, founded a few years before to address on-the-ground "police problems" directly, as well as pushed two referendums in the fall of 1972: the election of a Cook County medical examiner and greater transparency in the Chicago Police Board's appointments and monthly meetings. Coordinated by Roman Catholic activists John Hill and Betty Plank, the Alliance eventually sued the city and exposed the breadth of the Red Squad's activities. Many cities had such units, from New York to Denver, but none were more extensive than Chicago's. When it became clear that the

Red Squad's records might become public through a joint lawsuit by the Alliance and the American Civil Liberties Union, police officials destroyed thousands of individual and organizational files, and yet the fraction that survived and remain archived suggest a remarkably expansive, intrusive, and undemocratic enterprise found more often in dictatorships.[24]

Activism against state violence and suppression undoubtedly remained intertwined with other issues, given the role of the police in protecting the status quo and perpetuating inequality of all sorts. So much of the city's activism was in response to the harsh tactics of law enforcement—even within the police department, in the case of the Afro-American Patrolmen's League. But other kinds of organizing also informed the electoral realities of the era. After his flirtation with the 1971 mayoral race and rising conflicts with SCLC leadership in Atlanta, which wanted to reign in his unusual autonomy, Jesse Jackson officially resigned from the SCLC's Operation Breadbasket, the civil rights and selective-buying program established in 1966. As had been SCLC president Ralph Abernathy's concern, many of Breadbasket's several thousand supporters demonstrated more loyalty to Jackson by abandoning the SCLC and moving to his new organization, Operation People United to Save Humanity (PUSH). This effectively ended the SCLC's work in Chicago and dealt a major blow to an already-reeling civil rights organization seeking its place more than three years after Dr. Martin Luther King Jr.'s death. In Breadbasket's place was PUSH's nearly identical civil rights agenda, especially its program of selective-buying campaigns, negotiations, and covenants to encourage private companies' increased and varied hiring of African Americans. As reporter and Jackson biographer Barbara Reynolds observed, "The issues that confront the organization are mindboggling. They almost always divert the operation from its primary goals." Those issues, to name just a few, included spearheading protests against cuts to social welfare programs at the state and federal levels; sponsoring conferences on tax reform, the Black consumer, revenue sharing, and Black businesses; and advocating for a Black mayor, Black superintendents of schools and police, and a Black contractor to build the Carter G. Woodson branch library. The PUSH Teachers' Division emerged as a relevant actor in empowering Black teachers. Thus, Jackson's organization, whether it was called Breadbasket or PUSH, remained an important voice for social justice and equality in the city, even if the follow-through was often inconsistent—the same charge Jackson faced when he "ran" for mayor.[25]

PUSH touched on most concerns in the city in some way, but Jackson's network was certainly not the only social justice organization in town in the early

1970s. Others, in fact, routinely demonstrated more effectiveness in addressing specialized issues, from welfare rights and urban renewal to jobs, education, housing, and health care. For instance, the Chicago Welfare Rights Organization and the Latin American Defense Organization (LADO) reflected the priorities of the national welfare rights movement against welfare cuts and for income maintenance and more dignified treatment of clients. Those groups that were allies, if not part of the early Rainbow Coalition, such as Rising Up Angry and LADO, maintained several free medical clinics in the city and dovetailed their advocacy for basic health care with those of the Chicago-based Medical Committee on Human Rights, led by Quentin Young. Any number of coalitions worked on urban renewal and housing, such as the Campaign to Control High Rises and the Anti-Crosstown Action Committee, the latter successful in eventually blocking the displacement of 15,000 homes on the South and West Sides to build yet another highway. And labor unions, of course, remained a potent force, although most, including the city's increasingly Black municipal employees unions representing teachers and transit workers, usually made the practical decision to ally with the regular Democratic Party every four years. Only traditionally progressive labor organizations, such as those in the Coalition of Black Trade Unionists, could be considered a consistent part of the city's social justice network. And yet despite the array of issues at hand, activist talk routinely circled back to the foundational challenge posed by the Chicago Police Department—simple survival—which is why the transformation of Ralph Metcalfe remains a topic of discussion even today.[26]

Chicagoans, especially Black Chicagoans, decades later still talked about the epiphany Congressman Ralph Metcalfe had in the spring of 1972.[27] One of the gold medalists of the 1936 Olympics in Hitler's Germany and, more important to Daley, a Roman Catholic, Metcalfe was a rising star in the machine, becoming the Third Ward committeeman and then alderman, where he worked closely with ward secretary Harold Washington. When William Dawson died in 1970, Metcalfe succeeded him, underscoring Daley's confidence in the former athlete to tow the party line, including a rejection of most civil rights efforts, from Martin Luther King Jr.'s campaign to end the slums to criticism of the Chicago police during the 1968 Democratic National Convention. As alderman, Metcalfe tepidly called for a probe into the deaths of Fred Hampton and Mark Clark and was mercilessly booed as an opportunist during his public statements on the police's actions. Critics claimed that Daley himself wrote the remarks. Little seemed to change when Metcalfe became congressman, although he did join the Congressional Black Caucus, something Dawson never bothered to do. But

Congressman Ralph Metcalfe, *right*, appears at a downtown union rally in 1974 with Mayor Richard J. Daley, *second to right*, and others. Metcalfe had dramatically broken with Daley and the Democratic machine two years earlier over police violence, although the move did not mean he embraced the kinds of genuine reform activists had demanded. ST-11006193–0005, *Chicago Sun-Times* collection, Chicago History Museum.

when two Black South Side dentists, including one of Metcalfe's closest friends, Herbert Odom, were beaten by the police without apology or the acknowledgment of any wrongdoing, Metcalfe had had enough. He founded the Concerned Citizens for Police Reform, a multiracial coalition of church and community organizations, and declared famously that "it's never too late to be Black." Some observers doubted Metcalfe's commitment to the issue and believed he had mainly calculated that his organization on the South Side was strong enough to win on its own. But it was still startling that Daley's handpicked Black front man, someone he trusted far more than Dawson, had broken with him. Over the next several years, Daley repaid the favor by sending city inspectors to Metcalfe's offices and cutting most of his patronage jobs. But, significantly, Daley failed to defeat the popular Metcalfe electorally. When Metcalfe narrowly beat Daley's new man, Ervin France, in the 1976 congressional primary, Metcalfe seemed pleasantly surprised, ecstatically slapping backs and handing out money to precinct captains in his campaign office. Others, especially among African American politicos, took note that, more than anything, Metcalfe's victory meant that abandoning the machine, at least in certain circumstances, was not political suicide.[28]

METCALFE'S AWAKENING came only a month after thousands of African Americans from across the country attended the National Black Political Convention in the neighboring industrial city of Gary, Indiana—the first of its kind since the National Negro Convention Movement of the mid-nineteenth century. A symbol of postwar urban decay and the rise of Black political power, Gary and its recently reelected mayor, Richard Hatcher, hosted about 3,000 African American delegates and thousands of additional observers to this steel city just beyond Chicago's South Side. The delegates debated issues from busing to Israel to whether they should endorse New York congresswoman Shirley Chisholm's bid for the Democratic presidential nomination; they ultimately did not. And they talked openly about a race-based third political party, an attractive alternative given the rapidly whitening Republican Party of President Nixon and an increasingly multiracial yet tepid Democratic Party that still embraced conservatives hostile to racial justice. "Both parties have betrayed us whenever their interests conflicted with ours," proclaimed the Gary Declaration. "By now, we must know that the American political system, like all other white institutions in America, was designed to operate for the benefit of the white race. . . . We begin here and now in Gary. We begin with an independent Black political movement, an independent Black Political Agenda, an independent Black spirit." Black power poet and activist Amiri Baraka, one of three key organizers of the convention, endorsed a third party, as did a sizable number of delegates, especially those from the urban North and West. Mainstream Black newspapers such as New York's *Amsterdam News* called for one, as did Jesse Jackson. "Nationhood is the politics of multiple options," Jackson told a charged convention crowd. "One of those options must be a Black political party."[29]

But, in the end, delegates stopped short of endorsing one. Jackson quickly distanced himself from the idea, as the power of sitting Black politicians, most of them in the Democratic Party, proved too influential. In contrast to Baraka, his two convention co-organizers, Hatcher and Congressman Charles Diggs of Detroit, opposed a third party. Hatcher told the convention that he was "willing to give the two major political parties one more chance" in 1972 before he would "seriously probe the possibility of a third-party movement in this country." Meanwhile, state senator and future Detroit mayor Coleman Young threatened to lead Diggs's own Michigan delegation out of the convention if delegates endorsed a new organization. The impracticality of a race-based third party and the clear, albeit gradual, influence that African Americans had gained, particularly within the Democratic Party, eventually won out. Thus, the convention's final declaration embraced a distinct Black independence, but not a new party.[30]

Despite little clear mandate beyond the vague bumper-sticker slogan of "unity without uniformity," the male-heavy Chicago delegation, which included not just Jackson but also Metcalfe, Bobby Rush, state senator Richard Newhouse, and Alderman Bill Cousins, translated the convention's energy into an affirmation of political independence from the city's Democratic machine. As columnist Vernon Jarrett wrote in the *Tribune*, "It is not whom or what we conquered today, but also what we bequeath to those who would carry on the struggle." In addition to Metcalfe's break from the machine in April, Jesse Jackson and progressive Jewish alderman William Singer orchestrated a rare coup during the summer's Democratic National Convention (DNC). Using the so-called McGovern rules that encouraged greater diversity among convention delegates through demographic quotas, Jackson and Singer spearheaded an alternative multiracial, multigenerational slate to challenge Daley's Illinois delegation, made up overwhelmingly of white, male machine allies. Despite the rule changes, most political observers, both local and national, were stunned when the Credentials Committee and then the full convention recognized and seated the upstart delegation, driving a bitter and angry Mayor Daley into seclusion, complaining that groups like Jackson's were "destroying the Democratic party." The rejection was a remarkable embarrassment for a politician who had been a DNC kingmaker since the mid-1950s. Of course, South Dakota senator George McGovern, the rules' author and party presidential nominee, went on to win just one state in one of the most lopsided losses in the history of U.S. presidential elections—a campaign Daley half-heartedly endorsed because the mayor agreed far more with President Nixon than the progressive McGovern on issues from Vietnam and peace to civil rights and criminal justice.[31]

More broadly, Daley's humiliation at the DNC became just one more sign of the machine's vulnerability. Before Election Day, seventy-five members of the machine were under indictment. Many more indictments came down over the next two years, including ones of Tom Keane, the mayor's council floor leader; alderman and Keane law partner Paul Wigoda; and Daley's press secretary, Earl Bush. The city's police department, to which Daley's law-and-order politics were so closely tied, faced ever-increasing legal and community scrutiny, from the poor treatment of minority police officers highlighted by the AAPL to routine shakedowns of tavern owners to rampant police brutality and harassment. Daley and his sons, long seen as personally clean even if some of their associates were not, came under suspicion when newspaper reports exposed a shadowy real estate company owned by Daley and his wife, and favoritism around their sons' insurance license tests. Rather than deny favoritism, Daley complained, "If a man can't put his arms around his sons, then what kind of a world are we living in?" Daley was also slowing down physically. The following year, he suffered a stroke, which impaired his speech and sensory perception, prompting lengthy absences from the public eye, and heightening rumors about his fitness for office. What had started as a whisper had become a full-throated question: "Is the machine sputtering?"[32]

Despite these warning signs, few traditional political observers expected an African American revolt at the polls that fall. But that is exactly what happened when African Americans voted in record numbers for Republican Bernard Carey for state's attorney, making Edward Hanrahan, the architect of the Hampton-Clark murders, the first machine candidate during Daley's seventeen-year reign to lose a citywide election. While Republicans had enjoyed a sweeping national victory that year, Nixon's coattails alone did not explain Carey's victory. Despite the outrage among African Americans nearly three years earlier, the machine initially slated Hanrahan and only withdrew its endorsement in the primary after he faced a grand jury indictment for obstructing justice and conspiracy to present false evidence. Hanrahan still won the Democratic primary and thus was expected to cruise to victory in the fall. That seemed even more likely when, just two weeks before the election, a jury acquitted him on all counts. Yet he lost by more than 100,000 votes in what was seen as a major upset, especially since Democrats simultaneously won back the governorship. And despite initial media reports that mainly credited suburban white Republicans for the victory, it was African Americans, especially those on the South Side, who proved essential to Hanrahan's defeat. In a clear rejection of the state's attorney, less than 20 percent of African Americans voted for him. This was the case even though Carey himself was not particularly enlightened on criminal justice and race. "The Black community came together in a way that I've never seen before," observed journalist Lu Palmer, one of many African Americans who viewed Carey's victory as a sign of what could be, of the potential of Black independence.[33]

**HANRAHAN'S DEFEAT** was the clearest sign yet that the protests of the previous decade—school boycotts, Protest at the Polls, the Chicago Freedom Movement, the Rainbow Coalition, to name a few—may have finally had a decisive, cumulative impact on electoral politics in the city. This was particularly the case among African Americans. In the spring of 1974, Black independents made their most formal push yet for a Black mayor, forming the Committee for a Black Mayor. Founded by independent Black political and community leaders, the group sought to capitalize on the machine's troubles and community activism around police brutality, lackluster schools, and urban renewal, and announced an explicit goal of consolidating support around one candidate. "Black political power has gone beyond the talking stage," declared Charlie Hayes, longtime progressive labor leader, cofounder of the Coalition of Black Trade Unionists, and the committee's chairman. "We're tired of depending on other people who promise to serve Black needs but fail to deliver." Meeting secretly for several weeks before going public, the diverse group of more than thirty prominent African American activists and politicians included Jesse Jackson, Aldermen Anna Langford and Bill Cousins, and West Side community activists Brenetta Howell Barrett, Nancy Jefferson, and Danny Davis. The committee listed eight specific characteristics that a "creditable" candidate would have, including integrity, a record of service, intellectual ability, a willingness to put "community interest over personal ambitions," and a commitment to run. "We see our clear-cut responsibility to the Black community as one of changing illusionary political power to real concrete political power," stated Hayes, who then paraphrased Frederick Douglass's nineteenth-century dictum about power, "This cannot be given, it must be taken." Although focused on electing a Black mayor, the committee attempted to strike an inclusive, albeit awkward tone in reaching out to "those Browns, native Americans and white people of goodwill who desire to carve out the future with our help." The committee, especially Hayes, a leader in the United Packinghouse Workers who long believed labor rights were civil rights, knew they needed more than just African Americans to win.[34]

However, achieving any kind of consensus, even among those Black Chicagoans skeptical of the machine, proved a daunting task. The committee's first official order of business was to conduct a nonbinding survey of African American voters on their initial mayoral preferences. State senator Richard Newhouse, who had expressed openness to a draft, won a plurality and announced his candidacy in September. E. Duke McNeil, a committee member and respected criminal defense lawyer for the Black Panthers, had made history a month before as the city's first-ever Black mayoral candidate, only to withdraw in support of Newhouse. Two other African Americans also entered the race; but looming over the entire process was Ralph Metcalfe. The congressman's 1972 political defection over police misconduct made him an instant contender to mount a credible challenge to the machine's candidate, whether Daley or someone else, and for the committee's endorsement. He was a proven vote-getter with a strong South Side organization, and he enjoyed a broad popularity rooted both in his reinvigorated defense of the community and his Olympic folk hero status. Metcalfe faced intense lobbying to run, including by state representative Harold Washington, another contender who in a prepared statement to the committee called the congressman "the best candidate." Members of the committee agreed and endorsed the reluctant Metcalfe in early November. Despite these efforts and insider reports that he was tantalizingly close to running, Metcalfe retreated to the safety of his congressional district. "I am a witness to pressures from City Hall," Metcalfe said, pointing out the reality of the moment. "Anyone who has ever received a favor will be called upon to give a favor" for the machine and against him.[35]

The intrigue around Metcalfe's choice highlighted the long-running debate among African Americans, not just in Chicago but also nationally, over the best path to genuine empowerment—inside a corrupt political system or outside of it. After the decision to bypass Newhouse and others to endorse a hesitant Metcalfe, some dismissed the committee as a "Daley front." Newhouse was livid, calling the Black mayoral committee's impressive array of activists, a bit hysterically, a bunch of "Toms." Others more removed from the process were just as critical because they disagreed with those on the committee who viewed any Black mayor, even a pliant party regular, as a "step in the right direction." An unpersuaded Bill Cousins told the *Chicago Defender* that he and others were concerned that a "puppet Black mayor . . . would constitute no real change." Labor activist, educator, and committee member Tim Black, in a letter to Hayes, took the critique further. "At the same time, the group seems to have closed the door on other power options, because of the narrowness of the concept of 'Committee for a Black Mayor,'" Black wrote, citing Wilson Frost, the council's machine-aligned Black president pro tempore who was content to be little more than a symbol. "It has alienated a number of very useful Black people, and has almost completely shut out the possibility of alliances with other minorities and liberal or/and affected whites." He continued, "There may be a number of different groups who would like to see Daley dethroned, and the machine dismantled. Real Black empowerment will only be possible when that happens." After it was clear Metcalfe would not reconsider, the committee determined both Newhouse and white independent alderman Bill Singer were qualified. However, Hayes condemned as a "rough hurdle" Newhouse's initial opposition to the Equal Rights Amendment because it supposedly "distracted too many committed women" from attending to "broken families"—a position

Newhouse later reversed. Ultimately, more than twenty-five prominent Black leaders, including Metcalfe, endorsed Singer to be mayor.[36]

The deliberations of the Committee for a Black Mayor exposed what had tormented Black politics in the city for decades: African Americans and those opposed to unfettered machine rule remained quite divided on how to defeat Daley and his entrenched allies. Despite some fleeting successes at the national and state levels, a progressive multiracial coalition struggled to unseat conservative establishment Democrats locally. And when they did, as in 1972, they ended up electing a mainstream Republican who may not have had their best interests in mind either. As the next round of city elections approached in the winter of 1975, independent Black, Latino, and white Chicagoans attempted to get past the historic differences that so often divided them. By and large, they failed to win, either the mayoralty or most city council races. But in the process, activists invested in independent politics took an important step, one that highlighted the nuances between protest and politics and what factors needed to be considered if electoral politics were to be something more than just winning the spoils.[37]

## CHAPTER 3

# Winning by Losing?

Civil rights demonstrators make good marchers, but
poor politicians. Civil rights leaders can get a good
boycott, but they can never get out a good vote.
—Chuck Stone, Black journalist and activist, quoted in
Barbara Reynolds, *Jesse Jackson: America's David* (1985)

**W**hen Cha-Cha Jiménez announced a surprise run for alderman in 1975, the Puerto Rican activist remained candid about the goals of his new endeavor. "We don't necessarily believe that through elections we'll get our freedom," he told the radical newspaper *Rising Up Angry.* "The primary goal of the campaign is to build a base among the people. If we organize the people, the campaign will be a real victory."[1] His comment could have been a classic example of a candidate lowering expectations; the charismatic, red-headed twenty-six-year-old recently had emerged from hiding and a short jail sentence and was seen by most political observers as a longshot to win. But his remark also reflected the quandary of a longtime organizer pursuing elective office. His candidacy could be, as Jiménez suggested, another way to organize his North Side community, certainly a productive objective. Or perhaps his run represented how full participation in electoral politics—not just one driven by patronage—had become a primary component of first-class citizenship. Maybe it was a little of both.

In the mid-1970s, many electoral campaigns and their related community activism demonstrated both the rich potential and the acute challenges of transitioning from the protest culture of the city's freedom struggle to more formal politics. Independent, progressive African Americans had been running since at least the 1950s, but mostly as protest candidates; the name of the Protest at the Polls campaign of 1963–64 said as much. The city elections of 1975 represented a different calculation. It was the first year in which prominent individuals who identified first and foremost as activists in the city's freedom struggle had run for elected office and genuinely believed they could win. In particular, Al Raby, veteran of the SCLC-CCCO efforts of the Chicago Freedom Movement, was the favorite to win his race to succeed the retiring Leon Despres in the historically independent and progressive Fifth Ward, home of the University of Chicago. Several other council races were also notable, as two key members of the Rainbow Coalition, Jiménez and former Black Panther Bobby Rush, challenged machine-backed aldermen with vigorous grassroots campaigns in North Side and South Side wards. Meanwhile, an independent committee sought to add Chicago to the list of U.S. cities with a Black mayor, and Ralph Metcalfe, loyal soldier of the city's Black submachine and William Dawson's successor in Congress, successfully navigated his political independence from the city's white powerbrokers. Finally, Harold Washington—as well as the Polish community's Roman Pucinski—defied those same men who had sponsored them, challenging their choice to succeed Mayor Daley.

The Democratic machine proved its durability by winning all but Metcalfe's congressional race, including a surprisingly sizable victory by an aging Daley, who had sought an unprecedented sixth term in what turned out to be his last race. Despite rising expectations for a new civil rights and Black Power generation of politicians, this transition proved quite complicated. Perhaps most obvious was the machine's remarkable staying power, fueled by the business community; conservative, often transactional trade unions; and white ethnic voters. But other factors were just as important, including persistent, often personal, divisions among African Americans, the mundane but powerful advantage of incumbency, the "double-edged sword" that was personal charisma, and the uneven quality of the candidates' own grassroots work—the latter a particular irony for one-time civil rights and Black Power activists. These factors made it difficult for political independents to win, even as progressive African Americans made inroads against once-entrenched urban machines in other cities.

And yet warning signs for the existing political structure also loomed in Chicago—namely, the belief that these activists could address and mitigate such factors through more campaign experience, careful organizing, voter registration efforts, papering over of differences, and a bit of luck. A generation of activists, who had successfully undermined Jim Crow, eventually were able to wrest away at least some control from white politicos and their hand-picked Black and Latino lackeys. But this only occurred after they learned a series of difficult lessons about how to translate movement politics into more formal electoral efforts and political power. Most failed, especially the first, second, or even third time around. But many activist candidates effectively used these lessons to set the stage for greater Black and Latino empowerment in the coming decade. Bobby Rush, for instance, lost before he won. So did Harold Washington.

**BY THE MIDDLE** of the 1970s, most of the nation's major cities had seen reform mayors enter their city halls, a reflection of changing demographics, multiracial coalition-building with roots in the era's social movements, and a rejection of corrupt politics from urban machines to Richard Nixon's Watergate-compromised White House. With the exception of Frank Rizzo, Philadelphia's cop-turned-mayor who exuded a tough-guy persona straight out of 1970s vigilante crime dramas *Dirty Harry* and *Death Wish*, Daley appeared out of step with such national political trends; most of the nation's largest cities had either elected their first Black mayors, such as in Los Angeles and Detroit, or mildly progressive whites, as in Baltimore and New York.[2] Combined with Daley's age, ongoing scandals, and a national anticorruption sentiment, many independents were bullish about the potential of Bill Singer, a thirty-four-year-old Jewish lawyer and alderman from the North Side Lakefront who had announced his run sixteen months before the primary. As the sympathetic *Chicago Reader* noted, Singer was "the only man in recent time to defeat Hizzoner [Daley] at anything." Three years before, Singer briefly became a household name when he and Jesse Jackson persuaded the Democratic National Convention's Credentials Committee to seat a multiracial group of George McGovern delegates instead of Daley's mostly white delegation—a mortifying defeat for a party kingmaker, if not delayed justice from the interracial Mississippi Freedom Democratic Party's failed challenge in 1964.[3]

The DNC delegation reflected the coalition Singer hoped to put together in 1975—one that looked like the city's diversity of activism. The radical Rainbow Coalition may have disappeared years before, but others, often more reformist, had remained or emerged, including the electorally focused and predominantly white Independent Precinct Organization and the Independent Voters of Illinois, two groups that for years had sought ethics reforms, better budgetary oversight, and other "good government" objectives. Both, reflecting a mix of Republicans and independent Democrats, endorsed Singer's bid. Just like African Americans, the city's white "Lakefront liberals" had begun to turn on Daley, especially over the uptick in "pay-to-play" convictions over zoning and more mundane city services. According to one political scientist, Singer was the "classic reform candidate" who stressed better schools, tighter ethics and patronage rules, criminal justice reform, a more assertive industrial policy amid deindustrialization nationwide, and greater empowerment of neighborhoods across the city, not just Daley's Irish American enclave of Bridgeport or wealthy white communities on the North and Northwest Sides. But more than anything, Singer ran against the machine and its excesses—and hoped that a durable coalition of whites, Blacks, and Latinos could be built around this common foe.[4]

Singer was one of three independent candidates in the primary, but he was the only one perceived to have a viable citywide organization, with a presence in all fifty wards—unheard of for an independent organization in the Daley era. In addition to state senator Richard Newhouse, the Democratic primary also included former state's attorney Edward Hanrahan, who ran a barely veiled campaign of white racial hostility. Longtime political observers believed that Hanrahan had the potential to siphon enough white ethnic crime voters from Daley to make Singer competitive. Meanwhile, Newhouse, acknowledging that he had not unified Black support behind his candidacy, nor had the money or organization to win, still deemed his run a success because "it's been a way for people who never felt they had any power to feel they are politically important." Strikingly, the Black-owned *Chicago Defender*, disappointed in the lack of Black unity, endorsed Daley and credited him for keeping Chicago out of the "bankruptcy and economic chaos" that New York and other cities faced. The liberal-leaning Lerner weeklies, as well as the *Chicago Reader*, wrote positively about Singer, while the conservative, Republican-owned *Chicago Tribune*, which had endorsed Daley in three out of his previous five campaigns, chose not to endorse in 1975. Thus, while still considered an underdog, Singer and his backers remained confident about his chances. "We have the momentum," one supporter told the *Tribune* days before the election.[5]

In the end, as the machine had done so many times before, Daley beat Singer and the others handily—a deflating defeat for the city's independents. "What can I tell you?" Singer campaign manager Mac Hansbrough told reporters. "We got our ass kicked." Daley won with 58 percent of the total vote to Singer's 29 percent, as the machine poured resources into what had been considered Singer's strongholds on the North Side. Despite a well-financed citywide organization, Singer ultimately had little real street presence in predominantly Black wards, had not tapped any African Americans for the campaign's leadership, and made little effort to frame issues in terms of Black interests, according to William Grimshaw, a political scientist who had worked on the campaign. Singer fared particularly poorly in the "plantation wards" of the West Side, in which the Daley machine demonstrated its characteristic strength through a mix of patronage and voter suppression of the city's poorest African Americans.

Moreover, white ethnic law-and-order support for Hanrahan never materialized. While the mayor criticized what he called the media's "Singer bias," much
of the mayoral news coverage stressed "horserace" news rather than policy proposals, muddling Singer's reform message. Ultimately, independents resigned
themselves to another four years in the political wilderness.[6]

ON THE SURFACE, the races for alderman that year reflected a similar
result—most of the nonmachine politicians, including Al Raby, Bobby Rush,
and Cha-Cha Jiménez, lost. Even independent Black incumbent Anna Langford
fell, ushering in "the most subservient council in the city's history," predicted
the *Tribune* on election night.[7] Only independent aldermen Bill Cousins and
Dick Simpson were left, neither of whom identified as a civil rights activist per
se. Not one factor or issue swayed these elections; each ward had its own set of
circumstances. But these candidates' losses did prove instructive in how certain civil rights tactics could be used in an electoral context, and where the
traditional politics of incumbency, ideology, and personality emerged as decisive. Independents took these lessons and honed their strategies, eventually
applying them to a series of more successful campaigns later in the decade.

Raby, a leader in the Chicago Freedom Movement, delegate to the state's constitutional convention in 1969, and one-time education aide to maverick Democratic governor Dan Walker, campaigned on his civil rights work and ties to the
martyred Dr. Martin Luther King Jr. Long represented by alderman and tireless
Daley critic Leon Despres, the Fifth Ward included the University of Chicago,
the diverse community of Hyde Park, and the predominantly Black South Shore,
and had a history as a partially integrated liberal enclave, with Black residents
making up about 60 percent of its population, despite the university's efforts
at urban renewal. Describing himself as "primarily an organizer," the bearded,
some said beleaguered Raby stated that, in addition to traditional constituent
services, he was interested in "supporting and creating various organizations in
the community—tenant unions and block clubs, for example." Indeed, his campaign zeroed in on many of the same issues he had championed as a civil rights
leader in the 1960s: opposition to urban renewal and rapid condominium conversion, affordable housing, local control of the police department, and a consistent critique of Daley and pay-to-play governance. Ultimately, Raby wanted
to "maintain the independent tradition of the 5th ward," he told the *Chicago
Reader*. "The alderman of this ward has not only served as a powerful local voice
. . . but also as a critical analyst of the policies and overall management of the

city itself." Raby clearly attempted to position himself as the natural successor to Despres, admired in the ward and across the city for his impeccable record on human rights and ethics.[8]

As a civil rights activist, Raby was known for his "confrontational politics"—an image his three primary opponents tried to highlight as a negative—but his candidacy often took the opposite approach, one that reflected an attempt to make peace with electoral politics and work more within the system.[9] As a result, he at times took on the trappings of a traditional candidate—and a boring one at that—in a way that undermined his grassroots civil rights bona fides and contributed to his eventual defeat. One of three Black candidates in the primary, Raby won endorsements from the *Chicago Tribune* and *Sun-Times*, as well as several influential independent political organizations. While he won accolades from high-profile, charismatic civil rights figures, such as Jesse Jackson, Georgia congressman Andrew Young, and entertainer Sammy Davis Jr., some believed Raby relied too heavily on outside endorsements instead of the precinct-level groundwork necessary to win a ward election. "Raby had very little organized support within Black precincts," concluded the *Tribune*'s Vernon Jarrett. "Even his photograph with the sainted Dr. Martin Luther King Jr. helped little." There were several splashy efforts designed for the media but little sign of the voter registration or canvassing successful civil rights activism employed. Sidney Williams, one of Raby's opponents, told the *Hyde Park Herald*'s David Axelrod that "Al never really went into the Black areas and talked to people about what was on their minds. He just assumed that they would vote for him because he was Black and worked with Dr. King."[10] William Grimshaw underscored this point, arguing that successful independent Black candidates generally stayed out of the media and instead worked on "nuts and bolts" organizing for his constituents, "the same dedicated way that the machine worked its wards." Therefore, not surprisingly, even in a higher-turnout vote, Raby eked out first place with just 28 percent of the vote in a four-way race, just 500 ballots more than his closest opponent.[11]

In the runoff between Raby and Ross Lathrop, an administrator at the University of Chicago, a political neophyte, and the ward election's lone white, the roles of race and the machine grew more explicit. Both candidates also faced charges of being part of a "machine," and thus not a true representative of the fiercely independent ward. Raby fended off accusations of being a shill for Governor Dan Walker, an antimachine Democrat and corporate lawyer who in 1972 had defeated the party's preferred candidate and then the incumbent Republican. Walker had chaired a committee looking into the 1968 police riot and emerged as a rival to Daley, challenging the Chicago police, opposing the

Crosstown Expressway, and making unpopular state budget cuts in education and welfare. For his part, Lathrop unconvincingly denied he had support from Daley. Months later, well after Lathrop won, the *Hyde Park Herald* revealed that his campaign had received donations by machine-connected construction and engineering companies not in the ward. Raby and Lathrop also suggested that the other had quietly campaigned on racial lines. The poll results—for both primary and runoff—demonstrated such a divide. The wealthier and whiter precincts in central and east Hyde Park came out in significantly larger numbers for Lathrop, prompting Raby's campaign to try and rally historically low-turnout, majority-Black precincts west and south of the university.[12]

Although there were several reasons why Raby lost, including his personality and overconfidence, the accusations of racism and machine politics against a civil rights figure in such a diverse ward ended up tainting him more than Lathrop. As Raby himself admitted during a candidate debate, in response to a question about Walker's influence, "I don't have the luxury of having" political purity anymore. The moral clarity of his past activism was missing. But it was not replaced with the practical approach normally valued in an alderman either; more than anything, the alderman made sure basic city services were taken care of, the trash collected, potholes filled, often in exchange for votes for the organization. That mattered, even in the most independent ward in the city. Instead, Raby came across as neither idealistically inspiring nor politically practical, and it became clear that running for office was indeed different, even more difficult, than leading marches alongside Dr. King had been a decade before. In the end, the once-heavily favored Raby lost by 300 votes, with a large drop-off coming from precincts that were predominantly African American, poor, and underregistered. Predictions, perhaps hopes, that turnout would be higher proved wrong. As one resident wrote to the *Tribune* just days after the runoff—"The 5th ward—after 28 years—belongs to Mayor Daley."[13]

ANOTHER ALDERMANIC RACE featured Bobby Rush, the thin, bespectacled former Black Panther and comrade of the martyred Fred Hampton. Rush challenged machine-aligned alderman William "Butch" Barnett in the historic Second Ward, home of the famed community of Bronzeville just south of the downtown Loop and the power base for two of Black Chicago's first political giants, Oscar DePriest and William Dawson. By 1975 the ward had seen better days, marred by high crime, poor schools, and a lack of quality jobs; only four of the ward's twenty-six census tracts were not considered low-income. Tackling that intractable poverty and the issues related to it became the core of Rush's platform. "I'm touring every school in the ward," he told reporters. "They have become training schools for crime." Rush also leveled a sharp critique of the machine's incumbent, whose "vision has been blunted by the taste of polish from Mayor Daley's boots." The owner of a private security firm, Barnett was considered a "glorified coatholder" for the boss; for instance, the alderman gained notoriety for bucking most other Black aldermen and supporting improvements at the South Side's Lake Shore Club, which had no Jewish or African American members. Critics concluded that neglect by Barnett and his predecessors had led to many of the overwhelmingly Black ward's problems.[14]

Rush, despite being just twenty-seven when he announced his candidacy, was already familiar with the city's tough politics and had been a persistent critic of the machine for nearly a decade, much of it as a leader of the local Black Panthers. A founder of the party's Illinois chapter, Rush admiringly spoke of the rise of the charismatic Fred Hampton as chairman, his agenda to build a revolutionary multiracial coalition, and the chapter's dedication to community survival programs. "Fred moved people because most people felt as though he had a sense of conviction," Rush recalled years later. "If he said something, then you'd better watch out, within a few seconds he's going to be doing exactly what he said he's going to do." After Hampton's murder and a brief period underground in its wake, Rush finished his bachelor's degree at Roosevelt University in 1974 but struggled to find work because of his Panther past. After being denied positions at the Urban League and in state government, he went into insurance.[15]

Rush's close affiliation with the Panthers at times left a complicated legacy for his campaign, opening him to criticism by the mainstream media and police but also reflecting genuine grassroots experience and credibility with parts of the community. Even though the Panthers had closed their office in early 1974, Rush continually had to respond to aspersions from police and reporters, often in the *Tribune*, about the Panthers' perceived rhetoric of violence and socialism.[16] Citing the distribution of thousands of bags of food, pairs of shoes, and other benefits, Rush argued, "Our reputation with the people here has been excellent." Others questioned whether he had changed his philosophy dramatically to run for public office—a charge he also denied. "I still consider myself to be in favor of progressive change," he stated. "If you call that a revolutionary, that's what I am." Indeed, many of his policy positions were consistent with the Panthers' objectives and programs, from initiatives to help people with daily survival to criticism of the police and city officials. In an interview shortly after he announced his candidacy, Rush highlighted seemingly mundane yet important issues of funding for youth recreation programs, elevator repair in

public housing, and organized citizen's alerts to combat crime. The ward's crises had been "neglected by the present Alderman," Rush said, but "there exists
a lot of mechanisms to solve problems in the area of housing, city services, and
education. . . . The electoral process has legitimacy" to bring about necessary
change.[17]

Rush was not the first Black Panther to run for office—just the first in Chicago. In 1968, several Panthers from the original Oakland chapter ran on the
Peace and Freedom Party ticket, a symbolic third-party protest against the
Vietnam War. Eldridge Cleaver ran for president (with white Chicago Uptown
activist Peggy Terry as his running mate), Huey Newton for Congress, and
Bobby Seale and Elaine Brown for California State Assembly. They expected not
to win but to mobilize support for Newton's release from jail and against police
brutality and harassment more generally. But much like in Chicago, circumstances both nationally and locally changed during the next five years. Electoral politics seemed more viable after a series of Black mayoral victories in not
just Gary and Cleveland but also Newark, Detroit, and Los Angeles. Meanwhile,
in 1969 a record thirteen Black members of Congress established the Democratic Select Committee, later renamed the Congressional Black Caucus. On the
heels of the National Black Political Convention in Gary in 1972, the Panthers'
Central Committee decided that its members should run for office as serious
candidates and not symbolic protests. "We're going to use the existing institution to serve the people," Seale stated. "See, we're part of the system. You cannot
get out of the system." Several Panthers, many of them female, won seats that
year on local antipoverty agency boards in Berkeley and Oakland, and in 1973,
Seale ran for mayor and Elaine Brown for city council in Oakland. While they
did not win, their campaigns' prominent cooperation with Cesar Chávez and
the United Farm Workers proved a noteworthy example of electoral coalition
between Mexican American and Black activists.[18]

Rush also stressed his ability to build coalitions, again alluding to his work
in the Panthers, especially in Hampton's Rainbow Coalition. Rush had attended
the first and second National Black Political Conventions and had seen how coalitions could translate electorally. "In the 2nd Ward, I'm the individual who can
pull the forces together to create the kind of comprehensive coalition needed to
solve problems," Rush told the *Chicago Metro News*. "My Incumbent is a source
of division." Several independent organizations in the city agreed, endorsing his
candidacy, as much as they did Raby's. They included the Independent Voters
of Illinois and the Coalition for the Election of Black Independent Aldermanic
Candidates, an organization started a year before to find candidates with a
"commitment to improving the social, economic and political condition of the

Black, Latino and underprivileged community" of the city. The demographics of the Second Ward meant that Rush did not have to pursue a Rainbow Coalition exactly; in 1975, the ward was more than 90 percent African American. But Rush still sought to build alliances across classes and neighborhoods, and if elected he promised to work with anyone who wanted to empower underprivileged people—Black, white, or Latino. The ward also had demonstrated a willingness to support independence, electing Fred Hubbard in a 1969 special election— only to witness his conviction for embezzling more than $100,000 in federal funds and his replacement by Barnett in 1971.[19]

Rush's defeat occurred for reasons not entirely the same as Raby's. For some, Rush's affiliation with the Panthers remained fresh. "Most people had him trapped in a moment in time, politically and socially and otherwise," recalled then machine alderman Tim Evans, "when clearly Bobby Rush was moving beyond his ties with the Black Panther movement." Evans supported Rush, but quietly, making sure to meet in nondescript places so as to not be discovered by Evans's party backers. Rush had little money, demonstrated by an initial public gambit to raise campaign funds through soda bottle refunds. And while Barnett was not a particularly strong candidate himself, incumbency and the Daley organization were potent forces—at least in harnessing the resources to get the vote out among loyalists in the southern precincts' low-income high rises such as the Robert Taylor Homes. As the current ward alderman, Barnett could remind voters who provided basic services—often by denying those same services. A third candidate, Larry Bullock, did not help. Much like Rush, Bullock ran against the machine, criticizing the incumbent for his "unimaginative, do-nothing leadership" and ties to the scandal-plagued administration. As special assistant for government affairs in Operation PUSH, the twenty-eight-year-old Bullock was a credible independent but viewed as more mainstream than Rush, having narrowly lost the Democratic primary for the state House in 1974. Historically, machine candidates fared better with multiple challengers, and that helped Barnett survive. Bullock's PUSH background also neutralized the role Jesse Jackson might have played in the race; he endorsed neither Bullock nor Rush against the incumbent.[20]

With the help of Daley's surprising coattails, Barnett won 54 percent of the votes in the first primary, avoiding a runoff by about 400 votes against Rush and Bullock, who finished second and third respectively, in a race in which turnout was up by about 15 percent from four years earlier. Rush vowed to stay engaged in the community, which may have been why he appeared in the news later that year. Pulled over on what was called a routine traffic violation, Rush suddenly found himself facing a $4,000 bond, which he called "a dastardly act of attempted intimidation" by "city bosses." Eventually, the charges were dropped, quietly.[21]

**IT WAS THE RACE** in the Forty-Sixth Ward, however, that may have proven the most illustrative of how civil rights attempted to translate into electoral politics—a race one commentator called a "test-tube" for independent voting by not only African Americans but also working-class whites and Latinos.[22] Centered on the racially and ethnically diverse communities of Uptown and Lake View on the North Side, the Forty-Sixth Ward contest pitted machine-backed incumbent Christopher Cohen against Cha-Cha Jiménez, who would have become the first Latino elected alderman since William Emilio Rodriguez in 1915. Once boasting the busiest entertainment and shopping district north of the Loop, the ward by the 1960s and 1970s had become best known as "a port of entry and home for transients." Indeed, it was one of the poorest and most diverse areas of the city, where Puerto Ricans, Mexican Americans, poor whites from Appalachia, African Americans, Asians, and American Indians commingled. About half of the ward's census tracts were considered low-income but juxtaposed with some of the city's wealthiest along the lake shore.[23] The ward had never elected an independent to the council. Cohen, an attorney, lived in the shadow of his father, Wilbur Cohen, former secretary of the U.S. Department of Health, Education, and Welfare during President Johnson's War on Poverty. The son had a reputation for integrity and occasional independence, often voting "present" on a handful of the most controversial bills and literally wandering away from the City Council dais at strategic moments, rather than prompt the wrath of his poor constituents or perhaps his conscience. But that could work for only so long, and disgruntled activists sought a candidate who better represented the community's racially diverse, mostly working-class population. That candidate was Jiménez.[24]

In many ways, Jiménez's candidacy was a natural extension of the class-based antiracist coalition work he pursued in the 1960s with the Young Lords and the Rainbow Coalition. He built a platform around the working-class issues, especially opposition to urban renewal and police brutality, that had plagued the area's poor people as developers and city officials eyed transforming the neighborhood into a home for young, mostly white urban professionals. Despite gaining considerable attention—some would say, notoriety—Jiménez and the Young Lords lost the fight on the streets Puerto Ricans fondly referred to as

"La Clark" and "La División" and slowly moved north to the border of Uptown and Lake View. For many of these young men and women, it was yet another move, the fourth, fifth, sixth, forced by the redevelopment of once-affordable, albeit ramshackle, housing in different parts of the city; Jiménez had moved nine times by eighth grade. Just as Hampton, Rush, and the Young Patriots' Bill Fesperman had, Jiménez became a target for marginalization, if not elimination, in the early 1970s, went underground for more than a year, and eventually served a one-year prison term for stealing lumber to build a day care center. He returned to the community in 1974, ready to continue the fight even if that meant running for elected office.[25]

But as Rush, and to a lesser extent Raby, did that year, Jiménez attempted to blend this working-class street activism with more traditional electoral politics. Declaring his candidacy soon after his release from jail, Jiménez explained that it was poor people's time to elect their own, and not just "beg in protest to a deaf alderman who ignores our concerns. It is time that we have our own representatives on the City Council." The issues and rhetoric of earlier fights remained the same. "The city must abandon its master plan to systematically and callously remove Latinos and other poor from the inner-city and other desirable areas of Chicago," Jiménez stated. "The answer to eliminating slums is not to relocate them but to provide decent jobs, a decent standard of living and stable neighborhoods." If urban renewal was addressed head-on, Jiménez argued, then other issues plaguing poor neighborhoods like Lake View and Uptown, such as drugs, crime, and unemployment, would be alleviated. A first step, according to Jiménez, was the establishment of community zoning boards, a structure endorsed by independent aldermen such as the Northwest Side's Dick Simpson in which residents held greater sway over local land use. Jiménez also proposed a nonpartisan community service center that would help everybody, not just those who supported the machine or an individual alderman. Other policy changes would flow naturally from this shift in power to the people.[26]

Indeed, the campaign itself strove to reflect this kind of model of empowerment—to the point that immediate political victory did not seem necessary to achieve Jiménez's goals. Subsequent interviews with Jiménez and his campaign staff suggested that the process of community empowerment through voter registration, public hearings, and house meetings with the candidate were significant achievements in themselves. "We are using the elections to mobilize a lot of people" more than anything else, Jiménez told *Rising Up Angry*. As Jiménez joked years later, at the time, he was not even sure he was eligible to be alderman, due to his criminal record—a particularly rich statement considering the ethical challenges of many machine aldermen. Therefore, massive voter registration of the ward's working class—"an army of the dis-placed," as one canvasser put it—represented the ultimate success for the cam-paign. This was the first step in the establishment of a longer-term registration infrastructure that, organizers believed, could change the electorate. Rather than allow the residents of tony Lakefront apartment buildings to dominate ward politics with just 10 or 20 percent voter turnout, canvassers sought to per-suade the ward's working people that they mattered, too. That was a significant effort in Illinois, which made registration difficult by strictly limiting the power of deputy registrars and forcing most people to register downtown. Starting in 1973 with local elections for Model Cities boards, organizers started taking people there by the carload.[27] These efforts continued for Jiménez's campaign a year later.[28]

Many observers also sensed a different kind of campaign. Columnist Javier Navarro, writing for the local Lerner papers, called Jiménez's candidacy less of a traditional campaign and more of "a total social phenomenon." Paul Siegel, who had been organizing the ward for a couple of years before Jiménez's run, called it "the partyingest" campaign of which he had been a part. Every Friday and Saturday, the campaign held parties featuring salsa music, food, and the candidate himself to deepen community roots, build relationships, and recruit new campaign workers. The campaign even issued strategies for safe trick-or-treating on Halloween. The parties also helped highlight the campaign's diversity. Historically, the Forty-Sixth Ward had been one of the city's most ra-cially diverse because of Uptown's role as a gateway to newcomers, including poor white transplants from Appalachia and American Indians through the federal government's forced urban relocation program. But most did not vote before 1975, even for Appalachian transplant and Uptown activist Chuck Geary, who ran against Cohen four years before. Jiménez's campaign registered sev-eral thousand people and cobbled together a coalition of middle-class whites from the Independent Precinct Organization with largely working-class Puerto Ricans, African Americans, whites, and natives. This diversity was on display several times, most prominently during a "unity rally" featuring Jiménez, Dick Simpson, former alderman Sammy Rayner, radical white organizer Walter "Slim" Coleman of the Intercommunal Survival Committee, and Marcos Muñoz of the United Farm Workers. "The question is not whether we're working within the system, the question is whether we're working within the system to main-tain it or change it," Jiménez told the crowd. "I'm working within it to change it." More mainstream newspaper coverage, while generally hostile to Jiménez, still grudgingly acknowledged the campaign's creativity and Jiménez's unique candidacy as a former gang member.[29]

Cha-Cha Jiménez dramatically stands in front of Armitage Avenue Methodist Church—dubbed the "People's Church" by the Young Lords in 1969. Six years later, Jiménez ran for alderman in the Lake View–based Forty-Sixth Ward, borrowing heavily from his activist tactics, including informal block parties, as a way to recruit new people to the electoral process. ST-40001941–0023, *Chicago Sun-Times* collection, Chicago History Museum.

On the eve of the election, campaign volunteers really thought they had made headway in terms of overcoming the machine's structural advantages in the ward, including Cohen's incumbency. When the campaign began, organizers encouraged residents of the ward's high rises to "vote for the survival ticket," to which they responded, "Yeah, I'm going to vote for my survival," meaning the machine that provided basic services for votes. But pledges such as a no-strings-attached service center for the community made an impact. "When the people who voted against us realized that we actually meant it, and that they were entitled to the services however they voted, that was important, too," Siegel said. By February, white, often female gatekeepers in key buildings were wearing Jiménez's gold campaign buttons, trumpeting in English and Spanish "The

Dawning of a Brand New Day: Cha-Cha for Alderman." Such efforts, along with robust voter registration efforts, made the campaign cautiously optimistic.[30]

Such strides, however, were not enough to win. Jiménez won 27 percent of ballots cast in a three-way race against Cohen and mortician Darrell Quinley, who finished a distant third and, like Bullock in the Second Ward, split anti-machine sentiment. The race always had been an uphill battle against the machine's resources and Cohen's scandal-free incumbency. Despite his charisma and street credibility, Jiménez's checkered past remained an obstacle. Yet, Jiménez's showing far surpassed Geary's in 1971 and, consistent with earlier statements, he still considered the campaign a victory because it empowered people. In a year in which overall voter turnout declined slightly citywide, those showing up to the polls in the Forty-Sixth Ward increased by one-quarter and more than doubled in a few key western and central precincts in which Jiménez either won or was competitive. "Our campaign was able to involve many person(s) who had never even voted, had never even seen a voting machine," Jiménez told a magazine a few months after the election. "Our opponents, because they won at the polls, think that they have the right now to drive poor people from their home. We cannot allow that to happen." The community service center he touted became a reality, sponsored by Coleman's Intercommunal Survival Committee, and provided services such as legal aid, transportation to prison, and guidance on welfare and black lung. Moreover, Jiménez saw lessons for coalitional politics. "The 46th Ward was not primarily Latino so we had a coalition campaign," he commented.[31] Indeed, Jiménez's coalition became a model for the ward's politics in the 1980s and beyond. Twelve years later, the ward elected radical activist and *Keep Strong* magazine editor Helen Shiller as alderman and, in some minds, displaced Hyde Park as the heart of Chicago's progressive neighborhood politics for a generation. The coalition Jiménez's candidacy had begun to form for transparency and against urban renewal proved integral to that process.

THE 1975 aldermanic races were not the last forays into electoral politics by Al Raby, Bobby Rush, and Cha-Cha Jiménez, but they were for two of their opponents. After losing the Fifth Ward runoff, Raby remained active in Chicago before taking management positions in the Peace Corps in Maryland and Ghana. Raby reemerged in Chicago in time to manage Congressman Harold Washington's historic mayoral campaign in late 1982 and early 1983. Lathrop never achieved the independence "expected from a Hyde Park liberal," according to former Raby supporters, and lost his reelection bid in 1979. Neither Jiménez nor

Cohen would run for alderman again. "Poor Chris Cohen," as Paul Siegel referred to him, remained a rather hapless figure caught between the machine and his more progressive instincts. Disliked by party insiders—and his father's friends apparently—that backed him, Cohen left the council in 1977 to work for the administration of President Jimmy Carter. Meanwhile, Jiménez involved himself with the ward community services center he promised and vowed to run again. Instead, he was falsely accused and jailed for ties to the Puerto Rican paramilitary Armed Forces of National Liberation, which coordinated a series of bombings in the Chicago area, among other places. Jiménez was eventually acquitted but remained in jail through the process because he could not post bond. He would not resurface in Chicago politics prominently until 1982, when the successor organization to the Young Lords, the Puerto Rican Defense Committee, became the earliest Latino group to support Harold Washington's mayoral run.[32]

Meanwhile, Bobby Rush remained the most visible as he became enmeshed in the city's Black independent politics, eventually becoming a South Side alderman and then congressman. In 1976, Democratic governor Dan Walker experienced firsthand the risks of making an enemy of the mayor. That spring, Walker became the rare incumbent governor to lose a primary—to Daley ally and former Illinois secretary of state Michael Howlett. Daley, however, failed to dislodge Ralph Metcalfe from either his congressional seat or, more important for patronage, his position as Third Ward committeeman. Continuing the trend of greater Black independence, Tim Black, Anna Langford, Brenetta Howell Barrett, and others founded the United Black Voters of Illinois (UBVI)—which Rush joined—and once again looked to the local Republican Party as a possible alternative for governor. Former U.S. attorney James Thompson, who had won the GOP nomination handily, had built a powerful reputation for fighting corruption. Known as "Big Jim," the thirty-nine-year-old Thompson had racked up scores of successful corruption prosecutions against members of the machine, big and small, from Alderman Tom Keane to more than fifty Chicago police officers. Initially rumored to be running for mayor in 1975—an unlikely scenario for any Republican interested in winning—Thompson instead sought the governorship. Calling himself a "caged tiger" ready to do battle, Thompson dominated the campaign, first against his primary opponent, and then Howlett. In late September, the UBVI endorsed Thompson for governor. As much against the machine as for any other reason, Rush and other UBVI members also worked for Bernard Carey's reelection as state's attorney. Both Republicans won handily in November.[33]

Even more striking, perhaps, was the local Democratic machine's inability to deliver enough votes to presidential nominee Jimmy Carter, himself an anticorruption candidate who ran against the crimes of Watergate. While Carter eventually won a tight national contest against President Gerald Ford, it was the second election in a row in which the Democrat lost Illinois, confirming for many observers that Daley's national clout had faded. Few wanted to write him off completely, reflected by the *Chicago Sun-Times* editorial page's careful treatment of the issue: "This is not a political obituary for Richard J. Daley or his machine. You can wonder, however, if the organ notes are starting to be heard in the back of the chapel."[34] It proved prescient; Daley died from a massive heart attack six weeks later.

THE DEATH OF Richard J. Daley prompted the kind of tributes few others would receive beyond perhaps presidents, popes, and the occasional Hollywood star. The gruff, jowly septuagenarian was an unlikely celebrity, known for his malapropisms as much as the iron fist with which he ruled the city. And yet thousands of Chicagoans, mostly but not entirely white, solemnly viewed his casket and watched the funeral procession. Their children handwrote sympathy cards, as scores of political dignitaries, including Vice President Nelson Rockefeller, President-elect Jimmy Carter, and Senators Ted Kennedy and George McGovern, made pilgrimages to the city. Tributes to Daley's love for family, city, and Chicago sports teams filled the pages of local and national newspapers and television broadcasts. His viewing at the Nativity of Our Lord Catholic Church was treated as "a neighborhood event in which all Chicagoans were regarded as neighbors by the Daleys," wrote the *Chicago Tribune*. And while there were "a few in the crowd wearing mink coats . . . these were far outnumbered by those in work clothes." Again and again, commentators contrasted Daley's mythological "city that works" with the financially strapped New York. The comparison was unfair for a variety of reasons. As journalist Studs Terkel suggested, in the *New York Times* no less, "Chicago is the most segregated large city in the world aside from Johannesburg. An old multiracial neighborhood [the Near West Side] was destroyed in the name of 'education.' . . . Large realtors get tax breaks while small-bungalow owners pay through the nose. . . . Fear, as in other cities, is endemic."[35] And yet the label and comparison stuck.

Thus, Daley's death prompted numerous declarations that the "Age of Daley" was over. Such conclusions were right, in the sense that it was unlikely someone would be both mayor and chair of the Cook County Democratic Party in the future. No one would have that level of power again, not even Daley's son, Richard M., who became the city's longest-serving mayor a generation later. But in other ways, such declarations were at least premature. "Daley has left a legacy that is pure Chicago," wrote another of Chicago's famed journalists, Mike Royko, in the *Chicago Sun-Times*. "I'm not talking about his obvious legacy of expressways, high-rises, and other public works projects that size-conscious Chicagoans enjoy. Daley, like his town, relished a political brawl. . . . Well, he's left behind the ingredients for the best political donnybrook we've had in fifty years. They'll be kicking and gouging, grabbing and tripping, elbowing and kneeing to grab all, or a thin sliver of the power he left behind. It will be a classic Chicago debate."[36]

Setting aside the Chicago exceptionalism that Royko, and so many other Chicago writers, are known for, this observation *was* largely accurate. Within hours of Daley's death, a mad scramble among politicians and his would-be successors commenced—a process in which African Americans and other minorities found themselves mostly empty-handed at the end. If Wilson Frost, the City Council's president pro tem, had had his way, Chicago would have sworn him in as the city's first Black mayor, at least on an interim basis. "I am the acting mayor," he declared the evening Daley died. The fifty-year-old Frost, a cautious, low-key lawyer and former parole agent, was the alderman and committeeman in the South Side's Thirty-Fourth Ward and had run council meetings when Daley was ill. Known more for his machine loyalty and get-out-the-vote efficiency than his legislative achievements and leadership skills, Frost seemed to be the perfect compromise candidate in a demographically changing city. "He certainly wasn't a standard bearer for civil rights against the Daley administration," wrote the *Tribune*. "Rather . . . Frost described himself as a Black man who had worked within the system to get ahead." This version of Black Power—the quest for a Black mayor, any Black mayor, no matter the cost— greatly concerned independent activists. Frost was not ideal, but even those who routinely criticized him as too cozy to Daley and self-serving reluctantly rallied behind him and pushed others, including a council majority, to do the same. That required that they "show Frost that we could pack that ballroom (at the South Side's Roberts Motel) with people who would support him fervently, if he would stand up for mayor," journalist Gus Savage recalled. "At least stand to make the council vote. And he had agreed, if we could do what we said. And we succeeded. We packed the place." After several hours delay, Frost showed up, entering through the kitchen to avoid reporters, and pledged that he would stand for mayor. They roared with approval.[37]

And yet, even the moderate Frost was not satisfactory to Daley's white inner circle, who rejected the notion of any Black mayor. Before Frost could enter the mayor's office the day after Daley's death, security padlocked the doors and white Daley loyalists including Alderman Michael Bilandic, from the late mayor's Eleventh Ward, deliberated over how to proceed. In addition to African Americans' claim of a clear succession, the council's Young Turks led by white aldermen and ward committeemen Ed Vrdolyak and Ed Burke sensed an opportunity to challenge the Daley bloc's grip on power. For years, the Eddies, as the two young, ambitious politicos came to be known, complained of a tightly controlled organizational ladder that denied promotion to all but the most pliant individuals. Their challenge, thus, risked a split among whites when the council voted on a successor; most of the Black aldermen had committed to supporting Frost. Over the next several days, Black, Latino, and independent Chicagoans waited with growing frustration as the council blocs engaged in backroom negotiations, worried that they would not like the result.[38]

In the end, they were right. Despite his initial denials to the contrary, Frost had been involved in negotiations with white council members throughout the week after Daley's death. He eventually accepted the chairmanship of the council Finance Committee in exchange for his support for Bilandic as acting mayor, Vrdolyak as council president pro tem, and Walter Kozubowski as vice mayor, a new position created to placate the city's influential Polish community. Part of the deal was Frost's refusal to even be nominated from the floor, despite what he had told the crowd a week before. The new leadership lineup won 45–2, with only two white North Side independents voting against. Chairing the Finance Committee was a plum job personally for Frost, and arguably the most powerful one on the council and thus potentially helpful to Black residents. Contending that he simply did not have the votes to win, Frost exclaimed years later, "Why should I be the one to take the suicidal leap?" But independents, Black and otherwise, viewed his decision as cowardly. Those who had orchestrated the initial community support for Frost, such as Savage, tried to be conciliatory at the time: "Frost is not the main culprit. However, he should have stood, although he would not have won. The bitter and aging culprit is racism." Decades later, Savage was blunter. "Wilson Frost was a weak Tom," he stated flatly. "Strong as a committeeman. Had one of the strongest pro-Democratic wards in the city. But weak in terms of political convictions . . . let's say in terms of race loyalty." Frost had no regrets. "I played the cards that were dealt me," he said, "and I think I got the best hand at that particular time." That he chose to use the language of poker spoke volumes.[39]

**WHILE LEGAL QUESTIONS** swirled over the immediate succession process, Illinois law was clear that a special election had to occur within six months of a vacancy, which provided another challenge to a machine in transition. Not surprisingly, Acting Mayor Michael Bilandic, who had said he would not run to finish out the existing mayoral term, accepted a "draft" to do just that—a move that observers presumed reflected less of an actual draft and more of a long-term plan. While Bilandic became the city's first mayor of Croatian descent, in most other ways he represented "business as usual," as the *Tribune* put it. Living with his mother just a few doors down from the late mayor's house, the fifty-three-year-old Bilandic had attended a series of Roman Catholic schools and represented Bridgeport and the Eleventh Ward since 1969. Considered a "bland machine soldier" and "quiet soul," Bilandic was mostly known for expounding on his statistical analysis of council legislation. Most political observers at the time believed that he was simply a caretaker, keeping the seat warm until state senator Richard M. Daley, the late mayor's eldest son, was considered mature enough to run himself. Thus, rather than consolidate support leading up to the April 19 Democratic primary, Bilandic faced substantial opposition by two prominent politicians born inside the machine: former Congressman Roman Pucinski, the Polish alderman representing the Northwest Side's Forty-First Ward, and Black state senator Harold Washington from the South Side. Both had the potential to be imposing opponents, although neither were willing to condemn the party organization. Instead, they argued that, at its core, the machine was a positive force and only needed reform to fulfill the needs of white ethnics, in Pucinski's eyes, and African Americans, according to Washington.[40]

Pucinski, with a crop of white hair shaped into a mini-pompadour, had represented the Northwest Side of Chicago since the mid-1950s. Once a liberal Democratic congressman with a near 100 percent record on civil rights and anti-poverty programs, Pucinski had begun to move right as it became clear that the freedom struggle was as much about northern cities like Chicago as it was Mississippi and Alabama. In the 1966 wave election in which conservative members of both parties ran and won against President Lyndon Johnson's Great Society policies and his execution of the Vietnam War, Pucinski beat his Republican rival by a scant 3,750 votes. He had routinely spent most of his time taking care of the parochial needs of his district, which included opposition to the school marches of the mid-1960s, but on the heels of the Chicago Freedom Movement, Pucinski elevated the tone of white racial resentment, particularly against open housing and busing. In 1966, he aligned with segregationist congressmen against civil rights guidelines for schools, while a few years later, he rejected the placement of any public housing in his district. After giving up his seat to challenge Senator Charles Percy in 1972 and losing, Pucinski handily won a special election to the City Council the following year and became part of the Daley voting bloc. As a result, while Bilandic won the lion's share of formal endorsements during the 1977 campaign, Pucinski secured the support of a few police and homeowners groups, all in the name of "protecting" whites from integration.[41]

Washington's candidacy took a more circuitous route, a reflection of the deep political divisions among African Americans in the city. Soon after it became clear that Wilson Frost was content to chair the council's Finance Committee, two search groups, both chaired by Black labor leaders and financed by Black businessmen, emerged to find a viable African American candidate for mayor. One based on the South Side retained the core members of the unsuccessful, rather unwieldy Committee for a Black Mayor in 1975, including Chairman Charles Hayes of the Amalgamated Meatcutters and publisher Gus Savage. A third of the select committee's nine members were women—Brenetta Howell Barrett, Nancy Jefferson, and labor activist and priest Addie Wyatt—although the committee did not seriously consider endorsing a woman for the race. A second group chaired by Tommy Briscoe, general chairman of the American Postal Workers Union local, and state representative Jesse Madison came out of the West Side. After considering more than a dozen individuals each, in a rare sign of unity, the two committees unanimously endorsed Harold Washington. While technically still a member of the regular party organization, Washington had demonstrated significant, albeit calculated streaks of independence during his tenure in Springfield. A founder of the legislative Black Caucus, Washington had championed the Equal Rights Amendment, consumer protection measures, and opposition to state aid for parents sending their children to private schools, a common practice to avoid integration North and South—although Washington did not view integration as the primary way to achieve equal educational opportunity. Washington was also instrumental in making Illinois the first state, in 1973, to formally recognize Dr. Martin Luther King Jr.'s birthday as a holiday. And yet, as one biographer states, "No matter what he accomplished in Springfield, back in Chicago he helped turn out the vote for Metcalfe and the machine he was coming to despise." But Metcalfe was now independent. Or was he? Just hours before a formal unveiling of Washington's candidacy, Metcalfe, who again declined to run for mayor, shocked Washington and his supporters when he opposed his one-time ally.[42]

Metcalfe's intentions were murky. The official reason was Washington's 1972 conviction for tax evasion, in which the then state representative spent thirty-six days in the county jail. Claiming he had a "whole bill of particulars that he did not want to go into," Metcalfe told reporters, "I cannot support Harold

Washington. We need a candidate who will advance the interests of Black people and who will be a good mayor for all of the City of Chicago." But much more significant malfeasance by other associates had not stopped a Metcalfe endorsement before. Tommy Briscoe surmised it was the congressman's transparent attempt to return to the machine's good graces under a new mayor, while others saw it as a purely personal move—returning the favor after Washington chose not to endorse Metcalfe in his primary fight against the machine the previous year. Whatever the reason, Washington determined Metcalfe's opposition as fatal and announced his withdrawal from the race to a disappointed crowd who booed lustily when they heard Metcalfe's name. A reeling Committee for a Black Mayor made one last effort to endorse, settling on Robert Tucker, general counsel for Jesse Jackson's Operation PUSH. His campaign lasted two weeks, torpedoed after the *Tribune* reported on Tucker's personal debts and lawsuits stemming from a failed minority business venture in which $300,000 of federal money had gone missing. While he denied any wrongdoing, Tucker dropped out of the race soon after, blaming poor fundraising. For those who had worked day and night for more than a month to find a candidate, the experience was deeply demoralizing.[43]

But in mid-February, after being approached by Savage and a handful of other supporters with a petition of signatures to run, Harold Washington had a change of heart and entered the race as a self-proclaimed "people's candidate." Others called it more of a protest candidacy, as all but the most diehard supporters knew he would not win reentering the race so late. "We had no illusions about him winning," recalled Savage, who managed the campaign with little financial support. But "we felt that we could make a sufficiently good showing, that it would encourage people to go further." Similar to Singer and Newhouse two years earlier, Washington ran as a reformer, emphasizing more resources for the public schools and mass transportation; a stronger police review board and other criminal justice reform; greater neighborhood empowerment in Black, Latino, and working-class white neighborhoods not named Bridgeport; and a more transparent, democratic hiring and contracting process, one not controlled by a singular "boss." Washington's campaign literature, more than anything, emphasized taking "control" of their communities—not unlike earlier messages of Black (and Latino) power—in this case, from machine bosses.[44]

Unlike traditional reformers, however, Washington insisted that these could be accomplished within the regular Democratic organization, within the machine. "I'm not anti-Machine," he told the *Chicago Reader*. "Obviously, you have to have an organization. My purpose is to reform the Democratic Party, not to dismantle it or destroy it. That would serve no useful purpose." He also defended certain kinds of patronage, although not the sort that placed incompetent people in key jobs. "Why be concerned about the clerk, if you're not concerned about the fact that the mayor can give away hundreds of thousands of dollars in a contract?" he asked, proposing that, of all people, precinct captains needed freer rein to serve voters. While not surprising for someone who had been part of the machine his entire career, such positions risked dampening enthusiasm among white good-government supporters, including the *Reader* editors themselves. As a result, Washington faced tough questioning from members of the Independent Voters of Illinois (IVI). However, in a surprising move that may have indicated the IVI's own inherent weaknesses, an explicit intent to reach African Americans, or perhaps the weak quality of the opposition, Washington still won the organization's endorsement—the first Black mayoral candidate in Chicago to do so. It was an early indication that Washington might be able to attract votes across racial lines.[45]

Just as important, Washington's 1977 campaign proved a training ground for key organizers jumping from community organizing into electoral politics. According to the Black United Fund's Brenetta Howell Barrett, a veteran of independent politics and Washington's campaign scheduler in 1977, the two-month sprint that spring taught her more than any race she had been part of, including her own independent congressional run in 1964. "I thought it was a pretty good campaign considering the inexperience we all had, including Harold," who had never run for an executive position or for a seat outside of his nearly all-Black legislative districts on the South Side. She learned the small logistical things that went into preparing candidate events, while "it gave [Washington] a little bit of the taste" of what becoming mayor would entail. The campaign also represented the first time that Renault Robinson of the Afro-American Patrolmen's League—which provided Washington's security team—became directly involved in a campaign, helping build a grassroots network for the candidate and Robinson's own future political work. Meanwhile, Charles Hayes and Tommy Briscoe rallied progressive labor organizations representing more than 100,000 workers in support of Washington.[46]

Moreover, Washington's candidacy seemed a natural extension of the coalition work Cha-Cha Jiménez had tried to translate into electoral victory in the Forty-Sixth Ward. While Jiménez was caught up in legal troubles in 1977, Slim Coleman and Helen Shiller, of the Intercommunal Survival Committee (ISC) in the North Side's Uptown, rallied behind Washington's candidacy. Founded in 1970, the ISC provided Black Panther–style survival programs to the area's white working-class communities, ones that Cha-Cha Jiménez gave voice to, on urban renewal, police brutality and harassment, unemployment, and other issues. Washington's platform was a natural fit—and given Fred Hampton's efforts to build a Rainbow Coalition, the area's poor whites were unusually open to a Black candidate. In the ISC's endorsement of Washington in *Keep Strong* magazine, Coleman reinforced this impulse: "It is time that we in the poor and working White communities put the question of a person's race or color out of our minds and remember that the enemies of our enemies are our friends. . . . Harold Washington represents a real alternative." Similar to Al Raby's aldermanic race, Washington received more attention for the celebrity endorsements his campaign garnered than the grassroots organizing—or lack thereof—his campaign conducted. But just as in 1975, it was unclear if Aretha Franklin and Dick Gregory, not to mention Jesse Jackson (whose late support raised some eyebrows), had as much impact as the support of the ISC and other activists.[47]

As most expected, Bilandic won the primary, garnering 368,404 votes, or 51 percent, against Pucinski's 33 percent and Washington's 11 percent. Certainly, on its face, the so-called people's campaign appeared to be a failure. But as the *Tribune* reported the day after the election, neither of the main runners-up talked like they had just lost the election. Pucinski crowed, "Let no one write any epitaph for Roman Pucinski's political future," while Washington simply promised, "This is the beginning." He spoke of the plurality his candidacy won in five middle-class Black wards and the "ruthlessness" the machine used to win. While such optimism may have been a bit misplaced, since Bilandic even won the plurality of Black votes citywide on his strength on the West Side, there indeed were warning signs for those in charge. Precinct captains worked the hardest they had in recent memory, with 46 percent of voters saying they had been contacted by a party worker, and yet the charisma-challenged Bilandic mobilized a scant 18 percent of the city's voting-age population—the poorest showing by a candidate since Daley's first run in 1955. Only 27 percent of voting-age African Americans voted at all, for any candidate. Overall, Bilandic received more than 100,000 votes fewer than Daley in 1975. If low-turnout elections guaranteed a conservative, machine-dominated status quo, what would motivate a larger proportion of the population to come out in Chicago—a city with only a Black plurality—to follow in the footsteps of progressive, multiracial victories in other cities?[48]

IF THE RACES for mayor and alderman in the mid-1970s were any indication, then the answer to that question was substantial, genuine, and deep political coalitions, ones that reached across not just race, but class, neighborhood, and religion, too. That meant more grassroots organization and old-fashioned shoe leather, and less emphasis on high-profile endorsements and charisma. Those could help but were not sufficient in themselves. Moreover, any progressive coalition had to incorporate fully the city's most prominent racial minorities, according to independent observers and strategists at the time. In 1974, Peter Knauss wrote in the *Chicago Reader* that "only a multiracial populist coalition of poor whites, poor Blacks, Latinos, and the same white ethnic working and middle-class people who are locked out of power (even though the machine pretends to rule in their name and in their interests) which is united on a program committed to a new form of democratic socialism will stand a remote chance of controlling the mighty alliance of big business and the leadership of organized labor which makes the machine effective." Independent political strategist Don Rose, who had worked on Washington's 1977 campaign, agreed. One route to independent success is "recognition of the burgeoning Black and Latino population as the vehicle for social change" in the city, he said. Minorities can "become a new balance of power."[49] Intellectually, independents knew what they had to do. Mitigating political disunity among African Americans was just one task. Another piece of the puzzle began to emerge in the next two years, as it had in California, Texas, and the Southwest years before—namely, the rise of Latinos, especially Mexican Americans, as a potent swing voting bloc in city elections, not to mention the nation.[50]

## CHAPTER 4

# We Were Invisible

We were still debating, do you organize
around elections or do you have an election
to organize? It was still a cogent argument.
—Linda Coronado interview

I n the spring of 1977, Rudy Lozano, Jesús "Chuy" García, Linda Coronado, and other Mexican American community activists from Chicago traveled to Springfield to face their state legislators. The nation had been debating immigration, mostly from Mexico, which had exploded in the twelve years since the nation's doors had reopened in 1965. New president Jimmy Carter proposed both a broad amnesty of many undocumented immigrants in the nation since 1970 and sharp penalties on businesses that employed such workers— reforms that would pass a decade later. Illinois legislators joined the fray by proposing their own employer sanctions and limits to public services and education. Alarmed, especially after the state House of Representatives unanimously passed an employer sanctions bill, Chicano activists went to Springfield to stop what they viewed as discriminatory legislation. What they encountered shocked them. "In the state Legislature, we were invisible," recalled García. "People were looking at us, like, who are these people? There were not any of us down there—people who looked like us, had surnames like us." Indeed, out of 177 representatives, not one was Latino. While the anti-immigrant legislation eventually failed, in part because businesses opposed losing their cheap labor, the trip downstate transformed activists like Lozano and García. "We came back with a clear understanding how voiceless and powerless and invisible we were [outside of our immediate communities]," García remembered. "And we began the conversations about how do we participate in electoral politics."[1]

To that point, Latinos largely had steered clear of the city's infamous politics. Even after the Puerto Rican uprisings along Division Street in 1966, Latino activism focused on issues of urban renewal and jobs, not running candidates.

One reason was that careful gerrymandering by the Democratic machine ensured that, even with rapidly shifting demographics in some parts of the city, no council district drawn after the 1970 census was more than one-third Latino. But it remained striking that, in contrast to African Americans, who were overwhelmingly segregated into about a third of the wards and thus were able to elect their own, especially on the South Side, a smaller percentage of Latinos were more evenly dispersed on the Near North and West Sides. In addition, a sizable percentage of Mexican Americans—perhaps as many as half, according to some estimates—were not citizens and thus were ineligible to vote. Of course, the lack of a majority did not mean a Latino could not win; a multiracial coalition could have been built. But as Cha-Cha Jiménez's experience demonstrated, that was a tall order, even with an already-present community structure.[2]

Another rarely discussed reason also existed. For Mexican Americans like García and Coronado, who were naturalized citizens and part of the radical CASA-HGT (Center for Autonomous Social Action-General Brotherhood of Workers), the city's regular Democratic organization reminded them of Mexico's one-party system since the Mexican Revolution. The Institutional Revolutionary Party (PRI) had dominated that country's politics since the late 1920s—just a few years before the advent of Chicago's Democratic machine—and co-opted the government bureaucracy, military, labor unions, and major industries, many of which had been nationalized over the years. Dubbed the "perfect dictatorship" by Peruvian writer Mario Vargas Llosa, the PRI coupled massive state investment in industrialization and economic modernization with endemic corruption, rigged elections, and a general disregard for human rights. As a result, until the 1980s, formal political opposition remained largely ineffective. The parallels were not exact, of course. Nothing nearly as bad as the 1968 Tlatelolco Massacre, in which more than 300 students were killed, had occurred in Chicago. But the machine bore enough resemblance to turn off many Mexican Americans from even participating in Chicago's elections.[3]

The changing economic and political landscape of the 1970s, especially the attempts to curb immigration and the implications of living in the legal shadows during an age of economic anxiety, forced many Mexican Americans to reconsider. Poverty had declined considerably nationwide, thanks to the social movements of the 1960s, the expansion of Social Security, the creation of Medicare and Medicaid, and general economic growth. But poverty among Latinos had remained stubbornly high, with 33.2 percent nationally, and in Chicago 24.1 percent, living at or below the federal poverty level in 1980. Of even greater concern, perhaps, especially as deindustrialization accelerated, school dropout rates by the early 1980s had hit 21 percent among Mexican Americans.

Affordable housing also remained scarce, as urban renewal continued to displace poor people, pushing them into areas where crime touched most families, arson for hire was rampant, and the police were either routinely indifferent or openly hostile to their needs. Continued uncertainty around many individuals' citizenship status simply amplified these issues. By the end of the decade, Latinos overall made up 14 percent of Chicago's population and had formed more than 200 organizations to address community issues, one result of the Chicano movement of the late 1960s and 1970s. And yet, in contrast to municipalities in California and the Southwest, Latinos still did not have "anyone who looked like them" in the Illinois General Assembly or the Chicago City Council—people who came from their communities and who could champion their issues in more formal spaces of power. Even the 1979 election of Jane Byrne as the city's first nonmachine mayor in two generations had not translated into genuine opportunities for Latinos or other poor people in the city. After upsetting the incumbent mayor with broad independent support, Byrne quickly embraced her former rivals and betrayed those who had viewed her as a reformer, albeit a reluctant one.[4]

Therefore, in 1981, as affordable housing and anti–police brutality activists had begun to do in other parts of the city, a group of Southwest Side activists, including Rudy Lozano and Chuy García, founded the Independent Political Organization (IPO) of the Near West Side as a formal foray into electoral politics. While they recognized the potential pitfalls of such politics, Lozano also saw opportunity, especially in a post-Daley world. The next year, they rallied around a candidate who wanted not just to "organize the people," to quote Cha-Cha Jiménez during his 1975 council run, but someone who seriously believed he could win. Immigration lawyer and legal aid activist Juan Soliz did not end up the victor in his historic race for state representative, but he and his supporters set the stage for what came next: establishing Latinos—Mexican Americans, Puerto Ricans, and people of other nationalities—as essential citywide partners in the coalition to elect a progressive mayor.

THE WORK OF Pilsen activist Rudy Lozano epitomized the transition that some of Chicago's Mexican Americans made during the 1970s from the distinct, perhaps more idealistic path of cultural nationalism and the Chicano movement to an increasingly pragmatic politics of labor organizing and electoral coalition-building. Born in South Texas and two months old when his family moved to Chicago in 1951, Lozano was raised in Pilsen as the neighborhood underwent a dramatic shift from a mostly southern European ethnic enclave to a

Mexican American one. Lozano attended Harrison High School, where even as a teenager his leadership skills were on display. He organized youth activities through Hull House and, as a senior, helped lead walkouts at the school in 1969, part of a national movement by Chicano students demanding more Mexican culture and history in the curriculum and challenging policies that discriminated against students who spoke Spanish, even if they were bilingual. This activism continued when he became a student at the University of Illinois, Chicago Circle (UIC), an institution symbolic of the neighborhood displacement and urban renewal pursued by Mayor Daley and his allies. A multiracial neighborhood, which included the original Hull House founded by Jane Addams, had been demolished to make way for the brutalist, predominantly concrete circle-themed campus. Fittingly, Lozano and other students protested the university's dearth of Latino courses, faculty, and students, which led to greater awareness of Latino concerns at UIC and to the eventual establishment of the Latin American Recruitment Program—later called Latin American Recruitment and Educational Services—in 1975.[5]

But Lozano's heart, and thus much of his work, remained in Pilsen. Even as a university student, Lozano worked with the primarily women activists of Pilsen Neighbors Community Council, originally a white ethnic, Saul Alinsky–style organization that a new generation of Mexican American women had transformed into the leading voice calling for a new high school in the community. Parents and activists sought a new school for several reasons. Because of persistent crowding at nearby Harrison High, students attended multiple grades in the decrepit former Froebel elementary school before going to Harrison for their last two years. As parent Teresa Fraga recalled, Froebel "was dingy and dark. The bathrooms were in the basement and there were no lights. The walls had holes. The school was cold." In addition to the physical conditions of the school, activists worried about student safety, from the greater temptation to misbehave further away from home to the reality of crossing gang boundaries just to get to Harrison, which served the mostly African American South Lawndale community. As the Mexican population increased, so did tensions stemming from the area's racially identified youth gangs. Although most activists denied it then, Fraga was blunt about the role of race in oral histories later. "Our kids didn't want to go to Harrison," she said. "The school was mostly Black and they had many racial problems. So about 77 percent of Mexican kids were dropping out of high school after 10th grade."[6] Echoing Lozano's demands at UIC, parents also wanted more Mexican history and culture, as well as adult education, incorporated into the curriculum. "We want a school truly representative of the community," Lozano said at the time. "Maybe have it open 24 hours."[7]

District officials consistently denied community petitions for a new school, arguing that the city did not have construction funds and instead offered to bus Pilsen students to underutilized schools in even further-away predominantly Black neighborhoods.[8]

It was then when community activists turned to direct action. In the fall of 1972 and spring of 1973, the mostly women activists, including future Pilsen Neighbors presidents Teresa Fraga and Mary Gonzales, led protests and candlelight vigils of nearly a thousand people outside the Board of Education offices. Even more effective was a multiday boycott of seven schools, two of them predominantly Mexican American, that fed Harrison. The absence of nearly half of the schools' students risked a decline in state funding based on attendance and, thus, forced school officials to begin listening. In 1973, the school district committed to build a new high school in Pilsen, but the fight turned out not to be over. Factory owners on the chosen school site held out for more compensation for their property, prompting activists into action again, lobbying those who worked in the factory. More delays prompted another round of protests, vigils, and school boycotts, including the successful use of civil rights–style "freedom schools" to supplement what boycotting students missed in the formal classroom. Finally, the Board of Education began to buy land in 1975, and two years later, Benito Juarez High School—named after the beloved nineteenth-century Mexican president who championed public education—opened in the heart of Pilsen.[9]

Building a high school may have been the highest-profile effort in the community, but it was just one issue pursued by Pilsen activists that reflected the priorities of the national Chicano movement. In 1973, a coalition of Mexican and Puerto Rican workers formed the Association for Workers' Rights, which used direct action tactics to challenge workplace discrimination against Latinos by the Chicago Transit Authority and other government agencies. Young men of Mexican descent founded a chapter of the Brown Berets, a culturally nationalist Chicano organization from Los Angeles loosely modeled on the Black Panthers. An array of activists, including the Berets, helped transform Pilsen's historic settlement house called Howell House, which once assisted the neighborhood's Eastern European immigrants at the turn of the century, into Casa Aztlan and a space more tailored to community services for Latinos. In turn, Chicanas sought vital services for women and girls, such as reproductive health services and a domestic violence shelter, and founded Mujeres Latinas en Acción.[10]

For perhaps more radicalized people, such as Lozano and Linda Coronado, a trained teacher active in Mujeres Latinas, it was the plight of undocumented workers that most captured their imagination. Lozano left UIC without graduating, worked full time with undocumented workers through Legal Aid, and dabbled in work with the local La Raza Unida party, a Chicano-only political organization that fielded Chicanos in political races in the Southwest, most prominently Texas. La Raza Unida did not catch on in Chicago, where most Mexican Americans either eschewed electoral politics or, in the case of the small, conservative-leaning Amigos for Daley, backed the mayor's machine. In 1974, Lozano helped spearhead a local chapter of CASA-HGT. The Marxist-leaning organization founded by veteran labor organizers Bert Corona and Soledad Alatorre in Los Angeles "identified Mexican workers as crucial to the U.S. economy and integral to its work force," as one Chicano scholar puts it. "It sought to maximize workers' organization and participation in unions, as envisioned in its overall labor strategy." Originally a mutual aid society when formed in 1968, CASA altered its mission when younger activists took over the leadership and pushed the organization into far more assertive organizing among Mexican immigrants.[11]

As the son of immigrants, Lozano viewed this fight as personal and practical, especially amid the increasingly harsh rhetoric that scapegoated workers of Mexican descent—documented and undocumented—for the nation's rising unemployment and economic anxiety in the 1970s. These people were his family members, his friends, and often cultural and economic pillars of Pilsen. In late 1974, U.S. attorney general William Saxbe epitomized the challenges they faced when he told a group of Texas lawyers that the deportation of 1 million Mexicans, who he wrongly claimed did not pay taxes, would create at least as many jobs for unemployed Americans. While some, including the *Tribune*'s editorial page, embraced this claim about "illegal aliens" (the accepted term the media and government used to identify undocumented workers at the time), an array of labor, academic, religious, and activist voices, including Lozano's, challenged such assertions. "A 'scapegoat' is very convenient," wrote New York labor leader Henry Foner. "The illegal alien seems to have been cast in that role."[12] In response to Saxbe's claim about taxes, Lozano argued, "The undocumented worker contributes millions of dollars in Social Security which he can never receive as benefits due to his illegal status."[13] In Pilsen and Little Village, residents across the political and organizational spectrum bristled at what they saw as federal Immigration and Naturalization Service (INS) agents' racist targeting of Mexican-descended people. As if to prove their point, the local INS district director referred to undocumented workers as "wet Mexicans" and "a bunch of ignorant apes," while defending agency practices.[14] Other INS officials later confirmed that the agency almost exclusively operated in Mexican enclaves

Chicano movement activist Rudy Lozano speaks during a meeting of CASA-HGT (Centro de Acción Social Autónoma-Hermandad General de Trajadores or Center for Autonomous Social Action-General Brotherhood of Workers) in the mid-1970s in Chicago. By the end of the decade, Lozano had traded his leather jacket for a three-piece suit as he prepared to engage with electoral politics. ST-40001425–0011, *Chicago Sun-Times* collection, Chicago History Museum.

despite thousands of undocumented workers from Europe, Asia, and Africa in other parts of the city. Because CASA had deep roots in the area's community organizations through individuals like Lozano, it was trusted to take the lead in defending immigrants from Mexico and Central America. In addition to keeping tabs on the INS and law enforcement and providing legal assistance, CASA's work included the establishment of student and community committees in defense of farmworkers, primarily through produce boycotts and awareness campaigns, as well as a partnership—and, in fact, considerable overlap in membership and programming—with the Chicago-based Midwest Coalition for the Defense of Immigrants. It was this coalition that took a small group, including Lozano, Coronado, and Chuy García, to Springfield in the spring of 1977.[15]

While Chicago politicos obsessively followed the first mayoral race since 1951 without Richard J. Daley, Mexican American and Chicano activists watched the state legislature's actions with growing alarm. As in other state capitals, Illinois legislators introduced a series of bills targeting undocumented workers, most prominently one that sanctioned employers for knowingly hiring anyone who was in the country illegally, language supported by congressional Democrats and Republicans in Washington. Democratic president Jimmy Carter's immigration proposal touted employer sanctions, a denial of social services to the undocumented, and the introduction of employment identification cards. Carter did back a broad amnesty to those who had been in the country since 1970, and he appointed Leonel Castillo as the first Mexican American to head the INS, signaling a potential change in the agency's law enforcement. But after a couple of years, most Mexican American activists, both nationally and locally, dismissed these as empty gestures; Castillo himself resigned in disgust in 1979, and Latino activists more generally criticized the administration for not taking their issues seriously. Those in CASA remained quite critical of Carter's approach, calling for unconditional amnesty and, reflecting a national trend of increasing Latino unity on immigration, succeeded in getting their amnesty work endorsed by other local Mexican American organizations, including the less ideological Pilsen Neighbors and Mujeres Latinas. In a report on CASA activities in 1977, Lozano reminded the organization's members that others in the community, such as Casa Aztlan, often dismissed them as communists and had not always been that sympathetic to undocumented workers. "We must safeguard against being sectarian," he stressed, and respecting immigrants and combatting racism through unconditional amnesty was one issue that achieved that.[16]

At the state level in Illinois, however, amnesty was not on the table. Rather, the employer sanctions bill unanimously passed the Illinois House. While its backers argued that it prevented employers from exploiting undocumented workers—"equal to servitude," according to one legislator—Chicano activists viewed it as a racialized punishment of hard-working men and women.[17] "It forced us to go to Springfield to lobby against these bills," recalled Chuy García, "and I keep pointing to this experience as being a turning point."[18] Among the legislators they did meet were Chicago-area state senators Dawn Clark Netsch and Harold Washington, who sympathized with Chicano arguments against the legislation. However, Washington warned them that there were few other Black legislators who shared his concerns about protecting illegal immigrants because of the belief they took jobs that would otherwise go to working-class African Americans. In fact, machine-backed Black state representative James Taylor, a rival of Washington's, cochaired the state Legislative Investigating Committee inquiry into illegal Mexican immigration into the state. Capitalizing on anti-Mexican hysteria, the committee's report argued that Joliet, Illinois, a city forty miles southwest of Chicago and the focus of a recent newspaper exposé, was not alone in its role as a major distribution point for illegal immigration. As a result, Taylor's report advocated making another attempt to pass state employer sanctions legislation, offering examples from California and other states that had begun to take a harder line toward immigrants. This experience, combined with the unfulfilled potential of Harold Washington's mayoral candidacy earlier in the year, prompted Lozano to conclude that "we need to elect our own." Coronado's reaction was "What? . . . It was so counterintuitive to everything we had been doing the last ten years." But that was what they ultimately decided to do.[19]

First, however, Lozano became a labor organizer. Although clearly a natural fit for the gregarious Lozano, unions were not often allies to the undocumented. Labor alliances such as the American Federation of Labor–Congress of Industrial Organizations—including Cesar Chávez's United Farm Workers in California—routinely supported tighter restrictions on illegal immigration because employers used such workers to depress wages and break strikes. This then allowed otherwise progressive politicians to call for aggressive deportations of undocumented workers and other limits on services and employment, especially in a place such as Chicago where unions were so intertwined with the dominant political machine. Nonetheless, working with CASA again showcased Lozano's natural talent for organizing and connecting with people—and led to a position as a full-time organizer for Local 336 of the International Ladies Garment Workers Union (ILGWU), the one national union with a rich, albeit complicated, history of organizing such immigrants.[20] "He had a very good way of talking to people and letting them know he really believed in them," recalled Robert Starks, a white activist priest in Pilsen in the 1970s who frequently worked with Lozano. "I think he had a good way of communicating that this was not just somebody organizing them for the sake of the union. . . . He didn't look down on them, he wasn't trying to manipulate them."[21] Added Coronado, "Rudy was really an organizer—he believed in leadership development," not in seeking his "own fame and glory." Lozano's daily reports from the late 1970s reflected this respect for the workers, as he organized among mostly immigrants in the city's notorious tortilla factories. Organizing in an industry increasingly dominated by Latinos, the ILGWU expanded into factories that employed them primarily, no matter what the product. Many days, his work consisted of simple gestures toward the workers, small amounts of assistance or mentoring. The factories' owners routinely threatened workers with federal immigration raids and deportation, and Lozano found himself fighting the union itself about the projects he wanted to pursue. And he was not perfect. Coronado recalled his mistakenly attempting to unionize an already-organized plant. But Lozano's painstaking work, charisma, and integrity in the community eventually led to three successful votes to recognize the ILGWU at Del Rey, the city's largest tortilla factory. His approach also won the respect of other potential partners, especially African Americans.[22]

Early on, Lozano saw potential allies in the independent Black politicians who emerged in the 1970s. While CASA had an explicit campaign to build a durable Latino alliance, its ideological approach allowed multiracial partnerships to be explored. As a young Chicano activist, Lozano admired the accomplishments of African Americans during the freedom struggle. The curricular reforms demanded by African Americans at Harrison High and UIC were models for his own arguments for Mexican American and Latino inclusion. In 1975, Lozano was a driving force behind CASA's advocacy for a Black school superintendent rather than a Latino, at odds with Pilsen Neighbors' position. As Starks recalled, "CASA said . . . it's the Blacks' time now, but we want a Black with content," rather than a Daley machine hack. Manford Byrd Jr., a veteran African American district administrator and former teacher supported by most of the city's Black luminaries, including Jesse Jackson, did not receive the appointment, prompting many of his advocates to shake their heads. "The despairing, humiliating, tragic powerlessness of Black people in Chicago," wrote *Tribune* columnist Vernon Jarrett, "is so unreal, so unbelievable, and so unnecessary."[23] CASA's support, even if unpopular with some Mexican Americans, produced valuable capital for the future. As a field organizer for the ILGWU, Lozano built ties with African American union activists, such as Charles Hayes, Eloise Brown, and the Coalition of Labor Union Women's Johnnie Jackson, often advocating for both Blacks and Latinos in the city's sweatshops, even amid the immigration crisis of the late 1970s. African Americans also lived in neighborhoods adjacent to Pilsen and the increasingly Latino community of Little Village west of Pilsen, and thus made up part of the electorate in an increasingly Latino-centric ward. As Lozano began to translate his labor organizing into electoral work—including the Independent Political Organization, which he helped found in 1981—white and Black progressives from around the city became increasingly essential to Lozano's political ambitions.[24]

WHILE PILSEN EMERGED as an important organizing space for the city's growing Mexican American population, other issue-focused groups and networks embraced a wide range of activism that challenged, directly and indirectly, a Democratic organization in transition in the late 1970s. One of the most potent issues remained the fight for affordable housing and against urban renewal and "condomania" across the city, including the "mini-city" proposed in the Chicago 21 Plan. The latest in a long series of efforts by business elites to tame the city and protect the Loop from poverty and disorder, Chicago 21 called for a massive mixed-use development on the Near South Side to attract wealthier residents. Eventually called Dearborn Park, the development would have, in effect, created a barrier from the poverty of Bronzeville and the Second Ward. Similar to the actions of the Young Lords in the 1960s and to the ultimately successful opponents of the proposed Crosstown Expressway in the mid-1970s, a range of community organizations doggedly opposed such development efforts that displaced or isolated low- and even middle-income Chicagoans. Of course, not all opposition was as flashy as the Young Lords' 1969 takeover of the McCormick Seminary. In 1976, more than a dozen community organizations formed the Chicago Rehab Network to share information on how best to rehabilitate housing in a way that did not price longtime residents out of their communities. The information-sharing first took the form of a center offering technical assistance and training in rehabilitation employment, eventually gaining federal funding through the Comprehensive Employment and Training Act and other block grants. By 1979, nearly a thousand units had been upgraded in an affordable way. More striking politically was the increasing influence of this network of affordable housing advocates across the city, demonstrating how banding together rather than competing individually allowed them to overcome the city bureaucracy to secure funds, as well as work on broader housing policy. Four years after its founding, the network had grown to twenty neighborhood housing development organizations, a disproportionate number of them working in Latino communities.[25]

One was the Spanish Coalition for Housing, based in the predominantly Puerto Rican enclave of West Town west of the Loop. A product of the 1966 Division Street uprisings, the coalition initially worked on a variety of issues, including job opportunities before spinning off the Spanish Coalition for Jobs in the early 1970s to focus on housing. The group, with a professional staff of two and a large stable of volunteers, had succeeded in slowing down the demolition of affordable units on the Near Northwest Side by advocating for tenants' rights, offering assistance in self-help construction (such as how to find inexpensive materials), and providing leadership in the Coalition to Stop Chicago 21 and what they viewed as just the latest gentrification blueprint for the Loop. Through the Rehab Network, the coalition expanded and formalized its ties to a diverse range of like organizations across the city, such as the Black-led Kenwood-Oakland Community Organization on the South Side, the Eighteenth Street Development Corporation in Pilsen, and the multiracial Intercommunal

Survival Committee (ISC) and Heart of Uptown Coalition, led by Slim Coleman and Helen Shiller, on the North Side. And while they did not pretend that their work took the place of more sweeping public housing construction and policy from earlier in the century—or even adequately fought the market and government incentives to displace existing homeowners—activists with the Spanish Coalition for Housing and its partners saw their work as making a difference. "Some have been only momentary victories," wrote Bob Giloth, former director of the Eighteenth Street Development Organization. "The problem does not lie so much in the city's lack of capacity to initiate new housing policies for low- and moderate-income people . . . but with lack of follow-through and commitment by the city to minimize displacement and to foster neighborhood development."[26]

While housing activism tied these groups together, through community development corporations and opposition to urban development plans such as Chicago 21, several of the organizations pursued a range of interrelated concerns. After all, housing was so often inextricably linked to quality education, jobs, health care, and other needs. For instance, the Heart of Uptown Coalition—known as the ISC in Uptown until 1978—and the Westtown Concerned Citizens Coalition pursued a full range of services and avenues to empower its members. The ISC was founded in 1970 by Slim Coleman, who, despite his nickname, country drawl, and slicked-back hair, hailed from a middle-class Houston family and had graduated from Harvard University. After college, he came to Chicago in time for the protest culture of the late 1960s and moved to Uptown. There, Coleman faced many of the same challenges the community's less-educated residents faced in terms of housing and police harassment, and he responded by forming the ISC under the direction of the local Black Panther Party. The ISC, which aimed to primarily "serve the needs of the poor and oppressed white community" (which made up the majority of Uptown residents), used language and programming similar to those of the Panthers. It offered survival programs from tenants' and welfare rights organizing to other sorts of legal counseling and food cooperatives. Many services were tailored specifically for Appalachian migrants, such as health care, counseling, and legal support for black lung victims, as well as Sunday country music shows and other entertainment. The ISC embraced the coalitional and class language of Fred Hampton, routinely pointing out how policies impacted Black, Latino, *and* poor white communities. As the decade wore on, ISC activists, not unlike their Chicano counterparts, increasingly realized they had to provide not just cultural and survival services but also pursue actions more explicitly political. Those included petitions to remove state's attorney Edward Hanrahan in 1972 and opposition to a Regional Transit Authority, which would have weakened Chicagoans' say in the city's mass transit, in 1974. The ISC endorsed Jiménez's council bid in 1975 and eventually championed the candidacies of Helen Shiller, Paul Siegel, and other ISC members for local office in the late 1970s.[27]

One of the ISC's strengths was its ability to smartly communicate its activities and ideology through *Keep Strong*, a glossy-covered monthly magazine modeled after the explicitly political underground publications that circulated in Chicago, such as the *Black Panther* and *Rising Up Angry* newspapers. *Keep Strong*'s editor, Helen Shiller, had come to Chicago in 1972 and initially sold the *Black Panther*, efforts that allowed her to get to know the community, including tapping into Coleman's ISC. She was known for persistence, including one potential customer who, "worn down, [bought] one after the 17th knock on his door." In 1975, just months after Jiménez lost his council bid, Shiller launched *Keep Strong* as an official organ of the committee. Within two years, the monthly magazine was sold for twenty-five cents an issue in nearly 100 locations throughout Chicago and Milwaukee. The magazine highlighted issues specific to Uptown, such as standard features on welfare rights, tenant rights, community health, arson and police watch, "fighting City Hall," and the "slumlord of the month." Reflective of the ISC's everyman appeal—and long before mainstream newspapers—the magazine boasted an "on the street" feature, quoting regular people in response to questions such as "What do you think of four more years of Daley?" and "How did the movie 'Roots' affect you?" But *Keep Strong* integrated these locally oriented features into relevant coverage of a larger people's struggle beyond the confines of Uptown or even Chicago. Stories about the Ku Klux Klan in Harlan County, Kentucky, fuel shortages in West Virginia, and education budget battles in New York City directly resonated with the community's many recent Appalachian transplants to the Midwest's urban metropolis. Considerable attention went to the Black Panthers' work in Oakland, the moderate policies of President Carter, and international struggles against racism in Rhodesia and elsewhere. Reviews of significant popular culture, such as the documentary *Harlan County, USA*, the groundbreaking television miniseries *Roots*, Robert Altman's *Nashville*, and Merle Haggard's new bluegrass album made it into the pages, too. In contrast to so many of its counterparts among activist community publications and businesses, *Keep Strong* boasted enough community advertising and support to survive into the 1980s and became a vehicle for more successful progressive political candidates.[28]

Another such organization was the Westtown Concerned Citizens Coalition (WCCC) in another neighborhood considered a "port of entry" for migrants to

Editor and aldermanic candidate Helen Shiller adorns the cover of *Keep Strong*, the official organ of the Intercommunal Survival Committee. The magazine offered coverage of working-class residents of Uptown and surrounding communities in a way the city's dailies rarely did. Municipal Reference Collection, Chicago Public Library.

Chicago. Founded by the young, charismatic Puerto Rican pastor Jorge Morales, the WCCC operated out of a storefront location in the diverse but increasingly Latino enclave on the city's Near Northwest Side and blended Christian worship with social justice. "We instilled in them the idea that what we did on Sunday was basically to thank God and celebrate the victories from Monday to Saturday," stated Morales, who also led St. Luke's United Church of Christ. As a Chicago native, Morales had grown up familiar with the tactics of Saul Alinsky and Jesse Jackson. "I frequently went down to listen to Jesse" at Operation Breadbasket, and later PUSH, "and had some admiration for the Black church as an institution of empowerment and liberation," Morales said. "I think one of the ideas in my mind was how the Latino church could be such an instrument for Latino people in contrast to what the church had done historically . . . which had been an instrument of conquest." As a result, he said, "We created a theological understanding for the social activism that was taking place." Made up of no more than a couple of hundred people, the WCCC used direct action protest to tackle unemployment, affordable housing, and an overall sense of despair among Puerto Ricans that had prompted another small uprising the year before. Arson, while on the decline, had devastated an estimated 40 percent of the housing units in some parts of the community over the previous seven years, according to WCCC.[29]

Unemployment was an even bigger problem. As a result, the WCCC's first direct action was against the local post office for not hiring Latinos and thus violating affirmative action policies. It was ill-advised, Morales recalled, because it was not an "easily winnable issue," as Alinsky's philosophy dictated. But "we learned fairly quickly," Morales recalled. "There were times when we were beaten by the postal inspectors and the postal police." They found out where the postmaster lived and picketed his home, as well as slowed services with people buying fourteen-cent stamps with the same number of pennies. Their activism also required careful negotiation with other groups. "Part of our challenge, as we worked to increase Latino employment, was also to build relations with the Black community," he recalled. Facilitated by the Community Renewal Society's Tom Benedict, Morales engaged with Congressman Ralph Metcalfe and community leader (and future alderman and congressman) Danny Davis, who "were key to creating the linkages for communicating that we were not trying to take jobs from Blacks." The old saying that "there was always work at the post office" was often true among African Americans, and thus the Latino challenge could have been seen as a threat. Instead, Morales and others built lasting ties to Black community leaders by talking with them.[30]

Morales also partnered with Pilsen Neighbors, the Spanish Coalition for Jobs, and Alderman Dick Simpson on expanding job opportunities for Latinos. Simpson, a political science professor at UIC and another Texas native, had represented the far Northwest Side's Forty-Fourth Ward since 1971 and, by 1978, was one of just two bona fide independents left on the City Council. After spending several years pushing more aggressive and inclusive affirmative action policies, Simpson wrote in support of Latinos' administrative complaint to the federal Treasury Department's Office of Revenue Sharing. "As we seen [sic] in the federal lawsuits against the Police and Fire Departments, nothing will be accomplished until the flow of federal funds is cut off," stated Simpson. "Chicago is a city that will only treat human beings fairly if forced to do so by the federal government." Morales offered a litany of reasons why officials should consider blocking the $95 million the city would receive, including the slow pace of Latino hiring, the use of culturally biased testing, and the requirement to have a political sponsor (presumably from the machine) to apply for many city jobs. After Mayor Michael Bilandic and other city officials rejected the jobs numbers—and the *Tribune* perpetuated stereotypes of Latino laziness in its own dismissal—Morales retorted in a letter to the editor that "statements about Latinos having many little children, about many Latinos not speaking English and not being educated enough to hold city jobs, about 'illegal aliens,' and about deportations, are indicative of a racist tone which takes on an ugly and immoral spectre." Their efforts to improve job opportunities in the city went largely unheeded—at least as long as Bilandic remained mayor.[31]

Their activism, and the work of many other community organizations, eventually led them back to electoral politics; these men and women sensed opportunity—and power—despite the potential pitfalls. For the Intercommunal Survival Committee, electoral politics had never been very far away anyhow. Helen Shiller, who edited *Keep Strong* magazine from 1975 to 1980, ran for alderman in 1978. Chris Cohen, the Forty-Sixth Ward alderman who had beaten Cha-Cha Jiménez three years earlier but who machine officials never liked or found totally reliable, had become the regional director of the federal Department of Health, Education, and Welfare. After a judge ruled that city officials must call a special election to fill two council seats—ones that happened to be in wards no longer seen as machine strongholds—Shiller decided to run in the Forty-Sixth. Not surprisingly, her campaign prioritized the "neighborhoods first" approach championed by both the ISC and the growing network of community organizations with which it partnered—from greater accountability for the city's use of federal funds and community inclusion in the planning process to tenants' rights and local control of the police. "I have a proven record of community accountability," Shiller said at the time, framing her candidacy as classically, if slightly more irreverently, independent. "And that will be a breath of fresh air, perhaps best to be provided by the only independent woman in the council." Indeed, Shiller built on the diverse, largely working-class coalition that emerged for Jiménez by also subtly reminding those in the ward's wealthier precincts along Lake Shore Drive that she was as an educated Jewish woman conversant in the community's development projects and the pressures faced by small businesses. Similar to Jiménez's campaign, she held scores of coffee klatches with residents and devoted her limited resources to expanding voter registration. But unlike Jiménez, Shiller was a bit more "respectable," white, and educated and thus won endorsements from the *Sun-Times*, as well as from high-profile independents such as Harold Washington, former alderman Bill Singer, and state representative Ellis Levin.[32]

Not unlike dismissals of mayoral candidate Jane Byrne the following year, few observers, especially men, took Shiller seriously, which allowed her to make the race closer than expected. In its editorial endorsing heavily favored machine candidate and ward committeeman Ralph Axelrod, the *Tribune* devoted less than a sentence to Shiller, calling her "a community activist who runs primarily as a champion of the poor."[33] While accurate enough, much of the editorial and other coverage stressed Axelrod's organization and ties to Sheriff Richard Elrod. Only late in the campaign did Axelrod sense a real threat as Shiller campaigned with Singer and voter interest appeared high, prompting some last-minute vandalism of Shiller campaign posters and intimidation of her supporters. Ultimately, in a three-way race that included publicist Michael Horowitz, Shiller lost with 35 percent of the vote, coming within 2,000 votes of Axelrod. The result was close enough that, as the pages of *Keep Strong* show, she never stopped running for the seat, which was up again in 1979. That race, she recalled, was "much nastier," as Axelrod supporters labeled her an "anarchist" and tried to use race as a wedge by asserting that Shiller had several children with Black and Puerto Rican men in the ward. A suspicious fire also destroyed her election office. For her part, Shiller used the same grassroots tactics as she did the previous year and, with some anti-incumbent help from mayoral candidate Jane Byrne, actually outpolled Axelrod in the primary. She did not win 50 percent, however, and as the machine had done so many times before, the organization managed to drag Axelrod across the runoff's finish line by a scant 247 votes. After the nastiness of the campaign, Shiller swore that she would never run for office again.[34]

Meanwhile, the independents were all but written off. In 1978, outspoken progressives Ellis Levin, Michael Holewinski, and James Houlihan lost their legislative primary races to more conservative Democratic regulars. Harold Washington survived a machine challenge—in which two neophyte candidates also named Washington ran, in an old machine trick—by only 219 votes. Just two independents remained on the City Council. Predicting a "gloomy outlook" for the foreseeable future, the *Tribune*'s Richard Ciccone wrote, "Last month, the Independents suffered their worst election losses since their first encroachments on organization turf. There seem to be few reasons to expect a comeback."[35] And yet such predictions belied the actual weaknesses of the post-Daley machine and the groundwork the machine's grassroots foes had quietly made. Ironically, it would take one of the machine's freshly scorned members to do what independents by themselves had been unable to accomplish two years earlier.

WHEN JANE BYRNE announced her candidacy for mayor in April 1978, charging that "a cabal of evil men . . . had fastened itself to government," more than a few observers smirked. Not only were they unpersuaded that she could beat Mayor Bilandic, but she also had not long before been part of that same party organization. "We do not [to put it tactfully] expect Mrs. Byrne to win," wrote the *Tribune* editors. "In Mrs. Byrne's view, it seems, the machine turned sinister only after the death of Mayor Daley.... No doubt we can expect a campaign like this to produce some picturesque name-calling. We cannot expect it to turn up any very factual or convincing history." Black columnist Vernon Jarrett had similar suspicions that "Jane Byrne is no Joan of Arc," while others viewed her move as mostly paving the way for more substantial—and male— candidates to enter the fray. Indeed, the initial treatment of Byrne's candidacy was tinged with an amused sexism. Alderman Edward Burke said Byrne reminded him of his Aunt Bessie, "always fussing," while others more crassly called her a "menopausal bitch" who was going through "the change" in a very public way.[36]

This rather insular male group of journalists and politicos who wrote off Byrne, it turned out, ignored the factors that made her victory possible. They had paid little attention to the often-quiet grassroots work developed within and between the city's communities in the 1970s. Excluding Jarrett, few had taken seriously the increasing estrangement of some African Americans, even after Harold Washington swept the Black middle-class wards in his failed mayoral bid in 1977. In a point even lost on most scholars of Chicago and urban politics, the city's old-boy network of media and politics did not stop to think that its quick dismissal of Byrne reflected gendered assumptions.[37] And they certainly did not anticipate that the atrophying machine might respond with incredible incompetence to the blizzards that paralyzed Chicago in January and February of 1979. As unlikely as it was, Jane Byrne became the first mayoral candidate to beat Chicago's Democratic machine since 1931 and, in an oft-overlooked superlative, the first woman to run a U.S. city with more than a million residents.[38]

Hailing from a well-to-do Irish Catholic family on the city's Northwest Side, Jane Byrne always had ties to the city's Irish American political establishment, including Richard J. Daley, and it was this mentorship that became the foundation of her political career. After being widowed at age twenty-seven with a young child, Byrne joined the local presidential campaign of John F. Kennedy in 1960, but not through the regular Democratic organization. Daley, who was a friend of the family, later lectured Byrne that, if she had used the proper channels, she could have then landed a patronage job. Months after that conversation, his point made, Daley hired her as a midlevel bureaucrat in 1964 and then four years later as commissioner of the city's Department of Consumer Sales, Weights, and Measures, a little-known agency (even to Byrne) that insiders viewed as one of the city's most corrupt. According to numerous state and independent investigations, meat and produce scale inspectors routinely took bribes to allow stores to cheat consumers, while others skipped the inspections altogether and took second jobs on city time. Despite limited managerial experience, Byrne used her blunt, often abrasive style effectively in taking on the old-boy network, rotating inspection routes, firing or transferring some of the worst offenders, and periodically talking to the media about it. While she reported that Daley was absolutely giddy to make her "the first woman commissioner of any major city in the United States," he clearly had ulterior motives. As Gary Rivlin writes, Byrne's empowerment at Consumer Sales provided Daley with a small bit of cover as feminists ratcheted up their critique of the machine's male dominance. Exactly one of eighty Cook County Democratic Committee members was a woman. In a mostly ceremonial move in 1975, Daley even made Byrne cochair of the county Democratic organization.[39]

But all of this changed when Byrne's powerful patron died in December 1976. George Dunne, president of the Cook County Board of Commissioners, quickly maneuvered her out of the party leadership, and Michael Bilandic closed down her access to the mayor's office. Accordingly, her ability to run the Department of Consumer Sales as she had under Daley began to wane as well. Just like that, her influence was gone. In response, she demonstrated the "brass" that Chicagoans came to know her for. Framing herself as the guardian for city consumers and the authentic keeper of the Daley flame, she publicly accused Bilandic and his aides of pushing through an illegal taxi fare hike—and with violating the spirit of her mentor, Daley. Calling the City Council's approval of a fare increase "fraudulent and conspiratorial," Byrne stated that Bilandic "greased the way" by suppressing an independent audit of the city's cab industry. As proof, she supplied reporters with a notarized memo—written by herself months earlier—that included warnings from Daley to avoid the cab representatives so as not "to get yourself set up like that." A federal probe concluded there was no wrongdoing—conveniently just weeks before the 1979 mayoral primary. In the meantime, Byrne was fired for insubordination and, soon after, began running for mayor. Sour grapes over her treatment after Daley's death certainly played a role. But she also saw other factors at play. She believed that the overwhelming popularity of Proposition 13 in California—better known as the California tax revolt, which greatly limited officials' ability to tax property—reflected that "people everywhere are fed up with government," she told a reporter. "It will make people ready to vote against the public officials." While California seemed a long way from Chicago, the worsening economic conditions across the country infused the politics of less government and better government everywhere in the late 1970s. Such sentiments would help former California governor Ronald Reagan triumph nationally in 1980, and they did so for Byrne a year earlier, who sensed at least a chance against a machine uniquely hobbled under Bilandic.[40]

Few veteran independents believed Byrne was the real deal, given how Daley had groomed and protected her politically for more than a decade, not to mention her campaign's lack of organization, staff, or money. Yet many of those same independents slowly began to rally around her campaign late in 1978 when it was clear no one else would enter the race. Many African Americans remained offended over how the machine had blocked Wilson Frost, the council's Black president pro tempore and Daley's legal successor. While Frost would not be mistaken for a reformer, it was clear that he had been thwarted from becoming the city's first Black mayor because of his race. Prominent and respected African Americans such as labor activist Tim Black, West Side community leader and aldermanic candidate Danny Davis, and *Tribune* columnist Vernon Jarrett supported Byrne's run, as did white independents such as retiring alderman Dick Simpson. Don Rose, a local legend in independent politics because he had successfully managed several campaigns, also joined Byrne's team in January and gave it some of the professionalism the campaign desperately needed. Plenty of others remained skeptical. For instance, Helen Shiller, who was running for alderman again in the Forty-Sixth Ward, never mentioned Byrne in either *Keep Strong* magazine or her campaign literature. Black professor and South Side activist Bob Starks, when asked years later if he had supported Byrne, responded simply, "Heck, no." But he understood why some did. Latinos such as Rudy Lozano, Chuy García, and Jorge Morales also watched intently but remained neutral, unconvinced—and rightfully so—that Byrne was an ally. Instead, Elena Martinez, a Cuban American psychiatric social worker and campaign volunteer who had met Byrne just that spring, became the candidate's de facto liaison to Latinos. But while the campaign lacked traditional independent support and organization, it had more than enough volunteers, energy, and pent-up anger by those mistreated by the machine to take advantage of a blunder—if it presented itself. One of the worst winters in Chicago's history offered just that opportunity.[41]

The snow that began falling on New Year's Eve 1978, followed by more and more snow for the rest of January and into February, triggered a remarkably incompetent response in a town many loved to call the "city that works."[42] Fifteen inches was followed by twenty-two inches, and then subzero temperatures, all in a winter that produced eighty-seven total inches of snow—more than double the average annual amount in Chicago. Rather than systematically plow the snow, a basic function of a major city in the Midwest it would seem, the city government fell further and further behind. O'Hare International Airport closed

Mayoral candidate Jane Byrne poses with respected educator, civil rights activist, and labor organizer Tim Black, who endorsed her quixotic challenge to Mayor Michael Bilandic in 1979. She ended up winning a significant portion of Black votes, but hopes that she would enact policies friendlier to Black Chicago were quickly dashed. Timuel D. Black Jr. Papers, box 190, photo 094, Vivian G. Harsh Research Collection of Afro-American History and Literature, Chicago Public Library.

multiple times, as did the trains when the rails froze. During one storm, Mayor Bilandic ordered the closing of ten El stations, all in Black South Side communities, to move suburban trains faster to downtown. He claimed multiple times that the streets were plowed when they were not and ordered residents to move their cars to designated school parking lots to ease plowing—just to find those lots had not been cleared themselves. Amid the paralysis, the *Tribune* reported that machine crony Kevin Sain received a $90,000 city contract the year before to devise a new snow-removal plan, which had not been completed and made embarrassingly simple recommendations such as "remove the snow from major arteries." Byrne called it the "Great Sain Robbery." Day in and day out, the media, Byrne, and others hammered the administration for not getting a handle on snow removal. In desperation, two weeks before the February 27 primary, Bilandic tried to rally machine precinct captains and went off his normal lawyerly script, "likening criticism of his administration to the Crucifixion of Jesus, the mass murders of Jews, and the recent collapses of foreign governments" in Iran and Cambodia, wrote the *Tribune*. Exhorted Bilandic, often in a voice cracking with emotion, "It's our turn to be in the trenches, to see if we are made of the same stuff as the early Christians, the persecuted Jews, the proud Poles, the Blacks and the Latinos." The true believers applauded; most others believed Bilandic had sealed his doom.[43]

Byrne won the Democratic primary with 51 percent of the vote and a 16,775-vote margin, garnering more than 63 percent of the African American vote. The heavily favored Democrat went on to win the general election in April with 82 percent. Rather than celebrate, however, the Black and white independents who had supported her became alarmed at how quickly her tone changed. "This is the story of a political revolution that expired before it began," declared Vernon Jarrett—before, in fact, Byrne had even become mayor officially. While she did appoint Northwestern professor and lawyer Louis Masotti to head a transition team packed with reformers, including former independent aldermen Dick Simpson, Bill Singer, and Leon Despres, and outspoken Black activists Tim Black, Nancy Jefferson, and Addie Wyatt, Byrne also met behind closed doors with key machine aldermen Vito Marzullo, Ed Burke, and Ed Vrdolyak. Sure enough, Byrne fired Masotti and tried to bury the 1,000-page transition report that the team had compiled, which called for, among other things, sweeping changes to the makeup of city boards, as well as mechanisms for lower-income people to purchase condos. The transition team report only became available fourteen months later after *Chicago Lawyer* magazine sued and a judge ordered its release; Byrne reportedly never read the report.[44]

Meanwhile, a few African Americans tried to forge a relationship with the new mayor, but they had little to show for it. Renault Robinson, who had sued the city as president of the Afro-American Patrolmen's League, emerged as an unlikely yet vocal backer of hers, and was rewarded with a post on the Chicago Housing Authority (CHA) board. But as he warned her upon acceptance, Robinson aimed to remove controversial CHA director Charles Swibel, who was notorious for corruption and mismanagement over a more than fifteen-year reign. "My job was to get rid of Swibel," Robinson recalled. "And I told Jane that's what I was gonna do. I was gonna run him out. She said, good luck. You'll be doing me a favor." But when Robinson came close to doing just that, Byrne pleaded with him to back off. "I need him . . . I can't run the city without Swibel and [Ed] Vrdolyak." Without such allies, her legislation would be ignored, he recalled her telling him. Byrne then offered Robinson another position in the administration, which he declined, and he soon left the board. Other African Americans briefly held prominent positions in the city—in the Chicago Transit Authority, the police department, and on the school board—all to be removed by 1981.

Black Chicagoans were stunned by the betrayal, as Tim Black captured in one of his last letters to the mayor. "It was the Black vote that gave you the slim margin of victory in the primary election on February 27," he wrote. "Black people are waiting to see what you are going to do in appreciation of their confidence in you. . . . You could at least show good will and good intentions. Anything less will not." He then added, as a not-so-veiled electoral threat, "As a good Christian, I am sure that you are familiar with the Biblical statement that, 'The Lord Giveth and the Lord Taketh Away.'"[45]

Latinos, if anything, fared worse under Byrne and responded with their own activism. Elena Martinez, for instance, witnessed a change in Byrne immediately. The day after the primary victory, the woman who had been Byrne's main female confidante during the campaign suddenly had no access to the Democratic candidate for mayor. Two bodyguards materialized in front of her office door and Martinez, just like everyone else, suddenly had to make an appointment. In March, Martinez wrote Byrne a memo outlining several Latino issues, including the expansion of bilingual education, more jobs and contracts for Latinos, and city attention to neighborhoods like Pilsen and Humboldt Park. After two weeks of no response, Martinez stopped Byrne in the hall and warned her that Latinos were growing impatient, to which she retorted that, "Latinos did not vote for me . . . I'll answer them when I'm good and ready." Indeed, Latinos did not vote in large numbers generally and, of those who did, 55 percent had supported Bilandic, reflecting the interests of what scholar Mike Amezcua calls the "conservative *colonia*" of Latino, especially Mexican American business and homeowners. Only in the Seventh and Thirtieth Wards did Byrne win a majority. The day after Martinez's warning, Jorge Morales and members of the Westtown Concerned Citizens Coalition filled Byrne's campaign office and insisted on being heard, shouting, "No hables, no hables" at Martinez while Byrne struggled to respond to their demands. Much like her mentor, Byrne made promises—in this case, a greater Latino share of jobs and contracts—that she would not keep, and after the general election, Byrne severed ties with Martinez entirely. Under sustained pressure, Byrne eventually tapped lawyer Raul Villalobos for the school board and Joseph Martinez for city council, the latter of whom Byrne erroneously called the city's first Hispanic alderman. Neither, it turned out, were particularly qualified to speak for their constituencies. Despite some cooperative Black-Latino efforts on school board appointments, Villalobos faced withering criticism from many African Americans for his opposition to tapping the city's first Black school superintendent and other insensitivity toward the Black school experience. Similarly, observers viewed

Martinez, a Puerto Rican lawyer in powerful alderman Edward Burke's firm, as mostly a machine hack. "Joseph Martinez?" observed one Latino activist. "Never heard of him."[46]

COMPOUNDING BYRNE'S troubles with Blacks and Latinos was the election of Ronald Reagan as president in 1980 and a new census that, even with the most conservative count, proved Latinos would be a significant political force in the city during the next decade. The former governor of California and the most politically conservative president since at least the 1920s, Reagan had promised a retrenchment in domestic life by the federal government well beyond President Carter's own austerity policies. Reagan pledged massive tax cuts, a dramatic increase in defense spending, a more aggressive posture toward the Soviet Union and its allies, and a sizable reduction in the federal welfare state and other discretionary spending, from Medicaid to Amtrak to Aid to Families with Dependent Children, or welfare. "I pledge to restore to the federal government the capacity to do the people's work without dominating their lives," Reagan declared in his nomination speech in Detroit in July 1980. "Everything that can be run more effectively by state and local government we shall turn over to state and local government." While that may have aligned with Byrne's outlook, as most historians suggest, Reagan was also the candidate of white backlash—racial resentment masked by a sunny love-of-country optimism. "I believe in states' rights," Reagan told a crowd matter-of-factly at the Neshoba County Fair in Mississippi, using the euphemism for white supremacy just miles away from where three civil rights workers had been found murdered sixteen years earlier. One year later, Reagan reminded a group of police chiefs that "only our deep moral values and our strong social institutions can hold back that jungle and restrain the darker impulses of human nature."[47] Such racist dog-whistles included urban centers like Chicago, for which most observers predicted dire consequences from higher local taxes and slashed services and jobs from Reagan budget cuts. While not all the proposed reductions in urban spending occurred, the federal share of the city's general revenue dropped from 27 percent in 1978 to 12 percent by 1985. Byrne had not supported Reagan, or President Carter for that matter. Demonstrating an explicit Irish Catholic loyalty to the Kennedy family, Byrne had backed Massachusetts senator Ted Kennedy's failed liberal challenge to the centrist Carter in the 1980 Democratic primary and found herself with few allies after Reagan's victory. As a result of her weak political position—and a fundamental conservatism—Byrne offered the new president an olive branch, arguing that budget cuts were "unfortunate, but so is inflation," while quietly condoning the racist scapegoating embedded in Reagan's rhetoric and policies. It proved a sharp contrast to other big-city mayors as well as other Democrats in Chicago, including the city's newly elected congressman Harold Washington, who expressed his "deep distress at the regressive, antiblack, and anti–poor people actions" of the Reagan administration, policies that disproportionately harmed Blacks and Latinos in the city.[48]

For Rudy Lozano, despite his periodic success in labor organizing in the 1970s, this new reality cemented what he had begun to believe in Springfield in 1977: "We have to elect our own."[49] Amid national calls for Black-Latino-and-white unity against Reagan's cuts and a 1980 census indicating a robust Latino population in the city—14 percent versus 3 percent ten years earlier—Lozano and others found the Independent Political Organization (IPO) of the Near West Side. Along with Lozano, the leadership consisted of some of Pilsen's and Little Village's most dynamic organizers, including Chuy García, Linda Coronado, and Arturo Vasquez of Pilsen's Casa Aztlan. The organization's name echoed those of other antimachine organizations in the city, including the North Side's similarly named Independent Precinct Organization and the statewide Independent Voters of Illinois, and it promised to do similar work, especially in the Twenty-Second Ward, which had a Mexican American majority. Unlike other independent groups, however, Lozano's IPO made explicit commitments to coalitions with both African Americans and other Latinos—a reflection of the Twenty-Second Ward's demographics and part of a larger citywide strategy. While the ward was roughly 74 percent Mexican American in 1980, there were significant Black-majority precincts in neighboring North Lawndale and LeClaire Courts. Moreover, they decided that their "politics were going to be about change," recalled García, "that they were going to be a vehicle for empowerment and enfranchisement, that we were going to work in coalition with other groups. In our situation, it was mandatory because we did not have the numbers by ourselves given the immigrant status of many people in the community, that we would work in alliance through a multi-racial approach to our politics."[50] This reality translated into a multipronged strategy of aggressive voter registration efforts among Mexican Americans, the protection and advocacy of undocumented workers of all nationalities conducted by Casa Aztlan and CASA-HGT, and the continued cultivation of Black allies on the West Side and in community development networks across the city. Added to their Black labor connections were new allies such as activists Ronnell Mustin, Pat Dickson, and especially Danny Davis, who had translated his community leadership in Lawndale as a high school teacher and health center director into a success-ful race for alderman in 1979.[51]

Two of the most important activities in the IPO's first year were partnering with African Americans in their legal challenges to the proposed City Council maps based on the new census and backing Juan Soliz's independent candidacy for the State Assembly. Soon after the IPO formed in the summer of 1981, the City Council released the redrawn maps. In addition to Latinos' surge to 14 percent of the city's population, including two near-majority concentrations in Pilsen and Humboldt Park, the census determined that African Americans made up 39.8 percent of Chicago residents. But the new maps championed by Mayor Byrne and drawn by Tom Keane, the powerful alderman and Daley ally who once had been convicted of mail fraud in 1974, managed to reduce the number of Black-majority districts from nineteen to seventeen and to deny Latinos a clear majority in any ward. In what legal scholars call "fracturing," the Puerto Rican–dominated areas of Humboldt Park, Logan Square, and West Town on the Near Northwest Side were divided into six wards; the Mexican American communities of Pilsen and Little Village on the Near Southwest Side were splintered into four wards. Despite fierce criticism from these communities, the City Council passed the new maps with few changes in late 1981, ensuring a majority-white council of 60 to 65 percent despite a bare white plurality of 43 percent in the city. As one reporter stated, "In past generations, minorities may have accepted the remap with resignation. This time they took it to court."[52]

Blacks and Latinos filed three lawsuits, two by groups of voters and one by the political alliance of Aldermen Danny Davis and Allan Streeter and Jesse Jackson's Operation PUSH. Meanwhile, in a surprise maneuver at the time, the Reagan administration's Justice Department also challenged the maps and pe-titioned to join the legal challenges that had been consolidated into one law-suit. "As U.S. attorney, I cannot stand back and ignore obvious violations of the Voting Rights Act," stated U.S. Attorney Dan Webb. "We're not joining the lawsuit just to put the muscle of this office behind the issue. I have an obligation to correct an obvious injustice." While seemingly sincere in 1982, Republican advocacy of minority-majority districts within a decade had become a mostly cynical attempt to "pack" minority districts to dilute others held by moderate white Democrats, especially in the South. In the only such instance outside of the South that year, U.S. Circuit Court Judge Thomas McMillen ruled that the Chicago map was deliberately discriminatory and ordered a new one, sparking a process that went through several more layers of judicial review and even-tually led to special elections in 1986 and a political sea change in minority representation on the City Council.[53]

The IPO also helped Juan Soliz set the tone for his historic run in 1982 for state representative. While the organization's first major test did not result in an electoral victory, it demonstrated the kind of campaign tactics it might take to win in the future, including Rudy Lozano's aldermanic run in Pilsen's Twenty-Second Ward in 1983. The race pitted Soliz, an attorney with the Legal Assistance Foundation and the Midwest Coalition for the Defense of Immigrants, a native of New Mexico, and a relative newcomer to the area, against machine-aligned state representative Marco Domico. Despite having only arrived in Chicago in the mid-1970s, Soliz had built a reputation for advocacy of undocumented workers and new immigrants, representing them in a high-profile eviction case and raid in Edgewater, on the city's far North Side, and offering vocal critiques of a proposed federal guest-worker program. In the race, Soliz secured a rainbow of endorsements, ranging from Danny Davis, Art Turner, and the Reverend Willie Baker to labor stalwarts Art McBride, Frank Rosen, and the United Electricians local. Harold Washington also endorsed him. In fact, his most prominent campaign photograph shows him among African Americans, not Latinos, which may have been symbolic. While the campaign registered several thousand new voters, Soliz was not entirely accepted by Latinos. Nicknamed "Johnny Solo" by one reporter for his sometimes go-it-alone approach, including later alliances with the machine in 1980s runs, Soliz did not have a close relationship with either Lozano or Washington—a reality that may have fed a rivalry between the two activists, according to some observers. But most at the time chalked up Soliz's loss to the extraordinary measures taken by party regulars to disqualify him. Charging that Soliz did not file the proper change-of-address form and that he had forged signatures—a charge later dismissed—the Board of Elections threw him off the ballot. "I am not surprised at all," he told a reporter, speaking of machine shenanigans, including the unusual, menacing presence of veteran alderman Vito Marzullo, who just stared at the judge throughout the proceeding. Soliz ended up running as a write-in candidate and losing with 33 percent of the vote. Members of the IPO and its partners in Pilsen and Little Village committed considerable groundwork to the effort. And yet, "we really didn't know what we were doing," said Linda Coronado. "We really saw what the machine was like. . . . We didn't win, but we built a movement."[54]

While activists could have interpreted the election result as confirmation of why they should not engage with formal politics—and Coronado admitted to such doubts—they instead forged ahead. Within weeks of Soliz's defeat, Rudy Lozano and ten other Latinos, including two machine-backed candidates favored to win, announced their candidacies for City Council. Soliz's run, despite the machine's ugliness, was in fact seen as a triumph. The community rallied

116 | **We Were Invisible**

behind this newcomer and the machine went to great lengths to stop him. Yes, it had defeated him, but activists sensed an opportunity to send a message that they were not going away; Latinos made up nearly one-sixth of the city's population, and they would force the party organization to listen. African Americans drew a similar conclusion, as Black South Side congressman Harold Washington also announced his candidacy for mayor and made sure to include Latinos—as well as the poor whites and African Americans so often ignored in politics—in his campaign appeals. Latinos and their grassroots allies were "invisible" no longer.

## CHAPTER 5

# The Grassroots Challenge

[Byrne] was good for the spirit of the Black community.
She insulted the Black community enough so that
Lu Palmer . . . began to have voter education classes.
—Tim Black interview, HMDA

By the summer of 1982, a handful of activists had been meeting in the basement of Lu and Jorja Palmer's Bronzeville home for more than two years.[1] There, anywhere from ten to twenty Black intellectuals had met to discuss the latest transgression by Mayor Jane Byrne and to hash out a strategy to replace her with a Black mayor in 1983. This brain trust included Robert Starks, Al Sampson, Conrad Worrill, Tim and Zenobia Black, and other scholar-activists. But no one was more adamant about replacing Byrne than Palmer. Lutrelle "Lu" Palmer—a sharp-tongued, uncompromising, and unapologetic newspaper journalist, radio commentator, and Black nationalist— had led an ad hoc group to block Byrne's choice for Chicago school superintendent in 1980. After the courts ruled the choice ineligible, Palmer capitalized on their victory and formed Chicago Black United Communities (CBUC) as a voice for grassroots Black Chicagoans for whom the Urban League and other more conservative African American organizations did not always speak. CBUC described itself as "a people-based and people-controlled organization . . . structured to enable Blacks to become involved, to become more aware, to become more skillful, and to become more successful in confronting and solving serious social, economic, and political issues." CBUC's most prominent achievement, and the brainchild of Lu's wife, Jorja, was a series of Black political education classes in which participants learned to poll watch, run for office, fundraise—"all of the elements of politics," recalled Lu Palmer years later. By the winter of 1983, the classes had trained nearly 2,300 African Americans on the South Side. This was a fraction of the Democratic machine's estimated 35,000 soldiers, but Palmer's trainees made up the most significant political organization Black Chicago had seen outside of Congressman William Dawson's submachine a generation before.[2]

Alongside the political classes was a CBUC-sponsored survey of Black Chicagoans on who should be the first African American mayor of the city. While wholly unscientific, the survey distributed through Black churches, political clubs, and other institutions whittled an initial list of 92 names down to six potential candidates, including Palmer, Harold Washington, and Jesse Jackson. Then in July, thousands of Black Chicagoans packed Bethel African Methodist Episcopal Church to vote in what was called the "plebiscite"—a term many were not familiar with, but whose use the Palmers saw as part of participants' political education. The clear winner of the vote was Washington, whose charisma, legislative skills, and ability to win independently of the machine had made him a consistent favorite in previous informal polls, despite his previous mayoral loss in 1977. Washington attended the plebiscite and was invited to speak to the throng. But instead of accepting the crowd's draft, as Palmer had expected, Washington spoke broadly of "the plan, not the man." He would not commit to running, many guessed, because he enjoyed being a member of Congress too much. Soon afterward, at the most legendary of basement meetings, Washington affirmed his disinclination to run. As Starks, Palmer, and others remembered it, the room exploded into bickering. "It was almost necessary to keep him separated from some other people because they were going to go to blows," Palmer said about the evening. Washington listened until he had had enough and stalked out, disgusted. But before he left, he told them that he would only consider running if they registered 50,000 new voters and raised at least $250,000 in time for the fall 1982 campaign. Some observers thought Washington suggested such high numbers to avoid any sort of draft. But by November, both numbers had been exceeded, including nearly double the number of registrations. "They hit every target I threw at them," Washington told *Tribune* reporter David Axelrod. "What else could I do?" For more than three decades, this is the story that has been passed down—in oral histories, journalistic accounts, and scholarship—of the 1983 campaign.[3]

But while the story of the "conspirators," to quote one biographer, remains an essential part of Washington folklore, this narrative risks obscuring the larger economic and political context as well as the broader grassroots coalition that emerged in opposition to Byrne's reelection.[4] It was an expansive intraracial *and* multiracial alliance that elected Washington in 1983. Much like progressive coalitions in other cities across the nation, his election required a remarkable amount of organization not just among the African American factions so

Journalist and activist Lu Palmer, *right*, poses with then congressman Harold Washington. By founding Chicago Black United Communities and its political education classes, Palmer, his wife Jorja, and a handful of other Black organizers were instrumental in making a Washington candidacy possible. Harold Washington Archives and Collections, Pre-mayoral Photographs, box 3, folder 11, Special Collections, Chicago Public Library.

routinely highlighted in popular and scholarly narratives but also among key progressive Latino and white groups. Moreover, Washington's victory reflected contingencies that scholars and activists often do not adequately acknowledge, most prominently a white political elite which had evenly divided its support between the incumbent Byrne and Cook County state's attorney Richard M. Daley. Race, of course, was a central factor in the electoral contest, but, at least in the February 1983 primary, so was gender. Women remained a rarity in public office at the time, especially at the top of the executive branch.

All of this took place amid a larger discussion of the future of American cities, prompted by deindustrialization, crime, deteriorating infrastructure in roads and housing, rising inequality, and the worst economic downturn to date since the Great Depression. The latter was largely placed at the feet of President Ronald Reagan, whose economic policies were anathema to most Chicagoans and yet routinely embraced by Byrne. In this complicated atmosphere a sharply divided Democratic Party chose Harold Washington as the first African American to win a major party nomination for mayor of Chicago.

AFRICAN AMERICANS had played a central role in putting Jane Byrne in City Hall and, unlike her immediate abandonment of white good government reformers, there were small signs that she might return the favor, at least as much as her unpredictable politics allowed. In addition to appointing Renault Robinson and another prominent Black reformer to the Chicago Housing Authority board, Byrne's initial school board choices shifted the balance of power to a Black-Latino coalition for the first time in its history, even though for a generation the great majority of public school students had been African American and Latino. She began to offer a few more city contracts to Black business owners, such as food vending at city-sponsored neighborhood festivals. And Byrne increased both the raw number and percentage of African Americans and Latinos working for the city, although whites still held 69 percent of city positions in 1981 despite making up just 40 percent of the city's population. At the same time, Byrne used some of her campaign funds to resurrect the traditions of an older, more paternalistic era by providing low-income families with gifts of holiday food, Easter eggs, and Christmas trees and making cash donations to certain powerful Black churches. Such practices had drawn the ire of Protest at the Polls and other independents and had been in decline for years. That Byrne brought such practices back, remarked Lu Palmer, was "an insult" and "patronizing."[5]

More bizarrely, but consistent with her penchant for showy symbolism over substantive policy, Byrne and her husband temporarily moved from their Gold Coast apartment to the overwhelmingly Black Cabrini-Green public housing complex in the spring of 1981 to combat rising gang violence. Her presence— and that of her security detail—did produce a momentary decline in crime in the Near North Side complex made famous by the television show *Good Times* in the 1970s, and later the films *Candyman* and *Hoop Dreams*. The apparent decline in violent crime prompted widespread praise in the press for "our gutsy mayor." Wrote the *Tribune*, "Having the mayor as a neighbor should raise the morale of those residents who want to make Cabrini-Green a decent place to live." Not surprisingly, Byrne's own memoir dwelled disproportionately on her foray into Cabrini-Green. "Security and the recreational programs improved at Cabrini, and indeed at all the public housing complexes," she wrote proudly. "In the end, one statistic pleased me the most—not one murder occurred at Cabrini

Green until after I left the mayor's office." But not everyone was impressed by such tactics. Some Black leaders complained of a "police state" and the belief that "symbols with Black folks can take the place of substance." Others asked where the commitment was when the mayor moved out after only three weeks and did not repeat the stunt at any other complex, such as the equally troubled Robert Taylor Homes on the South Side. Despite boisterous protests led by Cabrini-Green activist Marion Stamps—"We need jobs, not [Easter] eggs," they chanted—Byrne's dramatic gesture initially worked politically; her approval numbers, which had dropped precipitously in two years, crept back toward 50 percent midway through her term.[6]

In many ways, her Cabrini-Green venture captured Byrne's approach toward African Americans in a broader way—a bold, highly publicized, and largely symbolic move quickly reversed or undercut by quieter decisions later. This pattern infuriated activists like Palmer. "The impression with Byrne is that she is working in the interests of Black people," he said in 1982, "when actually she is destroying our interests." In fact, Byrne's approach added up to "nothing less than a frontal assault" on African Americans, which took many forms. One was her steadfast support for the Chicago Police Department amid a record homicide rate and increasingly sharp rebukes of the department's corrupt and violent treatment of Blacks and Latinos. Early in her term, she had showily installed Black police official Samuel Nolan as the interim superintendent, only to ease him out months later and replace him with a young, white, brash political ally, Richard Brzeczek. Not that a Black superintendent would have magically solved the embedded racism and corruption of the department, but her treatment of Nolan underscored a belief in inherent Black criminality. This became more obvious in the years that followed the Cabrini-Green foray, most prominently when a Black suspect murdered two white police officers in the winter of 1982. The manhunt that followed was unprecedented and led by police commander Jon Burge, whose extreme techniques, including torture, were an "open secret." Byrne and her aides, according to one historian, "knew what they were getting when they unleashed Burge"—unspeakable brutality that no one, even a clearly guilty suspect, deserved.[7]

Another "deliberate insult," to quote columnist Vernon Jarrett, was Byrne's handling of the Chicago Public Schools. While Jarrett was writing specifically about the replacement of two Black Board of Education members with two conservative white women from the Northwest and Southwest Sides, Byrne's larger approach to schools reflected clear opposition to African American educational interests more generally. In May 1980, the fleeting Black majority named Kenneth Smith as the Board of Education's first Black president, and Byrne herself tapped Dr. Ruth Love of Oakland, California, as Chicago's first African American school superintendent. But as historian Elizabeth Todd-Breland notes, both could be considered "empty victories" as the real power lay in the newly appointed Chicago School Finance Authority, a five-person board of white corporate executives tasked with managing the school system's budget. After years of mismanagement under the Daley machine, the budget crisis had come to a head in 1979 when banks refused to lend $125 million to keep the system going. Not unlike what happened five years earlier in New York or a generation later in Detroit, the mayor turned to state and business leaders, who used the crisis to wrangle power away from democratically elected officials and put in place a corporate-style management structure. Austerity measures led to a 20 percent cut in Board of Education personnel, disproportionately impacting African Americans. The finance authority also fired the existing board members, to which Byrne responded by choosing two conservative white women. Observers viewed it as a blatant political play for white voters opposed to school desegregation. Comparing the move to President Richard Nixon's antibusing appeals a decade earlier, Jarrett wrote, "It is obvious that this woman is making a direct appeal to whites who resent and fear Blacks.... I have no doubt that this will get Byrne some new votes. But I don't believe that it will get her enough" to offset lost Black ones.[8]

Moreover, Byrne continually chose high-profile fights with Black political leaders and activists as part of her bid for white support. For instance, newly appointed Black alderman Allan Streeter in the Seventeenth Ward bucked instructions from his committeeman and opposed Byrne's white school board appointments. Under pressure from community groups, Streeter, a longtime precinct captain, argued, "The party wants us to sell our souls and give up our self-respect for what the white bosses want. I just couldn't take it." Instead, he aligned himself with ten other Black aldermen and voted against the two white appointees, but Byrne attempted to make an example of Streeter, fanning unfounded bribery charges and backing his opponent in a June 1982 special election. He still won. In 1982, Byrne again reversed course, this time on the Chicago Housing Authority board, and appointed a white majority, claiming they had superior managerial experience. Concluded a disillusioned Renault Robinson, who thought he had Byrne's ear when appointed, "They want us to sit there, looking intelligent but acting like dummies." And these were just the most high-profile cases. The mayor backed a state transit package that included a sharp fare hike for the disproportionately Black and Latino low-income riders of the Chicago Transit Authority (CTA). She made no effort to fix inequitable tax assessments that targeted Black and Latino property owners, prompting the founding of the Black Taxpayers Federation by Harold Washington and others. She even picked a fight with organized labor normally loyal to the machine, attempting to break two Black-led unions representing CTA workers; bus drivers remembered it a year later when they backed Harold Washington.[9]

Yet another attack on African Americans, as well as Latinos, was the dilution of minority voting power through the decanal ward reapportionment. As noted in the fourth chapter, the machine-controlled City Council and administration engineered a map that actually reduced Black-majority wards from nineteen to seventeen (out of fifty) and dispersed Latino voters into wards in which they had neither a majority nor a plurality. The map prompted three lawsuits, the most prominent by a multiracial coalition led by Black state senator Richard Newhouse in what became *Ketchum v. Byrne*, calling for twenty-one Black-majority and at least two Latino-majority wards. Even Ronald Reagan's Justice Department, not known for the defense of civil rights, joined the challenge.[10]

Despite the lawsuits, however, Byrne and her political allies had generally viewed Latinos—only 73,000 of whom were registered to vote in 1980—as more pliant and thus willing to cast their lot with the machine, especially after the mayor appointed Puerto Rican lawyer Joseph Martinez to a vacant City Council seat in the Thirty-First Ward. Similar to her outreach among African Americans, the mayor had begun showing up at community dinners and made a monetary contribution to the Latinos for Political Progress (LPP), an organization founded in the early 1970s to elect more Latinos to office. But vocal criticism by local and regional leaders persisted, and not just over the ward remap's dilution of Latino voting power in a city in which their population had doubled in ten years. Activists also targeted financial cutbacks to community health care clinics, substandard housing, and how Latino representation should be chosen in the first place. In addition to Rudy Lozano's IPO, which organized Mexican Americans, the Reverend Jorge Morales of the Westtown Coalition of Concerned Citizens joined other prominent Puerto Ricans, including Benjamin Reyes, Hilda Frontenay, Edwin Claudio, and Peter Earle, in founding the Political Action Organization (PAO) in Humboldt Park on the Near Northwest Side. Morales expressed skepticism that someone such as Martinez, who had not participated in any independent community organizations, including the LPP and PAO, should be appointed to represent the area on the City Council. Instead, Martinez's qualifications seemed to be machine loyalty, a Spanish surname, and a position in Alderman Edward Burke's law firm. "With this appointment, the mayor and the machine impose their politics on the people and do not respect the community," Morales said. "The Puerto Rican community goes from no representation to misrepresentation," added activist Arcelis Figueroa.

Martinez protested this characterization, arguing that machine and community interests were not mutually exclusive and that his community work was putting himself through school and being a precinct captain. "Nobody gave me anything," he stated. Well, except a City Council seat, many believed.[11]

Therefore, by 1982, Black Chicagoans and their progressive Latino and white allies had plenty of motivation to organize against Byrne's machine, not to mention conservative Republicans in Springfield and Washington, D.C., who championed draconian budget cuts amid the worst recession since the 1950s. While Lu Palmer and the newly created Task Force for Black Empowerment plotted a campaign to draft Harold Washington, grassroots activists in other parts of the city geared up to challenge the machine through a citywide coalition of community organizations. Yes, all politics could be considered local, to paraphrase U.S. House Speaker Tip O'Neill, but the wisdom of that view was sometimes overstated, even then. "If you fight in your community to save 10 units of low-income housing as the city destroys 1,000 units in other areas, what have you gained?" asked Curly Cohen, an Uptown activist, questioning the city's tradition of organizing that ended at neighborhood lines. Without some coordination, organizers risked working at cross-purposes, with neighborhood pitted against neighborhood. It had become increasingly clear to everyone, from Lu Palmer and Marion Stamps to Rudy Lozano and Jorge Morales, that a larger network was essential to bring about real reform in the city.[12]

A CENTRAL TENET of independents' strategy was expanding the voter base, a tactic effectively used by grassroots community activists across the country in the late 1970s and early 1980s. It had been tried before in Chicago, most notably by the Chicago Urban League in the mid-1970s. But while the league's modest efforts met some success, organizations such as the Association of Community Organizations for Reform Now (ACORN) had emphasized voter registration to greater effect in other cities.[13] To even consider running for mayor again, Washington had demanded that Palmer's organization register at least 50,000 new voters, which, in August, Palmer began to do through the People's Movement for Voter Registration. But other activists already had turned to registration work earlier that summer in response to state budget cuts. In what became the People's Organization for Welfare Economic Reform (POWER), an interracial coalition of community activists began to scour the city for new voters. Spearheaded by Slim Coleman, chair of the Heart of Uptown Coalition, and Nancy Jefferson, executive director of the Midwest Community Council, POWER represented twenty-one community groups responding to a reduction in general assistance grants for poor people. "We believed that if we got all our welfare people registered that elected officials would listen better," Coleman said. "Moreover, we had a captive audience because we knew exactly where each one of these people would come every month to sign their general assistance checks." In a twist on the kind of poor people organization long advocated by sociologists Frances Fox Piven and Richard Cloward, POWER organizers set up voter registration booths outside of every public aid office in the city, including library branches and unemployment lines, where recipients had begun to see smaller checks.[14] "We really didn't have to argue very much," recalled Coleman. "People would come out angry and say, 'Give me that thing. I'm going to register to vote.'" Arguing that they could create thousands more Democratic votes, Coleman persuaded the gubernatorial campaign of Adlai Stevenson III to pressure the party-controlled Cook County Board of Election Commissioners to train and provide deputy registrars at each location. In just five weeks in the summer of 1982, activists registered about 42,000 new voters of all races. POWER later sued successfully to enlist voters inside public aid offices, as well, to sustain the drive as colder weather approached.[15]

The work by POWER synched nicely with registration and related protest efforts by other African American groups. After Byrne's reappointment of three conservative white housing authority members, activists seriously pondered a radio show caller's suggestion to boycott ChicagoFest, the largest of the city's summer festivals. Initially named Taste of Chicago when it began in 1977, the twelve-day August event represented Byrne's interpretation of community—and a not-so-subtle way to promote her reelection. As mayor, Byrne prioritized such symbolism: Chicago as a big party and a fun place to live. But "the joke around town," writes Gary Rivlin, "was that her name took up more space on the bumper stickers and posters promoting the festival than the name of the event itself." In the whole scheme of things, ChicagoFest was a mostly white affair and not that important to African Americans, especially compared to legendary Black community events like the Bud Billiken parade festivities on the South Side's Dr. Martin Luther King Jr. Drive. The parade, started by the *Defender* newspaper and held since 1929, featured the city's top Black entertainers, drill teams, bands, and personalities and was considered the largest African American parade in the country. Much of the South Side literally shut down every August to accommodate Bud Billiken. In contrast, while Chicago-Fest included high-profile Black entertainment, it was a mostly white space.[16] Nonetheless, a Black boycott could still give the mayor a political black eye.[16]

Jesse Jackson, whose Operation PUSH had specialized in consumer boycotts with varying success throughout the 1970s, embraced the protest and became its face, for better or worse.[17] In early August, Jackson ceremoniously burned his ChicagoFest tickets at a PUSH meeting, and, soon after, the People's Coalition to Boycott ChicagoFest was born. Much of the boycott organization relied heavily on already existing activism, including by CBUC and other groups. Some activists were irritated that Jackson received the lion's share of the credit, and he did nothing to discourage that impression. But they certainly liked the result. Fears that it might hurt Black vendors or somehow make Byrne a sympathetic figure were not realized. In support of the boycott, Motown superstar Stevie Wonder canceled and forfeited his $160,000 payment. Kool and the Gang played under protest, wearing armbands, and many smaller acts simply did not show. African Americans stayed away, making up only a small percentage—perhaps as low as 1 percent—of festival attendees compared to 15 percent the year before. Their absence had a modest impact on total attendance, although festival officials said that bad weather was more of a factor. The *Tribune*'s editorial page declared the boycott a failure. But what the press and other white observers did not grasp was the organizational test the boycott had represented. African Americans largely respected the action—a sign of unusual Black unity—despite efforts to break it, such as the dumping of free tickets in African American neighborhoods. "Involvement in the boycott gave Black citizens a sense that they could act together effectively to assert their racial interests," argues political scientist Paul Kleppner. "By mobilizing community organizations and helping to change the outlook of the Black populace, the boycott experience paved the way for the voter registration movement to spread."[18]

Indeed, the timing could not have been better, as CBUC and other groups ramped up their voter registration into the fall and, this time, with more resources at their disposal. Ed Gardner, the owner of Soft Sheen Products and one of the city's most successful Black businessmen, quietly agreed to shift the company's advertising resources temporarily to the cause, charging its marketing department with creating an engaging radio and print campaign in support of registration; he ended up spending thousands of dollars. "The campaign was not for any specific politician," recalled Gardner, who framed the move as, among other things, good business. "It was primarily to improve the quality of life for Black Chicagoans because our strength, growth and dollar capabilities are derived from Black Americans. If successful Black businesses don't take steps to use their dollars in a constructive way to move Black Americans forward, then we cannot blame the major white companies." The result was the "Come Alive October Five" campaign, known for its catchy R&B-infused song and culminating with the namesake event on the last day voters could register before the November elections. Jesse Jackson, although initially miffed that he had not been included in Lu Palmer's earlier basement discussions, made a show of working with his community rival and put the full force of Operation PUSH behind voter registration. Key to the campaign's success, according to Gardner, was that organizational meetings were held not at PUSH headquarters but at Soft Sheen—"on neutral ground," he called it—to affirm more shared leadership.[19]

In addition to business leaders, prominent ministers and other members of the Black middle class used their own kind of persuasion to register voters, including even withholding some food pantry handouts and routine medical services to clients who could not produce a voter registration card. Nate Clay recalled walking up and down the corridors of Cook County Hospital looking for potential voters. Such tactics were coercive, to say the least. But Washington supporters insisted they were no worse than machine tactics and, in fact, succeeded in pushing many people to register. The drive produced more than 135,000 additional voters—about 125,000 of them Black, which brought the number of eligible African Americans to nearly 87 percent, compared to 70 percent in 1975. Numbers for whites and Latinos also rose, albeit more gradually, from campaigns by POWER and the Midwest Voter Registration Project, which targeted Latinos. The question remained, however, of how many newly registered voters would go to the polls.[20]

Jane Byrne was not on the ballot in November, but Governor James Thompson and other conservative Republicans she considered allies were. City politics certainly loomed large, even as the expansiveness of the voter registration campaigns of 1982 suggested that state and national politics also could not be ignored. On the eve of the election, the country remained mired in the worst economic recession since the 1930s, with a national unemployment rate of 10.1 percent, 17,000 failed businesses—the highest since 1933—and a notable rise in homelessness, crime, and demands for public services. In Illinois, 12.5 percent were jobless. Meanwhile, the cityscape seemed dingier, the city's future bleaker. Many neighborhoods, including tidy working-class and proudly middle-class communities such as Gage Park, Hyde Park, and Chatham, experienced some blight, including their share of rundown buildings, broken sidewalks and streetlights, and a modest rise in crime. The Loop, despite low crime overall and pockets of cultural vibrancy, battled perceptions that the opposite was true. Chicago elites, like their counterparts in New York, Detroit, and other northern cities, increasingly fretted about the city's future, and even the future of cities period. Chicago was, the *Tribune* declared dramatically, a "city on the brink." In response to the 1982 recession and such rhetoric, conservative politicians at both the federal and state levels had cut taxes, trimmed social service budgets, and advocated policies such as enterprise zones, which doled out incentives in exchange for fewer regulations and worker rights. Congressman Harold Washington and progressive Democrats were particularly sharp in their critique of policies they saw as severely disadvantaging cities, predicting that Republicans would pay dearly at the polls.[21]

They were right, probably more than they realized. Political observers and polls had not expected voters to punish "Big Jim" Thompson for the city's and nation's economic woes, and yet the heavily favored governor beat former U.S. senator Adlai Stevenson III by just a few thousand votes, with the outcome confirmed just days before the inauguration in January. Turnout did not quite match registration numbers, but among African Americans, it was more than twenty points higher than in 1975, with 55.8 percent voting. To sustain enthusiasm, activist groups had kept up the pressure in the run-up to the election, unveiling a new campaign called "Follow Through November Two" on Black radio and sponsoring a range of get-out-the-vote events. While the mainstream press heaped praise on party chair Ed Vrdolyak and the Democratic machine for the dominant turnout in Chicago on November 2, the credit really lay with the work of progressive activists to stoke the deep unpopularity of Republican policies during the recession. Only 3.5 percent of African Americans ended up voting for Thompson—a remarkable Black rejection of the party of Lincoln in his home state.[22]

IN THE TEN DAYS after the November election, both Congressman Harold Washington and State's Attorney Richard M. Daley announced their candidacies for mayor in the February 1983 primary, officially opening what would become one of the most written about political races in not just Chicago history but modern U.S. history as well. Often called both "ugly" and "revolutionary," the 1983 Democratic primary featured "a three-way race that," the *Tribune* editorialized at the time, "is genuinely in doubt." While both the *Tribune* and *Sun-Times* eventually endorsed Daley in the primary, early editorials suggested a real possibility of a Washington victory and, at the very least, credited the congressman with being the "man who forced Chicago to take a close look at itself. Just being a Black candidate with a realistic chance of winning, he has changed an election into a genuine hard-edged, conscience-pricking decision."[23]

Fresh off a resounding reelection as congressman, Washington did promise a different kind of campaign—he insisted he was not the "Black candidate" but a reform candidate for all of Chicago. While the room at the Hyde Park Hilton was full of African American professionals when he announced—"Black ministers, Black lawyers, Black doctors," as one reporter described it—what made the scene equally striking was the prominent presence of whites and Latinos. Standing on stage next to Jesse Jackson, Lu Palmer, and Renault Robinson were Slim Coleman, Rudy Lozano, and Jorge Morales, plus white independent politicians Bob Mann, Lawrence Bloom, and Barbara Flynn Currie. And it was that coalition that Washington emphasized, alluding to the summer and fall voter registration drives: "The people of Chicago have announced their willingness to become involved, to unify and to act. . . . For if I am to be mayor, it will be as the spokesperson of this new movement—not the mayor of just a political faction—but mayor of all Chicago." Going off script, he added that "we seek out the poor white who has been downtrodden. We reach out with open arms to the Latin community." Of course, he had said this, too, in 1977, and only a fraction of African Americans and far fewer whites and Latinos ended up voting for him. But this time, Washington had both a broader organization, a clearer track record on issues of Latino interest, and an obvious foil to run against in President Reagan, who remained deeply unpopular in Chicago.[24]

While Washington had achieved a lifelong dream of becoming a congressman, he discovered a political climate in the nation's capital that was remarkably hostile to his urban liberalism. Soon after he arrived in 1981, Washington found himself wielding influence far beyond his freshman status and became one of Reagan's most persistent critics, ranked by the *Congressional Quarterly* as the fifth-most anti-administration member in the U.S. House of Representatives. In his first year as a congressman, Washington proposed a 20 percent cut in Reagan's inflated defense spending, arguing that it could be better used in the nation's cities. He endorsed a nuclear freeze, and he became the most vocal and effective floor leader for renewal of the Voting Rights Act, which was about to expire.[25]

As a member of Congress, Washington proved a steadfast defender of not just African Americans but also Latino concerns. "He did two things in Congress," said Nena Torres, who later chaired the Mayor's Advisory Commission on Latino Affairs during Washington's administration. "One, he had supported immigration reform" by opposing the Simpson-Mazzoli legislation that made hiring an undocumented worker a federal offense and which critics argued would prompt workplace raids. Washington also "was one of the leading critics of the war in Central America." The Cold War proxy wars waged by Reagan in places like Nicaragua and Guatemala had become lightning rods for Latino criticism and prompted a sanctuary movement for war refugees within the United States.[26] In his rhetoric, Washington routinely linked the violence in Latin America with racial lynchings at home, calling them "the international environment in which race hatred spreads." Latinos also credited Washington for his work on the Voting Rights Act, in which he championed amendments to allow lawsuits challenging local at-large districts designed to dilute minorities' voting influence. Latinos used these changes successfully to force localities to adopt single-member districts in Texas, among other locales. The renewed Voting Rights Act also provided the basis for the *Ketchum* lawsuit by Black and Latino plaintiffs over Chicago's own redistricting, which eventually led to the creation of several Latino-majority City Council districts in Chicago in 1986. As he had done as a legislator in Springfield, especially toward the end of his career there, Washington built a legislative and political record in Congress as an unabashed and articulate defender of the powerless.[27]

Of course, in Chicago that was not the usual path to City Hall. Despite the respect Washington received in some elite quarters, the clear improvement in grassroots organization and unity among African Americans, and the potential represented by a burgeoning Latino population, the city's electorate remained largely unconvinced that he could become mayor. In poll after poll from November to January, Washington ran a consistent and distant third. His weak third-place finish in the 1977 race against another flawed incumbent was fresh in some people's minds, as was that campaign's disarray. Byrne and Daley also enjoyed greater name recognition in the city, which translated into a broader base of fundraising. Despite the rise in Black mayors nationally through the 1970s—not to mention Henry Cisneros's pathbreaking Latino victory in San Antonio in 1981—Blacks and Latinos had not become chief executives in cities with white majorities or even pluralities such as Chicago. The main exception was Los Angeles Mayor Tom Bradley, a business-friendly former police officer first elected in 1973 who was decidedly more centrist than Washington. Even Bradley, with his moderate record, lost the California governor's election in the fall of 1982—a loss routinely attributed to race. It was clear race was still perceived as a barrier, especially to attain executive power.[28]

Daley and Byrne had different challenges. Elected as state's attorney in 1980, the oldest son of the longtime mayor had built a reputation as a competent prosecutor who hired a fair share of women and racial minorities and had improved the office's approach to juvenile crime. As a state senator, he also had helped reform the state's mental health system. But while Daley enjoyed polling leads as late as the fall, more and more questions about his abilities emerged. Daley had been ranked one of the least effective senators in the 1970s by the Independent Voters of Illinois, especially weak on civil rights, election reform, and corruption—and this all before it became clear years later that, as state's attorney, Daley had ignored systematic police torture on the South Side. In contrast to Washington's prolific legislating, Daley had been best at killing legislation, especially reforms sponsored by independents, during his decade in Springfield. Moreover, those who respected his father were skeptical of the son's ability to fill his shoes, questioning his intelligence and political skills. "He has a great name," quipped Ed Vrdolyak, a Byrne ally who voiced the commonly held view that Daley got where he was because of his father. Patronizingly called Richie by the mayor and other opponents, Daley had long operated in the shadow of the Boss. Similar to his father, he had a painful speaking style, full of malapropisms, especially when he was nervous or pushed—to the point that he hired a Northwestern University professor to assist him in his oratory for the race. But many observers said he deserved credit for being politically astute. He blindsided Byrne by running for state's attorney in 1980 instead of circuit judge, to better prepare for a mayoral run, and though he valued loyalty over most other things, he was careful not to blast his rivals in public to contrast his style with Byrne's take-no-prisoners approach. This seemed to work, at least initially, as Byrne bounced from one conflict to another, while Daley built support among the business elite and those pining for the "simpler days" of his father. By November, however, Daley's nearly ten-point lead in the polls (averaging 34 to 26 over Byrne) had evaporated, prompting speculation that he might even run in April as an independent instead of challenging an incumbent mayor and party organization in the primary.[29]

This is because Byrne, after ricocheting from self-made crisis to crisis, had begun to make her own recovery in the polls—a transformation that reflected the role of gender, money, and national politics in the early 1980s. That fall, Byrne hired New York political consultant David Sawyer to help remake her image and, in a sense, reintroduce herself to the electorate. The first consultant of his kind to work on a local Chicago race, Sawyer was paid a cool $700,000 to create "New Jane," as the local press called her. Out were the floral print dresses, the unruly blonde hair, and the combative rhetoric; in were dark pants suits, carefully coiffed hair, and a softer tone. Some observers were unconvinced, even offended by the change. "The new Jane Byrne is Exhibit A in demonstrating a solution misbegotten in Manhattan for a campaign that is to be run in Chicago," wrote writer and novelist Eugene Kennedy in the *Tribune*. "Success, in their book, can only come through camouflaging one's personality, in this case, by making the unique Jane Byrne look like every other plasticized woman candidate in the country." Indeed, the emphasis on appearance was something only Byrne had to contend with in this race—a common experience for female politicians.[30] The mostly male reporting corps did not comment on Washington's heft, Daley's haircut, or really any other physical trait, reflecting a markedly different standard. Chicagoans routinely praised Byrne for her toughness—to the point that, as Kennedy put it, "Jane needs to be reminded that she doesn't have to be likable to be elected mayor, but she certainly has to be herself." Byrne retorted, "I haven't changed anything," while Sawyer allowed that the media campaign was about simply deemphasizing certain features. This was the "Real Jane," he insisted. And yet, they recognized an ugly gendered rhetoric lying just below the surface that needed to be countered. Just one of many unofficial Daley slogans suggested, "Ditch the Bitch, Vote for Rich." Columnists nicknamed her "Calamity Jane" and "Attila the Hen." And only Byrne was subject to an "opinionated psychobiography," according to Kennedy. Thus, despite some admiration for Byrne's willingness to brawl with the boys (and claims by some that she was treated like any other candidate), her poll numbers rose only after the "New Jane" media campaign blanketed the airwaves that fall and winter. Byrne and Sawyer planned to use her commanding $9 million in campaign funds to bury her reputation and win votes from across the city's racial and political spectrum.[31]

In contrast, Washington's initial objective was simply to demonstrate that he was relevant, and not just the Black spoiler in a race between two white heavyweights. Despite early praise of Washington after his mayoral announcement, the white press generally ignored the congressman, a coverage decision reinforced by Washington's distant third in both polls and fundraising. Observers presumed he would win a sizable Black vote on the South Side as he did in 1977 but little else, and that a key to victory for Byrne and Daley was coming in second among African Americans. While Byrne campaigned extensively in Black wards, especially churches, often alongside the handful of Black committeemen who had endorsed her, her policies had earned her a reputation for racial hostility. Meanwhile, Daley carefully avoided racial pronouncements. His standard stump speech to African Americans focused on crime and unemployment but did not reflect the nuanced understanding he showed of white neighborhood interests. Generally, he received polite responses; some African Americans might vote for him, but not enthusiastically. In a particularly blunt assessment, Washington told a Black audience that Daley was "a racist from the heart, toe to toe and hip and hip, just like his daddy. The difference being his daddy earned what he got." From the mayor's perspective, Washington's entry into the race was a godsend; he would undercut Daley's play for the anti-Byrne Black vote, which then forced the state's attorney to win even more white ethnic voters than he reasonably could do against the party-endorsed candidate. Joked one Democratic committeeman in July, "If I were Byrne, I'd send Harold a $100,000 campaign contribution."[32]

The mayor did not do that, of course, but it would have helped if she had. Despite some Black business money and enthusiasm, Washington's campaign was plagued by few funds and shaky organization. The day after announcing his mayoral run, Washington tapped Renault Robinson as his campaign manager—a decision he regretted immediately. "Renault didn't know anything about running campaigns and [it] was very obvious he didn't know anything," remembered Jacky Grimshaw, who coordinated precinct-level work for Washington. The persistence, courage, and obstinacy that Robinson showed in his leadership of the Afro-American Patrolmen's League did not translate into Washington's campaign, which reporters described as hopelessly disorganized. Pressured to "not blow this opportunity," according to one aldermanic supporter, Washington replaced Robinson with civil rights activist and former aldermanic candidate Al Raby. Viewed with suspicion by members of Palmer's CBUC, Raby did bring an ability to facilitate discussion among different factions, as he had tried to do during the 1966 Chicago Freedom Movement. Cerebral and low-key, Raby was not sure he was qualified for the position given his own limited and less-than-successful experience with electoral politics, but the campaign took shape after he came onboard.[33]

Raby managed two major accomplishments in the months before the primary. Perhaps most important, Raby moved the campaign's headquarters to North Dearborn Street in the Loop from its cheaper but lower-profile South Side location. The change incensed Palmer, who already believed Raby cared more about the interests of whites than his fellow African Americans, a charge Raby had heard eight years before when running for council. Raby did not, but both he and Washington understood that, to win, the congressman needed to compete citywide. A downtown office signaled that Washington really wanted white and Latino votes, too, and that his campaign was a serious investment for donors. The so-called 80-80 strategy—80 percent Black turnout, 80 percent voting for Washington—had been embraced by Washington's mostly Black advisers and remained central to the campaign. But, they feared, that strategy was not enough. If Grimshaw and the rest of the 1977 campaign team learned anything from that race, Washington's rhetoric of inclusion and fairness had to be matched by reality. "Your campaign talked coalition but didn't produce it," press secretary Steve Askin wrote Washington in 1977. That could not be repeated if he hoped to win.[34]

To avoid the disconnect, Raby's other main achievement was simply managing the campaign's "creative chaos," as he called it, made up of three disparate nodes of support: good government reformers, community development activists, and Black nationalists.[35] The latter, which included a number of Black organizations and formalized into the Task Force for Black Empowerment in November, were often dismissed by those downtown as the "47th Street Crowd" or "The Sound and Light Show." Because their voter registration work and over-all grassroots energy among African Americans made the 80-80 strategy pos-sible, Raby sought only to contain them, not sideline them. But their rhetoric and actions risked turning off supporters in other parts of the city. Accused of undue partisanship by his sponsor, Illinois Bell, Palmer lost his radio show, *Lu's Notebook*, the day Washington announced his candidacy. Palmer responded with an emotional critique of the show's sponsors, calling the move "dastardly," "diabolical," and "insidious." Playing the hardball politics that they had seen consistently conducted by white and Black machine types, the Task Force and its allies kept Raby up at night. Routinely, he found out from reporters that Daley and Byrne posters had been torn down or the Task Force had disrupted an event of another candidate. They were "doing their own thing," Raby said drolly, "quite separate from the [formal] campaign." Yet they were essential to Washington's victory strategy, and as other scholars point out, the campaign's ability to balance these efforts with minimal coordination was one of its most striking feats.[36]

INTEGRAL TO THE CAMPAIGN, but routinely less emphasized by exist-ing accounts, was the careful cultivation of good government reformers and community development activists of all colors. As biographer Roger Biles co-gently points out, Washington offered a genuine reform agenda, reflected by the innovative and remarkably detailed "Washington Papers." Most modern campaigns featured some sort of policy blueprint, usually produced in a short time by a handful of outside experts. More times than not, such documents were discarded after the campaign ended, at least partly because few people, including the candidate, had much invested in the process or the product. In contrast, the "Washington Papers" resulted from a thoughtfully coordinated research process by scholars, policy experts, and activists who remained part of the campaign and the eventual administration. Research was part of the campaign strategy. "These papers have to convey the image and the substance of new solutions that tap the capacities of citizens and communities to set goals and become active participants in their own governance," wrote Hal Baron, the chair of the campaign's Research Committee who held a doctorate in history, in December 1982. Research, continued Baron, "will enlist the participation of a wide range of organizations, businesses and interest groups. The preparation process for the issue papers will be indicative of the kind of inclusive and equitable issue definition and decision making that will take place under the Washington administration." Over the next month, fifteen issues teams, reflecting a range of views and backgrounds, submitted recommendations that were then refined by the committee and Washington himself.[37]

Fifty-seven pages in all, the document addressed everything from jobs and fiscal policy to health, art and culture, and education. A consistent theme was the role of neighborhoods and community input in city decision-making. This included the use of neighborhood development, or planning, boards to help allocate federal Community Development Block Grants, the establishment of community-based networks for mental health and substance abuse counseling, and collaboration with neighborhood organizations in retaining businesses, creating jobs through recycling and similar initiatives, providing preventative health care and senior citizens services, and rehabilitating existing housing stock. "The unwavering premise of Harold Washington's campaign is that the best solutions come from the communities themselves," declare the "Washington Papers." Moreover, the document not only symbolized the best of community-informed development ideas in the city but also cast in sharp relief the differences between Washington's governing approach and those of his opponents. Neither Daley nor Byrne had a comparable comprehensive document. While Byrne's approach to development—really everything—was rife with inconsistency, the Washington team offered a measured approach that took community voices seriously. Given the unusually democratic process followed to produce them, it was not surprising that the "Washington Papers" later became the foundation for the administration's aptly named development plan, Chicago Works Together, in 1984.[38]

The "Washington Papers," and thus the campaign, particularly spoke to progressive whites and Latinos with long-standing priorities in affordable and open housing, neighborhood-based economic development, quality health care and education, and healthy police-community relations. Byrne had not just infuriated and disappointed African Americans; scholars and activists also were crestfallen over the city's crass approach to development under her administration. Some had held out hope that, as a reform candidate who ran against the downtown elite, Byrne would offer a more balanced approach to economic development. Instead, she appeared to double down on downtown development schemes, such as the 1992 World's Fair, to enhance and insulate the Loop, even though the grand majority—as high as 80 percent—of the city's jobs were not downtown at all.

In response, the Chicago 1992 Committee, POWER, and the Community Workshop on Economic Development (CWED) joined older grassroots coalitions such as the Rehab Network and the Chicago Association of Neighborhood Development Organizations to advocate for a bottom-up, more democratic, and more neighborhood-based role in shaping development, in line with Harold Washington's neighborhoods-first campaign rhetoric. The Chicago 1992 Committee formed in the summer of 1982 to oppose the city's hosting of a World's Fair ten years later. Arturo Vasquez, a veteran Pilsen community activist in CASA and the IPO, was the committee's chair and viewed the World's Fair development plan as one more effort by corporate leaders to gentrify an existing working-class neighborhood. In the 1960s, it had been the Near West Side and then Lincoln Park; now, Pilsen and Bronzeville on the Near West and South Sides could be overrun by new development. Moreover, Vasquez was skeptical of the amount of city money to be spent on fair infrastructure "given the problems of the city . . . steadily deteriorating housing stock, its deteriorating infrastructure, its neglected parks, its deteriorating schools—is this what we want to do with the little money that we've got?" he asked. Fresh off their voter registration work, the organizations that made up POWER offered a similar critique. In a multiracial assembly in August in Uptown, they passed what they called a "people's" platform, made up of long-sought-after policy reforms that tried to shift the balance of power toward people not wrapped up in the machine, such as the direct election of school board members; citizen review boards to investigate police brutality; strict enforcement of building codes; and an antispeculation tax to reduce condo conversions.[39]

Similarly, the multiracial CWED emerged because city community development plans once again appeared to shut out local voices—this time under the auspices of state-designated enterprise zones. Embraced by politicians of both parties, the enterprise zones offered what their advocates called a market-based alternative to encourage development in otherwise depressed urban areas, through tax cuts and other business incentives. The theory was that such cuts led to investments in infrastructure and jobs for local residents, thereby reinvigorating such areas. But skepticism of the concept abounded among community development experts, who questioned its implications, especially amid federal cutbacks to social programs. Reflecting the Reagan administration's federalist desire to shift urban policy to the states, the GOP-led Illinois General Assembly proposed an enterprise zone bill in early 1982. A coalition of community development corporations in Chicago—representing predominantly Black, white, Puerto Rican, and Mexican American areas—responded by organizing the CWED to combat it. "We have acknowledged the need for reinvestment and establishment of job creating firms in our areas," stated the CWED board, "but we find the enterprise zone ... unsound in principle, uncreative and counterproductive for community revitalization." The CWED contended not only that enterprise zones risked taking valuable resources away from traditional social services but that they would "engender unproductive competition among communities," potentially pitting neighborhood against neighborhood for funds that might not even lead to jobs. In addition, the Illinois legislation called for "deregulation" of companies working within the zones, undercutting union protections, worker safety rules, health insurance, and other rights. The entire concept seemed to be just another way to cut taxes at the expense of the poor, these experts concluded. The CWED proved too late to influence the governor's race later that year—or to block the bill, which passed in December—but the organization reconstituted itself as the Chicago Workshop on Economic Development because, as CWED founder Robert Mier and director Kari Moe wrote, "An advocacy organization focusing on development policy was essential." If enterprise zones could not be stopped at the state level—indeed, the policy spread like a wildfire across the nation—maybe they at least could be blocked by a new mayor in Chicago.[40]

For progressive Latinos, especially Puerto Ricans, Washington also was the obvious choice early on. "I believed in Harold Washington," recalled Cha-Cha Jiménez, who returned to the city in 1982. "His whole theme of neighborhoods first was in line with what we believed in. . . . It fit right in with our philosophy. So, I just started organizing." The Reverend Jorge Morales, who attended Washington's campaign kickoff, agreed. As the Puerto Rican founder of the Westtown Coalition of Concerned Citizens and an affiliated church dedicated to social justice and the poor, Morales viewed Washington as a key ally in the fight against infant mortality, police brutality, unemployment, and under-resourced schools in the Near Northwest Side. "He understands that if you are poor it makes no difference in a class society whether you are white, black, or Latino," Morales said in 1983, "If you are poor you will be victimized by this political system." Jiménez saw allying with Washington as a continuation of the work he started in the 1960s, when he fought police violence, urban renewal, and general displacement of the poor in Puerto Rican neighborhoods. The issues were not altogether different. For instance, arson for hire ravaged areas like Lake View and Humboldt Park as it became a way for developers to clear dilapidated buildings and collect insurance. Jiménez viewed the Washington campaign as an opportunity to combat such practices but also to broaden the city's political discourse. "We wanted to raise the level of consciousness in the city," he recalled.[41]

While the city's smaller Puerto Rican community supported Washington in larger numbers, demonstrating the common ground they often had with the African American experience, other Latinos proved a harder sell. The city's small Cuban American population was made up of disproportionately conservative business owners and professionals who often saw themselves as white. Mexican and Central Americans were far less engaged with the political system and generally suspicious of a Black politics shaped by the machine. But Rudy Lozano, Chuy García, Linda Coronado, and others involved in CASA, the ILGWU, and the IPO had worked to change that dynamic, registering voters, building ties with progressive Black independents including Harold Washington, and stressing commonalities that Latinos and African Americans faced. Soon after Juan Soliz lost his write-in bid for state representative in November 1982, Lozano announced his own candidacy for alderman in the Little Village–based Twenty-Second Ward. Using his IPO base to challenge machine alderman Frank Stemberk, who was rumored to not even live in the ward, Lozano campaigned on Black-brown unity, alongside and for Washington, and stressed the practical benefits of this partnership. "Our ward is a community of ethnic neighborhoods rich in the history and cultures of Eastern European, Polish, Mexican, Latino, and Black people," one campaign flier stated. "I believe in working together so that our community can grow and receive our fair share of services." Lozano and Washington vocally opposed the school board's decision to close Harrison High, which served mostly Blacks and Latinos, and both showed up to protest the closing of a local Westinghouse plant as well. Even Palmer's nationalist CBUC endorsed Lozano. Juan Velasquez embraced a similar strategy in the Pilsen-based Twenty-Fifth Ward against longtime alderman and machine icon Vito Marzullo. But voter registration figures remained low in both wards compared to other areas. Byrne's strategic Latino appointments, a new attention to Latinos by party chair Ed Vrdolyak, and the machine's ability to make life uncomfortable in a community with so many immigrants—especially dark-skinned immigrants—made campaigning with and for Washington in Little Village and Pilsen, as Nena Torres noted years later, "pretty lonely."[42]

JUST SIX WEEKS BEFORE the primary, the Washington campaign still struggled to find its proper footing as most people thought that, while he might beat Richard Daley, Jane Byrne was too formidable. Despite the financial support of key Black business leaders, Washington had about one-tenth the money Byrne did, meaning he ran mostly radio ads. Critics resurrected the 1972 misdemeanor tax evasion conviction that dogged Washington's last mayoral run,

Harold Washington, Rudy Lozano, and Juan Soliz appear before a diverse crowd at a blues and salsa dance party benefit for the campaign, underscoring its multiracial appeal and echoing Cha-Cha Jiménez's campaign eight years before. Soliz would later emerge as a skeptic of some of Washington's policies. Copyright Marc PoKempner.

inadvertently reinforced by the candidate when he paid his annual Christmas Day visit to inmates at the Cook County Jail; one television commentator called it a "homecoming." Another station mean-spiritedly ran Washington's old criminal mugshot with the segment.[43]

Endorsements by key civic and labor groups were difficult to come by. Artists for Harold, the Women's Network for Washington, and other pop-up constituent groups may have reflected Washington's stellar legislative record on a range of issues, but more prominent political groups backed Daley or Byrne in the primary. Most organized labor—except for the Coalition of Black Trade Unionists and the occasional Black labor caucus—sat on the sidelines or placed the surer bet of endorsing the incumbent mayor or Daley, even most municipal unions that had fiercely tangled with Byrne. Despite Charles Hayes's pleas that "she [had] the worst labor record of all three candidates," two-thirds of Chicago Federation of Labor delegates backed Byrne in a raucous endorsement meeting; same with the police union. Even firefighters, whose union's president was jailed during a bitter three-week strike, remained neutral—a win for Byrne. Sticking with the machine, however flawed, was safest.[44]

The mayor also benefited from gender-based decisions. To many gay men, Byrne had been the first mayor in Chicago history to embrace them, albeit cautiously. Yes, police raids of gay bars continued, but she had championed an antidiscrimination ordinance—albeit a toothless one—and promised to walk in the gay pride parade if reelected. Some even argued that gay men liked her flamboyant governing style. The Chicago chapter of the National Organization for Women (NOW) also supported Byrne "because Byrne is a woman, has worked for ERA, and 'We have access,'" said board member Ann Ladky. Behind the scenes, Byrne had promised that she would help settle a class-action lawsuit by janitors on gender discrimination. But Ladky's explanation infuriated many progressive women, especially working-class women of color who lived the feminization of poverty. Black West Side activist Nancy Jefferson angrily suggested that NOW really represented white women, while Rebecca Sive-Tomashefsky called the decision short-sighted and argued that city policies under Byrne routinely penalized women in health care and the workplace. "What a terrible irony that you chose to make your first entry in city politics based on old-style politics of expediency," wrote a group of local NOW members to the chapter's leadership. "You have betrayed the hopes that so many women had that the women's movement could represent a broader vision of politics— one based on a recognition of the needs of all women." Not surprisingly, Black women—particularly concerned about public education, jobs, crime, and other issues that disproportionately affected women and children—were Washington's most steadfast advocates.[45]

High-profile endorsements by politicians and the media remained elusive, too. Less than a third of Black aldermen—Danny Davis, Eugene Sawyer, Tim Evans, Clifford Kelley, and Marian Humes—backed Washington early, and canny observers like Don Rose sharply questioned how committed machine politicians Sawyer and Evans really were. Even prominent white independents such as alderman Marty Oberman and state legislator Dawn Clark Netsch hedged their bets and endorsed Daley. North Side alderman David Orr, who had backed Washington in 1977 as a housing rights activist, declined to do so this time, citing a split among his own campaign staff. Only Hyde Park's Lawrence Bloom and Barbara Flynn Currie, white politicians representing mostly Black districts on the South Side, endorsed him. Those aldermanic candidates trying to make the leap from community activist to public office were the most likely to ally with Washington because of both organization and ideology, including Rudy Lozano, Juan Velasquez, Paul Siegel, and Marion Stamps. Former independent alderman Dick Simpson, who had left the council in disgust four years earlier, also embraced Washington's reform candidacy.[46]

Women grassroots activists such as Cabrini-Green's Marion Stamps were instrumental in Washington's victory by sharply undercutting Mayor Jane Byrne—including Byrne's brief and farcical residence in public housing—and by rallying Black voters to his candidacy. Harold Washington Archives and Collections, Mayoral Photographs, box 81, folder 39, Special Collections, Chicago Public Library.

Similar patterns emerged among state and national leaders, as well, convinced that the old Democratic approach remained the safest one. Surely, Washington had no real shot, some argued, and, besides, in a refrain that persists today, the party needed to win so-called Reagan Democrats, white and working-class, to compete again nationally. Despite a Black voter surge that nearly had made him governor in November 1982, Adlai Stevenson III backed Daley, as did prominent national Democrats considering White House challenges to Ronald Reagan in 1984. Senator Ted Kennedy backed the incumbent Byrne, while early frontrunner and former vice president Walter Mondale threw his support behind his "old friend" Daley. Mondale's decision prompted a furious response from Jesse Jackson, who called it "dumb, just plain dumb," suggesting that the eventual Democratic presidential nominee showed a "profound disrespect" to Black voters. This may have been the moment when Jackson seriously considered running for president himself. In the end, only liberal senator Alan Cranston of California and Tony Bonilla of the Texas-based League of United Latin American Citizens (LULAC) endorsed Washington. Asked why so few white liberals supported him, Washington concluded, "That race thing runs deep. There is no sense kidding ourselves about it. . . . By what stretch of imagination could a white progressive end up supporting Byrne or Richie over me?" Moreover, despite their initial praise for his bold vision, political skills, and experience, the press drew similar conclusions, unconvinced that Washington was viable or, in the case of the *Tribune*, realistic in his policies. The Black-owned *Chicago Defender* and smaller community papers backed him, but both the *Tribune* and *Sun-Times* settled on Daley.[47]

The press favoritism toward Daley was less surprising and more reflective of the broader set of conditions that shaped the primary race and made Washington's election possible but unlikely. And yet contingency still mattered. That is exactly how the January debates should be considered. Washington and Byrne were both on record supporting a series of debates before the primary, both confident that they could win them against the mush-mouthed Daley. Despite taking oratory lessons, Daley had seen the debates as a disadvantage until he fell behind in the polls and reversed his position, agreeing to four in late January. From the opening moments of the televised debate in a small auditorium at First National Bank of Chicago, both Washington and Daley assailed Byrne's governance of the city, including tax increases, job losses, and corrupt, patronage-laden inefficiency. In the most memorable line of the night, Washington charged Byrne with "destroying our city. Chicago can no longer afford Jane Byrne, because what is at stake is the very life blood of Chicago—jobs, jobs, jobs." While the ferocity of his rhetoric seemed to surprise Byrne, she coolly defended her decisions and pushed back against Washington's characterization of the city budget as a "fiscal time bomb." The city was in much better shape financially, she replied, than in 1979 and "has turned the corner when compared to other cities" such as New York, Detroit, and Cleveland. Just months before, Byrne may have responded angrily, but throughout the debate, she remained "professional" under the steady verbal barrage. Despite some initial jitters, Daley held his own and, in his thick Chicago accent, hammered away at Byrne's New York media strategy. Most white observers initially said that all three candidates performed well, but that the mayor did best.[48]

Yet, as the press corps had throughout the campaign, it miscalculated what voters, especially African Americans, were looking for. With at least a million people watching, Washington dispelled impressions of a campaign in disarray with a clear rhetorical and intellectual command of public policy. While the *Tribune*'s TV critic called both challengers' performances "wooden," he did allow that the congressman excelled when commenting off the cuff. More important, as Vernon Jarrett and others pointed out, his performance left Black voters increasingly convinced that Washington was the most articulate and knowledgeable and, thus, actually had a shot at winning. "What I liked about the brother was that he didn't have to think so hard to come up with the right answers," Jarrett quoted a Black city employee saying after the first debate. "You could tell that he'd been thinking about this city for a long time." Time would prove this assessment correct, as Washington began to consolidate Black support in February.[49]

The 1983 campaign had been shaped by the social movements of the 1970s, but it was only in early February that the primary campaign itself began taking the shape of a moral crusade, at least to outside observers. On the heels of the debates and shifting poll numbers, the campaign raised enough funds to start advertising on television—two spots that highlighted Washington's commitment to all Chicagoans, with the tag line "We can all win." But while Washington sincerely believed that, most powerful was the kind of energetic critique he gave to a mostly Black audience on February 6 at the new Pavilion at the University of Illinois, Chicago. In what was the largest rally of the campaign, a standing-room-only crowd of more than 12,000 supporters braved a day of snow to attend what numerous people can only describe as a quasi-religious revival, not a political rally. The congressman was joined by white U.S. senator Alan Cranston of California, seven fellow members of the Congressional Black Caucus, and a slew of local independent Black, white, and Latino officials and leaders. But it was Washington the crowd had come to see. After three boisterous hours of political speeches, humor, and music by "mariachi bands, folk guitarists, soul singers, and gospel choirs," the throng began to chant "Harold, Harold, Harold" for several minutes. Finally taking the stage, Washington responded, "You want Harold? You've got him!" The pulsating crowd roared at every barb he threw. Referring to his two opponents as Tweedledum and Tweedledee, Washington called Byrne a "flunky of Ronald Reagan" and questioned Daley's belief in "the divine right of kings. . . . We don't transfer the mayor's office from one generation to another," he shouted. His sharpest criticism targeted Police Superintendent Richard Brzeczek for the rampant police brutality poor and minority communities faced, prompting a lengthy chant of "Fire Brzeczek." The intensity and joy of the crowd stunned observers, as did the sea of campaign buttons and other paraphernalia being sold at the rally and increasingly witnessed throughout the city. African Americans who may have had little else in common sported the recognizable blue-and-white "Harold Washington for Chicago" buttons and greeted each other as old friends; those not wearing one were viewed with suspicion. Designed by the Heart of Uptown's Helen Shiller, the buttons bore a striking resemblance to Cha-Cha Jiménez's "Dawning of a New Day" buttons in 1975. She initially made 10,000, a supply that did not last long.[50]

Amid rising concern that Washington was gaining traction three days before the election, alderman and Byrne ally Ed Vrdolyak admitted what Chicagoans, white, Black, and Latino, had been saying—under their breath, behind closed doors, to each other, but rarely out in the open. In a supposedly closed-door meeting among machine precinct captains on the Northwest Side, the chair of the Cook County Democratic Party exhorted the hundreds of loyalists present about the significance of the February 22 primary. "A vote for Daley is a vote for Washington," Vrdolyak told them. "It's a two-person race. It would be the worst day in the history of Chicago if our candidate, the only viable candidate, was not elected." If he had stopped there, the impact may have been minimal. But he went on. "It's a racial thing. Don't kid yourself," Vrdolyak implored. "I'm calling on you to save your city, to save your precinct. We're fighting to keep the city the way it is." It turned out that two *Tribune* journalists, including David Axelrod, were outside the room but within earshot and reported Vrdolyak's comments the next morning. The situation was eerily similar to four years ago, when then Mayor Michael Bilandic's messianic pep talk during the blizzard highlighted how out of touch the mayor was and opened the door for Byrne. Now, it was Byrne having to explain what exactly her top ally and de facto campaign manager meant. She could not, but Washington did. Speaking of Vrdolyak, Washington stated, "He's raised the race banner." If Blacks did not have enough motivation before, this surely provided it.[51]

FEBRUARY 22 WAS an unseasonably mild day in 1983. As campaign workers and activists began waking up in preparation for the long day ahead, the temperature was already above freezing and would creep over 40 degrees by midday, with some clouds but no rain or snow. It seemed fitting, given the enormous amount of energy the three campaigns had expended that good weather would, if anything, encourage more people to vote. Indeed, Election Day represented the culmination of months—in fact, years—of work by activists across the city. While the three candidates and a handful of other people understandably received most of the attention, thousands of people had labored in their neighborhoods and precincts for this day. Washington aide Jacky Grimshaw estimated she had 10,000 official volunteers for the campaign, but that there were ten times that many working the streets. They were disproportionately Black women.[52] From activists in the Task Force for Black Empowerment, the West Side IPO, and the Heart of Uptown Coalition to labor, women's rights, and community development organizers to the soldiers of the new and old machines, Chicagoans had set aside much of their other work—whether it was for the city, their neighborhood, or something else—to get their candidate elected. That was how it worked in Chicago.

Both Byrne and Washington were certain that they would prevail that day. Television and internal poll numbers showed a clear but not insurmountable lead for the mayor, and yet signs throughout the day suggested the polls might be wrong. The weather had not discouraged people from going. Historically long lines persisted in Black precincts and wards. Brief panic ensued in the Washington campaign when a South Side–bound L train broke down during rush hour and residents of the Robert Taylor Homes reported receiving notices to stay in their homes because of spot inspections by housing inspectors. Dirty tricks, the campaign presumed. Seasoned campaign troubleshooters like Washington ally Richard Barnett worked eighteen hours that day, tangling with machine operatives over who could be an election judge and which voters were actually disabled and needed help in the booth. But by that evening, it was clear that all the prognosticators and political observers had missed the campaign's main story. The enthusiasm and energy among African Americans for Washington, despite his campaign's many organizational and fundraising challenges, had pushed the congressman over the top. After a historic voter turnout of nearly 70 percent—or almost 1.2 million people—Washington won 36.5 percent of the primary vote, followed by Byrne's 34 percent, and Daley's 30 percent. Washington had won the Democratic primary.[53]

Much debate among journalists and scholars followed about how Washington had succeeded. Was it the man or the plan? African Americans or a rainbow coalition? The incompetence of Byrne or the arrogance of Daley? The role of race or of gender? Of course, all of these contributed. Washington won by 35,887 votes, a plurality of almost exactly 1,000 more votes than the estimated combined support of whites and Latinos. The campaign came close to meeting its initial 80–80 goal in Black turnout and support; African Americans turned out close to 65 percent, but 85 percent voted for Washington, with more than 80 percent of every subset of African Americans—poor, middle-class, and so on—voting for him. Two other statistics underscored the lopsided nature of his Black support: Washington won every precinct in ten majority-Black wards, and, in five Black wards, he won by a larger margin than Daley did in his own Eleventh Ward—the home of Bridgeport and the traditional power center of his father's machine. On its face, then, it is more than reasonable to argue that African Americans swept Washington into the nomination, as most, if not all, scholars have contended.[54]

But the multiracial campaign that Washington insisted upon running remained consequential—and not just for the general election or for governance. Washington, Raby, and others in the campaign recognized that having prominent white and Latino supporters from community organizations around the city also persuaded Black voters that a Washington victory was possible. The visible presence of a Chuy García, of a Jorge Morales, of a Helen Shiller suggested that Washington could gain support and thus govern the entire city. Even though they lost, the competitiveness of the aldermanic races of Washington supporters Rudy Lozano, Juan Velasquez, and Paul Siegel increased turnout in each of those wards; in fact, a record number of machine aldermen were forced into a runoff by independent opponents.[55] Not to mention that the POWER coalition, in which whites and Latinos were central partners, had been instrumental in increasing voter registration by more than 100,000 in 1982 and early 1983.

Moreover, gender played a subtle but significant role in how voters judged Jane Byrne. Harold Washington's charisma, especially on display during his debate performances and on the campaign trail, contrasted sharply with Byrne's dry campaign persona, one she embraced only after being crucified for her previously bombastic style. If Byrne had verbally assailed Washington or Daley as they had done to her—and her advisers had recommended—would observers have called her unladylike and hysterical? Perhaps. What is clear is that Byrne chose not to attack either opponent frontally, something she later regretted. "My advisers were right, and I was wrong," she wrote in her memoir. "I lost sight of the fact that I was in a three-way race." Undoubtedly, Washington's personality made a difference, as well. Even Lu Palmer, who, as Gary Rivlin puts it, became so frustrated with Washington that he wanted to strangle him, admitted few other candidates could have pulled it off. Not Ralph Metcalfe, not Richard Newhouse, not Jesse Jackson. "When this charming, articulate, brilliant man began to move among the people, man, you couldn't stop it," Palmer acknowledged.[56]

But what nobody knew in the early morning hours of February 23, when Washington took the stage to claim victory, was that the fight had not ended. It would take all of his charisma, the voter registration and canvassing, the multiracial coalition, and other primary work to win as Washington faced the unlikely scenario of a competitive general election for mayor—something that had happened in Chicago only twice since the 1920s.

## CHAPTER 6

# Race and a New
# Democratic Coalition

The idea of a black mayor goes right to the heart of the
ethnic, blue-collar, bungalow owner's fears.
—Unidentified white committeeman, "Dems Seek Peace
with Washington," *Chicago Tribune*, February 24, 1983

The euphoria of winning the primary did not last long. Despite every initial indication from vanquished candidates Jane Byrne and Richard M. Daley, party chairman Ed Vrdolyak, and machine veterans like Vito Marzullo that Harold Washington was the next mayor, machinations behind the scenes suggested otherwise. It was clear that Washington, unlike his predecessor, had no interest in kowtowing to the machine he had just beaten. "I am the nominee. I expect the support of the Democratic committeemen," Washington told reporters two days after the election. "In the process of that expectation, one talks. We will talk." But he stressed that there would be "no erosion" of his campaign promises, including open government and an end to patronage. Byrne had said similar things, then caved. In contrast, Washington indicated that he meant it, and besides, as white ethnic residents told their committeemen, a Black mayor was unacceptable. As one unidentified committeeman told a reporter, "We can't go to people and ask for votes for Washington, especially since we've been telling them for two weeks that they should vote for Byrne over Daley to keep a black out of the mayor's office." Therefore, while Washington began naming a transition team, machine Democrats quietly looked for alternatives, sparking the most competitive general election in Chicago since Republican mayor "Big Bill" Thompson narrowly won reelection in 1919.[1]

While scholars routinely treat the primary and general elections that winter and spring as part of one larger, seamless process, there were important distinctions between the two races.[2] Despite the rising unity among African

Americans and the behind-the-scenes racism that culminated with Vrdolyak's blunt pleas on election eve, race and white supremacy played an even greater role during the seven-week campaign before the general election. Despite Chicago's reputation, much of the explicit racism in March and April genuinely shocked observers, particularly among white journalists, and yet also helped consolidate African American support for Washington. But the strategy by the Democratic nominee's supporters also changed significantly between the two elections, as Latinos and progressive whites became an even more important part of the coalition. Indeed, it would be this non-Black vote that propelled Washington to victory and signaled a further realignment of urban politics in the Age of Reagan. White ethnic voters found it easier and easier to vote for a relatively conservative Republican to block an African American from winning office, while a progressive multiracial coalition emerged to counter this trend, and vice versa. The 1980s would see this happen again and again, in New York, Philadelphia, and elsewhere, as broad, diverse coalitions eked out victories against more conservative candidates supported by once loyal urban white ethnic Democrats.

JANE BYRNE'S ACTIONS epitomized the duplicity and desperation Washington's opponents showed in the days and weeks after the primary. It was already too late for an independent to file for the general election. Ed Warren, the Socialist Workers Party candidate for mayor and an African American, reportedly rejected an offer of a $1 million and a city job to be replaced by a high-profile white candidate on the SWP ticket. Byrne initially appeared gracious in defeat. In a press conference the following day, she said that she "spoke to the congressman this morning to personally offer my congratulations and pledge my support for his candidacy . . . and I urge all my supporters to do the same thing." Washington affirmed her well wishes. But after returning from a Florida vacation in mid-March, Byrne predictably did an about-face and briefly entered the race as a write-in candidate—justifying the move as a way to "unify" an increasingly fractious electorate. Instead, people across the political spectrum met her announcement with fury and derision and argued that her moment had passed. "Getting write-in votes is harder than plucking hen's teeth," said Black committeeman and former supporter Robert Shaw. "She can't win and she'd look silly and racist trying." Washington was baffled. "She'd rather destroy the City of Chicago and her own party," he said, although his aides acknowledged that her candidacy would seal his victory by splitting any opposition. Even her old ally Senator Ted Kennedy of Massachusetts condemned the idea, flying to

Chicago to make his point, endorsing Washington and campaigning for him with a slew of Democratic Party state chairmen. A week later, after being booed at a mostly white nursing home on the Southwest Side, she withdrew.[3]

Rather, Vrdolyak and other leaders of the local Democratic Party settled on a once-unthinkable solution: rallying around Bernard "Bernie" Epton, the little-known white Republican nominee. First, it was Alderman Aloysius Majerczyk of the Twelfth Ward, followed by Vito Marzullo and powerful patronage chief and parks superintendent Ed Kelly. Then, half of the Democratic committee-men, including influential congressman Dan Rostenkowski, skipped a party endorsement session with Washington. Vrdolyak, Daley, and Ed Burke, chair of the City Council's Finance Committee, remained officially behind the Democratic nominee, but their workers had begun campaigning for Epton. It was not the first time that machine Democrats in the city had supported a Republican against a progressive member of their own party. As Marvin Holli and Paul Green point out, white Democrats had crossed party lines to support President Richard Nixon's reelection in 1972 and, in a few instances, Ronald Reagan's election in 1980. But those were presidential races; this did not happen in a local contest. Byrne and Vrdolyak had backed incumbent Bernard Carey for Cook County state's attorney in 1980, but that was simply an attempt to deny Daley a launching pad to challenge Byrne three years later. As was common in big cities with effective Democratic machines, such as Baltimore, Boston, and Detroit, Chicago's Republicans were perpetually sacrificial lambs—compelled to put up citywide candidates that would, in all likelihood, lose two or three to one to the Democratic nominee. That was what the GOP expected this time around when it nominated Epton.[4]

A native Chicagoan and Jewish insurance lawyer, Epton had been a longtime state legislator from Hyde Park, the beneficiary of a quirk in Illinois law that seated three legislators from each district—two from the majority party and the top vote-getter from the minority party no matter how few votes they received. For fourteen years, Epton served the heavily Democratic Twenty-Fourth district, home of the University of Chicago, and compiled a moderate record in support of civil rights, the Equal Rights Amendment, good government reforms for transparency and against patronage, and less taxes and regulations, especially in the insurance industry in which he worked. He routinely introduced legislation with Democrats, including Harold Washington, with whom he had a solid working relationship. Epton also was known for being eccentric and thin-skinned, especially when questioned by reporters. "He has been volatile and capricious," wrote David Axelrod about Epton during the campaign, "prone to inexplicable outbursts and fits of righteous indignation." He had been hospitalized multiple times in the 1970s for what he called "migraine headaches," but some questioned if his persistent agitation signaled some other malady. After the state switched to single-member districts, Epton returned to his law practice full time and moved north to the Gold Coast neighborhood; to avoid the embarrassment of not running a legitimate candidate for mayor, local GOP officials asked him to run for the nomination, which he did unopposed. But Epton did not expect or want to be the "Great White Hope" for "white racist Democrats," as he told the *Chicago Defender*.[5]

That changed when the national GOP showed interest in the race after white volunteers, many of them Democrats, began to flood Epton's campaign offices. Giving the nominee $200,000 in early March, Republican Party officials sensed a chance to reinforce the power and message of so-called Reagan Democrats a year before President Reagan ran for reelection. With the cash infusion, Epton hired a high-powered media consultant from Washington, D.C., bought considerable advertising time, and launched a withering rhetorical assault on his former colleague's integrity and judgment for his 1972 misdemeanor tax conviction. Washington himself had called his failure to pay $500 in taxes over four years dumb: "How does one explain stupidity? You do stupid things, you suffer the consequences," he said. But "the record says I am a first-rate public servant who has assiduously pursued his responsibilities to the public." While Washington admitted his errors and paid his dues—more than most in Chicago, neutral observers pointed out—Epton's campaign kept repeating the allegations. Internal campaign documents, including "The Case against Harold Washington," indicated that a steady attack on Washington's ethics, stressing the conviction, along with poor legal representation, making a false statement, and a handful of unpaid utility bills from the same time period, was the best and perhaps only way Epton could win. The conviction tripped up Washington in his 1977 mayoral run; it could work again, Epton's aides argued. Of course, the subtext was a cynical one, to associate Washington with white voters' deeply held stereotypes of Black criminality—a stereotype carefully built over more than a century in Chicago and other parts of the urban North.[6] Epton consistently referred to Washington as a "convicted felon," despite the clear inaccuracy of the claim. When corrected by reporters, the prickly Epton snapped at them and then doubled down on his misleading statements. And the strategy seemed to work, as whites who would have otherwise never voted for a wealthy Republican insurance lawyer for mayor openly considered supporting him. Even the famed columnist and iconoclast Mike Royko, who had dismissed the tax issue earlier, wrote on Election Day that he was undecided on who to support: the "kook" or the "crook."[7]

While Epton pursued a veiled strategy of Black criminality, even crasser forms of white supremacy emerged during the campaign and, to a certain extent, gave the campaign's subtler tactics some cover. White Chicagoans of all ages wore shirts and buttons, passed out fliers, and offered graphic quotes to stunned reporters that displayed their prejudice with pride. "Vote white, vote right" and "Whites for Epton" were some of the most tame. One flier suggesting a new police logo called "Chicongo Po-lease" featured a watermelon and asked if Renault Robinson would be police superintendent. Another suggested comedian Richard Pryor as fire chief and replacing downtown's Water Tower with Watermelon Place. One more, linked to a right-wing Cuban American group (with a wink and a nod from Vrdolyak), claimed Washington had been charged with child molestation—one of the few charges to which Washington responded forcefully, angrily calling it a "scurrilous, incessant low-life kind of attack. . . . Well, I've had enough." He vowed to Epton that he would "fight you day and night." Handbills routinely linked Washington to street gangs and the controversial Jesse Jackson, saying the PUSH leader would be the new mayor's main adviser, and that Washington would force historically white neighborhoods to integrate. A common theme was the fanning of fears that Chicago would become another Gary or Detroit, deindustrialized, destitute, and majority-Black. "Dear Neighbor, forget party lines," stated one letter that was distributed widely. "If you voted Democratic all your life this is one time you better switch if you value your home, community, and existing social life." Just in case, blockbusting real estate agents—as they had done for a generation in Chicago—started canvassing white neighborhoods for panicked sellers.[8]

Two moments during the campaign came to symbolize the level of racial animus and were covered heavily by the mainstream media. One was the series of highly produced commercials for Epton, which ended with the foreboding tagline, "Epton for Mayor. Before It's Too Late." The *Tribune* editorial page called it "disgraceful evidence of either insensitivity or outright exploitation. But the committeemen love it." Epton insisted that the commercials were about the city's impending fiscal crisis. But few believed him, given the racialized imagery on top of the campaign's not-so-subtle suggestion that Washington was a common criminal. Especially because the slogan did not specify an issue—it even confused Epton's own daughter—viewers could easily interpret it as a racial appeal and warning about electing a Black mayor. In Chicago political circles, the ad became as infamous as the racist "Willie Horton" commercial run by the presidential campaign of George H. W. Bush in 1988.[9]

Even more alarming was the incident at St. Pascal's Roman Catholic Church on the Northwest Side. Father Francis Ciezadlo had invited both candidates to speak during a community forum in the parish hall. Washington ended up coming on Palm Sunday with former vice president Walter Mondale, who had belatedly joined a phalanx of national party leaders in endorsing him. The frontrunner for the Democratic presidential nomination in 1984, Mondale had fallen in line, especially after Washington said the former vice president "had some explaining to do" after shunning him in the primary. At St. Pascal's, the two men were greeted by a freshly scrawled message of "Nigger Die" on the church doors and a jeering crowd of placard-waving Epton supporters, yelling, among other things, "tax cheat," "baby killer," and "carpetbagger," the latter meant for Mondale, of Minnesota. Washington and Mondale had been too late to attend the service, and the crowd's aggression cut the visit short. "There's hate here," one parishioner acknowledged, although the priest insisted most of the crowd were not parishioners. Before accepting the invitation, Washington's campaign team knew it could be a turning point. "If Harold did well in speaking to those parishioners it would play to his advantage, and if he didn't do well because of racism, it would also help us drive the message that the Epton campaign was fundamentally a racist campaign," recalled white media consultant Bill Zimmerman. "What we didn't know was how virulent it would be. It was a lion's den." Indeed, the incident's ugliness and Mondale's presence prompted the attention of the national press, which ran cover stories on "Chicago's Ugly Election," as *Newsweek* headlined. A similar incident happened a week later at another church. Epton, concluded most observers, had chosen the only possible path for him to win the election, and that was the road of racism.[10]

THE REPUBLICAN'S STRATEGY initially surprised Washington and his campaign, catching them flat-footed as they debated how to proceed. The campaign had never been as well-organized as some had wanted. While campaign manager Al Raby had brought some order, he was still a social movement organizer first and foremost, not a political chief of staff. And the first week, in which Epton complimented Washington's intelligence and work in Congress, concealed how nasty the race would become thereafter. By early March, it became quite clear that, to win, Washington had to further consolidate the Black base that ensured his primary victory *and* build a more durable coalition among Latinos, whites, women, LGBTQ communities, and other traditional Democratic groups that had supported him in smaller numbers in February. Some of this organizing had already begun in the fall, simply because Washington's team wanted to consolidate the Democratic coalition to, if anything, govern more effectively. It started in earnest, however, the night of the primary win,

Bernard Epton, the Republican candidate for mayor, greets supporters during the 1983 campaign. Many white ethnic Chicagoans who had never voted for a Republican supported him rather than back Harold Washington in his bid to become the city's first Black mayor. Richard Gordon photograph, Harold Washington Archives and Collections, Pre-mayoral Photographs, box 5, folder 4, Special Collections, Chicago Public Library.

when campaign staffers struggled to balance the presence of Jesse Jackson with other faces after the outspoken PUSH leader had taken the stage numerous times and led the crowd in "We Shall Overcome" and chants of "We want it all!" The overwhelmingly Black crowd at the high-rise McCormick Inn Hotel loved it, but Al Raby and other Washington aides recognized that these were not good optics to win over rivals and govern. Not only did such theatrics suggest Jackson played a larger role in the campaign than he did, but they also might signal to disaffected whites, Latinos, and some Blacks that the controversial Jackson would be a key player in the new administration.[11]

As it had been during the primary, managing Jackson would be one of the campaign's most important challenges. While he could mobilize African Americans for a cause, he also could mobilize whites against a cause—in this case, Washington's ability to govern or even win the general election. Epton's campaign capitalized on such fears. Columnist Mike Royko noted how many more letters he received about fears of Jesse Jackson in the two weeks after the primary, while the *Tribune* mentioned Jackson multiple times in an otherwise congratulatory editorial on Washington. Two days after the primary, Washington made a point to tell reporters that Jackson "won't have any role" in his administration and, somewhat disingenuously, "none in my campaign." When Black businessmen implored the PUSH leader to stick with rallies on the West and South Sides and to avoid issuing press releases during the primary, Jackson reluctantly agreed. Thus, when Washington took the stage at 2 a.m. on primary night, it took enormous self-control not to shove Jackson physically out of the way, Washington said later. The candidate eventually agreed to attend a Saturday morning PUSH meeting at the insistence of the Task Force for Black Empowerment, but even that had been up for debate. Washington had to expand his base or he would lose the general election.[12]

The question about how to handle Jackson came amid a larger debate that reflected the ongoing tensions around whose support Washington really needed to beat Epton. Was it simply consolidating the Black vote, as the Task Force for Black Empowerment insisted, because whites ultimately could not be trusted? Were whites, such as gay men and lesbians, and other Lakefront liberals, the answer? Or did the smaller but growing Latino vote hold the key to victory? Internal memos indicate this argument lasted the entire general campaign, as different factions continuously lobbied for the candidate's time and resources. Ultimately, Washington made a play for all Chicagoans, and not just rhetorically, as he had in the past. In early March, Washington empowered a rainbow of individuals that included white political consultants such as Pat Caddell, President Carter's pollster; Bill Ware, Washington's Black congressional chief of staff; Bill Berry, the former executive director of the Chicago Urban League, who headed up the transition team; and Rudy Lozano, Washington's close Latino ally who had missed a runoff in his aldermanic race in Little Village by seventeen votes.

They, and many other more informal advisers, helped campaign manager Al Raby craft a strategy that brought Washington to neighborhoods across the city, from white communities in the Northwest and Southwest Sides where people, at best, listened politely, back to Latino strongholds in Humboldt Park, Logan Square, Pilsen, and Little Village, where voters remained suspicious of Epton. John McDermott, the longtime editor of the *Chicago Reporter*, wrote Raby that Washington must make a more concerted effort to reach out to white Roman Catholics, one of the most reliable Democratic constituencies. "This is crucial not only to Washington's winning the election, but also to his ability to govern after April 12," McDermott wrote, adding rather presciently, "He must win decisively in order to have a solid working majority on the City Council. A narrow win could result in the loss of control of the City Council and leave him in a position of Mayor Martin Kennelly in the 1950s, who presided while the City Council actually ran the government." Washington certainly tried to meet whites on their own turf, such as during the annual St. Patrick's Day parade, when he marched with one of his few regular Democratic supporters, Cook County commissioner George Dunne. Washington donned a green boutonniere, tie, and "McWashington" pin as he and other dignitaries, including Byrne and Epton, marched. Washington's campaign calendar reflected a concerted effort to reintroduce himself to white audiences, leaning heavily on his charisma, his ability to talk to just about anyone, and his deep knowledge of community issues. In Parkview in the far Northwest Side, for instance, Washington deftly handled questions about the balance of services between neighborhoods, crime, and education. While some attendees came away quietly impressed, others simply could not get past their racism. "I'm probably a little on the prejudiced side," stated Lois Cioch, a Democrat and Epton supporter. "As a minority group they could have come up with something better." Despite Washington's efforts, most whites rebuffed him; as one Marquette Park resident told the *Chicago Reader*, he backed Epton because of "fear, fear of the unknown."[13]

Another route, largely left untaken by Washington's campaign until the last week of the campaign, was to fight fire with fire. While the mainstream media focused on the racist extremes among some Epton supporters, a critique of the Republican's temperament and, even more important, his historic friendliness to insurance interests went underreported and unaddressed by Washington or almost anyone else. Whispers that Epton must be sick somehow, to help explain his physical pastiness and ill-temper toward Washington and the media, gained media attention, especially when reporters discovered he had been hospitalized in a psychiatric unit in the 1970s. More troubling perhaps was a *Chicago Lawyer* investigation into what the watchdog group Illinois Public Action Council called Epton's "pervasive" conflict of interest regarding insurance policies considered by the legislature. As a handsomely paid attorney in private practice, Epton made millions running interference for the industry, fighting bills that regulated insurance rates, which would have assisted Chicagoans in lowering their abnormally high, discriminatory home and auto insurance rates, while he championed other bills that restricted consumer product liability claims, damages, and lawsuits. Most striking was Epton's opposition to a tough bill that would have banned insurance redlining in Black and Latino communities and created a mechanism to punish wrongdoers. Instead, he endorsed a toothless bill that banned the practice in name, but with no method for enforcement. This was in some ways worse than the sickening, overt racism that the media focused on, the *Chicago Reader* concluded. Epton's legislative record convinced Public Action's Robert Creamer that "he'll sell the city to the highest bidder, just as he sold his legislative seat to the insurance industry." And yet, the Washington campaign only began to reference problems with Epton's integrity in the last week of the campaign.[14]

No matter what the white response was, the campaign also recognized that Latinos were the voters Washington had the best chance to win over, ideologically and practically, through a constructive reform message. The efforts of Lozano, Puerto Rican activist Peter Earle, Linda Coronado, Nena Torres, and other Latinos, with the assistance of longtime Black allies on the West Side like Alderman Danny Davis, arguably made the most significant difference in winning the general election. Armed with more resources and renewed attention from the candidate, Lozano and Earle headed up a revamped and more formalized campaign for Latino votes. They pitched Washington to Latinos on a range of issues important to primarily Puerto Ricans and Mexican and Central Americans: improved services for and increased input from neighborhoods such as Pilsen, Little Village, South Chicago, West Town, and Humboldt Park; a new deputy mayor position to be held by a Latino, most likely Lozano; a new advisory panel and special mayoral assistant on Latino affairs; more "bilingual/bicultural instruction" in the schools; greater attention to affordable housing, including the establishment of a Chicago Housing Commission; and a greater share of jobs and contracts for Latinos, who remained greatly underrepresented in city government. "The essence of Harold Washington's campaign is to heal this city through a firm commitment to fairness and justice," wrote Aida Giachello and Raúl Hinojosa. "Toward this goal," they proposed a commission "with the purpose of ensuring the vital input and representation of Latinos in all levels of city government." The campaign also continued to emphasize Washington's strong congressional track record on issues such as immigration, voting rights, Central America, and sanctuary, which spoke to Mexican and Central Americans.[15]

But as Earle stressed in multiple memos soon after the primary victory, the strategy was really about turnout. "The strategic issue is not whether or not Latinos that vote will support Washington," Earle wrote, "but rather how many Latinos will vote, period. Unless Latinos believe they have a major stake in the election, large numbers may just stay at home." Latinos, especially Mexican Americans, already voted in much lower numbers than white and Black Chicagoans, so Epton's racist appeals and his lack of a Latino platform did not necessarily translate into votes for Washington. Moreover, Earle warned the candidate that Byrne's Latino supporters, such as the Northwest Hispanic Democratic Coalition in the Twenty-Sixth and Thirty-First Wards, had taken "a political line that Latinos should exercise a demonstration of potential political power by boycotting the election." This, however, appeared to be as much about

Byrne loyalists' desire to deny Washington some of the Latino voters he desperately needed to win. Meanwhile, other Latino voters risked being turned off by whiffs of Chicano nationalism held by Coronado and others who remained a disproportionate part of Washington's Mexican American base on the Near Southwest Side. Conservative elements of the community, such as Vrdolyak allies in South Chicago and members of the "conservative *colonia*," viewed their more radical counterparts with considerable suspicion. Either of these intra-Mexican scenarios could be devastating to the ability to win and govern, Earle concluded. Thus, Washington had to have an affirmative, culturally friendly, and relatively big-tent approach to persuade Latino voters to show up.[16]

Lozano and his allies won this argument, and the campaign made a concerted effort to reach Latinos in whatever way it could. Campaign materials were more consistently translated into Spanish, touting "Harold Washington para Chicago," and the campaign created a Spanish-language newsletter, *El Independiente*. Washington maintained a heavy schedule in the city's Latino communities in late March and early April, including a series of meetings with Latino business leaders and police officers, groups that had viewed him skeptically during the primary. Washington took a high-profile walk through West Town with Herman Badillo, a former Puerto Rican congressman from New York City who himself had run—and lost—his own historic bid for mayor in 1973. The campaign organized scores of other endorsements by nationally prominent Latinos, from Badillo and Maurice Ferré, the Puerto Rican-born, former six-term mayor of Miami, to New Mexico governor Toney Anaya and Los Angeles deputy mayor Graciela Martínez Davis. These outside endorsements were similar to those by national party figures such as Kennedy and Mondale in that they did not necessarily sway a lot of people in a local race, but the fact that prominent Latinos lent their prestige and experience to a race in Chicago meant a lot to Washington's young Latino supporters. Nena Torres remembered that it was Ferré who challenged them to define what they really wanted in a mayor, which prompted a more serious conversation about an advisory commission. Perhaps the most important endorsements turned out to be by Jorge Prieto, María Cerda, and Elena Martinez, all one-time Byrne allies and respected figures locally.[17]

The hardest work, of course, remained on the streets and in the communities, and this was how future alderman and congressman Luis Gutiérrez became a vocal advocate for Washington. His "garbage-can-delivering precinct captains" asked him to put an Epton sign in his window, and Gutiérrez, he admitted in his memoir, went a bit berserk. He accused them of being racist and vowed that, "I'm going to make sure Harold Washington wins this precinct."

Initially stunned, the men then laughed and responded that would not happen. Yet, Gutiérrez, his wife, and friends, not knowing much about local politics, managed to do just that: in a largely Puerto Rican precinct routinely won by the machine, Washington beat Epton by sixty votes. The experience inspired Gutiérrez enough to challenge the ward's Democratic committeeman, Dan Rostenkowski, the next year. Modesto Rivera, a Puerto Rican activist with the Heart of Uptown Coalition, recalled canvassing some of the roughest, most derelict apartment buildings in the city for Washington. "We were not afraid," said Rivera, who routinely carried a gun while doing voter work. "To us, everyone was a card-carrying voter. Prostitutes, junkies—what, they don't count? What you do for a living doesn't really concern us." Paul Siegel, a white organizer who had campaigned for Cha-Cha Jiménez years earlier and lost his aldermanic bid in February, said the same thing. The city's many rundown apartment buildings were electoral goldmines if organizers were willing to spend the time—and they were in this election. John Betancur, a Colombian who had moved to Chicago in the 1970s, recalled feeling bad that Washington's supporters were mimicking the machine playbook. "I hated myself because . . . all we're doing is playing the same game. But that's what worked," he said. "I had to do my homework about the problems on the block. Watch the alleys and see things. . . . I would go, 'Jesus, that hole in the corner. How long has that been there? Has anyone called the city? Do you have a block club? You guys know you have your right, you pay taxes. That shouldn't be there.'" It made Betancur a lot of friends. They needed to call City Hall but didn't speak English. So when "I made that call, they would vote for Washington."[18]

Other groups, such as the city's burgeoning gay population, concentrated in several Lakefront wards on the North Side, had similar experiences. Gay rights activists, especially white ones, had largely supported Jane Byrne because of her willingness to simply acknowledge them and their issues. But many eventually rallied, if somewhat reluctantly, behind Washington, who, as *GayLife* columnist Jon-Henri Damski wrote, is "someone they can personally identify with and admire." Downplaying his otherwise white male privilege, Damski argued that the discrimination they faced made them natural allies. "Gays and Blacks, once they overcome their initial fears—after all, in many cases we are the same—will probably come together in a sizable number to make April 12 a 'Black and White and Gay All Over Tuesday,'" he wrote, riffing off of some whites' more pejorative label for Washington's primary win, "Black Tuesday." But supporting gay rights laws as a legislator and congressman were not enough to overcome concerns about race, religion, and the campaign's unwillingness, it seemed, to say "gay." After more than a month of trying to coordinate, Washington, a week before the election, spoke to a gay audience for the first time. There, he recalled a conversation he had with the conservative congressman Henry Hyde from suburban Chicago. "Why would you be concerned with the rights of women when Blacks haven't got their rights?" Washington said Hyde asked him. "I said, 'Henry, when a person defends his or her own rights, it's just courageous and smart. But when you defend the rights of other people, you ennoble yourself.'" Washington did not persuade everyone in the room, even after he promised to address police brutality against gay men and to champion a broad city ordinance protecting human rights with a genuine enforcement mechanism. But Washington's willingness to address gay Chicagoans' issues on their terms and visit them on their turf—despite concerns about homophobia within the candidate's base—won him many gay converts.[19]

FOR MANY Washington supporters, April 12 could not come soon enough. Although they sensed that if the election had been held a week or two before, he may have lost, the campaign had simply been far less exhilarating, far more exhausting, and a pretty disconcerting commentary on race relations in the city. The campaign was finally over, and it represented a narrow but clear triumph, the result of weeks of grueling campaigning and community work and decades of grassroots organizing by African Americans and their progressive allies. With 1.29 million Chicagoans voting, Washington won 51.7 percent of the vote—a margin of 47,549—in the city's closest mayoral race since 1919. The election revealed, not surprisingly, a "degree of racial polarization" that only could be described as "striking," noted Paul Kleppner. Nearly 85 percent of African Americans turned out, surpassing both their participation in the primary and that of every other group. An astounding 99 percent of them voted for Washington. The congressman swept most South Side and West Side wards, garnering 99 percent of the vote in eight wards. Meanwhile, Epton predictably dominated on the North and Northwest Sides, receiving 95 percent of the vote in three wards. The contrast was even more striking at the precinct level; Epton won every precinct on the Northwest Side of the city. Clearly, just as in the primary, African Americans remained the heart of Washington's base.[20] Without them coming out in record numbers, he would not have been mayor. That narrative remains essential to understanding Washington's victory, especially when viewed as the culmination of Black Chicago's rejection of white machine politics— a process fifty years in the making.[21]

But while this transformation in Black politics was crucial to victory, the same must be acknowledged about the other elements of Washington's coalition—a reflection of the delicate balancing act progressive urban politicians like him performed in the 1980s. Scholars who call the discussion of other groups irrelevant risk missing the greater importance of Washington's victory. When viewed beyond the immediate context of Chicago, the importance of the fragile coalition he formed becomes increasingly clear. Without Latinos, without progressive whites, without gay men and lesbians, Washington would have lost—narrowly, yes, but he would have lost. Without them, his campaign may have been relegated to a footnote. Seventy-eight percent of Latinos and 12 percent of whites, disproportionately from the Lakefront wards on the North Side and in Washington's home of Hyde Park, backed the Democrat. Even though their turnout still did not top 50 percent, Latinos, most of whom were working class and lower income, had made up almost all of Washington's margin of victory, with an estimated 43,286 votes. A majority of each Latino group backed Washington, with 87 percent of Puerto Ricans leading the way; even a majority of Cuban Americans, disproportionately middle class, ended up voting for Washington. As a result, the Democrat won a bare majority in Little Village and the Twenty-Second Ward and a near majority in the Twenty-Fifth Ward, home to Pilsen. Moreover, while Washington lost the home wards of Vrdolyak and Daley, he managed to poll 34 percent and 25 percent in the Tenth and Eleventh Wards, respectively. In other words, some working-class white Catholics—whether out of party identity, opposition to Epton's fiscal conservativism, anti-Semitism, or something else—pulled the lever for a Black Democrat.[22]

Some election observers acknowledged the role of other groups right away, usually as part of recognizing the grassroots effort that made it possible—a position then reinforced by scholars.[23] Some argued that Latinos were key. Others made the case for white voters, including gay men and lesbians, who were increasingly involved in city politics, as well as those "good government" whites interested in fiscal and political reform and an overall weakening of machine politics. But the influence of white voters on the North Side has been overstated as well. As some scholars have argued, the so-called Lakefront liberals did not make *the* difference, as progressive whites did in cities such as Philadelphia and New Orleans.[24] It remained crucial that Washington's campaign emphasized Latino and white voters down the stretch. They made the difference between winning and losing, and the candidate's decision to campaign everywhere again signaled that Washington was not just the "Black candidate" with mainly South and West Side support. He was genuinely interested in their votes, and they took notice. Thus, the best way to describe Washington's support was a multiracial coalition *led* by African Americans, but with a crucial and diverse set of allies that allowed him to claim victory.

As to be expected, African Americans and progressive whites and Latinos were overjoyed and relieved by Harold Washington's victory, both in Chicago and across the nation. "Washington Wins, Dirtiest Election Is Over—Amen!," the *Chicago Defender* declared. More than 10,000 well-wishers packed McCormick Place and gave him a fifteen-minute standing ovation in the wee hours of the morning, while his triumph swept the national news and immediately stoked the discussion of a Black presidential candidate in 1984. In the city, Washington also had a new, more reform-minded council to work with, as seven machine-aligned aldermen were defeated in the general election by the likes of Bobby Rush, Anna Langford, and other independents. "The City Council will be a freer and much more independent institution," said Langford, who previously served when the Daley machine dictated most city business. "It means we have the ear of the mayor. We are not the enemies of the fifth floor anymore." But others were warier of the future. Survival had characterized the general election more than anything else, and it suggested that healing would take some time, as well as a lot of energy that already had been expended campaigning. "On February 23, I thought I could go on vacation," laughed Jacky Grimshaw, but instead, the election took six more weeks of hard work amid some of the ugliest rhetoric seen in the city's politics. For his part, Epton did concede the following day, but with the same edge he had used most of the campaign. "I wish Harold luck . . . he'll certainly need all the good help and talent he can get," Epton said, before twisting the rhetorical knife. "His expertise in the area of finances certainly leaves a lot to be desired. But maybe he'll learn to pay bills promptly and certainly pay his taxes promptly." The vanquished Republican's tone would be a warning sign of the continued resistance to come.[25]

As Washington, Grimshaw, and the rest of his supporters soon found out—as other Black politicians had before and after him—winning an electoral campaign was far easier than governing. This was especially the case when Washington's supporters, after surviving the roller coaster of two campaigns, then were blindsided when his mostly white political opponents did everything possible to kill his administration and agenda in their infancy.

## CHAPTER 7

# Fighting Wars of All Kinds

We spent too much time investing too much energy
into one person rather than sustaining the organizational,
institutional support that we had built up.
—Bob Starks interview, HMDA

**T**hey were called the Council Wars. Cleverly named by local comedian Aaron Freeman amid the release of *The Return of the Jedi*, the power struggle between the new Black mayor and a white council majority threatened to mire Chicago's government in permanent disarray. The Council Wars stalled most reforms, slowed appointments, and made a mockery of Chicago's "city that works" motto. And that was the point. Throughout the winter campaign, Harold Washington had promised to right the city's economic ship, including a concerted effort to end the political patronage and graft that greased just about everything.

Unlike his predecessor, however, Washington tried to stick to those campaign promises, painting a grim portrait during his inaugural address of a city in near financial ruin that needed to change its free-spending ways. "The immediate fiscal problems Chicago faces are enormous and complicated," the new mayor declared, revealing to gasps that the city's general fund and school and transportation systems were more than $500 million in the red. "My transition team advises me that the city government is . . . in far worse financial condition than we thought." As a stone-faced Jane Byrne sat behind him, Washington went on to prescribe a series of fixes, including the firing of hundreds of new employees. Conditions were not as dire as New York City's fiscal crisis of just a few years before, but the city's financial situation did force the new mayor into uncomfortable and unpopular decisions. Some of his good government supporters were delighted. But such pronouncements petrified others, friend and foe alike, alarmed at what reforms, especially the potential loss of patronage, could do to their wards and, more important, their political futures. Many warned that the speech damaged any chance at council "unity." "He came off like Attila the Hun," griped Thomas Cullerton, a veteran machine alderman who had backed Bernard Epton. "That's not going to help him win aldermen over."[1]

Indeed, one response was the formation of the "Vrdolyak Twenty-Nine." Organized by one-time Byrne allies Ed Vrdolyak and Ed Burke, the bloc of twenty-eight white aldermen and the council's lone Latino showed remarkable discipline over much of the next three years. Lined up against the mayor and his twenty-one council allies, which included the city's seventeen Black aldermen, the twenty-nine blocked or slowed most of the mayor's appointments and legislative priorities until 1986, when special elections in four wards upended the status quo. From the budget to gang crime legislation to a host of redevelopment projects, a sad pattern emerged. One of the mayor's allies would propose legislation and it would lose 29–21. An alternative by the council majority then was proposed and would win 29–21, only to be vetoed by the mayor. Since it took thirty-four votes, or two-thirds of the council, to override a veto, gridlock ensued. This occurred again and again. "The council wars can turn anything into just another device to increase the divisions of race and power that are paralyzing this city," wrote the *Tribune*'s editorial page, in response to a particularly wrenching death of a local high school basketball star in late 1984, "even the genuine and general impulse to save our young people from being gunned down in the street."[2]

While many whites claimed at the time that the Council Wars were a product of real policy differences, Vrdolyak's political opportunism, and even Washington's delay in calling party leaders personally after the election, most Chicagoans admitted race and racism were central. "There is no doubt in my mind that the issue is racial," said Milton Davis, president of South Shore Bank. "The history of this country is replete with the unwillingness of the white majority to share power with the minority." Ed Burke admitted as much. "None of this would have happened if Harold had come to us the way Byrne did," he said, as if Burke was king. Even after the racism demonstrated during the April election, Washington supporters were taken aback. "I was anticipating that Washington would face opposition from whites, but I had no idea that it would go to the depths it's going," said L. Roscoe Boler of the Westside Coalition for Unity and Political Action. Added educator Joan Wilson, "I thought it would be going on behind closed doors." In a meeting with community newspaper publishers, Vrdolyak claimed that Washington had a "three-pronged plan" to drive whites out and "blacken the city," in order to win reelection in 1987. The publishers were flabbergasted; there was simply no evidence to support the assertion. For three years, the Council Wars became synonymous with the city's dysfunction, racial

Mayor Washington and Alderman Ed Vrdolyak, leader of the opposition, share a lighter moment on the council floor in 1985. While Vrdolyak's race-baiting and obstructionism infuriated Washington, the mayor also considered him a worthy, wily opponent. Former independent alderman Leon Despres sits in the foreground. Harold Washington Archives and Collections, Mayoral Photographs, box 14, folder 26, Special Collections, Chicago Public Library.

hostility, and the lengths that white elites would go to thwart Black leadership and political power.[3]

While the Council Wars have received the most notice—and certainly were the most entertaining to a cynical press—they were both fueled and fought alongside many other racialized battles against the new mayor and his allies, forced upon them by changing national and regional political cultures. Washington stood out as a distinct reformer in an increasingly conservative political era symbolized by Ronald Reagan. Washington embraced a muscular affirmative action, greater citizen access to local government, neighborhood-based economic development, and more humane social services. These made a real difference to people left behind by previous administrations and who came out in record numbers for Washington. But facing the reality of governing, Washington grappled with the challenges that others who also benefited directly from a movement-style campaign had before, not to mention since. Was it inevitable that much of the vision of social, economic, and political justice sketched out on the campaign trail would be compromised? Would grassroots organizations that had seeded the campaign's approach suddenly be sidelined, forced to fight for their issues but with perhaps less leverage? And would many of his Black supporters, reluctantly, accept this reality because one of their own was finally in office? The answer, it seemed, to all three questions was yes.

Too often, Washington found himself backing policies that burdened his key constituencies, whether they were African Americans, Latinos, gay men and lesbians, or women. This occurred for many structural and political reasons—a poor macroeconomy driven by deindustrialization, a racialized federal retreat from urban spending and investment, numerous dysfunctional local institutions, and an array of supporters who expected immediate, even contradictory change. As he tried to reform some aspects of the city's governance, Washington was compelled to find resources to fight wars on welfare, crime, and drugs, often within the neighborhoods most supportive of him. His administration became tangled in the nation's ham-handed and ignorant response to the AIDS crisis. And the immigration politics of the mid-1980s posed their own risks, inextricably tying urban centers like Chicago to the Cold War proxy wars in Central America. Moreover, the remarkable grassroots energy and organization that had made him mayor was not sustained after the election. Activism continued, of course, and often to remind the administration of the vision Washington had promised. But governing proved much harder and required a different set of negotiations. Oftentimes, the blame could be left at the feet of Washington and his aides who acquiesced to get things "done." Activists, as well as regular Chicago citizens, themselves gave the city's first Black mayor a broad benefit of the doubt, especially amid the racialized political culture that fed the white council majority and the Reagan administration. But some of those same people were dismayed when Washington did not reward his supporters with patronage—despite signals that he would reject such old ways.

Ultimately, Washington fell short of fulfilling his ambitious vision of a fair, just city, especially in the first years of his administration. He was stymied not just by the racial politics of Ed Vrdolyak and white ethnics desperately holding on to power locally, as the narrative usually goes, but also by a potent form of white supremacy and neoliberalism championed by the Reagan administration nationally, which in turn helped fuel and empower the Council Wars that wracked city politics. Being mayor of Chicago was one of the great political prizes in American politics. Yet, to quote one of Washington's biographers, it seemed more and more like a "devalued prize," thanks to the unique social, political, and economic challenges of the 1980s. And such was the experience shared, in various forms, by his fellow Black and Latino executives across the nation in the 1980s, during the Age of Reagan.[4]

"THIS IS THE FIRST TIME. Before we were protesting," recalled José "Cha-Cha" Jiménez, who resurfaced in Chicago's electoral politics during the winter of 1983. "With the Harold Washington campaign, we felt like winners."[5] Indeed, Jiménez spoke for many in the days and weeks after Washington's April victory. After years of protest and incremental progress at best, neighborhood activists such as Jiménez had worked hard in precincts that normally had low voter turnout. After his victory, they viewed Washington as a real ally in City Hall. He was, at times. And yet that alliance did not prove as straightforward as some had expected. For every activist whose hard work translated into a public job or a timely favor from the new administration, there were many others who found themselves on the outside looking in. Some activists became part of the administration, such as Rob Mier, Linda Coronado, and Brenetta Howell Barrett. Others, most notably Lu Palmer and those considered part of his Black nationalist orbit, felt frozen out. So did more working-class supporters of the mayor, passed over in favor of middle-class professionals.[6] As the story of Jiménez and Latinos more generally illustrates, there were clear limits to the administration's partnership with the activists that put him in power—and not just about jobs, contracts, and private meetings with the new mayor.

Jiménez's journey offered an excellent example of this reality. After his aldermanic loss in 1975, Jiménez helped run the independent, nonpartisan community service center he promised during his campaign and vowed to run again. Instead, he was falsely accused of and jailed for ties to the Puerto Rican paramilitary Armed Forces of National Liberation, which coordinated a series of bombings in Chicago, among other places, in the late 1970s. Jiménez was eventually acquitted but remained in jail through the process because he could not post bond. By late 1982, the Young Lords became the Puerto Rican Defense Committee (PRDC) as well as one of the earliest Latino groups to support Harold Washington's mayoral run. Jiménez organized what many believed was the first Latino rally in support of Washington, attended by 1,000 Puerto Ricans in November. Along with other members of the PRDC, such as David Mojica and Modesto Rivera, Jiménez went on to work tirelessly for the campaign, coordinating canvasses in five wards with substantial Latino populations. While Jiménez brought credibility to the Black candidate's campaign among Puerto Ricans on the Near Northwest Side, he eschewed a higher-profile role given his controversial past. After the election, Jiménez made sure Washington attended a Puerto Rican–themed parade and festival—one of nine neighborhood-based festivals the city sponsored in place of ChicagoFest. As the guest of honor, Washington donned a *pava*, a straw hat traditionally worn by Puerto Rican *jíbaros* on the island, to the cheers of the crowd. Jiménez recalled joking with the new mayor that if he wore the hat, he could pass as Puerto Rican. But Washington never asked Jiménez to join the administration—something Jiménez did not begrudge the new mayor or his team. "After the campaign, I had no job," he recalled. "I didn't want a job with the city. Well, I wanted one with City Hall. But they couldn't do that" because of his past legal problems. He soon left town, never to live in Chicago again. Mo Rivera, another Puerto Rican "soldier" active in the campaign, was less polite about it. "None of us got shit," he said, disappointed that Washington had stuck to his promise not to trade jobs for electoral support.[7]

If any Latino was guaranteed to work for the new administration, it would have been Rudy Lozano. One of Washington's closest political allies, the Mexican American came incredibly close to pushing the Twenty-Second Ward's absentee alderman into a one-on-one runoff and, after losing, had been added to the transition team and touted as a future deputy mayor. The night of the election, Lozano predicted a new era was about to begin: "Washington created the conditions permitting the Hispanic community to coalesce. That's something we've all dreamed of." Lozano's admirers were left reeling and lamenting his unfulfilled potential after a gunman killed the thirty-one-year-old in his kitchen in June 1983, just a day after the triumphant Puerto Rican parade. Authorities quickly captured and charged gang member Gary Escobar, who was eventually convicted. But while thousands of people of all colors and backgrounds—from political dignitaries and union leaders to average working-class men and women in Pilsen and Little Village—mourned Lozano at a number of memorial services, questions and conspiracy theories swirled around his death. The press suggested that Lozano may have inadvertently crossed Latino gang lines when members worked on his aldermanic campaign or, more darkly, that the victim had not paid a cocaine debt. His friends and family swiftly challenged such explanations, saying it was likely a "political assassination" in response to his union work or even his support for Washington. "Saying it's gangs make [prosecutors'] job simple—a drugged-up gang member equals senseless killing," said Emma Lozano, Rudy's sister. "But if they looked at the way gangs are used in this neighborhood—gang members are hired all the time to make hits." Added Chuy García, death threats had been a constant, but ticked upward after Lozano ran for alderman. Washington distanced himself from such conspiracy talk, but activists remained concerned and, in July, established an independent citizens group to shadow the police investigation. The group included key independent figures and Washington supporters, including Alderman Danny Davis, state representative Art Turner, IPO activists Chuy García and Juan Velasquez, and the Heart of Uptown Coalition's Helen Shiller and Slim Coleman. While they claimed that they had confidence in the police, their actions suggested otherwise. The independent commission remained active for more than a decade, and even more than thirty years later, Lozano's former confidantes were skeptical of official explanations for his death.[8]

Despite Washington's expansive Latino support, Lozano's death left a vacuum not easily filled—a reminder of the coalition's fragility. As the Council Wars dragged on through the summer, so did inaction on opening up City Hall to Latino ideas and personnel. Even professionally qualified Latinos, such as Mexican American activist and bilingual teacher Linda Coronado, could not get an interview. She reconciled it by telling those Latinos who did work for the administration that "my responsibility is to keep you honest. If I can do that, I know you'll do good work for the community." But that required a loose network of activists, including Coronado and representing a range of Latino nationalities and communities, to pick up the mantle from Lozano and press the administration to follow through on its promises. Several months of negotiation resulted in little more than unfulfilled promises. The new mayor's aides, including Chief of Staff William Ware, worried about establishing a city commission on Latino affairs that the administration could not control and, thus, worked to block it despite the mayor's promise to establish just such a commission. Finally, the group decided it could wait no longer, organized itself, and called a press conference to announce an independent Latino commission. Born in response to a question posed by Miami's mayor, Maurice Ferré, about what Latinos in the campaign wanted to accomplish, the commission would, among other things, serve as an independent watchdog and grade the administration's efforts in their communities. The night before the announcement, Ware called Juan Velasquez's house, where Nena Torres and other prominent Latinos were meeting. "Juan answered the phone," Torres recalled. "And they threatened that we would . . . fall out of bed" with Washington, to which they retorted, "We're not in bed with anyone." Instead, they invited the mayor to the commission's unveiling the next day and, within a week, Washington had signed an executive order establishing a Mayor's Advisory Commission on Latino Affairs (MACLA). It was the first of several promises Washington eventually kept to this constituency—but only after considerable pressure.[9]

During the first several months of its existence, the commission continued to face efforts to marginalize it. While Torres was named executive director and most of the informal group of activists, including Velasquez, Coronado, Miguel del Valle, and Peter Earle, were tapped for the sixteen-member board, the mayor's office added one person "because [Ware] thought it would explode it," according to Torres later. But the addition, a known mafia figure, did not stay long. Other efforts to diminish the commission included initially denying it a budget, monthly access to the mayor, and anything more than a desk in the Commission on Human Relations office. But board members pushed back and won a temporary office on the sixth floor of City Hall and two paid administrative positions. The commission did agree to give the mayor two weeks' notice before making any major announcement, especially any criticism of the administration's hiring and other sensitive subjects; he received plenty of notice when the board issued its first hiring grades of "D" in 1984. "It was a reasonable request," Nena Torres said, and the process placated some aides' fears of a "runaway commission." What was less reasonable was the City Council's attempt to thwart MACLA by establishing its own Latino committee, whose members would be appointed by aldermen. Given that the council had just one Latino, machine stalwart Miguel Santiago, and had shown little care for Latino interests—even those in the conservative *colonia*—MACLA maintained a sturdy alliance with Washington, despite their differences. MACLA also became the model for the administration's other advisory commissions, including for women, gay men and lesbians, immigrants, and the city's small but growing population of Asian Americans.[10]

While the creation of MACLA may have irritated Washington aides—and sometimes the mayor himself, who called them "the high-schoolers" because of their grading practices—it certainly prompted more urgency to prioritize Latino interests and symbolism. "These are not your enemies," Torres reminded Washington, "these are your friends." In January 1984, the mayor named a top Latino aide, thirty-one-year-old Puerto Rican Benjamin Reyes. While Reyes's appointment won praise by Washington ally and fellow Puerto Rican Jorge Morales and others because "it will open other doors," the move outraged many, and not only because Reyes's responsibilities proved something less than a promised deputy mayor position. Many Mexican Americans, in particular, doubted Reyes's community bona fides. A Chicago native, Reyes had worked for several organizations in the city, including Continental Illinois National Bank, ASPIRA, and the YMCA; he had most recently worked for a housing development nonprofit in suburban Washington, D.C. Yet, according to Torres, she and other early backers of Washington "felt betrayed because they had lobbied the mayor to secure a high-ranking Latino liaison who had been part of the reform political movement." Instead, the mayor chose Reyes, "who had not worked on the campaign and had moved from the city during the general election." While he eventually endorsed Washington after the primary election, Reyes had not paid the same dues that Torres and others had. His duties were not even explicitly about Latino interests, he reminded reporters. "Is this going to be a Latino position?" Reyes said. "No. We're working to make this city a better place for everyone." That Reyes was yet another male chosen for a high-profile position in the administration also rankled the mayor's women supporters.[11]

In fact, the administration's lack of attention to women in the first year prompted concern more generally. Speaking for the Women's Network for Washington, coordinator Peggy Montes, just two days after the election, expressed consternation that only six of fifty-three members of the mayor's steering committee were women. "We want to share in the power and responsibility of your administration," wrote Montes. "Roles such as administrators, decision makers and being a part of the governmental process. In other words, we want parity. . . . Please, Harold, help end the sexism that is forever prevalent in our city." The multiracial Women's Network, founded by early Washington supporters Nancy Jefferson, Addie Wyatt, and Sid Ordower, had played a key role during the campaign. But Washington's initial round of appointments was not promising. Out of eight top aides, the mayor named just one woman, Sharon Gist Gilliam, a former commissioner in the Bilandic administration, whom he appointed deputy budget director. Activists pressed for an Office of Women's Affairs, with a cabinet-level leader, through organizations such as the nonpartisan Women United for a Better Chicago (WUBC) and the Women's Network. Such an agency, especially if established by ordinance, would ensure greater female representation across city government, as well as greater priority for essential services that affect women disproportionately, such as social welfare, schools, health care, and domestic violence prevention. But it took until January 1984 to establish a Mayor's Advisory Commission on Women's Affairs and it, too, fell short of expectations. In addition to the commission's not being established through legislation, and thus more temporary, "we were . . . dismayed by the distorted process by which the members were selected," wrote Kathy Lanahan and Gloria Donahue of WUBC. "Where are the women who work on the neighborhood/grassroots level who are consistently not given a voice in matters that affect their own lives?" Only Nancy Jefferson of the Midwest Community Council and a few others could be considered grassroots leaders, and thus this line of critique persisted until administration officials began to respond with greater urgency in 1985.[12]

It did turn out, over time, that Washington diversified city government in an unprecedented way, breaking the council logjam and tapping a record number of women and Latinos, especially for leadership posts. In addition to Gilliam and Torres, Elizabeth Hollander became the planning director and Brenetta Howell Barrett was made commissioner of consumer affairs. Jacky Grimshaw, Lucille Dobbins, and Brenda Gaines—all Black women, along with Gilliam and Howell Barrett—became influential voices in the administration, with Gaines serving as deputy chief of staff. Kari Moe emerged as another key figure, first as an assistant to the mayor and later as the city's commissioner of general services. By early 1987, the Washington administration boasted nineteen female department heads, Black, white, and Latino, almost all of whom were in their thirties and forties. The city also hired scores of additional women to become police officers and firefighters, the latter after research by the women's commission revealed that female applicants needed more training to pass the department's grueling physical examination. All of this took time and effectively increased pressure. At the end of 1985, according to a *Tribune* analysis, women actually made up a slightly smaller share of the city workforce than they had under Jane Byrne (19.2 percent compared to 19.4), despite women's comprising 38 percent of all those hired by the city. The discrepancy could be explained by Washington's initial layoffs of Byrne's eleventh-hour patronage hires, who were disproportionately women—a gap Washington managed to erase by the end of his first term. Moreover, one-third of Washington's informal "kitchen cabinet," called the Mayor's Policy Advisory Cabinet, were women and included respected figures such as activist Addie Wyatt.[13]

Latinos had a similar experience, particularly striking given the national political climate against affirmative action and federal urban funding, not to mention the Council Wars. While MACLA worked on many issues, it became best known for its semiannual affirmative action reports on jobs and contracts. The commission's first reports on city hiring were sobering at times, with some city agencies earning low grades in MACLA's first several reports. Washington received more praise for appointments to boards, commissions, and other high-level positions, but even there, Latinos were "caught in the crossfire in the council wars," MACLA contended. At least fourteen high-level appointments, including to the transit authority, planning commission, and library board, languished as council members fought over control of the city's agenda. By the beginning of 1985, while Reyes and Torres remained the most prominent Latinos in the administration, both MACLA and other independent analyses reported that the administration had hired more Latinos than any previous administration, at a rate of 11 percent of all new employees a year. "Mayor Washington's record on Latino hiring is particularly impressive because he was able to hire a total of only 989 employees in 1984, compared to Mayor Byrne's 6,252 new hires

Peggy Montes speaks at a meeting of the Mayor's Advisory Commission on Women's Affairs, as neighborhood activist Gale Cincotta looks on. Despite early concerns that Washington's appointments had been primarily men, the new mayor eventually tapped more women to top administrative posts than any Chicago mayor to date. Michelle V. Agins, Harold Washington Archives and Collections, Mayoral Photographs, box 22, folder 39, Special Collections, Chicago Public Library.

in 1981," wrote the commission, despite "budgetary problems resulting from cutbacks in federal monies." The administration also stacked up favorably to the council itself, whose hires were only about 5 percent Latino. None of this praise changed the fact that Latinos made up only 4 percent of all city workers by 1986, far below their estimated 17 percent of Chicago's population. MACLA estimated that Latinos would have to make up an astronomical one-third of all new hires over several years to meet parity relative to population. This reality helped inform MACLA's persistent complaints that African Americans received the most benefits in terms of city jobs. And they were not wrong.[14]

THE ONE DEMOGRAPHIC GROUP that appeared to benefit most immediately from Washington's election was African American men—a consistent trend in many of the new Black-led administrations in the 1970s and 1980s. In a *Tribune* analysis in late 1983, a shift in high-profile appointments proved the most apparent and immediate change between the Byrne and Washington administrations, with eleven Black and twelve white men in Cabinet-level positions, compared to three Black and twenty-two white men in Byrne's Cabinet. Indeed, Black men were some of the administration's most prominent and powerful figures beyond the mayor himself, including Washington's chief of staff William Ware, his assistant and future chief of staff Ernest Barefield, Police Superintendent Fred Rice, Corporation Counsel James Montgomery, Health Commissioner Lonnie Edwards, housing authority board chairman Renault Robinson, Human Services Commissioner Al Raby, and School Superintendent Manford Byrd Jr. Overall, African Americans made up about 58 percent of 3,671 new hires by the administration. This sounded impressive, and it was. But even in this case, the numbers were misleading. Such hiring constituted less than 10 percent of the city's workforce of approximately 41,000, meaning that after two years, Washington's intentional affirmative action policy had barely dented the racial breakdown in the city's workforce. In fact, similar to hiring numbers for women, the African American share of city jobs declined slightly between 1983 and 1984.[15]

This reality particularly drew the ire of Lu Palmer and the nationalist-leaning activists of the Task Force for Black Empowerment, much like their counterparts in Atlanta and other cities. A longtime proponent of a Black mayor, Palmer was far less loyal to Washington personally. Washington merely represented the best vehicle to the city jobs, contracts, and opportunities that African Americans long deserved but had been denied, the task force argued. Thus, when Washington made clear that fairness to all races was a central policy of his administration, Palmer was dumbfounded. "Fuck fairness" was his response. "Our communities are in competition for political advancement," Palmer observed about Latinos. "We both want to make up for past abuses. You have to make up your mind who comes first." Palmer was willing to say what many African Americans believed: that Latinos coolly viewed the new mayor as a practical chance for tangible economic and political gains. Of course, what was also true, but generally left unsaid, was Black activists like himself also grudgingly recognized Latinos' crucial role in Washington's victory. What Palmer had not expected was Washington's insistence on keeping him and his allies at arm's length. And, unlike Latino activists, they did not gain much influence over time. Instead, while the Task Force continued to meet most every Tuesday evening for thirty years, Washington rarely attended these meetings, instead relying on Bob Starks, a professor, longtime chairman of the Task Force, and an informal adviser of Washington, to brief him on what happened. Ultimately, its members felt increasingly marginalized by City Hall, in favor of organizations and efforts that rejected policies and projects that explicitly favored Black Chicagoans over others.[16]

Palmer turned out to be a flawed spokesman—and someone who came to symbolize a grassroots activism that was suddenly less relevant after the election was over. His grievances multiplied after Washington endorsed longtime progressive Black labor leader Charles Hayes to succeed him in Congress over Palmer, who up to that point had led in the handful of polls measuring the contest. Hayes ended up beating Palmer handily in a Democratic primary crowded with Washington supporters including Al Raby and Marian Humes. "The Washington machine violated the principles of the movement that elected him," complained Palmer, who skipped a "unity" rally the following day. A series of perceived personal slights, continuing disagreements over Washington's racial policies, and Palmer's own anti-Semitism—he raged about the "Hyde Park Jewish conspiracy"—during the next year led to his public break with the mayor in 1984. But it was not just a personal and political disagreement; the marginalization of Palmer was symbolic of the "balancing acts," to quote one biographer, that Washington and other big-city mayors of the time had to perform in order to govern. The casualty was a grassroots organizer who, despite his bombastic style and personality, had been instrumental in Washington's victory in the first place and spoke for an important, often marginalized segment of his support. To Starks, the sidelining of Palmer reflected a larger, perhaps inevitable decline of some of the mayor's grassroots coalition. Unlike other organizations, the Task Force continued to meet, discuss issues, and weigh in on politics, but its influence peaked in 1983. "Why should we have all these organizations," said Starks, trying to summarize other activists' thinking, "we got a Black mayor, right?" While he viewed that conclusion as shortsighted, it remained a powerful impulse. Meanwhile, the disappointment, even betrayal, that Task Force members voiced was something many never really got past, he recalled. And yet in retrospect, the mayor's tactical shift away from the Task Force and its members—already indicated during the campaign—seemed inescapable at some level.[17]

Some might dismiss the complaints of Palmer, Montes, Torres, and others as identity politics run amok, as conservative white politicians then and now charged. But in the practical context of municipal politics in Chicago and elsewhere, who was being hired and for what truly mattered—and often more than any other policy the administration could enact. Reasons went beyond the city's grand tradition of patronage. Jobs for women and racial minorities, simply put, were not going to white ethnic men, whose political patrons wielded a ferocious zero-sum politics, even while they vociferously denied it. And in the mid-1980s, city jobs were especially valuable because well-paying private sector positions—especially for those without a college degree—continued to dry up thanks to deindustrialization, which had claimed more than a quarter of a million jobs in the city the previous decade. Thus, municipal jobs and contracts played an outsized role for many of the era's Black mayors like Washington, not only because of historic denial of these opportunities to minorities but also because of the political and economic context that shuttered factories and left more and more Americans to fend for themselves.[18]

In his quest to diversify who received city contracts, Washington had arguably more success than with jobs, but this too was tempered by budget cuts as well as some questionable practices. In most big cities, and certainly in Chicago, a way for businesses to mitigate economic downturns was to secure and maintain lucrative contracts with city government, from construction to garbage collection to accounting. But as with jobs in the city, a disproportionate number of contracts historically went to machine-aligned companies and unions, often in no-bid, sweetheart deals. Waste Management and Consumers Tire & Supply Co. were classic examples of politically connected companies winning no-bid deals. With few exceptions, these contracts did not go to minority-owned firms—a practice the new administration aimed to change. And it did, doubling the percentage of contracts with minority-owned companies to more than 20 percent in its first year. These included local firms providing new garbage cans and guaranteed construction jobs for African Americans at the expansion of O'Hare International Airport; in fact, by 1986, the latter project employed 40 percent minority- and women-owned firms. But the pie was also smaller than it had been. In 1984, the city spent $100 million less in purchasing than it did in 1982, meaning the raw increase in spending with firms owned by African Americans, Latinos, and women was about only $20 million. More insulting but not all that surprising to Washington supporters, some of the contracts turned out to be won by paper-minority operations that served as fronts for white-owned firms. Other business owners claimed the city forced them to partner with a minority-owned firm to maintain their contracts. Such complaints brought about what the *Chicago Reporter* called "unanticipated benefits for taxpayers" by placing a public spotlight on the bidding process. The result was the establishment of a contract review board charged with examining any contested awards of more than $50,000, modeled after ones in Milwaukee, Baltimore, and other cities. Rather than an all-powerful mayor dictating contracts to his cronies, the public could at least see the process. "Never in the history of the city has the council been involved to the extent it has been now," stated

Washington, knowing that, despite a greater council role, he retained great sway over the board. Such transparency, it turned out, would help him achieve his goals of spreading the wealth among minority-owned city businesses.[19]

WASHINGTON'S EMBRACE of affirmative action policies, however much flawed in their execution at times, was just the most recognizable element of a larger promise to open up the city. As Lu Palmer learned, that promise could cut multiple ways. For instance, the mayor's endorsement of the so-called Shakman decree was praised by his predominantly white "good government" supporters, who long had viewed the machine's tradition of patronage hiring as corrupt, inefficient, and often racist. Michael Shakman, a civic reformer and independent candidate for the state's constitutional convention in 1970, brought his initial lawsuit against the Democratic Party of Cook County in 1969, claiming that the machine's political patronage employment violated the First and Fourteenth Amendments to the U.S. Constitution. After a long deliberation, the suit led to three judicial decrees outlawing politically motivated hiring, firing, and punishing of government employees, the last of which came down in April 1983 amid the general election. Machine politicians had outmaneuvered earlier orders in 1972 and 1979 by insisting on key exceptions to the ban; observers expected the same moves from Washington. Instead, after negotiating about 900 policymaking positions controlled by the mayor, he signed off on the compromise and later declared that "patronage is dead." U.S. District Court Judge Nicholas Bua was astonished: "Quite candidly, I never expected a settlement in this case."[20]

By signing the decree, Washington appeared to prioritize one constituency, and one kind of reform, over others. Not only did he please the white progressives of the Lakefront and the influential Independent Voters of Illinois, he also had—at least briefly—joined hands with the more conservative business community, even the city's Republican Party, which had complained of the patronage system for years but expected little from a former machine pol. Despite his affirmative action policies, the Shakman agreement made it far less possible to put deserving African Americans on the payroll for merit—let alone for nothing but their vote, as the Democratic machine had done so efficiently for its allies since 1931. The bloated four-man garbage truck crew and the eighteen-year-old building inspector faded into the past. This did not sit well with many of Washington's Black supporters. Niles Sherman, a Democratic committeeman and alderman, complained bitterly that summer that "those individuals who put the mayor where he is deserve something more than a pat on the back." They deserve "the spoils or rewards" of victory, he told a radio host. From the perspective of such supporters, Washington had sacrificed one of his most powerful tools to better the lives of working-class Blacks when unemployment among them remained in double digits. Even Washington admitted that "we got hurt" in the process. "We simply couldn't bring our people in prudently," he told the *Tribune.* "All we could replace were top agency heads. You couldn't go down where it counts." Indeed, former independent alderman Dick Simpson, who remained a careful observer of city politics after leaving the council, estimated that Shakman reduced the effective number of patronage jobs from more than 35,000 in 1983 to fewer than 5,000 in the early twenty-first century. It had made an impact. But ironically, this one reform—because it kept so many ineffectual machine hires in place, and the mayor's own people out—made it far more difficult for Washington to pursue other reforms, including those most beneficial to African Americans.[21]

Activists of all races interested in greater transparency in local government achieved at least some success. Northwestern University's Center for Urban Affairs and Policy Research, in conjunction with neighborhood groups across the city, for years had demanded a greater overall commitment to more information, provided in a more systematic way, and in a timely manner. This was underscored by the Washington transition team's own experience. According to the team's official report, "One of the most obvious and pervasive facts about Chicago city government that has repeatedly been evident in our research is that basic information needed to understand how the City works, to assess how well services are provided and to determine who is responsible for various city programs is incredibly difficult to obtain." This included basic budget numbers and names of personnel. One former alderman characterized standard procedure under Mayor Byrne as "an official policy to obstruct." In contrast, Washington's became the first Chicago administration to champion freedom of information (FOI) policies enacted by the state and city—catching up to other local and state governments across the nation. The process proved to be neither smooth nor efficient, partly because the administration's first freedom of information officer, the cackling, flamboyant Clarence McClain, resigned in a legal cloud. But as John Kretzmann, a professor at the urban affairs center, points out, FOI was an inherently limited tool because it was "basically a statement of willingness to react and respond, not to initiate," and often in an adversarial manner, such as the media's use of FOI to pry information from public officials. Thus, many in Washington's administration also strove for an "affirmative" approach to information, in which civic organizations were partners in collecting data—called Affirmative Neighborhood Information. This, too, started off slowly, with "bureaucratic inertia" slowing the process down, according to Kretzmann. Eventually, city agencies began cooperating with the initiative, but only after the mayor held a very public press conference announcing it in 1985. "This program," Washington told those in attendance, "is what reform is all about."[22]

At the same time, the city moved toward open hearings on other issues, most notably budgets and crime. Opening up the city budget process—even with some exceptions—was "one of the two most important structural changes he made," according to Helen Shiller, the longtime editor and Washington supporter who won her third try at alderman in Uptown in 1987. Rather than shaped and debated solely behind closed doors—with favors furiously flying back and forth—the proposed budget was made available a month in advance of a series of hearings in which the public could speak openly about the city's priorities. The mayor's foes on the City Council embraced the reform as well, since they no longer controlled the process; in the past, a machine mayor proposed a budget already shaped in closed-door meetings and the council simply rubber-stamped it. With Washington in City Hall, such a process was no longer desirable for either his foes or supporters. "This will be the most open and thoroughly debated budget since [Republican] Big Bill Thompson was mayor in the '20s," predicted Ed Burke, the new chair of the Finance Committee in 1983, and he was right. But because of the deficit left by Byrne, the council's recalcitrance, and continuing cuts in federal spending, Washington's first proposed budget proved so modest that his opponents found few openings for criticism. They still did, especially Burke, determined to undermine the mayor at every turn. After five weeks of wrangling over the proper balance of user fees, business head taxes, and job security rules, a budget passed. Washington called it a "magnificent first," but it still took years to start fulfilling the mayor's promises in housing, human services, and economic development.[23]

Moreover, in response to rising demands by community watch groups, the administration's Division of Human Services partnered with the police to hold hearings on the city's rising crime rates in early 1985. Like most major cities in the 1980s, Chicago was gripped by increasing gang crime, closely linked to the ongoing decline of opportunities and hope in a deindustrializing city. In 1984, such crime ranged from graffiti and loitering to drive-by shootings, increasingly driven by turf battles over drugs; the city estimated there were as many as 100,000 gang members in Chicago. Protests about the violence rose throughout the year, especially after the shooting death of high school basketball star Ben Wilson. In response, the mayor established the Task Force for Youth Crime Prevention under aide Michael Holewinski. Part of the process included twenty-five town halls in which citizens could speak openly about their safety concerns and what the city—the police department and other service agencies—could do to mitigate it. "We're hoping that together we can help fill the gaps you identify," Holewinski said at the opening hearing in Pilsen. "The best experts are in the neighborhoods." A remarkable cross-section of Chicagoans participated, expressing a wide range of concerns about crime and how to reduce it. Some were angry and pointed, extolling the city to "stop pampering gangs." "Some parents don't even know their kids are in gangs," as one exasperated man put it. Ignoring the socioeconomic roots of gang membership, some even proposed fining parents for their children's gang activity. But for as many people calling for tougher law enforcement, a seemingly equal number were conciliatory despite grave concerns. Calling gangs a "crisis," West Side activist Nancy Jefferson stated that it started with members of the community. "Every Thursday evening since last May we've been holding gang crime meetings," Jefferson said at a hearing. "We've involved gang members. No matter how undesirable, they are our children." Added Robert Jones, "It's a form of identity" for some youth. "When they're members of a gang they're somebody." In Pilsen, Edgewater, and elsewhere, residents called for more resources, for block clubs, youth centers, and antidropout programs. While these resources emerged slowly, just being heard was a critical first step.[24]

AS THE ADMINISTRATION touted reforms around access and process, dysfunction remained in many city agencies, including those with historic leadership. Affirmative action policies and high-profile appointments of Black and Latino leaders were important steps, but they proved unable to turn around several of the city's most notoriously corrosive institutions. For instance, the Chicago Police Department, Housing Authority, and Health Department proved remarkably difficult to change after years of neglect and corruption, and the continued struggles of each underscored the limits of racial symbolism under a Black executive—and the quandary those limits posed for his supporters, especially those of color.

When Washington appointed Fred Rice as the first Black superintendent of the Chicago Police Department, the mayor rightly declared it was a new day in the city. The symbolic importance of a Black superintendent was difficult to overstate, given the department's ruthless, often extrajudicial behavior to keep poor, disproportionately Black and Latino, citizens in line. In the 1960s, Chicago police officers became the rioters outside of the 1968 Democratic National Convention, the killers of Black Panthers Fred Hampton and Mark Clark in 1969,

Nancy Jefferson, a respected activist from the West Side, appears with Washington in the spring of 1983. Jefferson had worked tirelessly for a Black mayor since the 1970s and had cofounded the Women's Network for Washington. She remained an important grass-roots voice throughout Washington's administration. Harold Washington Archives and Collections, Mayoral Photographs, box 80, folder 64, Special Collections, Chicago Public Library.

and the armed robbers in the Summerdale scandal that briefly imperiled Richard J. Daley's reelection in 1963. In the 1970s, many officers were exposed as part of the notorious and shadowy Red Squad, a Cold War–inspired subversive unit that infiltrated and slandered progressive activist organizations of any consequence in the city. And in the 1980s, the police represented the front line of the Reagan administration's ever-expanding anticrime policies, especially the War on Drugs, in which even torture was an accepted tactic against Blacks. As some activists darkly joked and Washington's second police superintendent even bragged about, the city's largest, "toughest gang" was the Chicago police. On the campaign trail, Harold Washington promised to remove Superintendent Richard Brzeczek, whose officers openly campaigned for Byrne. In the waning days before the general election, Brzeczek predicted chaos would occur if Washington won. That did not happen, of course, but Brzeczek denied Washington the chance to fire him by quitting on inauguration day. Four months later, Rice, a twenty-year veteran of the department, became superintendent.[25]

Rice, however, was a safe choice for Washington. Lauded as an up-and-coming leader in the department in the 1970s, Rice was called a "cop who cared—but carefully" for his approach to police work. He made waves in 1974 when he integrated patrol teams in the Englewood district, but he remained largely an insider—"a conservative, old-school Black cop," as one author observed. He had never joined the Afro-American Patrolmen's League. Instead, Rice had led the 8,000-person patrol division, the department's largest, and was seen as someone who garnered respect among the department's rank-and-file and union leadership, unlikely to rock the boat too much. He also happened to be in line ideologically with the new mayor's neighborhood method for combatting crime, which included recognizing that the police were not the only consideration in reducing it. "Crime is due to many [factors] beyond the scope of police work," he said in 1979, including poverty, substandard schools, and broken homes. "All the segments of society have to bear the responsibility for checking the high crime rate." Four years later, Washington chose Rice to put a community-based approach into action with more police on foot instead of in cars. While this shift may have had a small positive effect on city crime rates, which remained stubbornly high, Rice was more successful in integrating the police's command structure with Black and Latino leaders and reducing overt politics in the department, such as officers reviewing voter rolls and other shenanigans that happened under Daley and Byrne. Observers credited Rice with ending the practice of aldermen choosing investigators in the Office for Professional Standards (OPS), which investigated charges of police misconduct. Washington "more or less stayed away from the police department," Rice boasted, "and they'd tell you I had the best tour of duty as a superintendent than anybody because I was free from politics from the mayor."[26]

This hands-off approach was admirable given previous politicization, but Washington's deference to Rice rarely led to the kinds of reforms the department needed or even the mayor campaigned on. Changing the face of leadership from white to Black, while leaving other aspects unchanged, did not transform the institution. And when change did come, it was in response to a lawsuit and the courts. For instance, North Side gay activists, who had embraced Washington, albeit belatedly, continued to complain that too many gay bars were targeted by the police, usually in cooperation with another law enforcement agency. Once a common occurrence, police raids had declined as federal corruption cases made the opportunities to extort cash from bar owners and patrons far riskier. Thus, according to historian Timothy Stewart-Winter, the last of the "old style" raids occurred in 1985—of Carol's Speakeasy in Old Town, during which patrons were made to lie down on the floor for two hours, with their photos later published in the *Sun-Times*. Such "outings" often led to lost jobs and other discrimination in the still rampantly homophobic culture of the 1980s. The raid led to a lawsuit and an out-of-court settlement. One departmental response to gay concerns was increased sensitivity training, including at roll calls.[27]

Criticism persisted over questionable police shootings and other forms of violence, including the high-profile death of an unarmed Chicago Housing Authority resident. The department under Rice defended its deadly force policy, considered one of the most permissive in the nation, because shooting a fleeing felon "is a deterrent," according to Rice's assistant, Edwin Bishop. Indeed, overall complaints to the Office of Professional Standards, including charges of excessive force, crept up in 1983 and 1984 to more than 7,000. But after the Supreme Court's ruling in *Tennessee v. Garner* tightened the acceptable legal context for deadly force in 1985, the department followed suit and saw overall complaints and instances of excessive force drop more than 20 percent in two years, to well below numbers from Byrne's mayoralty. Still, few complaints were sustained by OPS (100 out of more than 5,000), and many suspected the department routinely massaged its statistics, as police have historically done, by reindexing crimes downward. The point remained that, even with a Black mayor and police superintendent, Chicago continued to have many more police shootings and fatalities per capita than New York City and Los Angeles—despite a clear legal consensus that such aggressive policies were ineffective in deterring crime.[28]

In addition, other odious forms of police violence—including torture—persisted under the new administration. In the worst example of this, area police commander Jon Burge oversaw the torture of more than 100 suspects, most of them Black men, on the South Side. Between 1973 and 1991, Burge led a team of detectives who used "savage torture" such as electroshock, to quote city lawyers, to compel confessions, most famously in the wake of the 1982 shooting deaths of two officers. The ensuing dragnet and coerced confessions led to multiple convictions, as well as several civil lawsuits starting in 1989, eventually revealing the brutality of Burge and his men. As a savvy, careful officer with a bright future in the department, Rice never indicated any direct knowledge of such tactics, including when he was superintendent. While plausible, Rice had spent his police career on the South Side and, as anthropologist Laurence Ralph points out, Black officers faced extreme pressure to stay quiet or risk being professionally derailed. After 1982, especially, Burge and company "grew comfortable that supervisors approved their illicit interrogations," contends historian Andrew Baer. It is quite possible that Rice chose to look the other way, as state's attorney and future mayor Richard M. Daley appeared to do when his office routinely declined to investigate the circumstances of questionable confessions. Numerous grassroots organizations continued to pursue police accountability during the Washington administration—most prominently Citizens Alert, founded in 1967—but their influence proved trickier with a Black mayor and superintendent. Rice's unprecedented but still calculated openness assuaged activists to an extent, his leadership given the benefit of the doubt. More bluntly, as stated by lawyer Flint Taylor, who pursued litigation against the Burge ring for years, there was a perception—including by the police themselves—that Black citizens were better protected by the Black mayor (and his Black superintendent). That may have been true, to a point. But Washington, like other Black mayors across the country, faced enormous pressure to make nice with the police. That often meant the powerful, white-led Fraternal Order of Police, which could direct sizable campaign fundraising and manpower to elected officials it considered friends. While the police union never endorsed Washington, allowing a seasoned veteran such as Rice to run the department with little input or intervention may have appeased enough police defenders. And yet Jon Burge's operation was allowed to continue.[29]

The administration's handling of OPS, the agency tasked with investigating police brutality, shootings, and other unethical behavior, reinforced this failure. During the campaign, Washington vowed to abolish it; instead, he kept the office intact and in June 1984 named David Fogel, a criminal justice professor at Northwestern University, to run it. In his six years, Fogel was credited with being a reformer, even the occasional maverick. Three years into the job, Fogel offered the mayor a candid assessment of why OPS was a problem and could not just be reformed from within. "A good number of our investigators continue to be irremediably incompetent," he wrote. "They are part of the inherited politically corrupt heritage of pre-Washington days." He added that, "The troops love OPS. . . . The appearance of doing a thorough investigation with full due process (and endless unnecessary reviews) for all, actually operates to immunize police from internal discipline, increases their overtime, leads to an enormous 'paper storm' and has institutionalized lying. . . . I have come to the conclusion that OPS gives the appearance of formal justice, but actually helps to institutionalize subterfuge and injustice." Department annual reports and a *Chicago Reader* report on the torture scandal affirmed this, showing that OPS rejected 96 percent of citizen complaints in 1982, with minimal improvement in the years afterward. Despite such assessments, Washington, Rice, and public safety aide Mike Holewinski had little response to Fogel's concerns. At least Fogel could point to a decline in the number of misconduct cases and some increased professionalization in OPS. That, however, was short-lived, as the drug crisis hit Chicago—fueled by crack cocaine, the crystallized cousin of powder that could be smoked for as little as five dollars—and risked upending Washington's carefully cultivated if superficial image of a department on the mend.[30]

When drug-related crime surged in the mid-1980s, a punitive anticrime culture was already in place, both nationally and in Chicago, prompting a swift and aggressive response by Black and white politicians across the nation. Similar to federal and local officials in Washington, D.C., and Los Angeles, for instance, Harold Washington, Fred Rice, and much of Chicago's Black leadership increasingly turned to the language and tactics of war in response to a rise in violent crime in 1986 and 1987. Gang crime had remained a constant during Washington's tenure, hence the public hearings of the previous year. But while the experimental Philadelphia-inspired Crisis Intervention Network had reduced the number of homicides in Chicago through alternative means of enforcement, other forms of violent crime rose sharply. Assaults, for instance, were up 64.9 percent in 1986. And the worst was yet to come, predicted Susan Weed, executive director of the city's Health Systems Agency. "Crack hasn't hit Chicago yet in the epidemic proportions it has appeared in New York, LA and other coastal cities," she wrote, meaning that they still had time to prepare. Indeed, drug-related violence and arrests already had spiked in other cities, as had militarized responses—from armored personnel carriers in Los Angeles drug raids to calls for the death penalty for New York drug dealers. Even Black members of Congress were nearly unanimous in embracing the Reagan administration's draconian Anti–Drug Abuse Act, which set higher sentencing guidelines for crack over powder cocaine. By 1988, Washington, D.C., witnessed a full-blown drug war with a record number of homicides connected to drugs. In Chicago, Washington and his aides resisted such approaches, including demands for mandatory drug testing of city employees. But they grew increasingly nervous about the political potency of drug-related crimes, especially with his reelection campaign fast approaching. As early as 1984, Joe Gardner, working for the Political Education Project, Washington's reelection campaign, had expressed concerns that youth crime in general might be a liability. As the public hearings reminded them, crime concerned citizens across the city's racial and political spectrum, even though it disproportionately impacted Black and Latino communities. The administration thus rolled out a series of initiatives in the second half of 1986, amplified the U.S. Conference of Mayors' "D-Day in the War on Drugs" rhetoric, and promised a zero-tolerance policy toward drugs. Drug possession arrests and sentencing rose sharply in Illinois. In Chicago, 500,000 more arrests occurred in 1987, a rise of nearly 10 percent. Thus, by the end of his term, Washington's administration had joined Black officials elsewhere in "locking up their own," to quote one legal scholar, and contributed to the mass incarceration of a generation of Black and Latino youth.[31]

THE ONLY CITY AGENCY that rivaled the police department in dysfunction arguably was the Chicago Housing Authority (CHA), charged with housing more than 145,000 people—second only behind New York City's—and in desperate need of reform. Washington tapped Renault Robinson, cofounder of the Afro-American Patrolmen's League, a former CHA board member, and a longtime supporter of the mayor, as the new chairman. The choice came as a surprise, with some of Washington's most vocal critics expecting Robinson to be tapped as police superintendent. The CHA had long been led by the corrupt businessman and machine moneyman Charles "Flophouse Charlie" Swibel, who used the position to leverage better borrowing terms for his own private development projects, including the iconic honeycomb Marina City towers on the Chicago River. But more than simply a leadership change at the top, the agency needed a massive transformation in vision and daily services coupled with increased resources, the latter unlikely as the Reagan administration slowed funding and tried to abandon public housing in favor of the private market. The CHA, concluded a U.S. Department of Housing and Urban Development (HUD) report in 1982, "is in a state of profound confusion and disarray. No one seems to be minding the store; what's more, no one seems to genuinely care." To its credit, HUD demanded that Swibel go, but what he left behind was a mess. In fact, Harold Washington privately had little hope that CHA could be transformed. "The CHA didn't have a problem," he told an aide. "They were the problem." Symbolized best by the high-rise Robert Taylor Homes and Cabrini-Green, which Washington called "canyons of despair that should never have been built," the CHA became known for deteriorating physical structures, poor maintenance and service delivery, and rampant crime and drug usage. Most of the elevators did not work, the stairs had too many broken bulbs for residents to feel safe, and bugs were everywhere. These complexes were even immortalized in popular culture—negatively through the horror film *Candyman* and, in a reminder that they remained home to thousands, the TV sitcom *Good Times*. Indeed, CHA-run facilities were genuine communities of people who looked out for each other—something Robinson and Washington recognized and many of the CHA's white critics did not. Primarily women-led tenants groups made these communities livable through their own volunteer efforts. But they needed the city's help and resources and, thus, the appointment of Robinson, a trusted progressive activist, won initial praise to at least "keep it all together."[32]

Instead, Robinson's tenure was a debacle, which CHA residents and leaders blamed squarely on the mayor. Charging forward with ill-considered layoffs and other cost-cutting measures, Robinson made a bad situation worse for residents. In the two highest-profile decisions of Robinson's tenure, the CHA rightfully canceled an extravagant elevator servicing contract, but before lining up a replacement vendor, and then fired more than 200 heating-plant workers on the eve of cold weather. In the winter of 1984, less than 30 percent of the elevators operated properly, while a series of broken pipes plunged residents into bone-chilling temperatures in their apartments. Robinson was also charged with nepotism, hiring a brother-in-law who had a criminal record but no housing experience. A respected out-of-state housing expert, Zirl Smith, was brought in to take over day-to-day operations but eventually lost a public relations war with Robinson and was pushed out. The final straw was the CHA's failure to meet a key federal deadline, which led to the loss of a $7 million grant—the equivalent of almost 10 percent of federal subsidies received by the CHA. By late 1986, resident surveys affirmed the continued failures; about one-third of respondents believed conditions had deteriorated since Washington became mayor, while only 14 percent saw improvement. The CHA indeed had saved money as federal subsidies flattened, but at a terrible cost to residents' living conditions and the mayor's policy goals. Well-intentioned efforts to reduce homelessness and other initiatives never gained traction amid the agency's inability to address day-to-day living conditions. Longtime renovation projects languished. Just a month before the 1987 primary, Washington reluctantly conceded that his friend Robinson had failed and accepted his resignation. Washington's handling of the CHA was considered his first term's greatest failure by Black leaders and activists, partly because he seemed unwilling to work with community groups to find solutions. "If you want to criticize someone, talk to Jane Byrne, or Charlie Swibel, or Ronald Reagan," he retorted when challenged, a response that left activists and residents shaking their heads.[33]

THE 1980S also witnessed a series of public health challenges, in which neither the federal government nor the Washington administration seemed entirely up to the task. Washington's choice of Dr. Lonnie Edwards for city health commissioner yet again exposed the structural challenges the administration faced. Much like Washington's other top appointments, Edwards arrived with a strong pedigree, as a respected medical professional and administrator at Cook County Hospital. But, as one Washington biographer put it, Edwards was "a political novice," which proved a distinct liability in increasingly protracted fights over health care. Declining federal budgets for Medicaid and public health reflected an overarching conservative philosophy that the poor and sick were so because of their own decisions, especially but not exclusively when it came to AIDS/HIV treatment. But rather than embrace Washington's positions that shifted at least some of the blame to a mix of federal spending cuts and an overall neglect of health care—certainly accurate, to a point—Edwards regularly criticized the mayor for not allocating enough money to hire more food inspectors, public health nurses, and lead-abatement investigators. While more local spending was needed in these areas to overcome the health impact of chronic poverty and corruption, such critiques did not ingratiate Edwards with the mayor and his aides, especially Ernest Barefield, charged with keeping Edwards on message. Just as unwise, Edwards stumbled in his interactions with two important constituencies, both of whom faced acute health challenges: Latinos and gay men.[34]

Edwards received sharp criticism for his handling of infant mortality, an issue that had emerged in Chicago and across the nation. After nearly twenty years of steady decline, the national rate had evened out in 1984 at about 11 deaths per 1,000 live births—less than half of what it was in 1965 but still one of the highest in the industrialized world. The decline had coincided with a shrinking poverty rate and greater health care spending; thus, the arrest in infant mortality's decline prompted sharp accusations that Reagan budget cuts to Medicaid and other public health programs in 1981 and 1982—to help pay for lower tax rates for wealthier Americans—were to blame. This was the refrain in Chicago, where the rate of 16.4, while slowly dropping, remained one-third higher than the national rate and one of the highest in the country. Puerto Rican activists saw their community's infant mortality rate of 18.4 as a top priority. Austerity made policy innovation that much more important, but the city's initiatives failed to make a dent due to debilitating disputes among Edwards, state health officials, Latino activists, and the mayor's aides. For example, Edwards engaged in a sustained and caustic exchange with state health officials over the Infant Mortality Reduction Initiative. In a series of letters, Edwards accused state director of public health Bernard Turnock of "a continued tendency toward intellectual dishonesty" in their dealings, making false allegations, and disrespecting the Chicago agency. Earlier in the year, Nena Torres of MACLA warned Edwards that the commission was "disturbed by [his] lack of trust" in them. Most observers concluded that a better administrator and communicator could have made a difference.[35]

Similarly, Edwards struggled to address AIDS, even after medical professionals had gotten a better grasp of a once largely misunderstood illness. Rather than demonstrate a sensitivity to a key political constituency, Edwards's initial avoidance of the issue—and then his subsequent ham-handed treatment of the city's response to the disease—were more consistent with the Reagan administration's culturally conservative response to AIDS awareness and gay rights more generally. Behind the scenes, Reagan's aides were divided on how to respond, but the president infamously did not utter the word "AIDS" until years into the crisis. For some, Edwards's slow response was that much more galling because Washington's first chief of staff—the respected but private Bill Ware—had died from complications from AIDS in 1984. AIDS was not even mentioned among city government priorities in health care in 1984, only changing two years later, as Edwards explained to the City Council Budget Committee. "The department is taking a leadership role," he said, "not only in Chicago but also nationally, in controlling the spread of AIDS through a comprehensive program of protection, surveillance, and health education. Chicago now has 500 cases of AIDS, far fewer than other large cities." Gay rights activists disagreed, charging that Edwards delayed urgent state and federal funding to the Howard Brown clinic, which provided AIDS services; was slow to hire AIDS researchers despite money to do so; and was remarkably insensitive overall to the needs of AIDS patients amid an epidemic. In his first press conference on AIDS, Edwards not only suggested that men mainly contracted the disease from female prostitutes, which was untrue, but also that AIDS patients might need to be quarantined. Edwards's handling of the issue, according to the Illinois Gay and Lesbian Task Force, "borders on criminal."[36]

Gay rights activists, predominantly from the key Lakefront wards on the North Side, eventually forced the mayor's hand—despite skepticism among some Black supporters. Even though Washington had offered vocal support for a gay rights ordinance in 1986, this did not provide much cover for his administration's AIDS response. The ordinance failed as many of his Black allies on the council "showed their independence" from the mayor and endorsed a Black church consensus that condemned the ordinance as unnecessary, if not immoral. Meanwhile, the *Chicago Defender*, representative of the city's Black establishment, stressed that the biggest health concern in the Black community was hypertension, not AIDS, and that spending priorities should reflect this. The gay and lesbian community responded to such recalcitrance with more organizing, including Ron Sable's aldermanic race in 1987 and the founding of the pro-ordinance coalition Town Meeting. Again, Washington recognized that maintaining his coalition to govern and win electorally was a balancing act—and that one of the paths to reelection was through those same North Side wards. Therefore, while Lonnie Edwards proved controversial on many issues, it ultimately was a months-long campaign by gay rights activists—from Town Meeting to the Chicago Area Republican Gay Organization to the mayor's own Commission on Gay and Lesbian Issues—that pushed Edwards to resign.[37]

**DESPITE SOME MISSTEPS,** the range of challenges Harold Washington faced and attempted to address made him a potent symbol and voice in a national Democratic Party eager to slow, even stop, the "Reagan Revolution." Halfway through his first term, President Reagan appeared highly vulnerable. Amid a harsh national recession, in which unemployment neared 11 percent and more businesses failed than at any time since the Great Depression, Republicans in 1982 lost twenty-six seats in the U.S. House of Representatives and faced considerable headwinds in moving their policy agenda forward before the president ran for reelection. The 1981 income tax cuts proved popular, but they came at a cost in terms of weakened domestic programs and a ballooning national debt. Add to that a strong public impression that the Reagan administration was both callous and somewhat incompetent in both domestic and foreign policies; the deaths of 241 Marines in a terrorist attack in Lebanon in 1983 and the administration's science fiction–esque Strategic Defense Initiative—deemed "Star Wars" by critics—did not change this impression. In the winter of 1983, Reagan's approval rating was stuck at 35 percent. By summer, poll numbers had risen somewhat but suggested that a clear majority still believed he did not deserve reelection. The telegenic Reagan was personally charming, but many of his policies were not. "Ronald Reagan must be the nicest president who ever destroyed a union, tried to cut school lunch milk rations from six to four ounces, and compelled families in need of public help to first dispose of household goods in excess of $1,000," stated one economist. Wrote Chicago's own Mike Royko, more caustically, "Reagan's approach will achieve one of the basic goals of the conservative: Things remain basically the same. The rich stay rich and the poor stay poor, or even a little poorer." The result was sharp polarization, with record numbers of Black, female, and gay and lesbian Americans— instrumental to Harold Washington's historic coalition victory—opposed to Reagan and his policies. Democrats saw an opening—that is, if they could heal their own wounds.[38]

To make history in the spring of 1983, Washington had put together a winning coalition that overcame initial opposition to his primary candidacy by two top Democratic presidential contenders. Both former vice president Walter Mondale and U.S. senator Ted Kennedy had endorsed the more conservative

Richard M. Daley and Jane Byrne, respectively, over the progressive Black congressman. Only liberal California senator Alan Cranston, a longshot candidate for president, embraced Washington during the primary. Mondale and Kennedy did come around for the general election, unlike many white Chicago Democrats, but African Americans had not forgotten the slight. Just weeks after Washington won, Black political leaders including Atlanta mayor Andrew Young, prominent Detroit congressman John Conyers Jr., and civil rights luminary Coretta Scott King gathered for the first of several meetings in Chicago to discuss the possibility of a serious Black candidate vying for the chance to challenge Reagan. Much more intimate and elite than the National Black Political Convention in 1972, the 1983 gatherings included up to forty key Black political figures to discuss the viability of a Black presidential candidacy and if it should be inside or outside of the party. This debate, which also animated the 1972 convention, had continued more than a decade later in the pages of *The Black Scholar* and other publications, even though every prominent elected Black politician, including mayors and the entire Congressional Black Caucus, was a Democrat.[39] Those gathering in Chicago decided that, yes, a Black candidate was desirable and should run for the party nomination, but they had no preference for whom.[40]

While rumors suggested runs by Young, former Atlanta mayor Maynard Jackson, or Gary mayor Richard Hatcher could be credible, it would be forty-three-year-old pastor and civil rights leader Jesse Jackson who answered the call. Jackson had flirted with political office before—most notably the 1971 Chicago mayoral race against Richard J. Daley—but he had never actually run; many Black Chicagoans, in fact, were still angry with him for not trying that year and for not following through at other moments of coalition-building. Jackson's political commitments had never matched his deep oratorical skills. But his calculus changed in 1983 after watching Harold Washington do what many believed was impossible in the Windy City. Blacks seek "a renegotiation of our relationship with the Democratic Party," Jackson declared that spring. After creating more organization than he was usually known for, Jackson announced in November 1983 that he would seek the party's presidential nomination. This was still a time when candidates could enter a few months—rather than two years—before the Iowa caucuses. National media outlets gave Jackson no chance, as he entered a crowded field led by party heavyweights Mondale, Colorado senator Gary Hart, and Ohio senator and former astronaut John Glenn. "Jesse Jackson . . . will not become president of the United States, or even gain the Democratic nomination," wrote venerable Black columnist William

Raspberry. "I understand that," but he still supported Jackson's run. To many others, however, Jackson was seen as a spoiler, influential enough to divide Democrats when they needed to unite.[41]

While never considered a presidential candidate himself, Washington became a sought-after endorsement in the 1984 campaign—both because he was the mayor of the nation's third-largest city and thanks to his role in galvanizing others to run. And the mayor tried to capitalize on this influence. Surprising Jackson, who had been an enthusiastic albeit at times problematic supporter of Washington, the mayor withheld his endorsement. "We do not have the political luxury to be in any campaign behind a Black candidate who can't win," Washington stated in a terse statement frequently quoted then and since. "The task at hand is defeating Ronald Reagan." Achieving this goal, of course, would have greatly improved Washington's ability to govern, but his position also reflected considerable posturing. A quick endorsement of Jackson would become fodder for his white political opponents locally, most of whom endorsed Mondale, considered the likely nominee. Jackson, depending on if he ran as the "Black candidate," could undermine Washington's "fairness for all" agenda at home. Instead, Washington gathered thirty-six favorite-son delegates in the Illinois primary in March to take to the convention that summer with the hopes of winning concessions from the eventual nominee. Other Black mayors, such as Philadelphia's Wilson Goode and Detroit's Coleman Young, made a similar calculation before endorsing the former vice president. However, Washington found himself in a peculiar position given the overlap between his own supporters and Jackson's. Lu Palmer, Conrad Worrill, and other nationalists embraced Jackson's run early on, but so did more mainstream supporters on the City Council, such as Danny Davis, Ed Smith, and Allan Streeter. Jackson's appeal to not just African Americans but to a "rainbow coalition" that prominently included national Latino leaders, such as Tony Bonilla of LULAC and the National Hispanic Leadership Conference, also complicated Washington's decision. Jackson's opposition to the Simpson-Mazzoli Act, which criminalized employing undocumented workers—in contrast to Mondale's support for it— won over Latinos such as Chuy García. The longer Washington waited to endorse, it seemed, the more consternation increased among his allies.[42]

A few other unforeseen things also happened on the way to San Francisco that foiled Washington's plans. One, Jackson performed far better than anyone, including Washington and even Jackson himself, had expected. Garnering more than 21 percent of all votes, Jackson won several primaries and caucuses, and not just in the Deep South where Blacks made up a sizable part of the Democratic electorate. Washington also was not able to secure a stronger jobs plank in exchange for his favorite-son delegates and ended up offering a last-minute endorsement of Jackson. Even the Council Wars, which continued to plague the administration and Chicago politics in 1984, followed Washington to San Francisco. Ed Vrdolyak, the mayor's nemesis, a prominent Mondale supporter, and part of the Illinois delegation, managed to bait the mayor multiple times at the convention, including sharp words between Washington, Black reporter Ed Bradley, and an off-camera Vrdolyak, all caught live on CBS. Bradley had tried to get both men on camera together to address their inability to work with each other, but the mayor would have none of it, calling Bradley's maneuver "an insult to common sense" and refusing to even acknowledge a smiling Vrdolyak. Media observers condemned everyone involved, including Washington for his "snit." Lastly, despite his historic victory the year before, Washington was not given a chance to address the delegates because of his refusal to endorse Mondale. Meanwhile, Jackson delivered one of the 1984 convention's most memorable speeches—so memorable, in fact, that he ran again, with an even better showing, four years later.[43]

Thus, the Chicago mayor who did so much to shape the Democratic primary by inspiring Jackson in the first place was left marginalized in the end, at least temporarily. To add insult to injury, Mondale—dry as toast, compared to Reagan—lost in a landslide, even in Illinois. As it always does, Chicago voted Democratic and brought along the party's candidate for Senate, Paul Simon. National Democrats, in fact, expanded their House majority, which became more liberal—another reminder that Reagan's personality was more popular than his policies. But even in the case of Simon's victory, local Democrats disagreed over who deserved the credit, Vrdolyak or the mayor. The Council Wars continued and reflected the racial landscape the mayor faced. An estimated 50,000 white voters split their tickets to reelect Reagan, while Black and Latino turnout failed to match that of the year before—unusual for a presidential year. Washington's aides were left wondering whether the city, and the administration, could survive four more years of the conservative economic orthodoxy that was sure to come. Would the conservatives in Washington, D.C., despite being from a different political party, continue to empower and embolden the white council majority? It turns out that the administration would not only survive but thrive in the next few years. But it would be Latinos, despite their early differences with the administration, who proved indispensable by helping put an end to the Council Wars, ushering in a genuine multiracial governing coalition in Chicago.[44]

## CHAPTER 8

# Latinos and a Governing Majority

How well Mayor Washington performs will determine whether coalition politics can begin to work in this country. I think he's very conscious of his role in giving meaning to that objective.—Tony Bonilla, LULAC, "Mayor Hires Few Women, Hispanics at Top," *Chicago Tribune*, December 4, 1983

L uis Gutiérrez flashed a broad smile to the more than 1,000 supporters crowded into the Humboldt Park Civic Center in late April 1986. After one of the wildest elections in Chicago history—which is saying something—the thirty-two-year-old aldermanic candidate and Harold Washington ally could afford to grin. He had just beaten the machine's handpicked candidate, Manny Torres, by more than 800 votes in a runoff in the Humboldt Park–based Twenty-Sixth Ward, home of the largest concentration of Puerto Ricans in the city. "We have shown that when you steal an election, righteous indignation will prevail," a beaming Gutiérrez declared, reminding the crowd that he should have won a month ago in the primary. "When we started this campaign, we said the basis was family, church and community and that if we could bring those forces together in this community then we would succeed. The election in the 26th Ward would mean the death of the regular Democratic Party."[1]

In a city known for hardball politics, the 1986 special aldermanic elections remain perhaps the hardest-fought, most memorable electoral battles in recent Chicago history. The seven contests, especially the one in the Twenty-Sixth, featured well-financed armies of precinct workers, a flurry of back-and-forth accusations, extensive legal intrigue, and even violence, both real and alleged. The two candidates, as one reporter described, also offered "a contrast in styles."

Gutiérrez, short, skinny, and a little excitable, literally sprinted across the ward, speaking to voters in both English and Spanish and making his case for reform and for Harold Washington's vision of the city. The stockier, bespectacled, and by most accounts dour Torres—a former weightlifter and a longtime machine precinct captain recently appointed to the county commission—spoke mostly in English, demonstrated less command of community issues, and woodenly defended traditional ward politics. The contest almost ended in March, when Gutiérrez appeared to win a bare majority of the votes against Torres and a write-in candidate. But after scores of votes for the third contender were "found" in an unsealed ballot box—and another reportedly found in the Humboldt Park lagoon—a judge ordered the runoff.[2]

The entire campaign, including the twelve-day runoff period, rivaled the mayoral contest from three years earlier in its nastiness. Early on, Torres accused his opponent of support for the radical Puerto Rican Armed Forces of National Liberation and claimed that he had been the target of an unexploded bomb in his campaign office, as well as a shooting. Neither claim was substantiated. Meanwhile, Gutiérrez accused Torres of insider trading, refusal to pay child support, and drug possession, not to mention trying to steal the first election; Torres sued him for libel. Known gang members played prominent roles in both campaigns. Mo Rivera, a Gutiérrez supporter, self-described "soldier" in Slim Coleman's Heart of Uptown Coalition, and cousin of Torres's campaign manager, called it "the ultimate campaign.... I don't care what side you were in ... that was the best fuckin' campaign ever run." As with other machine-backed Latino candidates, an undercurrent swirled around Torres's community bona fides, including whether he could speak Spanish. Torres could but admitted in an election eve debate, hosted by a Spanish-language TV station, that he preferred English and answered most questions accordingly. Observers viewed that choice as his undoing; he lost the runoff 53 to 47 percent.[3]

Normally, such a race might be entertaining, quintessentially Chicago, one of lore for old men to debate in taverns across the city—but certainly not capable of creating a seismic change in city politics or representative of something larger. What really could match Harold Washington's primary and general election victories from three years before? Apparently, the intense campaign that ensued to flip four redrawn wards and swing them in favor of the mayor and his multiracial vision for a different Chicago. Gutiérrez's victory, combined with three other wins by Black and Latino candidates that spring, evened council support between Washington and his political nemesis, Ed Vrdolyak, at twenty-five votes apiece. If the two sides held, which they largely did over the next year, then the mayor would be able to break a tie and the impasse over appointments

Washington and Jesús "Chuy" García march during the 1985 Mexican Independence Parade. García, who won an upset victory to become the Democratic committeeman from Little Village in 1984, succeeded friend and fellow activist Rudy Lozano as the mayor's closest Mexican American ally. He would go to become an alderman and a congressman. Washington was the first mayor to actively and consistently embrace the city's Latino voters. Harold Washington Archives and Collections, Mayoral Photographs, box 17, folder 3, Special Collections, Chicago Public Library.

and other policies he had proposed for three years. The city's first Black mayor actually would be able to govern consistently.

The special elections were only made possible by years of grassroots work by African American and Latino activists, along with some key white allies, to envision a different city and then take that vision to court after the 1980 Census. In *Ketchum v. City Council of Chicago*, a handful of Black and Latino plaintiffs challenged an aldermanic redistricting plan that reduced minority representation despite population shifts that should have produced the opposite. In late 1985, after much legal wrangling, federal judge Charles Norgle approved redrawn lines and ordered new elections in the seven wards—three with Black majorities, four with Latino majorities—to be held in March 1986. Long anticipating the decision, a record eighty-seven candidates threw their hats into the ring for alderman and committeeman, including Gutiérrez, fellow Washington allies Jesús "Chuy" García and Juan Velasquez, Black hopefuls Marlene Carter and Percy Giles, and several machine-aligned candidates, from Torres, Miguel Santiago, and Juan Soliz to white incumbents Frank Brady and Robert Kellam, whose districts were redrawn considerably. Over an abbreviated campaign season, the city's political forces concentrated on a small portion of the city, recognizing that a handful of races could put an end to the Council Wars and change the direction of the city, even the nation.[4]

Once again, it was a cross-class coalition of grassroots activists and campaign workers in the city's Latino communities that would make or break a Black mayor's attempt to reform city politics and policy—first in the aldermanic elections, and then in the run-up to the mayor's own reelection campaign a year later. It was the starkest reminder yet to Washington and his diverse group of aides—including those who really did not like this reality—that African Americans and Latinos relied on each other, often uneasily, to wield power in the city. Chicago proved to be a microcosm for progressive urban political coalitions across the country—both in its fragility and what could be accomplished if coalition partners listened to and trusted one another. For a brief moment, governance in the Windy City provided just such a model.

FROM THE DEBATES over council redistricting to the growing number of Latinos in city government to the infusion of Latino culture across the city, a marked population shift in the twenty years since federal immigration reform in 1965 had become noticeable in Chicago. Spanish-language media and businesses flourished, while Spanish could be heard as much as Polish in the city's streets and workplaces. Parades and festivals such as the Mexican Independence Day Parade along Eighteenth Street in Pilsen and the Puerto Rican People's Day Parade and Festival in Humboldt Park had become iconic community events. And Latino stars began showing up regularly on the rosters of the White Sox and Cubs. English-language press coverage also signaled the growing importance of Latinos in the city's iconic politics. The *Chicago Reporter*, a highly respected monthly published by the Community Renewal Society and historically focused on racial issues, ran an extensive series on Latinos in Chicago, taking care to discuss the distinctive experiences of Mexican Americans, Puerto Ricans, Cuban Americans, and Latinos of other nationalities. Other members of the press, including the *Tribune*, also made an effort to understand the city's burgeoning Latino presence, albeit less comprehensively. "By the turn of the century, Hispanics will be the Chicago area's largest minority group ... but Hispanics are not, like Blacks, a single race with a common past," observed the *Reporter*'s Jorge Casuso and Eduardo Camacho, somewhat inaccurately. "The differences that divide Mexicans, Puerto Ricans, Cubans and other Hispanics are likely to remain intact, frustrating those who envision a united

Hispanic community." These divisions remained an ongoing challenge for the administration.[5]

After the initial drama around the establishment of the Mayor's Advisory Commission on Latino Affairs in early 1984, the Washington administration signaled how important Latinos were to his electoral coalition during the next several years. And this went well beyond simply achieving a fair share of jobs and contracts, which the council's lone Latino before 1986, machine-aligned Miguel Santiago, tended to emphasize. Certainly Latino-friendly policies sometimes took the form of key appointments, and, after a slow start, Washington won praise on that front. But, to community groups, of equal importance over time were city actions on economic development, jobs, education, and policing, as well as more robust roles that traditionally poor, underrepresented neighborhoods like Pilsen, Humboldt Park, and West Town could play in that process. "The problem of unemployment affects the Mexican and the Black communities also," observed pastor Jorge Morales, cochair of the transition team's Neighborhoods Task Force. "Everybody knows that there are certain schools in this city that get more money," but Washington would have to change that, he said. The mayor and his allies also demonstrated a greater sensitivity to undocumented workers at a time when they were increasingly scapegoated amid lost industrial jobs and fewer resources for social services. This sensitivity included his embrace of the new sanctuary movement, the dropping of a citizenship question on city job applications, and even the city's symbolic and monetary support of Mexican families in the wake of Mexico City's devastating earthquake in 1985. Combined with his earlier congressional embrace of an invigorated Voting Rights Act and the *Ketchum* challenge to discriminatory redistricting, Washington's administration politically empowered Latinos in the city like no one before him.[6]

Reflecting his campaign's neighborhoods-first rhetoric, Washington laid out a vision of economic development that contrasted sharply with that of previous mayors and benefited previously neglected communities, especially Latino ones. Rather than concentrate solely on a handful of signature downtown projects—something Richard J. Daley perfected with projects such as the Sears Tower and the UIC campus—the new administration's Department of Economic Development sought to balance investment between the Loop and the city's seventy-seven officially recognized neighborhoods. To make this vision a reality, Washington drew on an array of existing neighborhood networks and tapped white UIC planning professor Robert Mier to run the department. In 1978, Mier had founded UIC's Center for Urban Economic Development, a think tank providing technical assistance and mentoring to community organizations; four years later, Mier and his students started the Community Workshop on Economic Development (CWED), initially to respond to enterprise zones, a free market–oriented tool for urban redevelopment championed by conservatives. The C in CWED quickly came to stand for Chicago, and the workshop morphed into a permanent neighborhood empowerment organization and early incubator for ideas and activists in the mayoral campaign.[7]

Described as an idealist and iconoclast, a "high theorist with dirty hands," Mier championed "equity planning," which among other things empowered community groups in the development process. He was skeptical of traditional development programs, such as the rabbit hole of frenetically chasing new tech and related industries; not only did they not pay for themselves, he argued, but they also largely ignored working-class communities of color, the people most devastated by the economic crises of the 1970s and 1980s. "Whatever this department does ought to be judged by the standard of creating jobs for Chicagoans who are in need of employment," particularly African Americans, Mier said in 1983. Instead of lavishing financial incentives on real estate development for outside companies, he emphasized the use of federal Community Development Block Grant funds to retain industry and support small businesses, especially those outside of the Loop, in creating jobs. To do this, Mier transformed the antiquated department he inherited through a thorough reorganization, new technology—he introduced computers, for instance—and, in 1984, in cooperation with a cross-administration subcabinet of planning officials, a comprehensive development blueprint, *Chicago Works Together: A Development Plan*. Two innovations from the plan stood out—the Local Industrial Retention Initiative and Planned Manufacturing Districts, both of which allowed communities to take the lead in planning job-creating industry in their areas but with the kind of support only the city could provide. This meant hiring activists to work for the city. For instance, Pilsen organizer Arturo Vasquez, an outspoken critic of the city's pursuit of the 1992 World's Fair, administered the latter program, building on relationships with dozens of community organizations across the city, including local housing and business groups. While the former celebrated this new approach, it made downtown business boosters nervous. As one developer interested in building in Englewood said, "You can't make it happen without dealing with the banks. And they really are not interested in the neighborhoods." Or at least not until activists cajoled them into taking a different kind of risk.[8]

The administration's attempt to shift its focus to investment in neighborhood jobs proved a mild success at best, cut short by the mayor's premature death, and did not significantly alter the larger trend of deindustrialization, federal budgetary retrenchment, or even the flow of city funds to downtown. Yet, Mier and fellow development official Kari Moe argued, "We achieved a lot of what we set out to do. This included substantial work with neighborhoods, most involving concrete projects: facilitating community-based development, helping smaller businesses, and encouraging housing construction and rehabilitation." Despite cuts of nearly 40 percent in federal development funds, the administration built more housing units than during Byrne's time and, by 1986, oversaw the creation of some 16,000 jobs through ninety different types of financial assistance packages. For instance, residents of Little Village, Pilsen, Chinatown, and other communities threatened by gentrification cautiously embraced city funds and planning when invited as equal partners on tourism projects.[9]

Even when a plant shuttered, such as the Hasbro/Playskool factory on the West Side, the administration proved surprisingly responsive to community pressure and acted in a novel way. In 1980, the company had received $1 million in industrial revenue bonds from the Byrne administration to buy new equipment after promising to create more jobs at its West Side plant. Instead, layoffs happened almost immediately and, in 1984, the company announced the plant's closure and move to Massachusetts. Eighty percent of the nearly 1,000 workers were Black and Latino, and 60 percent women, factors that some observers believed drove the company's decision. But after being pushed by community organizations through the West Side Jobs Retention Network, the administration sued the company and won a settlement that at least provided substantial funding for worker retraining and an emergency fund for laid-off employees. The Playskool example, concluded Robert Giloth, a scholar and development employee at the time, "has a moral for urban populism. Organizing cannot stop just because reformers get elected to office. . . . But open, sympathetic government may make such organizing less painful, and victories more probable." Whether Playskool could be considered a "landmark settlement," as Mier called it, is questionable, but at least workers received more than they would have otherwise. The city also instituted an early warning system, so employees had advanced knowledge of a plant closure. Neither of these changed the fact that workers were out of factory jobs that likely paid more than the service positions they took afterward. And the firms that took the space Playskool vacated did not hire many of those workers. Yet the city's efforts to challenge corporate decisions in court was a striking contrast to approaches by previous administrations in Chicago and other industrial cities.[10]

Other development achievements reflected Washington's decision not to abandon all earlier projects dear to the heart of downtown boosters—including improved professional sports facilities—but to do so, he risked disappointing the neighborhoods he championed. Jane Byrne left many unfinished plans, much of which Washington felt obligated to follow through on, such as the construction of a new central library—eventually named for him after his death—and the transformation of Navy Pier into an entertainment district. Both were delayed but eventually completed, if anything, to help convince developers that he still cared about downtown. These proved less controversial, in part because Mier insisted that projects be pursued through what he called "a civic culture of cooperation." Toward the end of Washington's administration, Mier used such an approach when the mayor proposed new stadiums for the Bears and White Sox and the installation of lights at iconic Wrigley Field, home of the Cubs. Washington told Mier matter-of-factly that if any pro team left the city—even if just to the western suburbs—a Black mayor would never be elected again. A double standard existed, of course: Richard J. Daley had been able to survive the departure of the National Football League's Cardinals to St. Louis in 1960. Thus, working with neighborhoods, the administration demonstrated that "development with participation is not only possible, but also better for the whole city," wrote Mier. "An enlightened Wrigleyville speaks legions." It is worth noting that, looking back, Mier routinely emphasized the carefully sought-after compromises with the Cubs and middle-class activists in the North Side's toney Wrigleyville and Lake View to modernize Wrigley Field rather than the harsher decision to raze the Black working-class community of South Armour Square on the South Side to build a new White Sox stadium. While the latter indeed prevented the Sox from relocating—a cause that had prompted its own grassroots campaign by a multiracial, largely working-class group of fans to "Save Our Sox"—the stadium plan came at a bitter cost for residents of that neighborhood.[11]

The decision that best illustrated this "balanced approach," however, was the choice not to pursue the 1992 World's Fair—a decision that delighted community activists of all stripes and infuriated downtown business interests who had invested heavily in bringing the fair back to its so-called ancestral home. In many ways, the battle over the 1992 World's Fair also crystallized how neighborhood grassroots activists, especially Latinos, shaped economic development during the Washington years and provided an alternative to the emphasis on "downtown monuments," as Mier called them. The idea of hosting another World's Fair had captured the imagination of some Chicagoans. The city had held two of the most successful and iconic fairs, including the 1893 World's Columbian Exposition, credited with putting the city on the cultural map, the construction of Jackson Park and the Midway Plaisance in Hyde Park, and the striking symbolism of the White City pavilion at the dawn of the Jim Crow era. As a result, the 1893 affair has been the most studied World's Fair and even the setting for a best-selling true-crime book. The 1933 fair, while less known, also had been credited as an important economic stimulus (and distraction) at the height of the Great Depression. But times had changed. The prestige of hosting a World's Fair, or similar events such as the Olympics, had diminished because of their high cost. The fair in Knoxville, Tennessee, in 1982, had barely broken even and left a remarkable excess of infrastructure behind; the most recent at the time, in New Orleans in 1984, literally went bankrupt, losing $107 million in mostly public money. None of this stopped downtown boosters, including the chief executives of some of Chicago's top companies, who believed in the city's ability to host such an event in grand fashion, given its history, not to mention the opportunity the fair offered to remake the Near South Side and produce jobs and further investment long after the fair ended. Even some Black business elites, including the Urban League's James Compton, believed the project could jump-start positive redevelopment in that long-neglected area. "It is inconceivable to me that a project of this magnitude . . . will not create jobs and job skills," Compton argued.[12]

As the plans emerged, however, a cross-section of activists expressed alarm about the amount of public development funds that would be diverted to the project, its physical impact on several immediate neighborhoods, and the overall lack of community input in the process. Fair boosters asked for almost $1 billion of public money—about a third of the city's entire five-year budget for capital improvements—which would have left the city hard-pressed to pursue any other projects, including those that neighborhoods had sought for years. Moreover, the World's Fair Corporation proposed locating the fair in the Near South Side, on the Lakefront, bordering the largely working-class communities of Bronzeville, Pilsen, and Chinatown; revisions to the plan included demolishing parts of those neighborhoods to build parking lots and other facilities to support the fair. In response, activists led by Pilsen organizers formed the multiracial 1992 World's Fair Committee to protest the fair; by 1984, the committee represented more than thirty organizations. Few issues garnered more attention from the Mayor's Advisory Commission on Latino Affairs (MACLA). Despite more than a year of research and formal hearings, many Latinos were left frustrated at what Miguel del Valle called "the cavalier manner in which the World's Fair Authority has dealt with Latino concerns," calling its answers to residents' questions routinely "evasive and misleading." Thus, in early 1985, the commission formally condemned the fair, showing unusual pan-Latino unity. Representing organizations from the Latino Institute to the West Side IPO to

Pilsen Neighbors, the commission argued that the fair "promises more than it will actually deliver, and in fact is likely to have a series of negative repercussions on the city's Latino community." The previous month, 300 members of Pilsen Neighbors unanimously voted against the fair. In their effort to block the proposal, activists even embraced one businessman's bold idea to move the fair to the cheaper, industrial north shore of Lake Calumet on the far South Side.[13]

The fair placed the mayor in a precarious position. He had criticized the idea as a candidate; as mayor he remained noncommittal, establishing an authority in 1983 to continue fair planning but also allowing city departments to explore the issue to exhaustion. Meanwhile, African Americans remained divided on the wisdom of the fair. "The neighborhoods don't count," scoffed Lu Palmer at the arguments of fair advocates. "It's the rich and powerful grabbing the land and it's typical of Chicago." Others more quietly complained that, despite promises, only white-owned firms had secured contracts while minority ones continued to wait. But Black activists sensed considerable pressure to mute their criticism of the mayor's acquiescence to avoid offering any unnecessary ammunition to Washington's political opponents. Privately calling his consideration of the fair "a sellout of the neighborhoods," many publicly argued he had "no choice" but to placate business elites.[14]

Ultimately, Mier and the Department of Economic Development made it clear that they agreed with MACLA and other activists that the fair did not reflect their approach to land use. Maybe the fair would create short-term jobs, in construction and services to host the fair, and an extensive infrastructure left behind could be repurposed. But was it worth spending millions of city, state, and federal dollars to raze all or part of several neighborhoods, displacing thousands, especially given the economic and social history of such fairs? Mier and his staff concluded the answer was no. The demise of the World's Fair proposal moved slowly, with the World's Fair Authority finally shuttering in 1986. By the end, there was little doubt that Latinos and a grassroots-informed approach to economic development had pushed city officials to act.[15]

THE GROWING immigration crisis offered Harold Washington a different set of challenges as well as more opportunities for Latinos to flex their political muscle. As politicians in the nation's capital fiercely debated the future of major immigration reform—a concept on which the new mayor had cast doubt as its punitive nature became apparent—Washington made Chicago one of the nation's first sanctuary cities, part of the burgeoning movement of the same name. Started by religious activists and pastors, most notably Quaker Jim Corbett in

Tucson, Arizona, in 1981, the movement drew on the Bible's many examples of accepting the stranger, including Jesus—"I was a stranger and you welcomed me," wrote Matthew—in an effort to protect immigrants fleeing the civil wars in Central America, wars that U.S. Cold War policy had exacerbated, especially under President Reagan. The administration contended that these migrants, most of whom were Guatemalans and Salvadorans, came to the United States for economic reasons rather than political ones and were thus ineligible for asylum. But religious leaders of many faiths, civil rights figures, and labor leaders across the nation increasingly viewed sanctuary as both moral and justified, comparing it to the Underground Railroad. Chicago had already emerged as a leader. Wellington Avenue United Church of Christ in Lake View, which former alderman Dick Simpson happened to attend, had become the second church in the country to provide such sanctuary; by 1985, this relatively small parish had offered a transitional home to thirteen refugees over three years.[16]

Ongoing raids and other actions by the federal Immigration and Naturalization Service (INS) propelled activists to lobby Harold Washington, who as a congressman had been one of the fiercest critics of the president's Central American policy. Even María Cerda, the mayor's Puerto Rican director of employment and training, and two other city staff members were harassed for "looking" Latino in a well-publicized incident downtown. While ensuring that the "public good is protected," Washington stated, "we draw the line . . . when the actions of any agency infringe on people's fundamental human rights," referring to racial profiling by INS agents. Thus, Washington announced, the city would not share citizenship information with the INS nor would it keep a citizenship question on city employment applications. The subject of debate more than a generation later, citizenship questions routinely "create a chilling effect" for Latinos, documented and undocumented alike, to the point of discouraging many from participating in a program, applying for a job, or filling out a survey, even the decennial census.[17]

The response to Washington's order was predictable, winning praise from immigrant rights groups and criticism from conservatives. "Enacting the executive order, the mayor renewed his pledge to abide by the law," wrote Carlos Arango of the Midwest Coalition in Defense of Immigrants. "We would like INS officers and agents to do the same." In contrast, the *Tribune* editorial page called for more cooperation between City Hall and federal agents and to "not let his feud with the administration currently occupying the White House get in the way of . . . a valuable service." Later in the year, the *Tribune* sympathetically covered INS raids of taxi stands to combat illegal medallion sales, which netted 129 arrests and left dozens of abandoned cabs at O'Hare and Midway airports. Most of the cabbies arrested, however, were Nigerian and at least half of them were in the country legally. Not one white cab driver was questioned. While the executive order was a start, activists and some of the mayor's aides pushed him to codify sanctuary with legislation, which did not happen until 2006. "The obvious political intention is, of course, to educate Chicagoans on the issues relating to Central America and give a message to federal law makers from Illinois and elsewhere," wrote the administration's immigrant and refugee liaison, Randy Pauley, adding that South Africans, Ethiopians, and Haitians could be included as well.[18]

All of this occurred amid the passage of the Immigration Reform and Control Act (IRCA) in 1986, a long-debated law that granted amnesty to nearly 3 million long-term noncitizen residents but also tightened criminal penalties for the hiring of undocumented workers. The mayor had testified before Congress against the law for its "discriminatory potential." But, as Chicago resident Frank De Avila described, IRCA "was an emotional relief" for the approximately 155,000 Chicagoans who were eligible for regularized status: "Not to have that worry anymore that at midnight they'll knock on your door and off you go." IRCA did make life that much more difficult for the remaining undocumented. After its passage, Washington aide Kari Moe expressed concern that the INS would "make an example of the City" and challenge "the Mayor's 'defiance' of INS and his 'violation of his oath of office' by issuance of" the sanctuary order. Ultimately, IRCA did not translate into the kinds of raids and federal retribution that Moe and others feared. But it did lead to long-term wage loss and, ironically, a greater concentration of Latinos in the city because the increasingly militarized border compelled families to stay together and even buy homes. In fact, Latinos were far less likely to face an immigration violation in the years after IRCA than they were to face a drug arrest as part of the stepped-up War on Drugs.[19]

In contrast, the administration's outreach to earthquake victims in Mexico City in the fall of 1985 received widespread praise from Latinos across the city. On the morning of September 19, an 8.0-magnitude earthquake rocked Mexico's capital region, killing at least 10,000 people and destroying the homes of more than 250,000. Chicagoans were among the first to respond, with city officials putting a call out for donations of clothing, food, medicine, and money immediately and organizing a telethon in which even the mayor took a turn manning the phones. Chicago turned out to be quicker than the U.S. government, which had waited for a formal request for assistance—something slow in coming because Mexican officials feared that U.S. demands on immigration policy would be attached to any aid. In the end, the Reagan administration made no such demand, but political calculations remained for Chicago's mayor. Observers viewed Washington's actions as "politics, but it's good politics because it's honest," said Arturo Vasquez. "To the extent you're looking at a reform mayor, serving areas not addressed before, you're seeing a mayor busily paying off campaign promises." Much of the aid was then delivered to the Mexican Red Cross through San Antonio, organized by Henry Cisneros, the first Latino mayor of a large U.S. city. Such efforts attracted some criticism, with one publisher of a Spanish-language daily in Chicago resorting to stereotypes and calling a donation drive in Pilsen "the most stupid, ridiculous thing. . . . There are a lot of crooks down there." Nevertheless, Mexican officials appreciated the work enough to invite Washington and a delegation from Chicago to tour the Cuauhtémoc district, where the worst devastation occurred, as part of a longer cultural and economic visit to the country. The mayor accepted, going to Mexico in the fall of 1986 as he ramped up his reelection campaign. As the mayor had hoped, Latino voters took note. "The support he gave the community was really phenomenal," recalled Linda Coronado, adding that it "created tremendous respect for the mayor."[20]

EVEN BEFORE a federal judge ordered new elections in seven wards, it had become clear that Latinos such as Chuy García could be important players in city politics. After Rudy Lozano's narrow loss in the race for Twenty-Second Ward alderman and then his sudden death in 1983, his longtime friend, political ally, and campaign manager decided to challenge Alderman Frank Stemberk to become the ward's Democratic Party committeeman the following year. "I did it in part to keep [Lozano's] memory alive," García said years later. "We thought getting elected was one of the most important statements we could make in terms of justice, politically and socially, for Rudy. It motivated me to run then, and it still does." While the alderman was the ward's public face, the committeeman—sometimes the same person—held the real power through patronage and, as a supposed behind-the-scenes party official, the ability to keep financial supporters hidden. In some cases, such as the Forty-Sixth Ward's Joseph Gill, who served fifty years until 1972, a committeeman held the position despite a revolving door of aldermen. Put another way, writes Luis Gutiérrez, the committeeman was "the tough guy who runs the neighborhood."[21]

While less boisterous than Lozano or Gutiérrez, García was well-positioned to carry his slain friend's mantle. At age twenty-eight, García was already a veteran activist himself, leading protests in Pilsen and at UIC since the 1970s, and had taken a crash course on electoral politics, Chicago-style, since the founding of the West Side's Independent Political Organization in 1981. He also had deep connections to the ward's Black precincts with longtime friend Ronnel Mustin as his campaign manager. Meanwhile, Harold Washington had never forgotten how García and his wife, Evelyn, saved him from choking at an IPO event when he was congressman, not to mention that García's contest was an important proxy battle in the larger Council Wars. Washington threw as many resources as he could into the race, hired García for a city job, and visited the ward's vote-rich Chicago Housing Authority complex just two days before the election. Despite widespread shenanigans by machine forces, including the rejection of some 3,000 Latinos trying to register, García won the race by fifty-nine votes, sweeping the ward's handful of Black precincts and holding his own among the middle-class Mexican American business and homeowners, who tended to back more conservative white Democrats. García immediately became a shadow alderman in the ward, providing services that Stemberk should have had but without discriminating against those who did not support him politically. "I just started acting like the alderman," García recalled. "I lived in the community, I spoke Spanish, I was out and about, I was visiting the block clubs, I was in the alleys doing the cleanups with the people. We were doing the whole thing. We were removing graffiti, so people became very comfortable." This set García up well to run for the special election in 1986.[22]

Two other progressive Latino activists ran for committeeman in 1984 with less successful results but demonstrated how demographic shifts enhanced the fluidity between community activism and city government and politics during the Washington years. In the predominantly Mexican American Twenty-Fifth Ward, Juan Velasquez, a high school dropout who joked that he had to stop wearing denim to run, challenged the dean of the machine, Vito Marzullo. Once a gang member who grew up in the neighborhood displaced by UIC, Velasquez had turned a critique of police brutality into full-fledged community organizing in the early 1970s, working with everyone from youth in Pilsen to farmworkers in Florida. After losing an aldermanic race against Marzullo in 1983, Velasquez landed a city job—in classic Chicago fashion—in the Streets and Sanitation Department despite little engineering experience. But he had a reputation for making people, including Latinos, work or face transfer. "I've had to move some people around," Velasquez said in 1984. "Over in the electricity bureau there's about 10 guys who don't do anything but sit around the main office. We call them the 'untouchables.' I plan to put these workers on the street.... Make them work, dammit." The following year, Velasquez ran for committeeman, challenging Marco Domico, who was a longtime precinct captain and Marzullo's intended successor. Despite the ward's majority–Mexican American population,

Velasquez came up short again—a testament to the alderman's wiliness and perhaps the depth of his Mob connections. Neither Velasquez nor anyone else would ever beat Marzullo or his favored candidates. Instead, Marzullo's home was drawn out of the ward in 1986—the only surefire way to beat him, the alderman pointed out angrily—forcing him to retire at age eighty-eight.[23]

Meanwhile, in the Thirty-Second Ward, which was transitioning from Polish to Puerto Rican, the underfunded Luis Gutiérrez of Wicker Park was swamped by his opponent, Dan Rostenkowski, who was both ward committeeman and one of the most powerful members of the U.S. Congress, as chair of the House Ways and Means Committee. Gutiérrez ran a spirited campaign, however, staying, as he put it, "the 15 rounds" against Rostenkowski despite virtually every one of his neighbors having the congressman's bright orange and blue campaign sign in their window. Gutiérrez also ran without any real resources from the mayor, who did not dare cross Rostenkowski, the number one source of federal funds to the city. "He outmanned us, he outspent us, he outpostered us," Gutiérrez said admiringly after winning 27 percent of the vote. "He's a pro." But Gutiérrez did win a handful of Puerto Rican precincts and was competitive in Black precincts. Moreover, Gutiérrez's audacity and persistence struck longtime political observers, who were not surprised when the former social worker and cabbie gambled and moved his family to a house near Humboldt Park to run for alderman in the newly redrawn Twenty-Sixth Ward in 1986. He knew that he could win a new largely Puerto Rican ward—especially with a dedicated worker base, newly registered voters, and Washington's resources and allies fully behind him—and, in the process, provide the mayor with another critical vote on the City Council.[24]

The grassroots-induced *Ketchum* decision that led to another remap was momentous because it successfully forced the city to make significant minority representation on the council possible. But the fact the decision could conceivably flip council control and provide Harold Washington a working majority grabbed the attention of political observers from Washington, D.C., to Los Angeles. While casting doubt on what it called Chicago's "old-fashioned politics," dependent on diminishing patronage, the *Washington Post* acknowledged that the mayor's claims to reform "will be put to the test if his candidates win." Seven wards were redrawn to become minority-majority, with three expected to stay in the hands of machine-aligned candidates: Robert Kellam in the Eighteenth, Miguel Santiago in the Thirty-First, and Juan Soliz in the Twenty-Fifth. Soliz, the one-time Latino hero of independents who first ran for the Illinois General Assembly in 1982, had since won a state legislative seat with the machine paying off his campaign debts. Soliz insisted he was still independent, but he remained critical of the mayor's policies affecting Latinos and receptive to Vrdolyak's entreaties, arguing that "we can't afford the luxury right now of shutting the door on anyone." Soliz's approach, reflecting the thinking of some middle-class Mexican Americans, proved victorious by combining one-third of the ward's Latinos with nearly all whites to succeed the retiring Vito Marzullo, who had once called Latinos in his ward "rats." Soliz's rival Juan Velasquez had the dubious distinction of losing races for alderman and committeeman, the latter to Marco Domico. In contrast, three other white machine incumbents named Frank—Brady, Damato, and Stemberk—saw their wards changed radically. Only Brady ended up running for reelection and, as predicted, fell to Marlene Carter, a Black secretary backed by Washington, although it took a runoff to prevail.[25]

Of the three races, Chuy García's effort to succeed Frank Stemberk showed best how both demographic change and grassroots work altered the ward's representation. After becoming committeeman, García projected a vision of community that included a reputation for efficient and reliable service without demanding a quid pro quo. This offered a sharp contrast to the operations of the machine, which smeared García in any way it could, even resorting to red-baiting—an increasingly weak tactic amid the Cold War's unexpected thaw by President Reagan and Soviet general secretary Mikhail Gorbachev in the mid-1980s. That winter, García's foes published a map asserting that his campaign financing relied not on mainstream labor and Latino community organizations but rather on the Soviets by way of Cuba. Others, like rival candidate August Sallas, viewed García's "confrontation politics" as phony, designed to create conflict. Still others resorted to anti-Black racism, trying to hold García's alliance with the mayor against him and making the age-old argument that Latinos and Blacks competed in a zero-sum game for limited resources. Plenty of Latinos and Blacks believed that, but García once again swept the ward's handful of Black precincts. Ultimately, what made the difference was what García called his "rootedness. . . . I was the most bilingual of the pack . . . and I was able to paint a picture of progress for the future," he recalled, adding, "I think people had become more comfortable with Harold Washington by the '86 election," defusing some of his opponents' racial arguments. That García quickly responded to potholes, broken streetlights, and unplowed snow mattered, too. Thus, all of these factors combined to make García's campaign a model of success for a progressive Latino and, along with Luis Gutiérrez's victory, placed a Black mayor on the cusp of a council majority.[26]

Gutiérrez's triumph in April reinforced the centrality of Latinos in Chicago's progressive political coalition, and, even more than García's race, foreshadowed the contours of the mayoral election campaign in 1987. Of course, specific issues

Washington and Luis Gutiérrez, a Puerto Rican activist turned politician, campaign in 1986. Gutiérrez's hard-fought victory gave Washington a narrow majority on the City Council for the first time. In 1993, Gutiérrez became the first Latino to represent Chicago in the U.S. Congress. Michelle V. Agins, Harold Washington Archives and Collections, Mayoral Photographs, box 28, folder 42, Special Collections, Chicago Public Library.

in the ward mattered, especially the candidates' authenticity as measured by their comfort with Spanish and other elements of Puerto Rican culture. Gang and police violence, affordable housing, illegal dumping, and basic city services and infrastructure remained important issues; access to city jobs, even with new limits on patronage, always mattered as well. Yet the race remained largely a battle of surrogates with the mayor and his more inclusive vision on one side and Ed Vrdolyak's narrower "business as usual" approach on the other. "The Machine crowd cannot tolerate a Hispanic, or any minority spokesman, who can inspire his people, yet is not for sale," wrote *Sun-Times* columnist Vernon Jarrett. "They shudder at the thought of Gutiérrez standing in the City Council." Gutiérrez recalled winning some voters over by simply evoking opposition to the outspoken Vrdolyak and not saying his own name. Moreover, both Jane Byrne and Richard M. Daley signaled their future campaigns by stumping for Manny Torres, while Gutiérrez enjoyed the full-fledged support of Washington and his allies, from the grassroots workers of Slim Coleman's Heart of Uptown Coalition to the diverse set of organizers in the West Side IPO. And there was always Gutiérrez's nervously energetic charisma to credit. All, in fact, contributed to a narrow, historic victory, with the promise of a new era in Chicago politics.[27]

Just days after the new council members were sworn in in early May, the shift in power was apparent. Twenty-five Washington appointments that had languished in the council, some as far back as 1983, were confirmed. For the most politically sensitive positions, such as the nomination of Black artist and educator Margaret Burroughs to the Chicago Park District, the vote was 26–25, with the mayor providing the tie-breaking vote. Burroughs, cofounder of the DuSable Museum of African American History, and her fellow nominee, Rebecca Sive-Tomashefsky of the Playboy Foundation, represented the votes to remove machine stalwart Ed Kelly as parks superintendent, which would free up a valuable patronage line to the mayor, not to mention a shift in parks and recreation resources to minority neighborhoods. Kelly was notorious for directing most funds and workers to white middle-class communities on the North and Northwest Sides. Two confirmed appointments to the Chicago Transit Authority provided a similar opportunity, offering Washington and his allies the chance to influence the powerful CTA and its more than 12,000 employees and $600 million budget a year before his reelection. Other appointees received more support, with as many as twelve council opponents switching sides to confirm certain nominees. Overall, appointees approved on that first day included some of the leading lights in the city's independent and civil rights movements going back decades, including Tim Black, Addie Wyatt, and Guadalupe Lozano. In the coming weeks, more of Washington's appointees would win confirmation. Of even greater importance, his council allies approved a reorganization of the body, abolishing nine committees, stripping chairmanships from the mayor's most vocal opponents, including Vrdolyak, establishing a new Budget Committee with ally Tim Evans as chair, and defanging Ed Burke by weakening the Finance Committee's power. A lawsuit brought by Vrdolyak, Burke, and others cast uncertainty over the reorganization process but only delayed the inevitable. For the first time since April 1983, Harold Washington had a clear path to enact his reform agenda.[28]

IN THE SUMMER AND FALL of 1986, politics in the city took on a different tenor. Progressive Democratic forces appeared increasingly poised to win back Congress that November, while an assured mayor pursued his reform agenda with a narrow but consistent majority in the City Council and solid, if not always enthusiastic, grassroots support. Fueled by federal deficits and the emergence of the Iran-Contra Affair, in which the Reagan administration had illegally traded arms for Iranian hostages and cash to supply Nicaragua's counterrevolutionaries, national Democrats hoped to stanch six years of electoral and budgetary bleeding. The proposed federal budget had become more draconian each year, especially in terms of urban spending for cities like Chicago. The 1987 federal budget, according to the Washington administration, cut 45 percent—or $277 million—of federal funds to the city; the 1988 budget proposed whacking 52 percent of annual funds to Chicago, even while the Pentagon's funding and deficits steadily rose and budget-balancing schemes designed to counteract such efforts took further aim at discretionary domestic spending. Less emphasized by the media but just as damaging was the loss of state funding under Republican governor Jim Thompson. According to the Urban Institute in 1987, "State reductions outdistanced federal ones in every human service field examined except housing and community development. And, in at least one field, social services, state reductions cancelled out a modest turnaround in federal spending."[29]

As a result of both, years after leaving the nation's capital, Harold Washington remained one of the most eloquent defenders of urban spending. "The effects could hardly be worse if we were attacked by a foreign enemy," the mayor told a congressional committee in 1986. "That is why it seems to us that . . . Ronald Reagan has declared war on the City of Chicago." If the cuts went through, "we would be left with essential services only. . . . Our development agencies— housing, economic development, and planning—would face elimination." Some rhetoric was exaggerated, especially since the administration could shift the blame for tough budgetary decisions to the Reagan administration even when federal reductions did not materialize. In fact, the administration made sure of it, with budget director Sharon Gist Gilliam's department producing polished, glossy reports on how devastating proposed federal spending reductions would be to the livelihood of the city and Washington's priorities.[30]

Ironically, federal cuts, at times, propelled the mayor's reform efforts. For instance, to make ends meet in 1986, Washington pursued changes to the property tax, which posed an immediate challenge to his fragile council majority. His machine critics immediately labeled the proposal, which actually set a more transparent tax rate for the first time in modern Chicago history, as unacceptable, even though the 3 percent rate was lower than the effective rates during Jane Byrne's time. To pass the reform, Washington needed every one of the twenty-five votes, and only prevailed when one of his white council supporters, Burton Natarus, very publicly and reluctantly cast the deciding vote in favor. "There are going to be many people who are sore at me," Natarus said glumly. The city even briefly provided him with a twenty-four-hour police guard. But while some, mostly white taxpayers, *were* angry with Natarus and the administration, the additional revenue averted more than 10,000 immediate layoffs of city workers and kept funds flowing into the neighborhoods in unprecedented ways, especially after the administration let the World's Fair proposal wither and die. Grassroots initiatives around the city, from the collaborative antigang Crisis Intervention Network to the affordable housing work of the Bickerdike Redevelopment Corporation in West Town, enjoyed stable financial support from the city. In a rarity, each ward received roughly the same amount of resources for improvements such as streetlights, sidewalks, and trash cans, rather than a distribution sharply skewed by politics, race, and class.[31]

To underscore the change in power, once-controversial ordinances on tenants' rights, public ethics, and cab medallions received near unanimous backing. Long sought by tenants' rights activists, including Alderman David Orr, a one-time history professor, cofounder of the Rogers Park Tenants Committee, and one of the mayor's steadiest white supporters, a sweeping tenants ordinance won forty-two out of fifty council votes. Called a "breakthrough" by a city coalition of rights groups, the ordinance allowed tenants to deduct from the rent the cost of repairs made to their unit or even the cost of substitute housing. And while tenants were often confused about their rights, it remained an important tool to improve rental housing in the city. Alderman Danny Davis called it the "most progressive piece of legislation ever passed by the City Council." And the council did not stop there, unanimously passing two other Washington priorities: a tough new ethics ordinance cracking down on nepotism and requiring financial disclosures, as well as a far-reaching package reforming the city's lightly regulated, monopolistic taxi industry (including mandatory classes on politeness and city geography). Not coincidentally, the council approved both reforms in the weeks before the February 1987 primary, when voters arguably paid the closest attention.[32]

**INDEED,** this was Chicago and reelection was never that far away from officials' thinking, including the mayor's. This was especially true given the many machinations of Washington's rivals, much of them rooted in crass racial politics. Similar to her first campaign declaration against Michael Bilandic, Jane Byrne made her intentions to reclaim her old job known nearly two years before the election, in the spring of 1985, with the hopes of clearing the field. Analysts largely agreed that Washington had won the Democratic primary in 1983 only by successfully dominating the Black vote and splitting those of whites and Latinos between Daley and Byrne. This time, she hoped to be the only white candidate, forcing Democratic voters to choose between her and the Black mayor. "She's making anyone else" who considers taking on Washington "a spoiler," pointed out one of her advisers. "By going early, she's got a much better chance of getting Washington in a one-on-one." One-time Byrne allies like Ed Vrdolyak, recognized the wisdom of this strategy too and attempted to nudge her out of the way with the promise of a cushy party job and help retiring campaign debts. It was the kind of deal that worked for Alderman Juan Soliz, but Byrne rejected it and the subtle sexism it suggested.[33]

Meanwhile, allies of Cook County state's attorney Richard M. Daley read the same analysis and turned to a sneakier and, they hoped, more permanent scheme. They gathered thousands of signatures—many of them forged—to a petition calling for a nonpartisan mayoral race, with a runoff between the top two candidates if neither won more than 50 percent. The proposal was attractive in several ways. On its face, it was the kind of good-government reform pursued by independents for decades because it appeared to strip party politics out of the election. The proposal, however, was far more personal, because it denied Washington the benefit of running as the party's nominee, which many believed made the difference in the general election in 1983. Much like Byrne's calculus, Daley backers believed Washington could not beat a single prominent white candidate such as the state's attorney in a head-to-head race. Many of the mayor's own aides had similar worries and encouraged him to consider an independent run in the general election, presumably against not one, but two white nominees of both major parties. Republican governor Jim Thompson even floated the idea of a "unity" candidacy—white unity, that is—of someone like Congressman Dan Rostenkowski to run in a general election. And as late as November 1986, it appeared that the more partisan ploy might work, only to have the city elections board reverse an earlier decision on related referenda, passed by the new council majority, and set traditional party primaries for city offices. Unable to persuade Byrne to leave the race, Daley stayed on the sidelines, while Vrdolyak and Cook County assessor Thomas Hynes announced runs in the general election under third-party banners. In December, the mayor, a life-long Democrat, said he had never intended to run as anything else and filed to be the party's nominee. Byrne would get her one-on-one contest.[34]

Overall, the 1987 mayoral campaign has received far less attention from scholars and journalists, and for some understandable reasons.[35] As narratives go, it was neither the "first" of anything nor the emotional "David and Goliath" story that 1983 has often been portrayed as. Washington, running as an incumbent, had far more resources at his disposal—upward of $3 million for the primary alone, from not just a relative handful of African American business leaders but a wider range of corporate and union donors. As an incumbent, Washington had far more control of city agencies and the traditional sources of patronage, even if both were less than previous mayors had enjoyed and even if he had only won this power after the special elections in the spring of 1986. Prominent unions such as those representing the building trades and firefighters withheld their support, as did the Cook County Democratic Party itself, in an unprecedented move for an incumbent. But the Chicago Federation of Labor, representing an array of individual unions, backed the mayor and made up for some of the lost party workers at the precinct level; they included members of locals in the steel, garment, and auto industries, as well as the Teamsters, the Chicago Teachers Union, and those organizations representing Chicago Transit Authority workers, the latter of which were predominantly African American. Church support was similarly more robust four years later, with even conservative Black religious icons such as the Reverend J. H. Jackson, longtime nemesis of civil disobedience and the work of Dr. Martin Luther King Jr., endorsing Washington. Moreover, the widespread belief that Black Chicago could not beat the machine and win the mayoralty, a perception that had been prevalent until 1983, had weakened considerably. They were confident that Washington could win again.[36]

African Americans remained Washington's political base and he needed them to show up in their communities and at the polls, but the social movement effect that so many observers described during the 1983 campaign did not repeat itself. For one, a "movement" seemed unnecessary because of the many more resources Washington had. But, more important, Chicagoans' willingness to see the reelection effort as a movement also was unlikely. In the weeks and months before the 1987 election, African Americans and their progressive white and Latino allies remained solidly behind the mayor, but many of them were disappointed by what Washington had not accomplished. The grand majority viewed that as the fault of his racist opposition, Ed Vrdolyak and the rest of the council's "twenty-nine." But it also reflected what many progressive Americans encountered a generation later when another Chicagoan, Barack Obama, ran for reelection in 2012. The euphoria around what could be, the possibilities of something that had never happened, was missing in 1987; instead, it was a more sober defense of a solid record as mayor and tempered hope that it could be built upon. While Melvin Holli and Paul Green described Washington's reelection effort—actually his entire first term—as "bashing Chicago traditions," because it eschewed traditional machine politics, in some ways the campaign reflected previous ones by Byrne, Michael Bilandic, and even Richard J. Daley.[37] The diverse faces of the campaign may have been different, but some of its promises and certainly its approach to power were similar. And this, in and of itself, made the 1987 campaign more striking than most historians allow— its relative normalcy suggested a certain durability for the progressive urban coalition Harold Washington had put together, and for its replication in other cities and perhaps the nation. That perceived stability would be tested before 1987 ended, but for the third straight mayoral election, a multiracial coalition fueled by key grassroots activism, won an urban election in Reagan's America.

JANE BYRNE wasted little time. In July 1985, the former mayor announced her candidacy in front of the padlocked gates of Navy Pier, a symbol of what she called a lack of civic cooperation and a failed economic development policy that abandoned the downtown projects she, and every other modern mayor, had championed. Once home to, among other things, the offices of the city's notorious subversive unit, the Red Squad, this conspicuous pier jutting into Lake Michigan had been eyed as a rich target for redevelopment and the tourist attraction it is now known to be. Under Robert Mier's Department of Economic Development, however, plans for Navy Pier stalled—something Byrne promised to kickstart with festivals like the ChicagoFest that she widely touted and that were once held there. As one economic development aide wrote to Mier, "She is creating a myth through her campaign that says that Chicago used to be fun and it used to be safe; now it is unsafe and no fun."[38]

Indeed, in keeping with larger political trends in the 1980s, Byrne settled on marrying the two issues, hammering Washington on crime and overall quality of life in the city, all through a racialized lens. Drug-related gang crime had intensified in the mid-1980s as crack cocaine had started to flow into Chicago and every other major city in the country. Chicago's reported crime, including murders, had ticked up in 1986. As a larger trend, the raw number of murders had declined from the 1970s—666 in 1986 in contrast to an average of 816 in Byrne's time as mayor, although the murder rate had crept up from 28.7 to 32.9 per 100,000 people by 1990 as Chicago's population continued to decline. Both experts and activists found the police under Washington and superintendent Fred Rice to be more cooperative with the communities they patrolled, but crime numbers were still remarkably high and everyone seemed to have a story. African Americans and Latinos were disproportionately the victims of crime, and the tough-on-crime policies that often led to mass incarceration had been accepted, albeit often reluctantly, by most Black public officials, including Washington. Yet Byrne ran a series of commercials designed to sow panic among whites, and to a lesser extent Latinos, that they would be the next victim. One commercial spelled Chicago in what looked like white powder cocaine; others used stereotypical images of Washington as the "angry black man" and blamed him for racial divisiveness in the city—an effort both the press and Washington supporters decried. A couple of high-profile Washington backers, Alderman Dorothy Tillman and Judge Eugene Pincham, got into their own trouble when making more direct racial appeals. Pincham's warning that "any man south of Madison Street . . . who doesn't cast a vote for Harold Washington ought to be hung" was particularly appalling given the lynching imagery. Although he counted on a solid Black vote to win, as the incumbent, Washington distanced himself, trying his best to stay above the fray and make a deliberate appeal to all Chicagoans.[39]

Learning from both 1983 and 1986, the two campaigns recognized how sustained outreach in Latino communities translated into votes, but each approached these complex constituencies differently. Unemployed since leaving City Hall, Byrne showed up at every Latino festival, parade, and event she could across the city, and was the butt of more than a few jokes for taking Spanish lessons and haltingly asking Latinos for their vote in her new second language; she even practiced her Spanish in a series of local television commercials for Chi Chi's Mexican restaurants. Her efforts could be dismissed as token, symbolic ones, which in many ways they were, and she was sometimes hard-pressed to make clear distinctions between Mexican American, Puerto Rican, and other Latino experiences. But many still gave this Irish American pol credit for "trying," whether it was speaking Spanish or attending a community baptism, while they perceived that African Americans had done much better than Latinos under Washington. Underscoring that charge, admitted Washington ally Miguel del Valle, was "racism in the Hispanic community. . . . At times there is competition for resources between Blacks and Hispanics." As a result, some polls suggested that Byrne had made significant inroads, with about one-half of Latino voters leaning toward her candidacy as late as January 1987.[40]

While Byrne's efforts contrasted with Washington's, especially in how much more substantive his were, the mayor's aides also saw a primary victory going through Pilsen, Little Village, and Humboldt Park. It was particularly important in a head-to-head race that Washington receive the appropriate credit for Latinos' political gains the last four years. Prodded by the community, the administration had doled out more jobs, contracts, and federal block-grant funding to Latinos than any Chicago administration before it; Latinos were still underrepresented in city government, but they had made significant strides.

The mayor also had more high-profile surrogates, both elected and appointed. Officials such as aldermen Chuy García and Luis Gutiérrez, department head María Cerda, school board member and MACLA chair Linda Coronado, and state senator Miguel del Valle—the first Latino to serve in the Illinois Senate— were integral to the administration's strategic outreach in Latino communities because they showed tangible evidence of Latino gains, in terms of elections and policy. Emphasizing this message, Washington achieved another first by endorsing Puerto Rican lawyer, activist, and planning commissioner Gloria Chevere for clerk against the white machine incumbent, Walter Kozubowski. "She adds luster and dignity to my ticket," Washington said simply. But what made the decision so bold—and controversial among some Black supporters— was that Washington tapped Chevere over Bill Walls, a former Black aide to Washington who had the backing of Lu Palmer and other prominent African Americans. In her bid to be the first Latino nominated to citywide office, Chevere faced an uphill battle against Kozubowski, a mild-mannered, competent, two-term incumbent and machine ally of council stalwart Ed Burke. But the strategy was unmistakable in both its symbolism and ability to drive voter turnout. Achy Obejas, one of the few Latino campaign staffers, suggested that Washington concentrate on Puerto Ricans, especially through Black radio, because of Chevere's historic candidacy and the fact that they had a historically higher turnout rate as U.S. citizens compared to other Latinos. Indeed, about 70 percent of Latinos, disproportionately Puerto Rican, showed up during the primary because of her candidacy. "While she needs the mayor's support," wrote Obejas, "we can also use her to appeal to Hispanics, notably Hispanic women. We should be taking special account of this after the Byrne women flap," when Byrne falsely claimed that women of color primarily supported her. Along with Washington's reliability on sanctuary, humane immigration, and bread-and-butter labor issues, the campaign believed it could neutralize, even win a clear majority of Latino voters against Byrne, despite her overtures and lasting popularity among some of them.[41]

The 1987 campaign's rainbow approach, even more than in 1983, remained one of its most striking characteristics. Washington and his aides had no delusions that he could win a majority of white voters, but he did believe he could do better than the 12 percent support he received from whites against Bernard Epton in 1983. The five so-called Lakefront liberal wards on the North Side, where a disproportionate number of gay men, lesbians, and Jewish people lived, largely embraced the mayor's focus on reform. The mayor's Committee on Gay and Lesbian Issues emerged as a real advocate and forum for gay leaders to challenge discriminatory policies. A gay rights ordinance barring discrimination

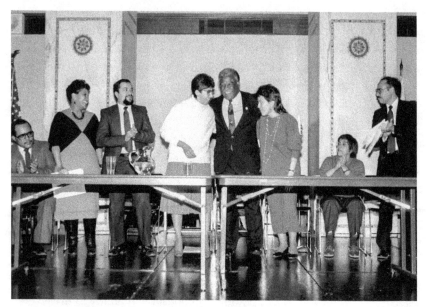

Linda Coronado, *left*, and Nena Torres flank Washington at a meeting of the Mayor's Advisory Commission on Latino Affairs. Although it took well into 1984 for the mayor to establish it, the commission was the first of its kind in the city and signaled a real commitment to this part of Washington's coalition, not to mention demographic changes in the city and nation. Latino voters largely paid him back in his 1987 reelection. Peter J. Schulz, Harold Washington Archives and Collections, Mayoral Photographs, box 48, folder 10, Special Collections, Chicago Public Library.

over sexual orientation only passed under his successor, in part because, while Washington "was committed in principle" to gay rights, "he was not going to sacrifice a whole lot," recalled Obejas, a Cuban journalist who also served as a campaign liaison to gay and lesbian activists. After the ordinance failed in 1986 by a wide margin in the council, Obejas recalled that Washington distanced himself, arguing, "It wasn't my ordinance." Part of this may have stemmed from unsubstantiated rumors—routinely spread by Washington's foes—about his own sexual orientation. He also considered other "kitchen table" issues to be more important. And yet his rhetorical support and mayor's committee did provide crucial groundwork for the eventual law. Combined with the end of police raids of gay bars and the creation of a department liaison to the community, Washington was certainly the most gay-friendly mayor of Chicago to date—albeit far surpassed by his counterparts in cities across the nation.[42]

Other groups also played a central role in campaign strategy. For instance, women of all colors remained Washington's most loyal constituency. An array of women's groups became active, from the local NOW chapter to the reconvened Chicago Women's Network, chaired by Addie Wyatt and considered by its members to be the "catalyst which helped to turn the [1983] campaign around and pick up momentum." The network also deftly countered Byrne's claims that she had substantial support from Black and Latino women. In fact, Black women were Harold Washington's most reliable supporters and for an array of reasons. The administration's focus on a "fair share agenda," as Slim Coleman called it, from women's health and jobs for low-income people to a fair distribution of services—none of which Byrne emphasized during her mayoral term—gave Washington an edge. "Many women voted for Jane Byrne [in 1979] because she was a woman," Wyatt said before the election, "but I think most feminists will give their vote to the mayor who did the most for them, and that was Harold Washington." The existence of the group Women Embarrassed by Byrne underscored this distinction. Moreover, Washington garnered formal support from Assyrians, Asian Americans (who were predominantly Korean and Filipino), and other ethnic immigrant groups, who benefited from the city's willingness to accept refugees and its attention to housing, crime, and the general welfare of such "port of entry" neighborhoods where new immigrants in the city lived. There were exceptions, of course, particularly among Asian Americans, who believed the administration largely ignored them in favor of Black and Latino interests. As for white ethnics in the Southwest and Northwest Sides, Washington remained a difficult sell, despite his remarkable patience with them. Some activists, such as Jane Mayer of Save Our Neighborhoods, a coalition founded shortly after his election to "defend" white communities, were pleasantly surprised by the administration's openness, the ease of working with Mier's Department of Economic Development, and even the mayor's embrace of a home-equity insurance program—which many offended Blacks rightfully called "insurance against Black folks." In fact, polling showed that a near majority of whites on the Northwest Side deemed the mayor's job performance either good or excellent. And yet, Mayer did not campaign for Washington—and most whites ultimately did not pull the lever for him.[43]

Despite some handwringing by his advisers and the general intrigue reported by the press, Washington's renomination was not in doubt in the last months of the campaign, with polls consistently showing him comfortably ahead of Byrne. Only once, in October 1986, when it appeared that the election might become a nonpartisan affair focused on rising property taxes, did polls show a statistical tie. But after that, the mayor held a steady 53 percent of the likely vote, which turned out to be his total in the primary. Voter turnout dipped from four years before, but the mayor repeated his sweep of Black wards and precincts and improved on his numbers among whites and Latinos, winning about 15 percent of white votes, especially in the Lakefront wards on the North Side, and 45 percent of Latinos (including more than 60 percent of Puerto Ricans). Byrne needed to win a clear majority of Latinos but instead squeaked by with just a 48 percent plurality; Chevere lost her bid for clerk but had boosted turnout, as predicted, in a way that helped Washington. Again, it took a multiracial coalition to win.[44]

Unlike in 1983, when Washington supporters could point to a handful of key moments—the debates, the UIC rally, and Vrdolyak's impassioned plea for white racial loyalty—that transformed the dynamics of the contest, Byrne never found such a moment. Knowing its importance four years before, Washington managed to avoid a one-on-one debate with Byrne. The beneficiary of paralyzing snow as a challenger eight years before, Byrne almost capitalized on weather again two weeks before the election. But unlike the incompetence of the Bilandic administration in 1979, John Halpin, Washington's veteran commissioner of streets and sanitation, had city crews working through the night to clear Lake Shore Drive from layers of lake-effect ice. Images of cars moving with ease on their morning commute punctured any hope Byrne had of lightning striking twice. Crime, taxes, and the continued woes at the Chicago Housing Authority, the latter barely mentioned during the campaign, did not galvanize enough voters to beat Washington, it turned out. In the end, she made a competent but uninspired run against a tireless campaigner with a broader, more diverse base of support and far more accomplishments than she had had during her four years as mayor. The city's major papers endorsed Washington, and it was the *Tribune* that may have summed up best the challenge Byrne ultimately could not overcome: "Though it is not easy to assess Mr. Washington's record as mayor, the same cannot be said of Jane Byrne. She was terrible. And although she cannot seem to remember all the terrible things she said and did, we can."[45]

UNLIKE FOUR YEARS EARLIER, Washington was not surprised by a competitive general election. Ed Vrdolyak and Thomas Hynes, along with Republican Don Haider, all former Democrats who had skipped the primary to take on the mayor in the general, tried to don the mantle of reform. While Haider, a professor at Northwestern University's Kellogg School of Business, could make a reasonable claim to be seeking reform, it was the wrong kind for most Chicagoans—lower taxes in exchange for privatized city services and fewer public jobs, all pitched in an earnest manner. Cook County assessor Hynes, who had been Byrne's budget director, a longtime ally of Richard M. Daley, and defender of disproportionate tax assessments of poor, mostly Black-owned property, struggled at times to explain why he was running, appearing unsure of himself during the candidates' one debate, and eventually dropping out of the race just two days before the general election. His campaign's most interesting—but ultimately unproductive—moment was his suggestion that Vrdolyak had Mob connections, a persistent but unsubstantiated assertion made for years.[46]

That left Vrdolyak, the one-time party chairman, to provide the most significant opposition under the Solidarity Party banner. Vrdolyak, of Croatian descent, started the campaign being chastised by a Polish man for sullying the name of the 1980s Polish freedom movement against Soviet domination. Washington's council nemesis went on to assail the mayor on all the issues Byrne had, but with a more theatrical, racially menacing tone. "Chicago is losing the war on crime because Harold Washington is more interested in registering criminals to vote than in arresting them," stated one of Vrdolyak's campaign fliers. Of course, in the alderman's framing, the criminals were always Black, as were the villains in Chicago's failing schools. It was the taxpayer versus the freeloader. To the alderman, the brother of two police officers, increasing police presence everywhere was the answer. To try and blunt criticism of his racial dog whistles, as well as peel off Black and Latino votes, Vrdolyak ran alongside two little-known candidates, African American John Thomas and Latino Alfred Sanchez, for city clerk and treasurer on the Solidarity ticket.[47]

While he expected Vrdolyak's more naked appeals to racism, Washington still remained saddened, even embittered by the tone. "He loved life," recalled Helen Shiller, "but he was very discouraged by the racism of that campaign." Yet, despite his opponents' attempts to polarize, the mayor managed to run a unity campaign of sorts in March and April of 1987. He collected endorsements from a series of Democratic presidential candidates, such as Senator Ted Kennedy of Massachusetts and Congressman Dick Gephardt of Missouri, as well as a handful of once-machine loyal aldermen, Bernard Hansen and Eugene Schulter. Jane Byrne gave a surprisingly robust endorsement of Washington in March for the "sake of unity," she said. "Having been a mayor of Chicago, I know that without it, it is difficult to govern." The mayor's campaign staff took no chances, however, continuing to raise money, combing CHA high-rises and other buildings across the city for voters, and registering people by the thousands at city facilities newly empowered to provide the service. While long-time aide Jacky Grimshaw organized volunteers, newly hired David Axelrod, who had traded in his reporter's notebook for political consulting, put together television and radio spots to highlight the mayor's accomplishments. Activists who were not already part of the administration or in an elective office, such as Conrad Worrill, Addie Wyatt, and Slim Coleman, continued to play important roles in galvanizing the grassroots. As Bob Starks of the Task Force for Black Empowerment stated at the time, "All of the people understand that, compared to four years ago, the spirit is not there. You need the formal campaign, but you also need a grass-roots campaign of street action. We need people who will not just come out to the polls but will bring someone else with them." Nevertheless, most objective observers concluded that the 1987 campaign, while perhaps more sanitized, even dull, had been more efficient.[48]

On April 7, the campaign strategy demonstrated its efficacy. A multiracial coalition, rooted in a unified Black community and partnered with a significant number of whites and a majority of Latinos, both Mexican American and Puerto Rican, made for a progressive engine during the so-called Age of Reagan. Not as many folks turned out, as activists such as Bob Starks feared, nor did the mayor consolidate many additional white votes; in fact, he received less white support, including in the Lakefront wards, than he had in the primary against Byrne. To the disappointment of the mayor and his aides, he gained just 13,000 additional votes in total between the primary and general elections, barely topping 600,000 and beating Vrdolyak 53.8 to 42 percent—despite job-approval numbers in the mid-60s. He carried twenty-seven out of the fifty wards, flipping only the Twenty-Fifth Ward and its Mexican American majority. Indeed, the vote difference in the general came almost exclusively from Latinos, who chose him more than three to one over his general election opponents. While it was not the mandate he had hoped for, it remained a comfortable win. Demonstrating an animation that often had been missing from the campaign itself, Washington on election night led a crowd of thousands at Navy Pier in an off-key rendition of "Chicago, Chicago, That Toddlin' Town." And Washington did not have just his own win to celebrate; his coalition solidified its hold on the City Council with at least twenty-seven allies, adding activist and publisher Helen Shiller from Uptown's Forty-Sixth Ward and attorney Raymond Figueroa in the Humboldt Park–based Thirty-First. With former neighborhood activists such as Shiller on the council, a progressive agenda on schools, neighborhoods, taxes, and development could really take shape. Little did Washington or his allies know that they would have only seven months to enjoy this new governing majority.[49]

## CHAPTER 9

# The Fragility of Coalitions

There really wasn't a Black-Latino coalition. There wasn't.
There was a Black, progressive-Latino, progressive-white
coalition. We ended up butting up with parts of the Black
coalition—they're a coalition, too. They're not monolithic.
—Nena Torres interview

In December 1987, just days after Harold Washington died from a massive heart attack and tens of thousands of mourners patiently waited outside City Hall to pay their respects, many of them had returned to the same place. But this time a different emotion and mood dominated. Sorrow had given way to angry disbelief. "We're making sure we have no deals behind no closed doors so that the dream of Harold Washington stays alive," one protester told a reporter. A week after the mayor had collapsed at his desk, agents of the Democratic machine had begun to push their way back into power. In the back rooms of City Hall, including at least one supply closet, the very same white men who had tried to thwart the mayor's agenda at every turn were close to winning enough votes to install Eugene Sawyer as the acting mayor. While dean of the Black aldermen, serving the Sixth Ward since 1971, Sawyer had been a machine loyalist until Washington's second mayoral run and was about the opposite in terms of personality and leadership skills. A seemingly disengaged, almost timid Sawyer, who had been nicknamed "Mumbles" by his detractors, could barely speak up for himself as he equivocated amid yelling and finger-pointing by Ed Burke and others. He did not want to be mayor? Too bad, Burke screamed at him.[1]

Meanwhile, upward of 6,000 people milled outside the building, with hundreds more inside, chanting, "Up with reform, down with the machine" and "Sawyer's in a Cadillac, looking like a Vrdolyak." Although condemned as a "mob" and a "bunch of creeps" by the mainstream press, those supporters of the Washington coalition and agenda who took to the streets sensed that the fix was in. They had shown up nominally in support of Tim Evans, Washington's floor leader on the council and another contender for mayor, but more than anything, they wanted the vision that had been affirmed in 1986 and 1987 to survive. They sought to maintain the grassroots, multiracial, neighborhood-based coalition that had made at least some headway in changing how the city was governed, despite so many obstacles. Sawyer may have been a decent enough man and the first Black committeeman to endorse Washington in 1983, but, they argued, he was not strong enough to defend Washington's achievements against the machine. Ultimately, he was the white man's choice. That was at least the calculation by Burke and his allies. Finally, at 4 a.m., after persuading the reluctant Sawyer to serve if chosen, the council voted 29 to 21 to install him as the next mayor, to serve until a special election in the spring of 1989. The multiracial Washington coalition, while relatively intact outside, fractured inside, with six African Americans joining most of the white aldermen—but no Latinos—in choosing Sawyer. The city had a new mayor.[2]

The selection of Eugene Sawyer has routinely become the narrative book-end to the Washington era. The in-fighting that followed within Washington's coalition, and the ability by machine forces—who viewed Richard M. Daley as the most obvious long-term successor—to exploit those differences, were able to hobble Sawyer's leadership. Well aware that many saw him as the choice of Burke, Vrdolyak, and company, Sawyer embraced most of Washington's policies and people over the following seventeen months, but with only mixed success. He was never fully trusted. And it quickly became clear how contingent electoral politics proved, how fragile coalitions could be, including the coalition that Washington had put together—not just between Blacks, Latino, and progressive white Chicagoans, as many in the press began to write, but among African Americans and among Latinos as well. Although we must be careful of subscribing to great man theory, Harold Washington's charisma certainly was one of the factors that made this progressive electoral coalition work amid the rise of political conservatism nationally. The internecine fights that ensued reflected what had lain below the surface but that Washington, by force of his personality and reputation, could smooth over. "Harold Washington was the glue that caused these differences not to rear their ugly heads," observed Conrad Worrill of the Black United Front. Without Washington, neither Sawyer nor any of his progressive allies could keep it together. Just a day before Washington died, progressive white councilman David Orr had his longest one-on-one conversation with the mayor, in which Washington made their cause's challenge clear. In response to progressive critiques about the pace of reform, he responded, "David, you and the others have to understand. I cannot do all of this by myself. There are still enormous challenges and a long way to go, and I need the reformers, the progressives, the liberals—I need them to be constantly out there fighting." Power in City Hall mattered less if the grassroots did not keep the pressure on themselves.[3]

Yet, it would also be a mistake to suggest that Washington's passing and his coalition's loss of most levers of power in 1989 to Richard M. Daley and his allies meant a return to a bygone era—that Chicago's experiment with a different kind of policy and politics was simply an interregnum, as some have contended, in the city and the nation.[4] In fact, some of the reforms that Washington's administration introduced ended up surviving, at least for a while, under a retooled machine designed for the 1990s and beyond. Changes to the city's political culture had staying power. Black and Latino Chicagoans remained better integrated in city government, as they did nationally, while overall Latino political power clearly increased. Working-class communities such as Pilsen and Humboldt Park survived, neighborhood school councils and open budget hearings continued, and big-ticket development projects such as new and renovated stadiums, the main library, and Navy Pier came to fruition despite Washington's neighborhoods-only reputation. Perhaps most important, the crassest elements of the patronage system disappeared, with far fewer jobs being sold by Irish, Italian, and Polish politicos than in the system Mayor Richard J. Daley ran a generation before.

Such changes did not necessarily promise a better, more equitable system, however. At the end of the 1980s, Chicago was on the verge of becoming a glittering global city. Far from its industrial roots, the city increasingly was attractive to tourists and investors from around the world, shaped by corporate money and neoliberal values rather than the outsized parochial interests of a generation or two before. The Washington coalition, in its fights with the vestiges of an old machine, inadvertently forced Mayor Richard M. Daley and corporate interests to adapt in ways that exposed the fragility of its own progressive electoral coalition, especially along racial and class lines. That became quite clear amid the internal fights over Sawyer's candidacy and abbreviated administration. Despite some clear policy achievements on LGBTQ rights, affirmative action in city contracts and jobs, and police accountability on torture, the coalition Washington had created could not easily be put back together to stave off a regular party organization that had learned from its previous losses and embraced just enough of Washington's reforms—especially in its symbolism—to cobble together a winning coalition at the polls. By winning most whites, a significant number of Latinos, and more conservative Black voters, the new Daley coalition managed to neutralize enough of the era's racial politics to win in

1989. Operating within the racially tinged national political culture that Ronald Reagan and his acolytes championed, Daley's Chicago offered an alternative to Washington's progressive coalition model: one for centrist whites to take back power, whether it was city halls in New York, Los Angeles, and Philadelphia, or the White House itself.[5]

IN THE MONTHS AFTER Washington's reelection, Chicagoans began to see what the mayor could and could not do with a small but significant electoral mandate, demonstrating that his larger electoral coalition in 1987 could deliver clear gains on some long-promised reforms, at least when pushed. At the same time, "business as usual" remained the practice on other fronts to the rising frustration of some of the mayor's longtime supporters. From Latino hiring and a human rights ordinance to a corrupt housing authority and a bloated, ineffective school system, activists of many stripes turned up the political heat on the administration that summer and fall, with mixed results.

Certainly, reformers could point to some progress. In addition to triumphs on taxi regulation and ethics in the winter, reformers orchestrated triumphs in the city budget process, economic development, control of the region's airports, consumer affairs, and even public schools. Usually a battle royale each year, the budget process became less acrimonious and more open as Washington and his allies took control and sidelined administration foes such as Ed Burke, who had previously used the process to embarrass the mayor. For the first time during his mayoralty, Washington proposed hiring a significant number of new city workers—1,000 in all—funded by a property tax increase. While tax hawks cried foul, the process continued to feature hearings in which ordinary citizens, not just machine hacks, could speak to city spending priorities—a lasting innovation praised years later by Helen Shiller, Bob Starks, and others for its spirit of transparency. Not too long before, the prevailing approach to budgets, really most legislation, had been to literally wave around a physical copy of what was being voted on and declare "now you've seen it," as floor leaders infamously did during the Daley machine. In contrast, as the *Tribune*'s conservative editorial board noted, Washington's "administration listens to more people, considers more conflicting goals and interests, and takes more pains to arrive at decisions than any Chicago government in recent decades."[6]

Indeed, as many Black mayors of the era discovered, Washington's stewardship of the budget created strange bedfellows—winning over elements of the white business community while placing certain neighborhood groups on the defensive. Despite high-profile public fights with powerful corporations like Commonwealth Edison, which Washington threatened with setting up a city-run electric utility, more and more downtown business leaders praised the mayor as "a positive force for fiscal reform," pointing to low payrolls, a recent rise in the city's bond rating, and support for big-ticket development such as new sports stadiums. Corporate leaders recognized that coordination with city officials, not chaos sewn by their more conservative council allies, could move development along, even amid the mayor's neighborhood-centric rhetoric. "We were starting to make progress," said one bank president after Washington died. "We were listening to each other more." Moreover, Washington's administration introduced the city to tax-increment financing (TIF)—in the central business district in 1984—diverting tax collection on rising property values for eventual redevelopment. Despite the mayor's reputation as "neighborhoods first," a disproportionate amount of development dollars still flowed downtown and to corporate interests in the neighborhoods through such schemes as TIF—a reality many activists noted with resignation at the time but most scholars and journalists have downplayed since.[7]

Much like the administration's work with the Cubs and White Sox baseball teams' desire for updated facilities, the mayor's championing of a new stadium for the uber-popular Chicago Bears, on the heels of their dominating Super Bowl victory in 1986, reflected such compromises. Of course, Washington could not let the Bears leave the city—to the extent that some claimed, including the mayor himself, that unwavering support for the Bears ensured his reelection. That spring and summer, city officials did their own "Super Bowl Shuffle," negotiating a new stadium on the Near West Side, just blocks from the UIC campus and an earlier generation's symbol of urban renewal. The proposed complex, next door to Rush University Medical Center, once again divided neighborhood activists, with longtime mayoral ally Nancy Jefferson of the influential Midwest Community Council pitted against other groups, primarily the clergy-led Interfaith Organizing Project concerned with displacement of poor Black residents. While not enthusiastic about the stadium plan, Jefferson pledged her support "if it's done right," reflecting both her clout with the mayor and his activist allies' willingness to give him the benefit of the doubt. The ultimate agreement, crafted by a fifteen-member committee, including Jefferson and Ernest Barefield, promised to compensate displaced residents fairly and build a neighborhood library with proceeds from luxury boxes—a deal residents reluctantly accepted. The political turmoil following Washington's death, however, scuttled the deal, with the state General Assembly deeming certain aspects as simply too generous to those displaced. Thus, the Bears remained in an increasingly antiquated Soldier Field, eventually renovated in 2003 in what most architects could only describe as a mind-numbing mishmash. For politicians of the time, however, echoing Washington, at least the team stayed in the city.[8]

Less headline-grabbing but arguably more effective in meeting progressive goals were administration efforts to retain city influence over the region's airports and to institute long-overdue reforms in the Department of Consumer Services. In collaboration with both business and labor leaders, Washington allies in the state legislature pushed back against regional control of O'Hare and Midway airports—a ploy that the mayor contended was yet another way his white critics tried to reduce city influence over a regional commercial engine. Of course, the about-to-be-expanded O'Hare did offer considerable tax revenues, contracts, and jobs—a reminder that even the most reform-minded politicians in Chicago had little incentive to abolish the patronage system; the airport was central to Washington's continuing affirmative action goals in hiring and contracts, with 40 percent of expansion-related contracts going to women- and racial minority-owned businesses. Besides, beating back regional encroachment had great symbolic importance, too—not unlike keeping the White Sox in the city. "Don't fool around with O'Hare airport," Washington warned his critics in the suburbs and downstate Illinois. "It belongs to us." Similar impulses at reform through transparency and control could be seen in the city's Department of Consumer Services, which regulated everything from taxis and nursing homes to restaurants and stores. Long considered one of the most corrupt city agencies—ironically once cleaned up by Jane Byrne as its commissioner—the department faced a new reckoning when longtime activist Brenetta Howell Barrett took over in late 1986. In addition to overseeing the expansion of cab medallions for independent drivers, Howell Barrett took on restaurant inspectors who routinely accepted bribes to overlook deficiencies. "One of the best things we were able to do was win just about all the cases . . . to get rid of those people," Howell Barrett stated, recalling one inspector who tried to defend himself by saying he only took ten dollars for himself per inspection. Clearly, it mattered, she said, because "his bribe could have cost people their lives by having them eat contaminated food." As Washington officials admitted, such corruption was common—most notoriously in building inspections and zoning changes; curtailing such practices became a new front for reform.[9]

**DESPITE SUCH DISRUPTIONS** in the status quo, other institutions and practices appeared largely untouched by reform, and by August 1987, months after his reelection, many Washington supporters had begun to lose patience. That was certainly the case with key constituencies such as Latinos, gay men and lesbians, and the Black women who made up the majority of leadership and members of the influential Chicago Teachers Union.

Latinos were perhaps the most frustrated. Despite Washington's establishment of the Mayor's Advisory Commission on Latino Affairs in 1984 and his endorsement of Gloria Chevere for city clerk in 1987, many viewed the mayor as once again dragging his feet on a range of Latino priorities in hiring, housing, and health care. Even mild-mannered leaders such as longtime ally Chuy García were perplexed. "I'm puzzled by it," García said, months after Washington's reelection. "I was expecting things to happen faster. . . . By now I thought we'd be beyond a lot of the issues we're still talking about." García's anger boiled over most publicly in an exchange on the council floor with Dorothy Tillman, a Black alderman from the South Side, regarding her support for a referendum to block the use of Illinois National Guard members in the U.S. proxy wars in Central America. According to García, she and other Black council members withheld their support in exchange for a loosening of recently passed ethics laws, but this is not how one should treat an ally. "We don't fuck with apartheid," he told her, referring to similar positions on South Africa, "so don't you go fucking with this bill." The referendum eventually passed with overwhelming Black support, but the process the episode illustrated symbolized the larger issue of Latino marginalization. Throughout 1987, García, Luis Gutiérrez, and MACLA members increasingly pointed out that—despite influential Latinos on the council and board of education—none of Washington's department heads or close advisers were Latino after the recent departures of Ben Reyes and Nena Torres. Latino hiring and contracts continued but at a pace much slower than needed to match their share of the population. Moreover, the city's Housing Department historically had viewed "housing as a Black problem," according to one longtime housing activist at the time, rather than one that impacted all poor people. "They're picking the wrong fights," the activist said of the mayor's housing commissioner, fights that often treated housing units as a zero-sum game. "It's not between poor people of different colors," the activist noted, "that's not where the real fight lies." Similar conclusions about resources were drawn about policy choices regarding infant mortality rates, of particular concern to Puerto Ricans. Concluded García, "Some people inside the administration have the idea that Latino progress can only come at the expense of Black progress, but I don't buy that. . . . Some people argue that in order to pay Peter you have to rob Paul, so their attitude is that it's tough luck on Peter."[10]

Indeed, this proved a prevalent attitude among some Black leaders even after Washington's reelection. In addition to Tillman and Lu Palmer, long critical of Washington's definition of fairness, administration insiders such as Jacky

Grimshaw were also skeptical. As head of the city's office on intergovernmental affairs and a Washington confidante since the 1970s, Grimshaw criticized openly the mayor's support for Chevere over a Black candidate for clerk, and then actively tried to block his endorsement of a Latino-majority congressional district in the heart of Chicago. "We had to put someone in the limo to make sure that she did not change the speech," Nena Torres recalled. "That was the level" of opposition within the administration. She added that David Axelrod, who had managed his 1987 campaign, also "was on board with that, checking Latinos," albeit for different reasons. "He wanted to de-racialize everything around Harold," not unlike Axelrod's efforts with future candidate Barack Obama. Not only did key Washington aides view these policies as a zero-sum game, but too many also believed the activist hierarchy trope that Latinos had suffered less and were thus less loyal and less deserving than African Americans. Of course, Latinos were not a monolith by any means. More conservative Latinos, especially some Mexican Americans and Cuban Americans, who were disproportionately represented among business and homeowners, as well as Spanish-language newspapers such as *El Heraldo*, proved quite critical of Washington. As a result, while Washington may have complained at times that Latinos were "a little too pushy or moving too fast," he ultimately sought to use his charisma to smooth over growing policy differences among his coalition partners—a habit that came back to haunt his allies eventually.[11]

The administration faced similar challenges from the Chicago Public Schools (CPS) and the influential Chicago Teachers Union, whose sizable Black female leadership and membership had made the union a key constituency for the mayor's reelection. During his first term, Washington had built up some goodwill with teachers by finally tapping longtime favorite and insider Manford Byrd Jr. to run CPS as the system's second Black superintendent—and, frankly, by not being Jane Byrne, who antagonized African Americans with her appointments and policies. As he did on a range of urban issues, Washington also offered a sharp rebuttal to Reagan administration education policy, captured in the 1983 report *A Nation at Risk*. The report largely blamed public schools and teachers for the nation's ongoing economic challenges and called for a return to "basics," including an abandonment of bilingual education and teacher tenure. U.S. education secretary William Bennett singled out Chicago as "the worse" schools in the nation, calling them "an educational meltdown." In response, Washington retorted that, "Mr. Bennett has a lot of gall to be criticizing Chicago public schools or any other school system," since the president "has literally dismantled public education in this country. Mr. Bennett speaks from a very poor point of view." Federal education funding had indeed slowed, but frustrated teachers knew it was more complex than that. The mayor had not matched his rhetoric with any real financial investment or policy commitment to improve schools or outcomes for students of color, who were the majority in CPS. Despite material gains in other parts of the nation, even in the former Jim Crow South, Chicago schools remained woefully uneven in quality, at a time when deindustrialization, rising poverty, and acute unemployment among youth made schools that much more important yet seemingly inadequate in how they prepared a new generation. In 1985, 32 percent of Chicago youth were unemployed, and 51 percent of Black men ages sixteen to nineteen were jobless; the Washington administration predicted that 43 percent of students entering school that year would eventually drop out.[12]

In response, the administration convened an education summit in 1986 to discuss how schools could better translate their work into steady jobs after graduation. What emerged held some promise—a Learning Works Compact, the brainchild of Washington's chief policy adviser, Hal Baron. Modeled after similar programs in Boston, Baltimore, and Pittsburgh, the compact called for local industries to promise full employment to qualified graduates if Chicago Public Schools could make progress toward improving the dropout rate, attendance, and basic skills. Baron himself was surprised with "a level of participation" in the summit by business leaders and CPS "that is beyond our original expectations." But two problems undercut the agreement in principle. Summit organizers invited forty mostly elite leaders to participate, including Roman Catholic Cardinal Joseph Bernardin and Amoco chief executive officer (CEO) Richard Morrow. While many Black and Latino leaders, such as Operation PUSH's Willie Barrow and the Latino Institute's Mario Aranda, did attend, missing were some of the most important stakeholders—parents and teachers, who brought critical insight into how such a compact could work in communities. Moreover, as Washington aides had warned, there was an inherent mistrust between CPS superintendent Byrd and Peter Willmott, chair of the business-oriented Chicago Partnership for Education Progress and CEO of department store chain Carson Pirie Scott. Byrd, like the mayor and most school administrators and teachers, believed systemic goals could only be attained with millions more in funding, at which Wilmott and other business leaders balked, claiming that CPS needed to eliminate administrative bloat. While both were correct—more funding *and* more efficiencies were needed to achieve their common objectives—the business community's attitude struck a mostly Black CPS leadership as one more effort by white elites to dictate the terms when African Americans were in charge.[13]

Watching the first summit mostly from the sidelines, teachers and parents wanted more than just rhetoric, a handful of well-meaning people of color in power, and empty promises from the business community. They wanted more resources and tools to help children and families. As rising poverty and crime touched more Chicagoans, public schools were often asked to be the stopgap, providing not just an education but also food, security, and stability. Yet, as best-selling studies from the time such as Jonathan Kozol's *Savage Inequalities* and Alex Kotlowitz's *There Are No Children Here* powerfully argue, the schools were ill-equipped to do so. The nation's schools "are routinely called on to provide solutions to personal, social, and political problems that the home and other institutions either will not or cannot resolve," wrote the authors of *A Nation at Risk.* "We must understand that these demands on our schools and colleges often exact an educational cost as well as a financial one." And while per-pupil spending remained constant between 1970 and 1988, changing federal policies threatened the resources teachers had. After failing to reach a new contract agreement in September 1987, teachers walked out for the ninth time in eighteen years, keeping 431,000 students home for four weeks.[14]

What transpired in the community during those four weeks proved remarkable, as a range of grassroots organizations, powered by activists, parents, and educators primarily of color, demanded not just better teacher pay but also a more holistic reform of Chicago Public Schools. Seasoned community veterans such as The Woodlawn Organization's Leon Finney and others organized marches and rallies outside City Hall and the Board of Education while educators, such as Chicago Urban League education director Dr. Gwendolyn Laroche, advocated for more parental and community involvement in the schools. Another coalition formed freedom schools for students at home, while still others called for children to be transferred to suburban schools. As Elizabeth Todd-Breland notes, "A grassroots education reform coalition was developing with significant Black leadership, and Washington's summit would have to respond." And it did, in a way that surprised observers.[15]

In October, after a record nineteen-day strike, teachers narrowly approved a new two-year contract, winning a small raise and slightly smaller class sizes in primarily Black and Latino schools, in exchange for 1,700 layoffs. But the real achievement of the strike and subsequent negotiations was a greatly revamped and expanded education summit, designed to capitalize on the widespread public consternation with CPS. As Hal Baron put it, "The summit was b.s. until the strike." This time, more than a thousand activists, parents, teachers, and civic and community leaders would hash out what a new, more equitable and effective CPS might look like. And, unlike the first attempt, this summit included a Parent Community Council (PCC) made up of a majority of Black and

Latino parents, for once accurately reflecting the number of CPS students of color, who by 1986 represented more than 80 percent of enrollment. For the next several months, the PCC had relatively equal footing with administrators, teachers, and business leadership to propose and debate proposals to reform the structure. Observers marveled, sometimes decades later, at what they witnessed, such as a working-class mother speaking as equals with Amoco executive Gene Cartwright and others about their vision for a reformed CPS. "We parents made a promise we would make that process go to its limit," stated chairman James Deanes, a Black parent from the West Side, at the first of ten regional hearings held by the PCC. "We are going to keep that promise." Indeed, similar to efforts on crime and the budget, the hearings invited open comments from the community, in which citizens proposed a range of ideas to reform schools, from more local control and additional early education programs to incentives to keep seasoned teachers in the classroom.[16]

While "children-first" rhetoric predominated, the process was ultimately shaped by interracial and intraracial complexity. Working-class parents' persistent mistrust of white business leaders—many of whom sent their kids to private schools—also turned toward the Black professional class that included Manford Byrd, union president Jacqueline Vaughn, and many of the city's Black politicians, who seemed more interested in protecting their own turf than in true reform. "Too often, the system and Byrd seem unable to relate to poor children and poor parents," said Coretta McFerren, coordinator of the grassroots People's Coalition for Education Reform. "So what if we're poor or uneducated?" she asked. Washington aide Toni Preckwinkle, a year before, assessed Byrd as not "willing to set goals for the system, take risks, or implement changes." At least in this context, Harold Washington seemed an exception, both because he had empowered the parents in the first place—"I'm with the parents," he declared amid the process—but also because he succeeded in remaining largely above the fray. "He would be a champion, [but] not a leader" on the details of school policy, Baron pointed out. After Washington died suddenly, participants heaped praise onto him and his vision to help kids and tried to persuade Eugene Sawyer, whom they greeted skeptically, to stay dedicated to the process. And while Sawyer did try, he simply did not have Washington's political skills or, frankly, the interest to navigate participants' differences. Thus, the summit process began to splinter in the winter and spring of 1988 along racial and class lines. The eventual reforms proposed to the Illinois General Assembly, which had to approve any major structural change to the school system, championed transparency and decentralization but without more resources.[17]

Arguably the most important reform was the creation of the local school councils (LSCs). The councils offered an "unprecedented degree of control to parents and communities," according to Todd-Breland—an important counterweight to the arrogance of CPS central administration and what was, after all, an unelected Board of Education; school principals had to remain accountable to communities in ways they never had been before, with an estimated 40 percent of new principals chosen by LSCs in their first five years. Each council included the principal, six parents, two teachers, and two community members, with an astounding 312,000 parents voting in the first LSC elections in October 1989. Participation never met that highwater mark again and dropped precipitously in the late 1990s, but the councils continued to receive credit for bringing more democracy to the system, if not the radical improvements that many parents and educators had hoped for—a tall order without the resources to match.[18]

Not everyone praised the school councils, then or later. While they certainly empowered some working-class Black and Latino parents, particularly undocumented parents who did not vote otherwise, the LSCs "didn't have a political champion" to maintain the original goals of greater participation leading to more equitable achievement, Hal Baron said years later. Instead, wealthier, predominantly white schools used the councils to gain even more influence and resources for their kids, while many Black community activists and educators lamented decentralization's impact on Black educational leadership. Teachers and school administrators, in many ways, had been the backbone of the Washington coalition, not to mention the city's Black middle class. Some supporters worried, understandably, that this new school reform—while injecting a level of democracy and local control into the system—would inadvertently undermine an area of long-term stable employment for middle-class African Americans in Chicago. And while certainly not the only factor in the gradual sidelining of professional Black educational power, the councils did contribute to this trend.[19]

AS WITH PREVIOUS policy fights, Harold Washington's battles over the city budget, education, and housing were part of a larger national debate about the state and future of urban America, one the mayor hoped to influence even more in his second term. That effort included a surprise early endorsement of the Reverend Jesse Jackson's second presidential run in 1988. Washington's decision contrasted sharply with his actions four years earlier in which he withheld his endorsement of Jackson in the hopes of currying favor with frontrunner Walter Mondale, to no avail. Indeed, Washington's September endorsement became the leading edge of the Black political establishment's reappraisal of

Jackson, around whom many more Black officials rallied. Most commentators, white or Black, still did not believe the "Country Preacher" had a viable path to the nomination, but they acknowledged his strengths as a candidate. Jackson had demonstrated that he was not just a charismatic orator with a strong following only among African Americans but also as someone who could speak eloquently and broadly across races about the shortcomings of Reaganism, especially its domestic failures. One *Tribune* columnist implored reporters to stop asking Jackson if he could win, and no less than the conservative *Tribune* and *Wall Street Journal* editorial pages praised his retooled message "playing up issues of economics in a serious effort to broaden his base across racial lines." His was a populist pitch toward African Americans, Latinos, white liberals, and other members of his Rainbow Coalition. That coalition, of course, had some similarities to Washington's in 1983 and 1987. And after nearly seven years of the Reagan administration's miserliness toward urban America, the Iran-Contra Affair and other scandals, and its poor treatment of Black Americans specifically, many including the mayor saw his fellow Chicagoan as an important and influential voice in what should have been a strong Democratic year.[20]

Fittingly, Washington's endorsement came at a labor rally at the General Electric Hotpoint plant in suburban Cicero. An estimated 1,400 sheet-metal workers attended to hear the mayor and Jackson speak amid rumors that most of the workers were going to be laid off, their jobs heading to a nonunionized plant in Alabama. It was the perfect setting for two of the most prominent Black politicians in the country to remind union members of all colors that the neoliberal policies championed by Republicans and many Democrats cost them their jobs, their livelihoods, and their dignity. "I've looked over the entire country and seen how the candidates are responding to these cries of help from within our cities, and none of them are doing the kinds of things that they should do," Washington declared. "We need someone . . . whose voice is loud and clear like a clarion call." While the plant's hourly employees were mostly Black and Latino, he knew that white ethnic union workers were a key part of the coalition Jackson needed to make a real run for the nomination. Washington privately did not believe Jackson would win but saw his campaign as strategically important—both to placate the mayor's home base of supporters and to underscore the damage federal policies had wrought on the nation's cities economically and culturally. The latter proved particularly potent, it turned out, with Jackson outperforming the eventual nominee, Massachusetts governor Michael Dukakis, on Super Tuesday, securing the second-highest number of delegates and handily winning the presidential caucuses in Michigan and several state primaries across the South.[21]

As part of his effort to raise the profile of urban poverty in the presidential election, Washington also stepped up his rhetoric on the ongoing housing crisis. Washington had finally begun to focus on the issue, long seen as one of the biggest failures of his administration to that point. Despite overseeing the building of more affordable units in the private sector than his immediate predecessor, his administration contended with the ever-more-dysfunctional Chicago Housing Authority, of which Washington had to fight HUD to keep control. The agency's problems may not have denied him a second term, but grassroots activists who had muted their criticism in his first four years were determined to push the mayor to greater reform and accountability in ways that empowered tenants, who were disproportionately Black women and children. One answer was handing over more management to residents, a federal experiment the CHA agreed to try in the LeClaire Courts complex. Residents were confident it could improve their lives even if some "thought we were crazy," said Irene Johnson, chair of the LeClaire Residential Management Corporation. "If we get the proper training, we can handle it." But there was a catch: resident management relied on eventually selling the units to the same tenants as part of a privatization scheme championed by the Reagan administration, something that had not proved effective in St. Louis and other cities that had tried it over the previous decade. While such tenants' efforts often reduced crime temporarily, this was hard to sustain with few resources, especially in buildings that had been poorly designed and maintained in neighborhoods where poverty endured—the case of nearly all public housing in the city.[22]

While Washington acknowledged some level of mismanagement and encouraged citizens like Irene Johnson to get involved, he trained most of his energy on criticizing the Reagan administration's commitment to shrinking federal spending on social services. More than anything, he contended, the housing crisis was the result of massive cuts to federal HUD grants and a persistent, racist message that those who lived in subsidized housing were lazy freeloaders prone to crime and drug use. Alton Miller, his press secretary, called Washington's problems with Reagan policies "fundamental and at times almost obsessive"—an interpretation echoed by prominent commentators at the time and many scholars since. And yet, the problem was more complex than simply recalcitrant federal policymakers. As historian D. Bradford Hunt points out, while new construction of public housing stopped, actualized HUD spending on existing housing did not decline until the 1990s. But the perception was that it had, in part because so much other federal funding *had* shrunk that disproportionately impacted those who lived in public housing, from food stamps to education, which led to higher poverty, unemployment, homelessness, and crime. Internal policy memos painted a grim picture of the city's challenges, as did ethnographies of the expanding underground economy on which people increasingly relied to survive. And, so, on the heels of his Jackson endorsement speech about the scourge of urban poverty, Washington traveled to the nation's capital to champion an ambitious spending plan to tackle the worsening housing crisis. The U.S. Conference of Mayors endorsed a "breathtaking" $25 billion plan to upgrade both private and public housing, build more affordable units, and make it easier for families to buy single-family homes—advocacy in which Washington took on a more urgent tone. "Candidates will not be able to duck" this issue in the upcoming campaign, Washington vowed. This renewed focus on housing even played a prominent role the morning before Thanksgiving, in what turned out to be his last day alive. Washington was scheduled for a CNN interview on homelessness with Mitch Snyder, an activist with the D.C.-based Community for Creative Non-violence, followed by a groundbreaking ceremony for a new affordable housing development by the Kenwood-Oakland Community Organization. Aides later commented that the mayor had been surprisingly out of breath at the event—just the last of many warnings about his deteriorating health.[23]

While not a major issue during his reelection campaign, the health of the sixty-five-year-old mayor increasingly concerned his closest advisers. What made Washington so popular and such a good campaigner also put him at risk physically. The mayor rarely cooked, choosing to eat out instead; this was part of his always-campaigning, charismatic persona, a man about town, to a certain extent. Years later, Chicagoans—routinely without prompting—recalled seeing the mayor eat high-fat, salty comfort foods, from fast-food cheeseburgers to multiple kidney-and-steak pies at the Red Lion. Michael James, longtime owner of the Heartland Café in Rogers Park and a Washington supporter, recalled him eating fried fish at an event there in 1987, while *Tribune* reporter John Kass, who covered his last campaign, commented that the mayor's limousine routinely stopped at fast-food joints between rallies. By November 1987, Washington was an estimated 100 pounds overweight. He had quit smoking but his favorite pastimes were reading and eating; physical activity beyond the campaign six months before happened less and less. An autopsy revealed that his heart was two-and-a-half times bigger than normal, straining to pump blood through arteries that were 90 to 95 percent clogged; his doctor said he was a perfect candidate for bypass surgery. Dempsey Travis, his friend and confidante who had bought the mayor a treadmill the previous Christmas, told Washington prophetically a week before his death, "You're going to be mayor as long as you live. Only you can hurt yourself."[24]

Whatever the signs were of poor health, Washington largely ignored them. And on November 23, 1987, while going over the day's schedule with press secretary Alton Miller, Washington suffered a fatal heart attack at his desk. It might sound like hyperbole and yet it was not: His death threw the city's political world into chaos.

"SEVEN WRETCHED DAYS" after Washington's sudden death—seven days of remarkably callous maneuvering by the political class while much of the city mourned—Acting Mayor David Orr handed the reins of the city over to the soft-spoken choice of Washington's political foes, Eugene Sawyer. Edging out Washington floor leader Tim Evans in a familiar 29–21 vote, Sawyer offered a sharp contrast to the charismatic Washington. As his detractors would repeat over the next seventeen months before losing the 1989 primary, Sawyer was neither charismatic nor courageous, an old Chicago pol who had been content to stay on the sidelines and serve his ward and himself as part of the machine. Sawyer had been the first Black committeeman to endorse Washington in 1983, and the mayor later tapped Sawyer to be president pro tempore of the council. Presumably the mayor had confidence that Sawyer could do the job, if called. But Sawyer was malleable in a way that Washington and progressive council members such as Orr, Danny Davis, Helen Shiller, and Chuy García were not. Could he be trusted to maintain the mayor's fragile coalition and pursue his agenda? Many had their doubts, especially if it appeared he had struck a deal to win the bloc of twenty-three white machine aldermen.[25]

Tim Evans emerged as Sawyer's primary rival, not necessarily because he was the most progressive or the most like Washington. That would have been Danny Davis, a Black West Side alderman, former teacher, and community activist with multiracial ties across the city but who showed little interest in becoming mayor at the time (and was genuinely grieving the loss of his friend). Rather, Evans, an Arkansas native first elected in 1973 to succeed his mentor Claude Holman in the Fourth Ward, had been a reliable member of the machine well into the Byrne administration. He had distanced himself from her, and Mayor Bilandic, on certain civil rights issues, especially on policing and later redistricting, but always in a calculated way. Evans endorsed Washington's bid in 1982; unlike Sawyer, however, he played little role during the campaign. But he became a loyal ally of Washington's and, as one profile put it, was "easily one of the brightest, most articulate, and best-educated members of the Washington bloc." Many believed him more capable than Sawyer of keeping together Washington's multiracial coalition to win citywide elections and

*From left*, Alderman Tim Evans and Acting Mayor Eugene Sawyer appear with the Reverend Jesse Jackson as a sign of Black unity soon after white aldermen orchestrated Sawyer's selection as mayor in 1987. In reality, the rivalry between Evans and Sawyer over who was better positioned to fulfill Washington's legacy weakened both as candidates against a resurgent machine less than two years later. Antonio B. Dickey, Eugene Sawyer Mayoral Records, box 90, folder 11, Special Collections, Chicago Public Library.

enact reforms. Observed Leon Despres, longtime council reformer, "When you were there in City Council you could sense without any difficulty the aldermen who were with Harold Washington because they had to be, and those who were with him with enthusiasm and energy. Evans was enthusiastic." Evans, added Alderman Larry Bloom, "has internalized the progressive agenda." What Evans could not do, however, was bridge the widening intraracial gap among African Americans generationally and ideologically. While the younger Evans garnered support of a young, more progressive generation of Chicagoans, he had made his share of enemies as Washington's floor leader. Many older African Americans, including six key Black aldermen once loyal to the machine, chose one of their own in a practical governing alliance with the white majority. Many Washington adherents predicted doom under the new mayor, persuaded that he would demonstrate loyalty to his machine patrons more than anyone else.[26]

And yet as mayor, Sawyer attempted to embrace much more of Washington's program than expected, even if he did not have the political muscle in the council, the trust of key neighborhood activists, or the gut beliefs and charisma to make most of it happen. Sawyer, as the *Chicago Reader* observed, was a politician without a real base, not unlike Jane Byrne a decade before. "The only way to stay mayor is to be more like Harold than Harold," stated one top administration official, and doggedly pursue Washington's agenda. Sawyer himself agreed to "move the Harold Washington agenda; whatever I thought Harold would do, I would do, like the Gay Rights Ordinance. Harold wanted that passed." Indeed, despite his earlier opposition, Sawyer championed a retooled and expanded human rights ordinance in what could be considered his administration's signature accomplishment. While skeptical of his pledge to reconsider, journalist Achy Obejas observed that gay and lesbian rights organizations across the city and state had steadily gained political influence since the earlier 1986 defeat and that Alderman Bill Henry, an early supporter and now Sawyer's floor leader, might usher the new ordinance through. "It'll be up to us not only to make new alliances," Obejas wrote in December 1987, "but also to make sure all our allies, progressive and otherwise don't desert us. The gay rights bill is no longer a radical idea." Indeed, major cities across the country had passed similar ordinances, Obejas observed, and Chicago could be next, if Sawyer viewed its passage as essential to winning a full term as mayor. And he agreed. The new mayor concluded that his only potential path to victory was to hold on to the Lakefront wards, home to a growing concentration of gay men and lesbians, who had become increasingly politically active in response to the AIDS crisis and the nation's creeping conservatism. But passage of the ordinance took nearly a year of hard, sustained work. Achieving a majority required not only its expansion into a human rights bill that included military discharge, marital, and economic status, but also voter registration drives by Norm Sloan and the Lesbian/Gay Progressive Democratic Organization, as well as Sawyer's individual cajoling of mostly Black council members. In December 1988, after three tries, eight council members, four white and four Black, flipped their previous votes and backed the human rights ordinance. Several, including Ed Burke, candidly cited activists' growing electoral clout as the primary factor, although Sawyer claimed the most credit in the end.[27]

Sawyer enjoyed a few other victories as well—albeit ones launched by Washington and his council allies and close aides. For instance, many on the council grudgingly credited Sawyer for pushing through the 1988 budget, which included $66 million in property tax and sewer fee increases to plug a budget deficit, in his first weeks as mayor. The new mayor's inherited and fragile multiracial coalition held up against a series of attempts by white aldermen to eliminate the new revenue and, with it, many city jobs and initiatives targeting

Washington and aide Kari Moe meet with the Commission on Gay and Lesbian Issues. While the mayor did not pass a human rights ordinance, gay and lesbian activists give him credit for viewing them with dignity and helping set the stage for passage of an antidiscrimination law after his death. His successor, Eugene Sawyer, capitalized on this work to pass an expansive antidiscrimination bill in 1988. Harold Washington Archives and Collections, Mayoral Photographs, box 80, folder 20, Special Collections, Chicago Public Library.

educational, housing, and health care inequalities. While the downtown business community did not embrace the record $2.7 billion budget, Sawyer did win praise for finishing negotiations to allow night Cubs games and for being generally more conversant with development interests. He is "not as contentious or polarizing as Washington," said conservative businessman Tom Roeser. "It's easier for him to reach out and make contact . . . yet he seems to be carrying out Harold's agenda." Indeed, Sawyer kept many of his predecessor's department heads and aides, such as Brenetta Howell Barrett, Hal Baron, Sharon Gist Gilliam, Rob Mier, and LeRoy Martin. Howell Barrett, who praised Sawyer as "intelligent" and "underrated," recalled that he did not interfere with the changes she had begun to make in consumer affairs, such as holding a taxi medallion lottery at McCormick Place that effectively broke the monopoly enjoyed by two local taxi companies. Meanwhile, Sawyer allowed Baron to move forward with school reforms, including the establishment of the local school councils; Washington's absence was felt, but the LSCs did get off the ground. Budget director

Gilliam became Sawyer's chief of staff, drawing wide praise among both Washington supporters and political observers, while Martin stayed on as police superintendent. Moreover, the *Tribune* reported, the appointment of Vincent Lane as Chicago Housing Authority director "has resulted in some of the most aggressive management of the CHA in years."[28]

Yet, at least for Sawyer's political future, the human rights ordinance proved the high-water mark of his administration. Relatively few Chicagoans had believed Sawyer could really maintain Washington's vision and program, and they were right. Sawyer simply did not enjoy the base that Washington had boasted. African Americans remained actively divided between the acting mayor and Tim Evans, and many more Latinos and progressive whites—including Washington stalwart Luis Gutiérrez—remained highly skeptical that Sawyer could lead the city. The specters of both his predecessor and his likely primary opponent, state's attorney Richard M. Daley, who was better prepared than six years before, cast long shadows over Sawyer's every move. In what political scientist and one-time independent alderman Dick Simpson dubbed the "War of the Roses," the City Council proved hopelessly dysfunctional in governance, something that Sawyer—a longtime creature but not leader of that body—could not tame. As Alderman Raymond Figueroa said, "The City Council seems so bad because we are so bad." Indeed, the council during an eight-month period studied by Simpson and his associates revealed more divided votes than any other time in the modern political history of the city—a total of 284. While division does not necessarily reflect dysfunction, the kinds of divisions during Sawyer's tenure did. "Aldermen vote against measures because of petty personal reasons, race, self-interest, or merely to vote against proposals presented by opposing bloc aldermen," wrote the authors, instead of votes based on ideology. "This factionalization of the council prohibits the formation of large coalitions into simple voting blocs," meaning it became incredibly difficult to pass legislation. Even "routine resolutions congratulating couples on their fiftieth wedding anniversaries"—an odd use of the council's time—were blocked because of personal grudges. Tough ethics legislation, community development funding to neighborhoods, and general professionalism by council members were the real victims.[29]

Many Chicagoans, Black, white, and Latino, rightfully blamed Sawyer for the council's inability to govern. Especially in contrast to Harold Washington, "Gentleman Gene" appeared meek, indecisive, generally unwilling to fight for what he believed in. "Black people don't want no whispering," contended Alderman Robert Shaw, who was one of only six Black council members to vote for Sawyer a year before. "I believe Gene Sawyer to be a fine person . . . probably someone nice to go to dinner with. But that doesn't have anything to do with political leadership." Provocatively citing Machiavelli, Shaw added, "He said the king doesn't need to be smart but should always appear so. I strongly recommend 'The Prince' to Eugene Sawyer." The mayor stumbled repeatedly in personnel choices, sometimes hiring the wrong people, sometimes keeping others on for too long. As expected, Sawyer had a different inner circle of aides, replacing Barefield and Grimshaw with controversial machine loyalist Erwin France. Although talented, as Sawyer's chief consultant, France often appeared to be mostly out for himself, charging the city for what the *Tribune* called "weak mush." In a highly criticized move, the mayor replaced María Cerda at the city's manpower training agency with development director Arturo Vasquez, prompting accusations that he was trying to drive a wedge between Puerto Ricans and Mexican Americans. "It will totally destroy any shred of credibility [Sawyer] had left with the Hispanic community," Alderman Luis Gutiérrez said angrily. "There are going to be political consequences, electoral consequences to pay." More likely than a deliberate plan to divide, Cerda's firing reflected Sawyer's general mistaken impression that all Latinos were the same—a blunder that would cost him. Even more alarmingly, Sawyer's handling of aide Steve Cokely, a key liaison to Black nationalists whose anti-Semitic remarks galvanized the media for days, suggested that Sawyer also could not make a decision. Charging, among other things, that Jewish doctors were secretly injecting HIV into poor Black children, Cokely kept his job for nearly a week after the story broke as Sawyer dithered over how politically damaging it would be among Blacks to fire him. Black nationalist and Jewish voters were part of any winning coalition Sawyer could put together, but his inability to act decisively underscored the impression of him as a weak, feckless leader.[30]

Ultimately, the drip-drip-drip of these incidents and Sawyer's worsening position jeopardized both the coalition that Harold Washington had built and, in turn, appeared to put at risk many of his mayoralty's hard-fought legacies. Six years after his first unsuccessful run for mayor, State's Attorney Richard M. Daley had just won another race easily and seemed well-positioned to win City Hall. In the eyes of whites and a growing number of Blacks and Latinos, he appeared ready to achieve a political "restoration," a new Daley machine.

JUST SIX YEARS AFTER helping coordinate a united Black front crucial to Washington's victory, Lu Palmer sounded the alarm early about the 1989 election. "WE ARE IN JEOPARDY OF LOSING THE FIFTH FLOOR OF CITY HALL TO WHITES," the *Metro News* columnist wrote in all caps in March 1988. "And if this happens, we cannot blame white people. We can only blame ourselves." In fact, as it turned out, there would be enough blame to go around. African Americans did remain divided between Sawyer, Tim Evans, and a new-look Richard M. Daley—many still sore from the political machinations following Washington's death. Party committeeman elections bore this out in March, as half of the Black committeemen who voted for Sawyer lost. But the acting mayor had also lost ground among independent, Puerto Rican, Mexican American, Lakefront liberal, white, and Jewish voters. On the strength of the human rights ordinance passed just months before the election, gay men and lesbians should have been more solidly in Sawyer's camp. Instead, the mayor's insistence on keeping Health Commissioner Lonnie Edwards, who resigned but then did not actually leave, despite his appalling record on AIDS—nine years into the pandemic, as ACT UP–Chicago reminded him—cost Sawyer valuable votes there, too.[31]

Bad feelings over how the council chose Sawyer in December 1987 continued to linger among many of Washington's most fervent Black supporters a year later—an ominous sign for the incumbent, who needed to consolidate African American votes the way his predecessor had. Younger reformers such as Aldermen Bobby Rush and Danny Davis, as well as activist Nancy Jefferson, threw their support behind Tim Evans's candidacy, while an older cadre of Black council members, Operation PUSH's Jesse Jackson, Black ministers including Addie and Claude Wyatt, and the Task Force for Black Empowerment eventually backed the incumbent. "Sawyer has sought to be a healer," Jackson declared. "Even his political adversaries and those who disagree with him like Gene Sawyer." And, in a sense, this was true. Opposition to Sawyer did not always show up in council votes on public policy, but it appeared elsewhere—in the media, the grassroots, and more obscure places. Any perceived miscue by the mayor in favor of a machine-connected developer or an uninspiring speech (of which there were many) became an issue. A debate among Democrats over the proper and legal time to hold the next election—1989 or 1991—became a proxy war between Evans and Sawyer advocates, with the former wanting a quicker election and the latter more time to prove himself. When Evans, struggling in the polls, withdrew from the Democratic primary to run in the general election as an independent under the banner of the Harold Washington Party, he refused to endorse Sawyer over Daley—even though he knew that Sawyer might return the favor by not endorsing Evans if the mayor lost. The decision "doomed Sawyer's already long-shot candidacy," wrote one observer. Most of Evans's prominent advocates also declined to endorse, all of which reflected the belief that Sawyer's selection in December 1987 was about political expediency, and not the mayor's weak claims that he acted selflessly to "keep the seat" in Black hands, as he repeated on the campaign trail.[32]

Meanwhile, Latino voters once again demonstrated their relevance—and complexity—to progressive coalitions in Chicago and beyond. That the city's Latinos split their vote relatively evenly during the state's Democratic presidential primary between favorite sons Paul Simon and Jesse Jackson was another warning sign for Sawyer and a potential opportunity for his rivals. Consistent with past elections, Puerto Ricans had favored Jackson nearly two to one, while Mexican Americans voted about 60 percent for his white counterpart; the eventual nominee, Michael Dukakis, also won a significant number of votes. Latinos did not vote in a bloc by any means, and it was perilous to expect that they would. It was also clear that many Latinos could not be expected to automatically vote for the Black candidate, even if they had largely favored Washington, especially to white Democratic alternatives. After missteps such as María Cerda's firing and weak Latino hiring overall, Sawyer's campaign ramped up its efforts to win over Latino voters. But as with most of his campaign efforts, it was too little, too late. Sawyer had few high-profile Latino advocates and little strategy to mobilize them in his favor.[33]

Instead, even the most progressive Latinos who had once supported Washington announced their support for Evans, or even Daley. Aldermen Chuy García and Raymond Figueroa, state senator Miguel del Valle, as well as Lupe and Emma Lozano—Rudy's widow and sister—all viewed Evans as Washington's true successor, even if some Latinos did not trust aides Jacky Grimshaw and Ernest Barefield to have their best interests at heart. The most consequential if not entirely surprising endorsement, however, came from Alderman Luis Gutiérrez, who had become perhaps Sawyer's loudest critic among Latinos. In January 1989, he officially embraced Richard M. Daley's candidacy, praising the state's attorney for his "progressive pragmatism" and the alderman's role in a future Daley administration. "I will have a great influence in determining the thrust and tone of the Daley administration's progressive and liberal agendas," he told reporters in front of a colorful portrait of Harold Washington. Many observers, however, interpreted the decision by "the traitor" as simple opportunism—a recognition that the acting mayor was likely to lose to Daley and that supporting either Sawyer or Evans would mean squandering the chance at remaining an alderman or, even better, becoming the city's first Latino member of Congress. Gutiérrez later confirmed that he indeed asked for such help—in fact, to challenge long-term Congressman Dan Rostenkowski again—but Daley said no. Some were not so sure. Either way, Gutiérrez's actions contrasted sharply with García's, who remained loyal to Washington's vision by backing Evans and then lost reelection himself to a Daley ally in 1991. On a larger scale, García lamented what Gutiérrez's decision signaled. "Now a lot of people are going to be doubting how reliable Hispanics are in coalition building," he said shortly afterward. Of course, one person's decision should not undermine all the work that progressive Latinos had pursued with Washington, Danny Davis, and other Black leaders who had long track records of cooperation. But García turned out to be right about the symbolic power of Gutiérrez's shift to Daley. While it was expected that more conservative Latinos would embrace Daley, Gutiérrez's decision helped cement many Black Chicagoans' long-standing suspicions that Latinos were, in the end, unreliable partners.[34]

Similar stories played out for other parts of the Washington coalition as well, and Sawyer's low-key campaign did not give many much reason to reconsider. "I'm not Harold," the candidate conceded. "He was a great person and I really admired him, but I can't be Harold and I'm not even going to try. . . . I'm just going to try and be a good Eugene, and maybe that will measure up somewhere someday." That made sense, to an extent. A generation before, Ralph Abernathy, Dr. Martin Luther King Jr.'s successor at the SCLC, who had unique skills of his own, tried to emulate King with only limited success. Better to be oneself than to try and offer a tepid, forced imitation of the real thing, Sawyer concluded. But in 1989, in a polarized city, Sawyer's quietude was not a winning electoral formula. In contrast to Washington or even Daley, Sawyer's campaign did not have the same kind of energy or street-level organization beyond Black wards whose committeemen endorsed the mayor. The city's largest labor federations and most of their member organizations sat on the sidelines, if anything quietly working for Daley behind the scenes. Jewish groups still smarted from the Cokely affair, as did gay voters angry about the city's AIDS program. Black Chicago remained divided. Community organizations across the city sat on their hands, decimated by funding cuts by the Sawyer administration. Not surprisingly, then, the kinds of grassroots voter registration efforts that Washington enjoyed never really got off the ground for Sawyer, with the number of eligible voters staying flat across the city. This was an ominous sign for the mayor, who needed more voters in the city's West and South Sides to balance out expected losses among whites and Latinos elsewhere. While Sawyer did have competent consultants working for him, he had neither "Washington's powerful, unifying presence," to quote the National Black United Front's Conrad Worrill, nor the broad connections or respect across the city that his predecessor had developed. After all, Sawyer had been an alderman with a workman-like reputation for sixteen years but few real policy accomplishments. And in contrast to 1983, there were no huge, memorable rallies, no catchy campaign jingles, no pivotal debates, no head-scratching racial blunders by his opponents, not even an election-bending snowstorm, to change the campaign's dominant narrative. Sawyer might be a nice man, but only Daley could restore order and unify the city.[35]

To be sure, Rich Daley was not a charismatic figure either, but he did not have to be. Thanks to the work of a talented and well-compensated team led by consultants David Axelrod and David Wilhelm and respected Black reporter Avis LaVelle as spokesperson, the state's attorney ran a more polished campaign than he had in 1983. The malapropisms and vague policy answers persisted, but a steady hand—not to be mistaken for an enlightened or particularly accomplished one—as the county's top prosecutor and the simple math that he was not going to split the vote this time with another prominent white candidate, helped Daley immensely. Throughout the second half of 1988, he took on the image of inevitability with fawning media coverage, numerous endorsements, strong fundraising, and impressive poll numbers, with Black voters divided and majorities of white and Latino voters saying that Daley could unify the city after six years of race-based turmoil. That such an argument was more than a little self-serving and misleading irked many of Washington's supporters; most independent observers believed it had been largely intransigent white leaders like Ed Vrdolyak who polarized the city, not Washington or Sawyer. Daley, meanwhile, had done nothing to mitigate the Council Wars himself. Yet the argument seemed to work.[36]

Moreover, the mayoral primary came just months after the national Democratic Party's third-straight presidential loss, in which party stalwarts cast doubt on the future of liberalism. While Michael Dukakis performed better electorally against Vice President George H. W. Bush than his previous counterparts had against Ronald Reagan, the loss still stung—including how the infamous Willie Horton commercial and other racist dog whistles by the Bush campaign undermined Dukakis. The election result prompted considerable soul-searching in the party. The centrist Democratic Leadership Council (DLC), formed in 1985 by moderate "New Democrats" from the Sunbelt such as Arkansas governor Bill Clinton, ratcheted up their intraparty critique of liberal orthodoxy, including progressives' defense of the welfare state and cultural liberalism and their critique of Pentagon spending and corporate influence. While careful to don a proreform, even progressive, veneer during the campaign, Daley also accepted plenty of corporate donations and a neoliberal centrism as the path forward for the city and nation. Daley, commented the *Reader*, "has often done the 'right' thing when it was politically easy"—from open government to school spending, he took the politically expedient approach, which usually meant the one supported by the white majority. But his record as state's attorney and his campaign emphasis on a vague unity and "quality of life" issues such as crime, taxes, and development underscored his neoliberal bent. Fittingly, Tennessee senator Al Gore, another DLC figure and future vice president, delivered the keynote at the Cook County party's unity dinner for Daley.[37]

Despite a last-minute spate of endorsements and tightening polls, Sawyer could not pull off a primary victory—and it was not even close. Daley outpolled Sawyer by 101,647 votes, winning 55.3 percent of what turned out to be the lowest turnout in more than a decade. As expected, Daley rode whites to victory to "an extraordinary degree," according to political scientist Paul Kleppner, making up more than 95 percent of Daley's primary coalition—an unheard-of percentage for a winning mayoral candidate. And while he was expected to run up impressive numbers in the predominantly white Northwest and Southwest Sides of the city, he also performed surprisingly well in the so-called Lakefront liberal wards where the city's gay and Jewish populations were disproportionately concentrated and where Harold Washington had been relatively competitive. Revealing his weakness among white progressives who had once backed his predecessor, Sawyer lost these wards by more than thirty points. In contrast, Black and Latino voters demonstrated their displeasure and showed up in much smaller numbers than previous years. Sawyer did garner an equally commanding 97 percent of Black voters, but there were far fewer of them voting or even registered. The acting mayor also managed a small plurality of Latinos (49.6 to 49.1 for Daley), a split decision that effectively neutralized any attempt to recreate the Washington coalition. "Gutiérrez's choice," wrote the *Tribune*'s Jorge Casuso later, "paid off." As Daley celebrated, the *Tribune* praised the two candidates for running respectable races that did not inflame racial sentiments the way whites had in 1983. "This was not a racially divisive campaign," the editorial board insisted, and yet it was quite clear who had supported Daley. Black and Latino voters made up less than 5 percent of Daley's coalition that night. It seemed clear that he simply did not need them.[38]

**DESPITE THE** potential intrigue of Tim Evans running under the Harold Washington Party banner and Ed Vrdolyak as a Republican, the general election played out similarly: with a sizable Daley victory thanks to overwhelming white support. Evans, in contrast to Sawyer, had fewer resources or opportunities and less time to penetrate the mantle of inevitability that Daley took on. While Daley had raised millions, Evans used mostly shoe leather and free television and radio programming to spread his warning of the machine's return. "Daley is getting ready to reopen his father's plantation," Evans told a rare raucous crowd at the UIC Pavilion late in the five-week campaign. But Daley's slick organization, superior media presence, and inclusive racial rhetoric made it difficult to pin the old machine label on him. Meanwhile, Evans could not pretend to lead a unified Black front; neither Sawyer nor many of his respected Black supporters chose to back Evans, staying either neutral as the acting mayor did or, in the surprising cases of Alderman Anna Langford and activist Marian Stamps, backing Vrdolyak's quixotic bid—a reflection of how personal the Sawyer-Evans schism remained among Blacks more than a year after that infamous council vote. As most national party leaders did, Democratic National Committee chair Ron Brown, the first African American to hold that office, broke with ally Jesse Jackson and also backed Daley. And while most high-profile whites and Latinos from the Washington coalition, such as David Orr, Helen Shiller, and Chuy García, continued to favor Evans, this time they appeared out of step with those who showed up at the polls. Among Latinos, "Older and more conservative constituents—who were regular voters—often resented their portrayal of Hispanics as an underprivileged minority group that shared common interests with blacks," observed reporter Jorge Casuso. "Instead [they] . . . viewed themselves as part of an immigrant American tradition" similar to the Irish—an overly simplistic yet attractive conclusion to draw that led many to support the Democratic nominee.[39]

As expected, Daley won resoundingly, outpacing Evans by nearly 134,000 votes and winning 53.9 percent in the three-way general election. As Sawyer had, Evans won Black voters overwhelmingly, but they simply proved far less motivated than when Washington was on the ballot—with turnout down 24 percent from 1983 and 19 percent from 1987. Evans also performed worse among the other two essential elements of the coalition—progressive white and Latino voters—than Sawyer, even with the controversial but entertaining Vrdolyak on the ballot, too. The key instigator of the Council Wars had faded considerably since his heyday of needling Washington. After improbably winning the GOP primary as a write-in, Vrdolyak pitched himself as the true white ethnic's candidate but failed to gain traction with that very constituency. Seemingly weary on the campaign trail with almost no organization or funding, "Fast Eddie" Vrdolyak had become "Past Eddie," joked columnist Steve Neal, and ultimately proved a nonfactor in the race. Meanwhile, a solid majority of Latino voters backed Daley, as Luis Gutiérrez had predicted, while white Lakefront voters also flocked to the Democratic nominee, giving him a striking 72 percent of their votes.[40]

It may have been incongruous for longtime Chicagoans to witness those North Side wards—which once teemed with white reformers gunning for the machine—backing anyone named Daley, but as former alderman Bill Singer observed nearly two decades after he was the independents' darling, "Lakefronters also may not be as liberal as everyone thought." That could apply to Singer himself, who made his own peace with the new machine after leaving office. And it was certainly the case as the gentrification of the North Side, once fought by Cha-Cha Jiménez, the Young Lords, and their allies, continued unabated. The mostly white, middle-class professionals who were transforming Lincoln Park, Wrigleyville, Lake View, and other Near North Side neighborhoods did not remember Boss Daley or the worst impulses of his machine. They may have embraced diversity—satisfied by the campaign's Black campaign spokeswoman and Luis Gutiérrez's high-profile endorsement. But, ultimately, they cared most about the urban quality-of-life issues that the younger Daley promised to address—crime, taxes, schools, even beautification—and not the more uncomfortable, persistent issues of racial, class, and gender inequity that Sawyer and then Evans attempted to highlight, albeit awkwardly. And with that, one fragile coalition of Black, Latino, and white crumbled and another apparently more durable, white-centered alliance took its place, shaping the city's course—and, in many ways, reflecting the nation's journey—well into the twenty-first century.[41]

# Legacies and the New Machine

One Chicago is symbolized by flowerpots and Ferris
wheels and good jobs and communities where police
respect the citizens. The second Chicago is still plagued
by a lack of jobs, poor schools, and police less tolerant
of youths who dress and talk differently than they do.
—Bobby Rush, congressman and 1999 mayoral candidate,
quoted in *Chicago on the Make* by Andrew J. Diamond (2017)

After winning the 1989 special election, Richard M. Daley would serve twenty-two years as mayor and become the longest serving in the city's history, surpassing his father by a year. Routinely praised as one of the nation's best mayors in the mainstream national press, Daley, his administration, and the machine he reconstituted in his image—one built for the 1990s and beyond—transformed the city into a powerful, vibrant, but remarkably unequal global city. Chicago became a symbol of the neoliberalism that swept American policymaking in both parties at the national level, symbolized by the policies of President Bill Clinton and the resurgent New Democrats, who wrested the party away from more traditional urban and labor pols—a strategy designed to beat the Republican stranglehold on the White House started by Ronald Reagan by neutralizing traditional GOP issues of crime, welfare, and taxes and spending. It was Clinton who announced that "the era of big government" was over. But it would be a mistake to credit or blame Daley and his allies for the city's transformation entirely. Rather, many of the policies—or seeds of them—started in the Washington administration and were an ironic result of the remarkable grassroots coalition that the city's first Black mayor built.

In 1989, Daley ran on a unity message, but what did unity mean in practice? Over time, it became clear that it meant not a wholesale rollback of Washington's initiatives but a governing strategy that emphasized transactional politics that reflected principles of equity and fairness rhetorically more than in practice. One scholar deemed Richard M. Daley's "unity" to be "machine politics, reform style." Even though his electoral coalition had been largely white and Latino, Daley was careful to include Blacks among his initial round of cabinet appointments in key areas such as schools and parks and to ensure that Blacks received a significant share of lower-level city jobs and contracts, less than under Washington and Sawyer but more than under previous white mayors. Rather than token appointments or alliances with a key powerful figure like his father's with William Dawson or Ralph Metcalfe to mitigate Black dissent, Daley worked with a variety of African American figures in city, county, and state government to "keep the peace." Also building on Washington's initial efforts, Daley fully integrated Latinos into the political structure of the city and machine as their share of the population fanned out across the city and jumped to 19 percent in the 1990 census. This integration included continuing the Mayor's Advisory Commission on Latino Affairs and championing a Latino-majority congressional district to be held by ally Luis Gutiérrez. Those who sat on Daley's Latino board, however, were cut from a different ideological cloth, dominated by conservative Cuban American and Mexican American business owners and members of his Hispanic Democratic Organization, not former Chicano movement participants. Similarly, as gay men and lesbians became more visible and politically influential across the nation in the 1990s, Daley begrudgingly became more of an ally, providing regular funding for AIDS work and championing LGBTQ cultural programming; while he only marched in the city's annual pride parade once, in 1989, he did host pride-themed events at City Hall. Rick Garcia, director of Equality Illinois, was clear-eyed about Daley's support: "The mayor gets on our issues not ahead of everyone else but when we have the votes."[1]

Some of the small "d" democratic principles that Washington emphasized also survived in some form, including the democratically elected local school councils, general budget transparency, and a reduction in the worst forms of race-based patronage under the still-enforced Shakman decree. "Despite the hatred and the internal tensions, Washington left an important legacy," stated Nena Torres in 2003. "The inclusive nature of his government lives on. It would be difficult to go back to the times when appointments to important boards and commissions went only to white people." Other Washington allies and long-time observers of city politics—from Bob Starks to Helen Shiller to the *Reader's*

A large poster of Harold Washington looms over Mayor Richard M. Daley during a 1997 memorial service at City Hall to commemorate the tenth anniversary of Washington's death. Even though Daley was firmly ensconced as mayor by that time, the memory of Washington and his surviving policies remained popular. ST-10001712–0070, *Chicago Sun-Times* collection, Chicago History Museum.

Ben Joravsky—generally agreed on this point. Commented Joravsky in 2009, Daley is "not going to put his Black allies in a position where they're forced to choose him over their communities in any sort of symbolic showdown. He's careful to avoid riling up Black voters with controversial appointments or inflammatory statements." Instead, Daley kept up appearances by hiring Blacks for high-profile positions and then slowly marginalizing them and narrowing which city contracts were eligible for affirmative action. He hid behind color-blindness when he laid off Black employees disproportionately in the public schools or displaced them when public housing was "transformed" (knocked down). And, not unlike Washington, Daley largely left the police department to its own devastating devices—a catastrophic decision but one consistent with officials across the political and racial spectrum in the 1990s and early 2000s.[2]

Economic development efforts in both the Loop and the neighborhoods, for which Daley received the lion's share of the credit from the political establishment and white voters, reflected the sharpest shift in priorities by the new mayor—although, even there, a certain level of continuity persisted from the Washington and Byrne administrations. While Washington and his economic development team, headed by scholar-activist Robert Mier, went to unprecedented lengths to engage and incorporate the grassroots in decision-making, the first Black mayor did not ignore downtown, as his critics suggested. Projects under Washington's watch included new stadiums, a new library, the redevelopment of Navy Pier, and the rehabilitation of the theater district. Efforts to stem industrial job losses with new investments outside of downtown had mixed results at best—in part because such work was not sustained after the mayor's death. When Daley became mayor, priorities quickly changed as elite, predominantly white interests in the Loop started to wield their traditional influence over city investments, including the passage of a new, expanded tax-increment financing (TIF) ordinance in 1990, which redirected tax revenues from rising property values for redevelopment. The practical result, as the *Reader* bluntly wrote about the city's first TIF in 1984, was "a slush fund controlled by the mayor [and] to compensate for that lost revenue, the schools, parks, county, etc. are forced to raise their tax rate," burdening ordinary city taxpayers. Harold Washington's administration approved the first TIF, which had become a popular, ostensibly "progressive" way for cities to fund redevelopment and address blight as federal urban renewal monies dried up during the Reagan era. But Daley relied too much on the tool to gentrify large swaths of the city, replacing lower-income housing, mom-and-pop businesses, and light industry with higher-end homes, corporate offices, and retail chains—the latter primarily catering to urban professionals and offering only low-wage service jobs to working-class Chicagoans—while watching taxes rise. Investigations by the *Reader* revealed that TIFs had siphoned off $1 billion in revenues during just a three-year period in the 2000s. Unequal tax assessments that disproportionately burdened the working class continued unabated as well. Symbolically, Daley himself moved into a townhouse in the rapidly gentrifying South Loop, which had benefited from a TIF. Yes, such redevelopment did beautify the city in the form of elegant streetscapes, flower boxes, and urban trees, not to mention premier gathering spaces like downtown's Millennium Park and the Near West Side's United Center for Michael Jordan and the Bulls, who dominated professional basketball in the 1990s. But at what cost? "Neighborhoods are hurting," observed Chuy García in 2016. "Chicago is still a city that is struggling to overcome the segregated patterns of housing. The divide between the haves and have nots is greater today."[3]

Especially after winning reelection resoundingly in 1991—against longtime Washington ally Danny Davis and a still-fractured Black political establishment—

Daley doubled down on "building the city of spectacle," as one study refers to his mayoralty. But building the high-gloss city that attracted young middle-class professionals, global corporate interests, and tourists from around the world came with two other concerning policy trends that Harold Washington had seeded but Daley accelerated: the militarization of the police and the corporatization of schools. Daley retained Washington's second police superintendent, Leroy Martin, a Black officer who epitomized the tough-on-crime, no-holds-barred policies embraced by most mainstream politicians of the era, white, Black, and Latino. Martin endorsed curtailing basic constitutional rights, even bizarrely praising authoritarian Chinese penology, while Daley himself muscled through legislation at the state level that reflected the national crime policies championed by President Bill Clinton, then senator Joe Biden, and much of the Black Congressional Caucus. As legal scholars Michelle Alexander, James Forman Jr., and others have shown, such policies proved extraordinarily tough on young offenders and gang members of color and only accelerated police militarization and brutality, mass incarceration, and a generation of curtailed economic and educational opportunities. Not surprisingly, instances of excessive force by the police rose under Daley, with fewer officers held accountable. Meanwhile, Daley refused to accept any responsibility for Chicago police commander Jon Burge's torture ring, which in the 1980s had provided his state's attorney's office with scores of coerced confessions. "I was not the mayor," stated Daley, shifting the blame to his predecessors. "I was not the police chief. I did not promote this man in the '80s." Daley fought being deposed in the case for years. In many ways, as Eric Klinenberg demonstrates, the city response to the catastrophic heat wave of 1995 epitomized the inhumanity that infused city services when responding to poor people, especially Blacks, in need. An estimated 739 people died during a week of 100-degree days—a disproportionate number of them Black and elderly, often trapped in their sweltering, oven-like homes by unrelenting poverty, social isolation, poor services, and street crime. Compounding the problem, men and women died because ill-trained police officers—many resentful of new community police initiatives that emphasized the "soft labor of feminine social workers"—failed to come to their aid in a timely manner and instead spent precious resources conducting the department's normal wave of drug arrests, even as people succumbed to the heat.[4]

Education reform also became inextricably tied to a neoliberal vision for the city. Long a target for reform by activists, most notably during the school walkouts of the 1960s over segregation and uneven resources, the future of the schools came to a head a generation later. In the wake of the 1987 teachers strike, promising efforts to empower parents and teachers in the 1980s by

Washington and Sawyer through the local school councils inadvertently fed other, more corporate schemes to decentralize and privatize the Chicago Public Schools. To diminish Black political power in the Chicago Teachers Union, CPS central administration, and the LSCs, and to attract more upwardly mobile white families to the city, Daley championed educational reforms that had become increasingly popular among elites of both political parties nationally in the 1990s. Through legislation he crafted in 1995 with the new Republican legislative majority in Springfield, Daley blunted the reforms from seven years before, retaining the LSCs but simultaneously opening the city's first charter schools, reorganizing (and thus slimming down) CPS with corporate management models, and incorporating accountability measures only bean counters could love—all under the supposedly innocuous umbrella of "school choice." Some Black and Latino parents and officials went along, with the hopes of improved educational choices for their children. But the practical result was the sidelining of traditional constituencies with the most relevant educational experience and knowledge—much of them Black, Latino, grassroots, and represented by unions—and the eventual 2013 shuttering of dozens of schools in minority neighborhoods by Rahm Emanuel to close a TIF-induced budget gap. This all happened while a former Chicago schools chief under Daley, Arne Duncan, sought to apply the corporate vision of "school choice" and "race to the top" as President Obama's secretary of education; it was more like a "race to the bottom," according to critics. The promise of inclusive participatory democracy and opportunity ultimately had been skewed in favor of corporate, primarily white benefactors.[5]

Such policies on economic development, policing, and education, not surprisingly, reflected the priorities of those who financially supported Daley and Emanuel. To finance its campaigns in the 1960s and 1970s, the first Daley machine relied on a coalition of real estate developers, construction firms, building-trade unions, and other downtown business elites interested in and invested in government contracts and development deals, along with an older, more closely knit network of ward-based organizations, where patronage work and "street money" flowed. In contrast, both Byrne and Washington won upset victories with shoestring budgets, with Washington's 1983 effort primarily reliant on donations smaller than $150 and only a handful of larger gifts from Black business leaders and liberal out-of-state groups; not surprisingly, both of their reelection efforts saw a significant influx of spending, expected for an incumbent by those doing business with the city, including trade unions, developers, and other downtown interests. But unlike either Byrne or Washington, Richard M. Daley's 1989 campaign looked like an incumbent's, especially based on the contributions he received from bankers, lawyers, consultants, developers, and many others who did not live in the city but had considerable economic interest in its future. Daley's largest contributor in 1989, for instance, was J. Paul Beitler, a major downtown developer and suburban Winnetka Republican who did not hide his disdain for racial hiring equality, economic development in the neighborhoods, or any kind of manufacturing. Instead of old-school patronage, in which primarily white members of the working class received city jobs for precinct-based machine work, "pinstripe patronage" became common, with lucrative legal, consultant, and insurance work doled out to connected firms. Nepotism, Mob-connected contracts, and outright bribery still occurred; the "hired truck" scandal of the late 1990s and early 2000s, in which truck crews were paid to do little to no work, looked like a scandal from the 1950s. But it was the sophisticated graft among service-based professionals—what some call the "global economy"—that really epitomized the new machine. And that pattern took a toll on democracy. As independent alderman Joe Moore of Rogers Park once observed, "When you see people close to the mayor leaving government and making megabucks, it contributes to the already large amount of public cynicism that exists."[6]

Indeed, Daley's style seemed to work for those Chicagoans willing to vote— the operative word being "willing." The number of people voting, in both percentage eligible and raw total, declined each municipal election cycle. After beating Evans and Davis, Daley went on to win four more elections, including against local Black luminaries Bobby Rush and Roland Burris. Rahm Emanuel, chief of staff in the Obama White House and a relative outsider himself, consolidated Daley's corporate support to win two terms of his own and become the city's first Jewish mayor. But each year under Daley, turnout dropped, with just 33 percent of voters showing up in 2007. Turnout in Emanuel's open, contested election in 2011 and his runoff against Chuy García four years later both edged past 40 percent. But the trend was unmistakable, especially among Black voters.[7]

IN THE SPRING OF 2019, Lori Lightfoot made history when she became the first Black woman and openly gay mayor of Chicago. A former federal prosecutor, corporate lawyer, and political neophyte, Lightfoot had been considered a longshot in a crowded field to succeed the two-term Emanuel—a field that included several high-profile figures from political scion Bill Daley and former police superintendent Garry McCarthy to Cook County board president Toni Preckwinkle and former schools chiefs Gery Chico and Paul Vallas. For the first time since 1983, a Daley on the mayoral ballot lost, leaving Lightfoot in a runoff against Preckwinkle, a veteran Black politician who started her political career as an aide to Harold Washington. The runoff—a format implemented two decades before to prevent the kind of narrow three-way primary victory that Washington achieved a generation ago—pitted two Black women against each other; as the *Chicago Reader* declared, "A Black Woman Will Lead Chicago." After Lightfoot pulled off a second upset, beating the once-favored Preckwinkle, the *New York Times* commented that her victory "signaled a notable shift in the mood of voters and a rejection of an entrenched political culture that has more often rewarded insiders and dismissed unknowns." Other outside observers agreed that the city's political establishment had been challenged and lost, while Lightfoot herself called her election as "a movement for change."[8]

Yet, many locals were not so sure. Neither candidate could be considered a "true blue progressive," to quote the *Reader*, or someone willing to challenge the city's commitment to neoliberalism that led to school and clinic closures, a regressive tax burden, continuing police violence, and enduring poverty in many of the city's Black and Latino neighborhoods—especially when such a challenge was politically risky. While each candidate had taken a different path to the mayor's race, both had ties to Richard M. Daley's new Democratic machine. After Washington's death, Preckwinkle adapted to the machine's return and won the first of five aldermanic terms in 1991, beating Tim Evans in the Fourth Ward, and later became president of the Cook County Board and Democratic Party chair. While known for progressive causes such as affordable housing, police accountability, and a living wage ordinance—not to mention being the occasional lone dissent on early budget votes—Preckwinkle increasingly backed the mayor's economic policies and became a "chief flag waver" for Chicago's failed bid to host the 2016 Olympics, a bid that looked a lot like the proposed 1992 World's Fair boondoggle. Of greater concern were Preckwinkle's ties to Alderman Ed Burke, the one-time Washington nemesis who had served on the City Council since 1969 and found himself caught in a federal corruption and extortion probe—as so many of his Chicago peers before and since had, including Ed Vrdolyak. "Her political brand," according to one writer, "had been badly damaged by the Burke scandal."[9]

In contrast, Lightfoot had never been elected to public office. She had the support of one-time independent heavyweights Dick Simpson and consultant Don Rose, but she also had held numerous appointments under Daley and his successor, Rahm Emanuel, including chief of the Chicago police's oft-criticized and now-defunct Office of Professional Standards, and later as president of the

Chicago Police Board and chair of the Police Accountability Task Force. These roles appropriately placed Lightfoot in the middle of the nation's debate over police violence against Black citizens, most egregiously the graphic 2014 murder of Laquan McDonald by Chicago police officer Jason Van Dyke, famously caught on video that was suppressed by the Emanuel administration. As chair of the task force, she sharply criticized police practices, calling the "community's lack of trust . . . justified" and arguing that the police's "own data gives validity to the widely held belief that the police have no regard for the sanctity of life." But she still came under fire by activists, including the Black Youth Project 100, for her inability to hold the police accountable beyond well-chosen rhetoric. Capturing many Chicagoans' skepticism, one columnist wrote, "Chicago will be run by a black woman. But is it ready for reform?"[10]

The question was a valid one. The last time a reform mayor was elected, lasting change proved difficult to sustain. Moreover, while Lightfoot's victory certainly upended conventional wisdom, it would be a mistake to see her election as a clear mandate. While on its face 2019 had some similarities to 1983, the structural challenges Lightfoot faced seemed even more daunting, while her base of political power proved far narrower. Voter turnout across the city was just 35 percent in the primary and an even more pitiful 33 percent in the runoff, with still lower participation among African Americans and Latinos. These numbers were less than half the turnout in 1983 or 1987. Moreover, with an initial fourteen-person field, neither of the top vote-getters received more than 20 percent. And in a two-woman race that Lightfoot won overwhelmingly with 73.7 percent, her 386,039 votes fell several hundred thousand votes short of Washington's numbers in similar head-to-head campaigns. In both races, Lightfoot did manage to win a cross-section of support, with strong showings in overwhelmingly white, middle-class North Side communities—indeed another reason why her progressive bona fides came into question—as well as the majority of Black and Latino votes in the runoff. But a central question remained: Why such low turnout, especially with such an initial diversity of choices?[11]

This discontent and disillusionment with the political process could be seen as a clear, albeit not inevitable, product of more than a generation of neoliberal politics and policies by Daley, Emanuel, and the modern Democratic Party both locally and nationally. While allowing some of Harold Washington's affirmative action policies and more symbolic efforts to stay in place, neoliberal politicians rebuilt a leaner, meaner machine and oversaw the city's transformation into a gleaming example of twenty-first-century inequality. Plenty of energy remained in the streets and among the grassroots, from teacher union activism to the Black Lives Matter protests of police violence that went well beyond Laquan McDonald's murder. But this energy struggled to infuse electoral politics in the way that the social movements of the 1970s and 1980s eventually did. In eight straight elections starting in 1989, the moderate white mayoral candidate won, soundly beating his Black (and in one case, Latino) rival. That streak may be over for the moment, but this electoral reality proves one of the most complicated legacies of the Harold Washington era.

AFTER HIS DEATH, many of Harold Washington's protégés and contemporaries continued to operate in the politics and policymaking of Daley's Chicago, often as the few truly progressive voices in city, county, and federal government for a more inclusive, participatory vision in a decidedly different era. Most adapted to the new regime to survive politically, carving out a few key issues to champion while going along with other aspects of Daley's corporate agenda for the city. Luis Gutiérrez became Chicago's first Latino member of Congress in 1992 and emerged as a leading voice for immigrant rights and one of the more reliably progressive votes—admittedly much of it in the House Democratic minority—before retiring after thirteen terms. After a stint as a county commissioner and a spirited but unsuccessful mayoral run against Rahm Emanuel in 2015, Chuy García succeeded Gutiérrez as the city's sole Latino U.S. House representative four years later. Danny Davis and Bobby Rush also became members of Congress in the 1990s, the latter winning the seat once held by Washington, Metcalfe, and Dawson. Toni Preckwinkle championed affordable housing on the City Council for twenty years, while Uptown's Helen Shiller fought developers for six terms as alderman. After eleven years as an independent alderman, David Orr served as Cook County clerk for twenty-eight years. Others, such as Kari Moe, Hal Baron, Linda Coronado, Brenetta Howell Barrett, and Jacky Grimshaw, pursued change through nonprofit work, political consulting, and public service, while Bob Starks, Nena Torres, and Dick Simpson returned to the academy. Slim Coleman, along with his wife and Rudy's sister, Emma Lozano, became a Methodist pastor and a passionate defender of the sanctuary and immigrant rights movements.

A new generation of activists have followed in their footsteps and, in numerous ways, challenged the compromises Washington's acolytes were forced to make both during and after his administration. Activists of all colors continue to organize for police reform and accountability, the Movement for Black Lives,

immigrant rights, affordable housing, a living wage, LGBTQ rights, quality education, and environmental justice, and have managed to diversify the City
Council to a certain extent—not unlike how the national Democratic Party
has tried to change in recent years. Instead of a handful of lonely independents
shouting in the wind, as had been the case during much of the last half-century,
a robust, multiracial "democratic socialist caucus" exists, demanding that the
mayor, whether she likes it or not, have an open dialogue and fulfill her progressive campaign promises. If neighborhood activists and their allies in city and
county government can sustain their coalition, agree to disagree on certain
issues, work together, and genuinely open up the city, both inside and outside
City Hall, then perhaps voter turnout and participation will rebound and a new
era of democracy will blossom. The extraordinary turnout in the 2020 federal
elections in Chicago, and the dynamic community activism and street work
that seeded that result, suggests the possibility.[12]

This all may sound quite idealistic, especially for Chicagoans trained to be
clear-eyed, perhaps cynical, about the transactional nature of politics. But the
alternative is as stark as it has ever been in modern U.S. history. In the twenty-
first century, we have been reminded that liberal democracies are inherently
fragile—and not just in historically developing countries in Africa, Asia, and
Latin America, but also in Europe and North America. The challenges the
United States has faced since at least 2008 have been some of the most desta-
bilizing since the nation went to war with itself over slavery in the 1860s. There
are many potential threats to the U.S. system, from crises such as pandemic,
war, and financial instability to rising inequality, white supremacy, and a new
plutocracy—much of it on display in Chicago. As disturbing as the January 6,
2021, insurrection at the U.S. Capitol was, most political scientists and legal
scholars argue that a rapid collapse of democracy, replaced by an authoritarian regime, remains unlikely. Rather, "a more subtle, incremental erosion" of
competitive elections, the rights to political speech, assembly, petition, a free
press, and a general rule of law are the far more likely path to "constitutional
retrogression" and eventual authoritarianism in the United States.[13] A primary
way to hasten such "democratic backsliding"—and one that our counterparts
in Chicago a generation ago and since can attest to—is through growing cynicism and complacency brought on by broken electoral promises and missed
opportunities. If a broad democratic coalition such as the one that lifted Harold Washington to power in 1983 cannot prompt real, sustained reform and
a greater quality of living for its supporters due to a variety of factors—from
structural barriers to rampant corruption and racism to a decline in grassroots,

social justice organizing—then the belief in the efficacy of democracy may very well erode over time. If complacency and cynicism are allowed to settle in, fewer and fewer people will participate in any form of politics—movement, electoral, or otherwise.

And who will have won then? Few but autocrats and their patrons.

# Acknowledgments

Like every book, this one has many more influences than the single author whose name appears on the cover. In fact, this book has two, maybe even three separate origin stories. One begins with a fundraising letter in late 2008. In the weeks after then senator Barack Obama won the presidential election on the backs of an impressively multiracial Democratic coalition, I received a note from the Durham People's Alliance, a local progressive advocacy organization in North Carolina. The organization's cochairs wrote that, while it was okay to celebrate Obama's historic victory, there was much more work to do. The worst thing, the letter warned, would be to sit back, relax, and become complacent, overly confident that now that the good guys would hold the White House and Congress (not to mention the governorship and state legislature), progressives could shift their focus to other work. It was not the time to "sit on our butts," they wrote.

I have thought about that message many times over the years since—especially as Obama's political rivals did everything in their power to obstruct his presidency, while he and his allies largely dropped, even discouraged, the grassroots organizing efforts that made his improbable victory possible. Presidential historians and other scholars will surely offer more nuanced insights into Obama's campaigns and administrations in the coming years and decades; in fact, they have already begun to do so. But for this historian, the frustrations of the Obama era underscored a larger truth: electoral politics alone will not bring greater freedom. Without continued grassroots activism outside of the halls of power, winning elections, even in the exciting, satisfying fashion that Obama did, will not produce the world those activists sought. Even in a city where politics seems to be everything.

And this brings the story to (well, keeps the story in) Chicago. While I was writing and researching my first book, many participants in the Chicago Freedom Movement of 1966 and the Poor People's Campaign two years later became reenergized, this time by an electoral campaign featuring Harold Washington. Al Raby, one of many 1960s activists to campaign for Washington, explicitly connected the two, calling Washington's historic mayoral campaign in 1983 nothing less than a continuation of Dr. King's work in Chicago. At that moment in the archive, I realized that the Harold Washington movement and moment

deserved a new sustained look. And it provided an excuse for me to keep returning to a city I came to love.

I do have a confession, however: I have actually never lived in Chicago for any
substantial length of time. It would be fair to call me an outsider. And yet I feel
I have known the city in a sense since I was child, in part because my grand-
father, Keith Sinninger—a small-town midwesterner who lived with my parents
and me at the end of his life—spent his formative years in the city. That's where
he met my grandmother, Zella Soltow, received a college education over seven
long years, and inexplicably shot rats as a nighttime security guard during the
1933 World's Fair, among other things. He was, ahem, a cantankerous old man,
to say the least. But he talked about the city he knew—the gritty Chicago of the
1920s and 1930s—so vividly that it captured my teenage imagination. Perhaps
it was then that I came to believe that Chicago, not New York, was the truly
American city.

Therefore, I want to first thank the people of Chicago, especially those men
and women of the Windy City who shared with me their stories and experiences from the 1970s and 1980s. They did not have to help me piece together this
history, but they did, and with great generosity and candor. They include Hal
Baron, Brenetta Howell Barrett, Tim Black, Linda Coronado, Chuy García, Jacky
Grimshaw, Michael James, Cha-Cha Jiménez, David Mojica, Modesto Rivera,
Helen Shiller, Paul Siegel, Dick Simpson, Bob Starks, and Nena Torres. A special
shoutout goes to friends and historians Erik Gellman and Katie Turk, who more
than anyone, other than my family, supported this project—from draft-reading
to research-trip housing to cold-beverage drinking. The same goes to two of my
favorite Chicagoans, Liz and Joe Fitzgerald, who were always ready to decom-
press with me after a long day of research.

I am grateful to everyone who read all or part of the manuscript in its
many chapter and conference panel forms and helped shape my understanding of both Chicago and my work's implications beyond the city. They include
an incredible array of scholars of the city and urban politics and life more
generally: Richard Anderson, Peter Cole, Lilia Fernández, Jeff Helgeson, Devin
Hunter, Austin McCoy, Tim Mennell, Juan Mora-Torres, Melanie Newport, Liesl
Orenic, Charles Payne, Christopher Reed, Andrew Sandoval-Strausz, Amanda
Seligman, Timothy Stewart-Winter, Elizabeth Todd-Breland, and especially
Simon Balto and Jakobi Williams, the not-so-anonymous reviewers of this
book. I also continue to learn from an array of other scholars of social move-
ments, Black and Latino politics, and the law, including Brian Behnken, Carlos
Blanton, Ally Brantley, Rob Chase, David Cline, Matt Countryman, Jon Dueck,
Mike Ezra, Patrick Jones, Adriane Lentz-Smith, Chuck McKinney, Brian Murray,

Marc Rodriguez, Phil Rubio, and Katie Wells. Deserving special mention is our virtual Latino reading and cocktail group, full of brilliant scholars I am honored to know: Lauren Araiza, Lori Flores, Rudy Guevara, Felipe Hinojosa, Max Krochmal, Sarah McNamara, and Christian Paiz. I look forward to seeing all of you again in a conference hotel lobby soon.

The University Writing Program at George Washington University in D.C. has been my academic home for nearly ten years and its many fine scholars and pedagogues have provided both professional comradery and immeasurable friendship along the way. Of particular note is my interdisciplinary pandemic happy hour gang, made up of writing studies scholars and physicists (!), who started meeting virtually most Friday nights in March 2020 and continue to keep me sane years later: Bethany Cobb Kung, Kavita Daiya, Evie Downie, Harald Griesshammer, Danika Myers, Rachel Riedner, Alexander van der Horst, and Zak Wolfe. Many others in the University Writing Program, the Departments of History and American Studies, and the D.C. Labor History Seminar also deserve mention, including Eric Arnesen, Jay Driskell, Leon Fink, Wade Fletcher, Tom Guglielmo, Carol Hayes, Chris Klemek, Randi Kristensen, Derek Malone-France, Sara Matthiesen, Joe McCartin, Phyllis Ryder, Katrin Schultheiss, Caroline Smith, Michael Svoboda, Phil Troutman, and Angela Zimmerman. And my remarkable students, too many to name here, keep me both grounded and reminded of why this work matters.

My deepest gratitude goes to the editors, archivists, and librarians who helped bring the entire book together down the stretch. My editor, Mark Simpson-Vos, as well as Brandon Proia, María García, Thomas Bedenbaugh, Valerie Burton, Alex Martin, and the rest of the talented team at UNC Press, have done it again, providing the right amount of support an author needed throughout the process. Yes, the pandemic slowed things down here and there, but I was always confident that I remained in good hands. The same goes for Justice, Power, and Politics series editors Heather Thompson and Rhonda Williams, who have long been supportive of my work. I conducted the majority of my research at the Harold Washington Library Center and cannot praise the professionals there enough. Maybe I am biased because I am the son of two reference librarians, but so be it! Thanks to Glenn Humphreys, Roslyn Mabry, Michelle McCoy, Johanna Russ, Morag Walsh, and Sarah Zimmerman for all of their assistance. I am also grateful to librarians at other institutions who helped me, including Peter Alter, Ellen Keith, Colleen Layton, and Lesley Martin at the Chicago History Museum; Beverly Cook, Cynthia Fife-Townsel, and Beth Loch at the Woodson Regional Library's Vivian Harsh Research Collection; Val Harris, Scott Pitol, and research assistant Marla McMackin at the Daley Library of the University of Illinois, Chicago; and Leigh Rupinski in Special Collections at Grand Valley State University. Humanities scholars cannot do their work without extra funding—and it's increasingly in short supply—so my appreciation goes out to GW, Duke University, the National Humanities Center, the Black Metropolis Research Consortium, and the Newberry Library for their financial help.

Finally, I want to thank my many friends and family who have nothing to do with academia. Researching and writing an academic book is a rewarding but difficult task, even in the best of times; during a global pandemic, an insurrection just miles from our home, and any number of other challenges we have faced over the last several years, finishing the book just seemed impossible. But thanks to our numerous friends in Arlington, Virginia, we had brief moments to escape, over a meal, a firepit, and meaningful service to the community. We feel appreciated and understood and that means a lot. As for my family, we are a team. While we might argue bitterly over a ridiculously drawn-out game of Catan, we come together and support each other when it counts. My parents, Ed and Judy Mantler, instilled in me a deep appreciation of the past from an early age. My amazing, busy, and inquisitive kids, Zella and Dash, gave me just enough space to finish this book, not to mention inspiration for a more just future. And my partner, Christina Headrick, an activist herself, kept us informed and safe in a world seemingly gone mad. Love and peace to you all.

# Notes

## Abbreviations

| | |
|---|---|
| ACW | Rev. Addie Wyatt and Rev. Claude Wyatt Papers |
| BE | Bernard Epton Papers |
| BHB | Brenetta Howell Barrett Papers |
| CC | Christopher Cohen Papers |
| CH | Charles A. Hayes Papers |
| CSS | Community Services Sub-cabinet Records |
| CUL | Chicago Urban League Records |
| DS | Dick Simpson Papers |
| DSS | Development Sub-cabinet Records |
| ESM | Eugene Sawyer Mayoral Records |
| GP | Government Publications |
| HH | Henry Hampton Collection |
| HMDA | HistoryMakers Digital Archive |
| ISS | Illinois State Senatorial Records |
| MACLA | Mayor's Advisory Commission on Latino Affairs Records |
| MC | Mayoral Campaign Records |
| MLK | Dr. Martin Luther King Jr. Papers |
| MR | Municipal Reference Collection |
| PEP | Political Education Project Records |
| PSRS | Public Safety/Regulatory Sub-cabinet Records |
| RG | Robert Giloth Papers |
| RL | Rudy Lozano Papers |
| RM | Robert Mier Papers |
| SA | Steve Askin Papers |
| TB | Timuel D. Black Jr. Papers |
| YL | Young Lords Collection |

## Introduction

1. "'We Have Won,' Washington Declares," *Chicago Tribune*, February 19, 1983.

2. Rivlin, *Fire on the Prairie*, 103. Unless otherwise noted, this book cites the revised edition of Rivlin's book on Washington, written in 1992 and updated throughout to connect Washington to the election of President Obama.

3. Biles, *Mayor Harold Washington*; Winston, dir., *Punch 9 for Harold Washington*. For other biographical accounts, see Levinsohn, *Harold Washington*; Travis, *Harold*; Miller, *Harold Washington*; and Chandler, *Harold Washington and the Civil Rights Legacy*.

4. Holli and Green, *Bashing Chicago Traditions*, 17.

5. For detailed accounts of how the machine worked—and how African Americans historically worked inside of it—see Manning, *William L. Dawson*; Grimshaw, *Bitter Fruit*, 136–38; Rakove, *Don't Make No Waves*, and *We Don't Want Nobody Nobody Sent*; Royko, *The Boss*; Rivlin, *Fire on the Prairie*, 51–53.

6. From the daily campaign and election coverage of the *Chicago Tribune* and *Sun-Times* to the most contextualized book-length accounts of Harold Washington's election and administration, analysis almost exclusively credits the interconnected rise of independent Black political power and decline of the Democratic machine after Mayor Richard J. Daley's death. Even *Fire on the Prairie*, written by the *Chicago Reader*'s Gary Rivlin and considered by many to be the best of the many Washington books, emphasizes these factors. Other accounts by journalists, sociologists, and political scientists—nearly all written in the 1980s or early 1990s—frame Washington's campaign and administration similarly. Rivlin, *Fire on the Prairie*; Grimshaw, *Bitter Fruit*; Kleppner, *Chicago Divided*; Holli and Green, *The Making of the Mayor*, and *Bashing Chicago Traditions*; Alkalimat and Gills, "Chicago—Black Power vs. Racism" and *Harold Washington and the Crisis of Black Power*; Starks and Preston, "Harold Washington and the Politics of Reform in Chicago"; Clavel and Wiewel, *Harold Washington and the Neighborhoods*; Nolan, *Campaign!*; Clavel, *Activists in City Hall*, 96–145.

7. Mantler, *Power to the Poor*; Krochmal, *Blue Texas*; Araiza, *To March for Others*; Brantley, *Brewing a Boycott*; Brilliant, *The Color of America Has Changed*; Behnken, *Civil Rights and Beyond* and *The Struggle in Black and Brown*; Stewart-Winter, *Queer Clout*.

8. Other scholars have framed multiracial coalitions among Blacks, Latinos, Asians, and progressive whites, including Jews, largely through success. See Ortiz, *An African American and Latinx History of the United States*; Ogbar, *Black Power*, chap. 6; Pulido, *Black, Brown, Yellow, and Left*; Bernstein, *Bridges of Reform*; Mariscal, *Brown-Eyed Children of the Sun*, chaps. 5 and 6. McWilliams, *Brothers under the Skin*, remains a classic study in this vein. On failure and the sometimes parallel but separate nature of these struggles, see Behnken, *Fighting Their Own Battles*; Foley, *Quest for Equality*, "Partly Colored or Other White," "Straddling the Color Line," and "Becoming Hispanic"; Clayson, *Freedom Is Not Enough*; Whitaker, *Race Work*, chap. 6; Vaca, *Presumed Alliance*; Luckingham, *Minorities in Phoenix*; Skerry, *Mexican Americans*.

9. Several broader accounts of Black politics in the city highlight the importance of Black activism a generation before, including King's visit to the city. Grimshaw, *Bitter Fruit*; Todd-Breland, *A Political Education*; Balto, *Occupied Territory*; Gellman, *Troublemakers*; Diamond, *Mean Streets*; Helgeson, *Crucibles of Black Empowerment*, 238–76; Williams, *From the Bullet to the Ballot*, 195–99.

10. Johnson, *Revolutionaries to Race Leaders*, xxiii. Tracing the "winding historical path" that Black Power takes, Johnson calls for a "renewal of political antagonism" lost in the 1970s. See also Ture and Hamilton, *Black Power*; and Joseph, *Waiting 'til the Midnight Hour*.

11. Sugrue, *Sweet Land of Liberty*, 500; Marable, *Race, Reform, and Rebellion*, 122–23, 132–33; Countryman, "From Protest to Politics," 813–61.

12. Mantler, "Rainbow Reformers," 221–23, 226, 232; Stewart-Winter, *Queer Clout*, 132–52; Balto, *Occupied Territory*, 222–55; Fernández, *Brown in the Windy City*, 131–261; *Keep Strong*, March and June–July 1978.

13. Sandoval-Strausz, "Latino Landscapes," 804–31, and *Barrio America*; Judd, *Simp-*

son, and Abu-Lughod, *The City, Revisited*, chap. 10; Francis-Fallon, *The Rise of the Latino Vote*, 310–85.

14. While there are too many to list here, the field of carceral studies has demonstrated a clear history of systematic state violence toward Black Americans, in particular, one that has not let up since the 1960s. Balto, *Occupied Territory*; Hinton, *America on Fire*; Felker-Kantor, *Policing Los Angeles*; Losier, "The Public Does Not Believe the Police Can Police Themselves"; Murch, "Crack in Los Angeles"; Thompson, *Blood in the Water*; Berger, *Captive Nation*; Chase, *We Are Not Slaves*.

15. Katz, "Why Aren't U.S. Cities Burning?" (quotes), and *Why Don't American Cities Burn?*, 78–100. The "long civil rights movement" paradigm signaled a lasting shift in the historiography and periodization of the freedom struggle, including multiracial coalition-building and carceral activism. Hall, "The Long Civil Rights Movement and the Political Uses of the Past." A few examples include Sugrue, *Sweet Land of Liberty*; Jeffries, *Bloody Lowndes*; Countryman, *Up South*. See also notes 8 and 9.

16. SNCC's early work in Mississippi started with voter registration; King routinely faced criticism, including in Birmingham and Selma, for compromising with white supremacist officials too quickly. Carson, *In Struggle*, 45–51, 74–81, 157–61. Meanwhile Black Power activists, such as Oakland's Bobby Seale and Chicago's Fred Hampton, were far more strategic than popular memory gives them credit for.

17. According to Reed, "The new Black elite's political capacity presumed acceptance of overarching programmatic frameworks and priorities . . . defined by the pro-growth, pro-business interests that reproduce entrenched patterns of racial inequality." Reed, *Stirrings in the Jug*, 5 (quote), 79–115; Marable, *Race, Reform, and Rebellion*, 147. Others have argued that a detached Black political elite touched by corruption emerged but mainly after systematized, mostly baseless challenges to their political legitimacy by whites in the 1970s and 1980s. See Musgrove, *Rumor, Repression, and Racial Politics*; Musgrove and Jeffries, "The Community Don't Know What's Good for Them," 305–28.

18. Sean Wilentz coined the term "Age of Reagan" and is one of several historians who downplays the alternative politics of the time. Wilentz, *The Age of Reagan*; Troy and Cannato, *Living in the Eighties*; Troy, *Morning in America*; Hayward, *The Age of Reagan*; Ehrman, *The Eighties*; Patterson, *Restless Giant*; Jenkins, *Decade of Nightmares*. Others still use the term but greatly complicate the fortieth president's centrality to the narrative. Martin, *The Other Eighties*; Rossinow, *The Reagan Era*.

19. Martin, *The Other Eighties*, 3–14, 19–24, 31–34, 131–36, 171–88; Foley, *Front Porch Politics*, 165–76, 280–300; Brier, *Infectious Ideas*; Lorentzen, *Women in the Sanctuary Movement*.

20. Foley, *Front Porch Politics*, 5. At times, Foley seems to use the term so expansively as to describe almost any activism from the time, including movements on the right. But while some activism might be driven by perceived threats to one's livelihood or home, such as antibusing advocacy and local antitax efforts, many are often pushed by larger interests such as those of corporations.

21. Cowie, *The Great Exception*, 209–29; Cohen, *Making a New Deal*, 285–86. The end of "the era of big government," was famously declared by Bill Clinton in the 1990s, but Reagan conservatives had made it their mantra after taking power in 1981. And yet just the opposite happened, as the Pentagon, domestic law enforcement, and the carceral state ballooned under Reagan, especially through the War on Drugs, dwarfing any shrinkage

of the state elsewhere. See Novak, "The Myth of the Weak American State"; Rossinow, *The Reagan Era*; Kruse and Zelizer, *Fault Lines*; Lassiter, "Ten Propositions for the New Political History"; Kazin, *What It Took to Win*.

22. "It's Been No Picnic, Mayor Says," *Chicago Tribune*, March 16, 1985. Richard J. Daley (1955–76) had been mayor the longest in Chicago's history until his son Richard M. Daley surpassed him by a year (1989–2011).

23. Green and Holli, *Restoration 1989*, vii–xii; Grimshaw, *Bitter Fruit*, 197–224; Diamond, *Chicago on the Make*, 203–321. Diamond, unfortunately, takes this too far, suggesting that the rise of a neoliberal machine was, in fact, inevitable.

24. "Chicago Mayor Lori Lightfoot Says Video of Adam Toledo's Fatal Shooting by Police 'Incredibly Difficult to Watch,'" *Chicago Tribune*, April 15, 2021; "2 Years after Her Election, Chicago Mayor Lori Lightfoot Hasn't Yet Fulfilled Key Campaign Promises," *Chicago Tribune*, April 2, 2021; "Lightfoot Turns City's Infrastructure into Weapons against Protesters," *Chicago Reader*, November 18, 2020.

25. Kwame Anthony Appiah, "The Case for Capitalizing the B in Black," *Atlantic*, June 18, 2020; Nell Irvin Painter, "Why White Should Be Capitalized, Too," *Washington Post*, July 22, 2020; Laws, "Why We Capitalize 'Black' (and Not 'White')," *Columbia Journalism Review*, June 16, 2020; Guzmán, "Latino, the Word," 143–45; de Onís, "What's in an 'X'?," 78–91.

## Chapter 1

1. Rustin, "From Protest to Politics."

2. D'Emilio, *Lost Prophet*, 393; Rustin, "From Protest to Politics"; Dittmer, *Local People*, 302 (quotes). Rustin, in the essay's penultimate paragraph, reiterated that they should have accepted the two-seat compromise the Democrats offered.

3. That year saw several symbolic candidacies. In addition to Tijerina, other prominent participants in the Poor People's Campaign, for instance, ran for office to highlight issues from the campaign, including Hank Adams, Flo Ware, Grace Mora Newman, Gilberto Gerena Valentín, and Peggy Terry. Mantler, *Power to the Poor*, 189, 211.

4. Marable, *Race, Reform, and Rebellion*, 122 (quote); Rustin, "From Protest to Politics"; D'Emilio, *Lost Prophet*, 403–4; Jeffries, *Bloody Lowndes*, 207–8; Sugrue, *Sweet Land of Liberty*, 498–502; Black and Black, *The Rise of Southern Republicans*; Navarro, *La Raza Unida Party*. Matthew Countryman is quite critical of Rustin's rejection of nationalism in Black politics, which he argues reflects Black Power in crucial ways. Countryman, "From Protest to Politics."

5. Lawson, *Running for Freedom*, 148–49; Francis-Fallon, *The Rise of the Latino Vote*, 308–11; Sugrue, *Sweet Land of Liberty*, 501–3.

6. Drake and Cayton, *Black Metropolis*, 376–77.

7. Wilkerson, *The Warmth of Other Suns*; Grossman, *Land of Hope*; Hirsch, *Making the Second Ghetto*; Seligman, *Block by Block*; Black, *Bridges of Memory*; Drake and Cayton, *Black Metropolis*.

8. Cohen and Taylor, *American Pharaoh*, 35–36; Diamond, *Mean Streets*, 28–33; Grossman, *Land of Hope*, 259–60.

9. Anderson and Pickering, *Confronting the Color Line*, 46–49; Satter, *Family Proper-*

*ties*, 39–41; Connolly, *A World More Concrete*; Cohen and Taylor, *American Pharaoh*, 34; Helgeson, *Crucibles of Black Empowerment*, 31.

10. Drake and Cayton, *Black Metropolis*, 379 (quote); Green, *Selling the Race*; Baldwin, *Chicago's New Negroes*.

11. Garb, *Freedom's Ballot*, 187–222; Anderson and Pickering, *Confronting the Color Line*, 50–52.

12. Most of the city's first generation of Black political leaders were born in the South, including Mitchell, Dawson, Earl Dickerson, and Harold Washington's father, Roy. This slowly changed over the next forty years, but key figures of Washington's era, such as Lutrelle "Lu" Palmer, were also born in the South. See Black, *Bridges of Memory*.

13. Helgeson, *Crucibles of Black Empowerment*, 54 (quote); Manning, *William L. Dawson*.

14. Rakove, *Don't Make No Waves*, 107–8.

15. Helgeson, *Crucibles of Black Empowerment*, 249 (quote); Cohen and Taylor, *American Pharaoh*, 58–61.

16. Travis, *Harold*, 49–51; Rivlin, *Fire on the Prairie*, 28, 30.

17. Gellman, *Death Blow to Jim Crow*, 47–62, and "Carthage Must Be Destroyed"; Helgeson, *Crucibles of Black Empowerment*, 55–62.

18. *Chicago Defender*, February 26, 1955 (quote); Cohen and Taylor, *American Pharaoh*, 143–45; Grimshaw, *Bitter Fruit*, 100–102, 108–12.

19. Albert Janney, "The Chicago League of Negro Voters," undated (quotes); Helgeson, *Crucibles of Black Empowerment*, 206; Beito and Beito, *Black Maverick*, 168–89; Tyson, *The Blood of Emmett Till*, 86–89, 136–43, 191–92.

20. "Dawson Backed by Voters League," *Chicago Defender*, February 7, 1959.

21. "Rallies Negro Voters after Loss," *Chicago Tribune*, March 27, 1960 (quote); Janney, "To Increase the Power of Negro Voters," June 1959; "Primary Sets New Low" and "Leads Negro Business Men in Civic Drive," *Chicago Tribune*, March 6 and August 29, 1959; "Credits League with Spuring [*sic*] Vote," *Chicago Defender*, December 16, 1959; Helgeson, *Crucibles of Black Empowerment*, 207–8; Despres with Heise, *Challenging the Daley Machine*, 90; Black, *Sacred Ground*, 85.

22. Gellman, *Troublemakers*, 105–18; Ralph, *Northern Protest*, 21–22; Danns, *Something Better for Our Children*; Todd-Breland, *A Political Education*, and "Barbara Sizemore." Adam Green offers a more qualified assessment of the boycotts but does argue that they proved more consequential to the city's civil rights activism than Emmett Till's murder and its aftermath. Green, *Selling the Race*, 208–9. For school boycotts as a national phenomenon across the urban and suburban North, see Theoharis, *A More Beautiful and Terrible History*, 31–62; Sugrue, *Sweet Land of Liberty*, 163–99, 449–92.

23. U.S. Commission on Civil Rights, *Report*, 365; Chicago Urban League Research Department memo to director Edwin C. Berry, Hearings and Statements on Racial Segregation file, January 18, 1962, GP; Todd-Breland, *A Political Education*, 26–27.

24. Danns, *Something Better for Our Children*, 25–27; Rury, "Race, Space, and the Politics of Chicago's Public Schools," 129–30; Ralph, *Northern Protest*, 15–18; Mantler, *Power to the Poor*, 49–50; Gellman, *Troublemakers*, 94–104.

25. Todd-Breland, *A Political Education*, 26–30; Ralph, *Northern Protest*, 19–33, 70–71; Danns, *Something Better for Our Children*, 25–27; Anderson and Pickering, *Confronting*

*the Color Line*, 84–102; Cohen and Taylor, *American Pharaoh*, 334–37; Diamond, *Chicago on the Make*, 158–64.

26. Accounts of the civil rights organizing that preceded the Chicago Freedom Movement, for instance, rarely mention the electoral challenges that coincided with the school protests. Ralph, *Northern Protest*; Danns, *Something Better for Our Children*; Anderson and Pickering, *Confronting the Color Line*; Finley et al., *The Chicago Freedom Movement*.

27. Helgeson, *Crucibles of Black Empowerment*, 251; Black, *Sacred Ground*, 88–89; Fremon, *Chicago Politics Ward by Ward*, 120 (quote). "Seven Women Eye Exclusive City Council Offices," *Chicago Tribune*, January 14, 1963; "Negro Voters to Meet Here in Conference," *Chicago Tribune*, February 29, 1960; "Mitchell Asks Minimum Wage Law Support," *Chicago Tribune*, April 6, 1960; "Parker's Death Is No Lynching," *Chicago Defender*, May 6, 1959; "Plan Help for Boycott Victims," *Chicago Defender*, September 3, 1960; "Minority Groups Form Alliance to Oust 27th Ward 'Outsiders,'" *Chicago Defender*, February 16, 1963; "Charlie Chew; The System Bustin' Man," *Chicago Defender*, October 20, 1970.

28. Black, *Sacred Ground*, 85; Fremon, *Chicago Politics Ward by Ward*, 193; Grimshaw, *Bitter Fruit* 20 (quotes). "Ald. Ben Lewis Led Three Lives," *Chicago Tribune*, March 17, 1963; "Hunt Ald. Lewis' Slayer," *Chicago Tribune*, March 1, 1963; "The Murder Chicago Didn't Want to Solve," *Chicago Reader*, March 2, 2021; Hirsch, *Making the Second Ghetto*; Seligman, *Block by Block*; Grimshaw, *Bitter Fruit*, 119–22.

29. "Polls Unit Slates Confab November 9," *Chicago Defender*, November 7, 1963; "Congressional Hopefuls Back School Boycott," *Chicago Defender*, February 24, 1964 (quotes). Brenetta Howell Barrett interview; "Group Begins Effort to Oust Rep. Dawson," *Chicago Defender*, October 14, 1963; "New 'Rights' Group a Phony?," *Chicago Defender*, January 27, 1964; "If You're on ADC or Live in Public Housing, You Can VOTE; Call Us If They Threaten You," *Chicago Defender*, January 20, 1964; "Protest at the Polls Lashes at BGA and the IVI," *Chicago Defender*, June 11, 1964; "Unit Seeks to Oust Ben Willis," *Chicago Defender*, March 6, 1965; "Dawson Is New Group's Target," *Chicago Tribune*, October 7, 1963.

30. Grimshaw, *Bitter Fruit*, 115; Cohen and Taylor, *American Pharaoh*, 296 (quotes).

31. "Private Office of Adamowski Is Burglarized," *Chicago Tribune*, March 28, 1963 (quote); "Victory Margin for Mayor Is Far below His 2 to 1 Goal," *Chicago Tribune*, April 3, 1963; "Adamowski Hits Hard on Rising Taxes," *Chicago Tribune*, March 31, 1963; Grimshaw, *Bitter Fruit*, 115; Cohen and Taylor, *American Pharaoh*, 297–300; Pacyga, *American Warsaw*; WBEZ, "Can Chicago Brag About the Size of Its Polish Population?"

32. Mantler, *Power to the Poor*, 50–51; Cohen and Taylor, *American Pharaoh*, 317–20, 343; Gellman, *Troublemakers*, 125.

33. "Blasts City's War on Poverty," *Chicago Tribune*, April 14, 1965 (quotes); Mantler, *Power to the Poor*, 50–52; Gellman, *Troublemakers*, 125.

34. Gellman, *Troublemakers*, 130 (quote), 127–36; "Picket Daley's Home Again," *Chicago Tribune*, August 4, 1965; "3rd Night March on Daley," *Chicago Defender*, August 4, 1965; "Vietnam War Protest Is Staged by 16,000," *Washington Post*, and "Thousands of Students in Capital Protest War," *Los Angeles Times*, both April 18, 1965.

35. "Aide of Dr. King Sets North Trip," *Chicago Defender*, August 21, 1965; Bernard Lafayette, in Hampton and Fayer, *Voices of Freedom*, 299; "Dr. King Starts Drive in Chicago," *New York Times*, July 25, 1965 (quotes). "Arrest Gregory, Raby at 'Vigil,'" *Chicago*

*Tribune*, June 8, 1965; Cohen and Taylor, *American Pharaoh*, 337–38, 347–48; Branch, *At Canaan's Edge*, 321.

36. See Ralph, *Northern Protest*; Finley et al., *The Chicago Freedom Movement*; Anderson and Pickering, *Confronting the Color Line*, 150–340; Deppe, *Operation Breadbasket*. For early narratives by participants, see Garrow, *Chicago 1966*.

37. The Summit Agreement's one bright spot was arguably the Leadership Council, charged with monitoring fair housing in the city and assisting residents through "coordinated service, advocacy, and legal service programs." During its nearly forty-year existence, the Leadership Council helped thousands of African American families secure better homes. And yet, by 2001, the council reported that 94 percent of Blacks in the city still lived in what the organization called "low-opportunity areas." White, "The Leadership Council for Metropolitan Open Communities," 141, 148.

38. Ayers, "Summit Agreement"; Anderson and Pickering, *Confronting the Color Line*, 273–74, 277; Gellman, *Troublemakers*, 143–61; Mantler, *Power to the Poor*, 56–57; Timuel D. Black letter to King, April 3, 1967, in box 5, folder 32, MLK. Black was president of the Chicago chapter of the Negro American Labor Council.

39. Rivlin, *Fire on the Prairie*, 13, Rose, "The Rise of Independent Black Political Power in Chicago," 264; "New Chicago Civil Rights Group Forms," *Chicago Tribune*, September 8, 1965; "King Says He Is Not Leading Anti-Daley Bid," *Chicago Tribune*, March 26, 1966 (quotes). *Jet*, August 25, 1966; *New York Times*, January 16, 1967; Anderson and Pickering, *Confronting the Color Line*, 228; Branch, *At Canaan's Edge*, 442, 507–11; "Raby Launches Vote Drive to Register City Negroes," *Chicago Daily Defender*, May 11, 1966; "Dr. King Replies to Daley Charges," *Chicago Tribune*, November 4, 1966.

40. Rivlin, *Fire on the Prairie*, 31–34, 36 (quotes); "Rep. Washington Calls 'Stop-Frisk' Dangerous," *Chicago Daily Defender*, June 27, 1968; Travis, *Harold*, 74.

41. "White Backlash Vote Beat Me: Douglas," *Chicago Tribune*, December 6, 1966 (quote); "Percy Favored on 3 Issues, Poll Reveals: Voters Think He Can Do Better Job," *Chicago Tribune*, November 3, 1966; Biles, *Crusading Liberal*, 192–99, 203–4; Jones, *Selma of the North*; Sugrue, *The Origins of the Urban Crisis*; Countryman, *Up South*.

42. "Gregory Comes Out for Percy," *Chicago Daily Defender*, November 7, 1966; "The Outlook," *Chicago Defender*, November 19, 1966 (quotes). "White Backlash No Big Factor in Vote, King Says," *Chicago Tribune*, November 10, 1966.

43. "Post-election Gloom Pervades City Hall; Future in Doubt," *Chicago Tribune*, November 10, 1966; Grimshaw, *Bitter Fruit*, 122–25 (quotes).

44. For instance, the latest anthology on the CFM and its legacy says surprisingly little about police brutality in Chicago politics. The same goes for Rivlin's updated biography on Harold Washington, *Fire on the Prairie*. For better treatments of the subject, see Stewart-Winter, *Queer Clout*; Balto, *Occupied Territory*.

45. Satter, "Cops, Gangs, and Revolutionaries," 1118; "Candidates Answer *Defender* Questions: 8th Ward," *Chicago Daily Defender*, February 21, 1967 (quotes). Rose, "The Rise of Independent Black Political Power in Chicago," 264; Satter, "Cops, Gangs, and Revolutionaries," 1110–34; Brenetta Howell Barrett interview.

46. Cohen and Taylor, *American Pharaoh*, 457 (quote), 453–56; Kleppner, *Chicago Divided*, 6; Gellman, *Troublemakers*, 170–74; "The Riot," *Chicago Tribune Magazine*, July 28, 1968; Seligman, "But Burn—No."

47. Renault Robinson (quote), Edward "Buzz" Palmer, and Howard Saffold interviews,

HMDA; Satter, "Cops, Gangs, and Revolutionaries," 1110–15; Balto, *Occupied Territory*, 240–46.

48. Balto, *Occupied Territory*, 220; Perlstein, *Nixonland*, 324–25 (quotes). Grimshaw, *Bitter Fruit*, 116–17; Cohen and Taylor, *American Pharaoh*, 476–78; "Police Battle Demonstrators in Streets," *New York Times*, August 29, 1968; Gellman, *Troublemakers*, 182–86.

## Chapter 2

1. Wilkins and Clark, *Search and Destroy*, ix (quote); Haas, *The Assassination of Fred Hampton*; Alk and Gray, dirs., *The Murder of Fred Hampton*; Mantler, *Power to the Poor*, 235–36; Balto, *Occupied Territory*, 222–23, 231.

2. "Hampton Probe Demands Mount," *Chicago Defender*, December 13, 1969 (quote); Wilkins and Clark, *Search and Destroy*, vii–xii, 3–13; "Police Brutality Exposed," *Chicago Tribune*, November 4, 1973; Balto, *Occupied Territory*, 160–62, 192, 197–200, 204–7.

3. Fred Hampton, "The People Have the Power," in Marable and Mullings, *Let Nobody Turn Us Around*, 480 (quote); Mantler, *Power to the Poor*, 208, 231–32; Williams, *From the Bullet to the Ballot*, 125–66; Ray Santisteban, dir., *The Rainbow Coalition*.

4. Fernández, *Brown in the Windy City*, 3–5, 34–37; Fernández, *The Young Lords*, 16–21.

5. Gabriela Arrendondo makes the oft-ignored point that many Mexicans—men and women—went north for adventure, and to get out from under their fathers and the patriarchy of traditional Mexican culture. Arrendondo, *Mexican Chicago*, 26–28.

6. Innis-Jiménez, *Steel Barrio*, 39; Arrendondo, *Mexican Chicago*, 153 (quotes). Arrendondo, *Mexican Chicago*, 15–79, 154–57; Innis-Jiménez, *Steel Barrio*, 20–25, 38–39, 78; Fernández, *Brown in the Windy City*, 29–43, 72; Rodriguez, *The Tejano Diaspora*. See also Flores, *The Mexican Revolution in Chicago*; Año Nuevo de Kerr, "Chicano Settlements in Chicago" and "Mexican Chicago."

7. Arrendondo, *Mexican Chicago*, 55–57, 171–73; Fernández, *Brown in the Windy City*, 27–28, 64–67.

8. Fernández, *Brown in the Windy City*, 91–92 (quote), 93–129; Sandoval-Strausz, *Barrio America*, 23–42; Podair, *City of Dreams*; José "Cha-Cha" Jiménez interview, December 19, 2011.

9. Amezcua, *Making Mexican Chicago*, 112–18; "Chicago's First Hispanic Alderman"; Diamond, *Mean Streets*, 91–97, 197–212; Padilla, *Puerto Rican Chicago*, 125–44; Toro-Morn, "Boricuas en Chicago."

10. For instance, see Sugrue, *Sweet Land of Liberty*, chap. 10. This omission began with the initial findings by the National Advisory Commission on Civil Disorders, better known as the Kerner Commission. Other than a passing mention to making "good the promises of American democracy to all citizens—urban and rural, white and black, Spanish-surname, American Indian, and every minority group" in the report's introduction, the commission only addresses a Black-white divide—ignoring the significance of the Division Street disorder. This occurred despite Illinois governor Otto Kerner serving as the commission's chairman. National Advisory Commission on Civil Disorders, *Report*, 2.

11. "The Cause of Riots," *Chicago Tribune*, June 15, 1966 (quote). While exonerating the police, the editorial went on to blame President Johnson, Senator Robert F. Kennedy, the late President John Kennedy, and "national magazines" for being responsible for the violence.

12. Méndez, "A Community Fights Back"; Fernández, *Brown in the Windy City*, 163; "2 Sides 'Wooing' Puerto Ricans," *Chicago Daily Defender*, June 20, 1966 (quotes). "Rev. King Asks Latin Leaders to Join March," *Chicago Daily Defender*, June 16, 1966; "Spanish Americans Slate Protest March," *Chicago Daily Defender*, June 27, 1966; "First Puerto Rican Protest March" and "Let Them March," *Chicago Daily Defender*, June 28, 1966; "Puerto Ricans March, Present Demands," *Chicago Daily Defender*, June 29, 1966; "Thousands Join Dr. King's Rally at Soldier Field," *Chicago Daily Defender*, July 11, 1966; *Jet*, June 30, 1966; Obed López Zacarías interview.

13. Méndez, "A Community Fights Back"; Fernández, *Brown in the Windy City*, 167–69, 176–85; Padilla, *Puerto Rican Chicago*, 144–79, and *Latino Ethnic Consciousness*, 48–54; Walton and Salces, "Structural Origins of Urban Social Movements," 243, 245; Amezcua, "A Machine in the Barrio," 102. See also Francis-Fallon, *The Rise of the Latino Vote*, esp. chaps. 3 and 4.

14. Fernández, *Brown in the Windy City*, 183 (quote), 176–85; José "Cha-Cha" Jiménez, interview by Mervin Mendez; Flores-Rodríguez, "The Young Lords, Puerto Rican Liberation, and the Black Freedom Struggle," 62–63; Fernández, *The Young Lords*, 13–37.

15. Flores-Rodríguez, "The Young Lords, Puerto Rican Liberation, and the Black Freedom Struggle," 63; "Business Men Are Told about Seminary Sit-In," *Chicago Tribune*, June 1, 1969 (quotes). "Parley Fails, Gang Holds Seminary Unit," *Chicago Tribune*, May 16, 1969; "Five-Day Sit-In at McCormick Seminary Ends," *Chicago Tribune*, May 19, 1969; Fernández, *Brown in the Windy City*, 187–92; Fernández, *The Young Lords*, 37–48; Hinojosa, *Apostles of Change*, 31–55.

16. The New York chapter, which became the Young Lords Party (YLP), has received the most scholarly consideration—perhaps because it was in the nation's media capital and had a more ideologically focused and formally educated membership. Johanna Fernández, among others, argues that the YLP had longer-lasting influence than its Chicago counterpart. Both, in fact, influenced their cities in important ways, including Chicago's Rainbow Coalition, but it remains important to note that, despite the promise and symbolism routinely emphasized by scholars, the Rainbow Coalition was also contingent. "Great man theory" does not adequately explain the coalition's existence, as Andrew Diamond suggests, but it remains unclear who beyond a relatively small cadre of individuals genuinely bought into the arrangement. Johanna Fernández describes more rank-and-file buy-in, especially in New York. Mantler, *Power to the Poor*, 233–34; Diamond, *Mean Streets*, 309; Fernández, *The Young Lords*, 42–47. See also Lee, *Building a Latino Civil Rights Movement*, 205–8; Serrano, *The New York Young Lords and the Struggle for Liberation*; Fernández, "Between Social Service Reform and Revolutionary Politics."

17. Mantler, *Power to the Poor*, 208 (quote); Fred Hampton, "The People Have the Power," in Marable and Mullings, *Let Nobody Turn Us Around*, 480; Alk and Gray, dirs., *The Murder of Fred Hampton*; Rice, "The World of Illinois Panthers," 50–51, 54; Santisteban, dir., *The Rainbow Coalition*.

18. *Rising Up Angry*, July and August 1969; Rice, "The World of Illinois Panthers," 50–52, 54–56; López, "LADO," 22–27; Obed López Zacarías interview; Santisteban, dir., *The Rainbow Coalition*; Hinojosa, *Apostles of Change*, 42–43.

19. Donner, *Protectors of Privilege*, 90 (quote); Mantler, *Power to the Poor*, 235; Baer, *Beyond the Usual Beating*, 117; Williams, *From the Bullet to the Ballot*, 170–80; *Black Panther*, May 19, 1969; *Rising Up Angry*, July and August 1969; Obed López Zacarías and José

"Cha-Cha" Jiménez interview, December 19, 2011; Wilkins and Clark, *Search and Destroy*, 26–27.

20. "Hampton Probe Demands Mount," *Chicago Tribune*, December 13, 1969 (quote); Wilkins and Clark, *Search and Destroy*, vii–xii, 3–13; William O'Neal, in Hampton and Fayer, *Voices of Freedom*, 531–32.

21. *Rising Up Angry*, Mid-Winter, Early Spring, and Summer 1970; *Jet*, December 18, 25, 1969; Wilkins and Clark, *Search and Destroy*; Austin, *Up against the Wall*; Diamond, *Mean Streets*, 308–10; Mantler, *Power to the Poor*, 236–37; Balto, *Occupied Territory*, 224, 250–54; Santisteban, dir., *The Rainbow Coalition*.

22. Deppe, *Operation Breadbasket*, xxvii–xxix; Gellman, *Troublemakers*, 209, and "The Stone Wall Behind."

23. "Jesse Details Mayoralty Goals," *Chicago Daily Defender*, February 8, 1971 (quote); Kleppner, *Chicago Divided*, 74–75; "Rev. Jackson Gives Support to Friedman," *Chicago Tribune*, April 5, 1971; "Daley the Winner—BIG," *Chicago Tribune*, April 7, 1971; "Jackson Sees Bid as Answer to City's Black Voter Apathy," *Chicago Tribune*, February 8, 1971; Reynolds, *Jesse Jackson*, 209–32; Baer, *Beyond the Usual Beating*, 118–19; Rivlin, *Fire on the Prairie*, 58–59; Fremon, *Chicago Politics Ward by Ward*, 116–17, 293.

24. Williams, *From the Bullet to the Ballot*, 170–72; Stewart-Winter, *Queer Clout*, 92; Baer, *Beyond the Usual Beating*, 122–23; "Elizabeth Plank, 1924–2006," *Chicago Tribune*, May 11, 2006; "The Quiet Quest of Alliance to End Repression," *Chicago Tribune*, April 13, 1975; "Coroner Post Up to Voters," *Chicago Tribune*, November 7, 1972. Jakobi Williams's study offers the most extensive engagement with the surviving Red Squad files, held at the Chicago History Museum archives, which for years had strict limits placed on it by a federal judge because of the incendiary and false conclusions routinely recorded by Red Squad agents.

25. Reynolds, *Jesse Jackson*, 277–80, 351–52; Deppe, *Operation Breadbasket*, 187–92; Fairclough, *To Redeem the Soul*, 396–97; Todd-Breland, *A Political Education*, 116–25.

26. "Political Activity Isn't Dead," *Chicago Reader*, September 27, 1974; "Why Crosstown Plans Raise Opposition," *Chicago Tribune*, October 9, 1972; Obed López Zacarías interview; López, "LADO"; Todd-Breland, *A Political Education*, 117–20; Mantler, *Power to the Poor*, 236–37.

27. "Two Panels on Chicago Police Misconduct Found the Same Problems 43 Years Apart," *Chicago Reader*, April 20, 2016; "Cleaning Up a Police Culture of Cover Up," *Chicago Tribune*, April 15, 2016; Axelrod, *Believer*, 30. Officer Jason Van Dyke's shooting of Laquan McDonald in 2016, in which he shot McDonald sixteen times in so-called self-defense, prompted journalists to draw parallels to the rough treatment of two South Side dentists.

28. "Metcalfe Vows to Fight Daley on Police," *Chicago Tribune*, May 7, 1972 (quote); "Probers See Site of Raid on Panthers," *Chicago Tribune*, December 21, 1969; "Black Politicians Ask Death Probe," *Chicago Daily Defender*, December 10, 1969; "Emotions Flare at Hearing; Boo Jesse, Metcalfe," *Chicago Daily Defender*, December 22, 1969; Rivlin, *Fire on the Prairie*, 30; Fremon, *Chicago Politics Ward by Ward*, 36; Kleppner, *Chicago Divided*, 86–87; Grimshaw, *Bitter Fruit*, 137–38; Losier, "'The Public Does Not Believe the Police Can Police Themselves,'" 4.

29. "The Gary Declaration: Black Politics at the Convention," in Marable and Mullings, *Let Nobody Turn Us Around*, 494–95; "NBPC Made Few Decisive Decisions," *Milwaukee Star*, March 16, 1972.

30. *Amsterdam News*, March 4, 1972; "Blacks at Parley Divided on Basic Role" and "'We Met, Therefore We Won,'" *New York Times*, March 12, 1972; "Set Permanent Political Unit," *Chicago Daily Defender*, March 13, 1972; Woodard, *A Nation within a Nation*, 205–17; Ben Chavis and Ivanhoe Donaldson, in Hampton and Fayer, *Voices of Freedom*, 581–82; Mantler, *Power to the Poor*, 239–42.

31. "What Analysts Overlooked at the Black Convention," *Chicago Tribune*, March 19, 1972 (quote); "From Chaos Comes Progress," *Chicago Tribune*, March 17, 1972; "Chicago Legislators Back Gary Meeting," *Chicago Daily Defender*, March 11, 1972; Reynolds, *Jesse Jackson*, 250–59; Cohen and Taylor, *American Pharaoh*, 521–24.

32. Kleppner, *Chicago Divided*, 81; Peter Knauss, "Is the Machine Sputtering?," *Chicago Reader*, September 27, 1974 (quotes).

33. Rivlin, *Fire on the Prairie*, 19 (quote); Kleppner, *Chicago Divided*, 75–78; Reynolds, *Jesse Jackson*, 272; "Carey Is Only Republican Office Winner in County" and "Blacks, Suburbs Bane of Hanrahan," both *Chicago Tribune*, November 9, 1972.

34. "Black Mayoral Candidate Sought for 1975 Race," *Chicago Tribune*, July 15, 1974; Charles A. Hayes, "Press Statement," July 9, 1974, box 1, folder 9, CH (quotes). Cohen and Taylor, *American Pharaoh*, 532–39; Kleppner, *Chicago Divided*, 78–81.

35. "Metcalfe Out, Hits Machine," *Chicago Tribune*, December 4, 1974 (quote); "Poll Shows Newhouse Is Top Black Candidate," *Chicago Tribune*, September 21, 1974; "Metcalfe Blacks' Choice for Mayor," *Chicago Tribune*, November 10, 1974; "Metcalfe Reported Ready to Announce Mayor Bid," *Chicago Tribune*, November 27, 1974; Harold Washington, "Statement to Committee for a Black Mayor," September 14, 1974, box 1, folder 13, CH; Travis, *Harold*, 88–90.

36. "Hits Mayor Race Delay," *Chicago Defender*, July 31, 1974; Tim Black letter to Charles Hayes, November 5, 1974, box 91, folder 15, TB; "The Invisible Man," *Chicago Reader*, September 13, 1990 (quotes).

37. "Black Mayor Group Called 'Daley Front,'" *Chicago Tribune*, November 25, 1974; "Daley Unqualified, Black Group Says," *Chicago Tribune*, February 13, 1975; "25 Prominent Blacks Will Join Singer Race," *Chicago Tribune*, January 19, 1975; "Mayor Group Called 'Toms,'" *Chicago Defender*, November 12, 1974; "Committee Plan Was 'Bankrupt,'" *Chicago Defender*, December 2, 1974.

## Chapter 3

1. *Rising Up Angry*, January 5–26, 1975.

2. Countryman, *Up South*, 312–22; Colburn and Adler, *African American Mayors*; Lombardo, *Blue-Collar Conservatism*.

3. "William Singer: The Only Man in Recent Time to Defeat Hizzoner at Anything," *Chicago Reader*, June 28, 1974 (quote); "Panel Denies Convention Seats to 59 Daley Delegates," *New York Times*, July 1, 1972. The *Reader* title proves misleading since Jesse Jackson played as much of a role as Singer. "He is talented. He is enthusiastic. He does his

homework," wrote the *Chicago Tribune*. The newspaper's editorial page surprised the political class when it declined to endorse Daley for the fourth time; it also did not endorse Singer, who the editors doubted could run the city. "No Endorsement for Mayor," *Chicago Tribune*, February 16, 1975.

4. Grimshaw, *Bitter Fruit*, 126 (quote); "William Singer," *Chicago Reader*, June 28, 1974; "An End to High Rise Blight," *Chicago Reader*, August 9, 1974; "Political Activity Isn't Dead," *Chicago Reader*, September 27, 1974; "The Quiet Quest of the Alliance to End Repression," *Chicago Tribune*, April 13, 1975.

5. Kleppner, *Chicago Divided*, 89; "Singer's 'Machine' Smells Upset, Presses Daley Hard," *Chicago Tribune*, February 16, 1975; "It's Daley," *Chicago Defender*, February 22, 1975 (quotes). In what is otherwise a careful, nuanced study of race in Chicago politics, Kleppner blames "collective self-doubt" among African Americans long under the heel of the machine for their inability to unify and elect one of their own—an overly simplistic, dubious notion. "City, Top Aide Guilty on Patronage Charge," *Chicago Tribune*, January 29, 1975; "Singer a Dark Horse Running Hard to Beat a Favorite," *Chicago Tribune*, February 9, 1975; "No Endorsement for Mayor," *Chicago Tribune*, February 16, 1975; "A Unity You Haven't Seen," *Chicago Tribune*, February 23, 1975; "William Singer: The Only Man in Recent Time to Defeat Hizzoner at Anything," *Chicago Reader*, June 28, 1974; Peter Knauss, "Is the Machine Sputtering?," *Chicago Reader*, September 27, 1974; "Can Cocky Duke McNeil Soul Strut All the Way to City Hall?," *Chicago Reader*, October 25, 1974; "For the First Time in 20 Years, Richard Daley Is Running Scared," *Chicago Reader*, February 21, 1975; "No Black Unity—No Black Mayor," *Chicago Defender*, February 8; "Jesse Says Newhouse Is 'Our Aspiration,'" *Chicago Defender*, February 24, 1975; Cohen and Taylor, *American Pharaoh*, 541.

6. "The Machine Was Out to Teach Singer a Lesson," *Chicago Reader*, February 28, 1975 (quote); Grimshaw, *Bitter Fruit*, 126; "Daley's Campaign Tied It All Together," *Chicago Tribune*, February 27, 1975; "The Independents: A Scenario for Success," *Chicago Tribune*, April 13, 1975. Between late January and late February, the *Tribune* alone ran more than ten stories and editorials on the race's polling, a significant amount then, if not in today's world of ubiquitous polls. *Chicago Tribune*, January 30 and February 15, 16, 17, 21, 23, 24, and 27, 1975.

7. "A Mandate for Mayor Daley . . . a Subservient Council," *Chicago Tribune*, February 27, 1975.

8. "Bitter Campaign Rages in 5th Ward," *Chicago Reader*, February 14, 1975; "Election '75," *Chicago Reader*, February 21, 1975 (quotes). "5th Ward: Lathrop vs. Raby," *Chicago Reader*, March 28, 1975; "Alderman Hopefuls Ask Localized Police," *Chicago Tribune*, February 3, 1975; "The Activist: Al Raby," *Chicago Tribune*, April 17, 1983; "How They Won the First Round and What They'll Do to Win the Second" and "An Election Analysis," *Hyde Park Herald*, March 5, 1975; Bradley, "The University of Chicago, Urban Renewal, and the Black Community."

9. Raby's one white opponent, Ross Lathrop, tried the most to make Raby's organizing style an issue. "Election '75," *Chicago Reader*, February 21, 1975.

10. Before becoming a political aide and consultant, Axelrod started as a journalist covering community politics at the local Hyde Park weekly, near the University of Chicago—important early lessons for what was to come. Axelrod, *Believer*, 25–37.

11. "Rules Politicians Should Memorize," *Chicago Tribune*, April 4, 1975; "The Election: A Perspective," *Hyde Park Herald*, April 9, 1975; Grimshaw, *Bitter Fruit*, 124 (quotes). "Raby Receives Endorsement from Jesse Jackson," *Hyde Park Herald*, January 22, 1975; "Despres Discusses 5th Ward Candidates," *Hyde Park Herald*, January 29, 1975; "Raby Gets Support of Rep. Bob Mann," *Hyde Park Herald*, February 12, 1975; "An Election Analysis," *Hyde Park Herald*, March 5, 1975; "IVI Endorses Raby" and "Notes from Raby Camp," *Hyde Park Herald*, March 26, 1975; "The Election: A Perspective," *Hyde Park Herald*, April 9, 1975; "What's a 5th Ward Vote Cost?," *Chicago Tribune*, February 24, 1975; "The Activist: Al Raby," *Chicago Tribune*, April 17, 1983. According to official election returns, 18,103 voted in the Fifth Ward primary, compared to 12,497 in 1971, Despres's last election. Chicago Board of Elections, Commissioners' Canvassing Sheets, 5th Ward Alderman, February 23, 1971, and February 25, 1975, MR.

12. "Honesty Gets Lost at Election Time," *Chicago Tribune*, February 19, 1975; "What's a 5th Ward Vote Cost?," *Chicago Tribune*, February 24, 1975; "Foes Have Similar Aims in Tough 5th Ward Race," *Chicago Tribune*, March 24, 1975; "Rules Politicians Should Memorize," *Chicago Tribune*, April 4, 1975; "Bitter Campaign Rages in 5th Ward," *Chicago Reader*, February 14, 1975; "Election '75," *Chicago Reader*, February 21, 1975; "5th Ward: Lathrop vs. Raby," *Chicago Reader*, March 28, 1975; "The Election: A Perspective," *Hyde Park Herald*, April 9, 1975.

13. "What's a 5th Ward Vote Cost?," *Chicago Tribune*, February 24, 1975 (quote); Chicago Board of Elections, Commissioners' Canvassing Sheets, 5th Ward Alderman, February 25 and April 1, 1975, MR; "5th Ward Is Daley's," *Chicago Tribune*, April 11, 1975 (quote); "Al Raby: The Activist," *Chicago Tribune*, April 17, 1983; "Raby, Lathrop Gird for Contest," *Chicago Defender*, February 27, 1975; "Al Raby Gathers Wide Endorsements," *Chicago Defender*, March 22, 1975; "Their Fingers Crossed," *Chicago Defender*, April 1, 1975; "Raby, Jones Losers," *Chicago Defender*, April 2, 1975; Axelrod, *Believer*, 34–35.

14. "2nd Ward Candidates Have Various Paths to Goal," *Chicago Tribune*, January 28, 1975; "Ex-Panther to Run for Council," *Chicago Tribune*, November 22, 1974 (quotes); "Bloc Vote Stuns City Council," *Chicago Defender*, June 13, 1974; "Revolt in City Hall?," *Chicago Defender*, June 15, 1974; Fremon, *Chicago Politics Ward by Ward*, 30; U.S. Census Bureau, *1970 Census of Population, Supplementary Report*, x–xiii.

15. Bobby Rush interview, HH (quote); Williams, *From the Bullet to the Ballot*, 92–103; Haas, *The Assassination of Fred Hampton*, 97–99; "The Radical Departure of Bobby Rush," *Washington Post*, May 3, 1993.

16. Media perceptions of the Panthers were routinely simplistic. While some members of the party seemed to fetishize violence, an image reinforced by the open brandishing of guns at the California state capitol and elsewhere, Rush, Hampton, and others were quite careful to use the language of armed self-defense. One hits back only when one is hit. Austin, *Up against the Wall*, xxi–xxiii.

17. "Ex-Panther to Run for City Council," *Chicago Tribune*, November 22, 1974; "Bobby Rush, Candidate HQ's Vandalized," *Chicago Metro News*, December 7, 1974 (quotes); "Murder in the City," *Chicago Tribune*, January 13, 1975; "Quinn's Got to Go, PUSH Exec Says," *Chicago Tribune*, February 10, 1975; "IVI 'Prefers' Bobby Rush," *Chicago Defender*, February 5, 1975.

18. Araiza, *To March for Others*, 144 (quote), 140–66; "Panthers Sweep Berkeley

Elections," *Black Panther*, June 10, 1972; "Chicago Model Cities Election—December 19th People's Candidates Campaign for Public Offices," *Black Panther*, December 7, 1972.

19. "Bobby Rush, Candidate HQ's Vandalized," *Chicago Metro News*, December 7, 1974; "CEBIAC Endorses 16 Aldermanic Candidates," *Chicago Metro News*, February 8, 1975; "IVI Prefers Bobby Rush in 2nd Ward," *Chicago Metro News*, February 15, 1975 (quotes); Bobby Rush interview, HH; "Illinois Black Leader Raises 'Open Convention' Question," *Chicago Tribune*, March 18, 1974; "Dem Heavies v. GOP Gadflies," *Chicago Tribune*, January 2, 1975.

20. Doug Cassel, "Is Tim Evans for Real?," *Chicago Reader*, March 16, 1989; "Bullock in 2nd Ward Contest," *Chicago Defender*, November 26, 1974 (quotes); "Ex-Panther to Run for City Council," *Chicago Tribune*, November 22, 1974; "2d Ward Gets Third Candidate," *Chicago Tribune*, November 23, 1974; "3rd Hopeful Enters Race in 2d Ward," *Chicago Tribune*, November, 26, 1974; "2nd Ward Candidates Have Various Paths to Goal," *Chicago Tribune*, January 28, 1975; Larry Bullock interview, HMDA. The extent of Jackson's influence remains in question, too. His endorsement did not make the difference for Raby, for instance, and his endorsement of Singer, rather than a Black candidate, prompted dismissals of what he could actually do for candidates. "Jesse's Political Influence in Question," *Chicago Tribune*, January 13, 1975.

21. "Rush Rips 'Bosses' for Arrest," *Chicago Tribune*, November 10, 1975 (quotes); Chicago Board of Elections, Commissioners' Canvassing Sheets, 2nd Ward Alderman, February 23, 1971, and February 25, 1975, MR.

22. "Election '75," *Chicago Reader*, February 21, 1975.

23. Eight of the ward's census tracts were considered "low-income" by the 1970 Census. While majority white, the ward was made up of roughly 18 percent "Spanish speaking"; 8 percent "other," including Indian, Japanese, and Filipino; and 6 percent Black. Much like the city as a whole, the ward saw a decline in whites by 1980; Latinos made up 22 percent. U.S. Census Bureau, *1970 Census of Population, Supplementary Report*, xii, 1; Fremon, *Chicago Politics Ward by Ward*, 308.

24. Fremon, *Chicago Politics Ward by Ward*, 303–4; U.S. Census Bureau, *1970 Census of Population, Supplementary Report*, x–xiii; Paul Siegel interview; Leon Despres, "Four Machine Good Guys: At Least Sort of Good, Sometimes," *Chicago Guide*, box 15, folder 225, CC.

25. José "Cha-Cha" Jiménez interview, December 19, 2011; Paul Siegel interview; Jiménez, "Statement of Candidacy," June 20, 1974, box 1, folder 12, and *Rising Up Angry*, January 5–26, 1975, box 1, folder 15, YL. See also Williams, *From the Bullet to the Ballot*, 125–66; Enck-Wanzer, *The Young Lords*, 27–29, 161–62; Rivera and Jeffries, "From Radicalism to Representation."

26. Jiménez, "Statement of Candidacy," June 20, 1974, quotes, and Jim Chapman et al., "A Letter from Independent Campaign Workers for José Cha-Cha Jiménez," box 1, folder 12, YL; José "Cha-Cha" Jiménez interview, December 19, 2011; Paul Siegel interview.

27. The federal Model Cities programs reflected more community control of federal antipoverty programs, and often set up opportunities for activists to experiment with low-profile electoral efforts first, such as in Oakland. Self, *American Babylon*, 242–43.

28. Jiménez campaign materials, box 1, folder 12, YL; *Rising Up Angry*, January 5–26, 1975; Paul Siegel interview.

29. Paul Siegel interview; "Jimenez Campaign Rolling Well," *Lincoln Park–Lake View Booster*, October 9, 1974; "Work within System, Cha Cha Urges Latinos," *Lincoln Park–Lake View Booster*, December 18, 1974, box 1, folder 15, YL (quotes). "Black, Latino and White Chicagoans Join in Unity Rally," *BPINS*, October 19, 1974, box 1, folder 15, and Halloween letter, box 1, folder 13, YL; "Variety Sparks Race for Alderman in 46th," *Lincoln Park–Lake View Booster*, February 16, 1975; "IVI Endorses Jimenez and Hoellen," *Chicago Sun-Times*, January 23, 1975; "Jimenez Worker Arrested in Drug Raid," *Uptown News*, February 11, 1975; "'Cha-Cha' Wins IPO Endorsement," *The Booster*, January 8, 1975; "Jimenez Reports," *Chicago Tribune*, February 12, 1975; "Diverse Candidates Run in 46th Ward," *Chicago Tribune*, February 20, 1975; "Crime, Better Housing Issues of 3 Candidates in 46th Ward," *Chicago Daily News*, February 17, 1975, box 15, folder 225, CC. While local newspapers routinely mentioned Jiménez's gang background and criminal charge, Cohen did not bring either up. Years afterward, Jiménez spoke conciliatorily of Cohen's decision not "to bring up the past." Later, however, he suggested that Cohen brought nine police officers to their multiple debates as a way to contrast his position on crime control with Jiménez's "shady" background. José "Cha-Cha" Jiménez interview, December 19, 2011.

30. Paul Siegel interview.

31. "An Interview with Jose Cha-Cha Jimenez," *Keep Strong*, July 1975, box 26, folder 416, CC (quote); Paul Siegel interview; Chicago Board of Elections, Commissioners' Canvassing Sheets, 46th Ward Alderman, February 23, 1971, and February 25, 1975, MR; *Keep Strong*, December 1975; "Election Marked by Fierce Fights in Number of Aldermanic Races," *Chicago Tribune*, February 25, 1975. According to election returns, 16,451 voted in 1975, up from 12,932 in 1971.

32. José "Cha-Cha" Jiménez interview, December 19, 2011; Paul Siegel interview; "A Model of Resistance," *Keep Strong*, January 1976; "11 Indicted Here in FALN Blasts," *Chicago Tribune*, December 11, 1980; "Raby Goes to Ghana," *Hyde Park Herald*, July 25, 1979.

33. "Thompson: 'I Feel Like a Caged Tiger,'" *Chicago Tribune*, March 7, 1976, (quote); "Walker Concedes Loss, Studying 3d Party Bid," *Chicago Tribune*, March 18, 1976; "Black Unit for Thompson," *Chicago Tribune*, September 29, 1976; "Black Vote Not in Anyone's Pocket," *Chicago Tribune*, November 10, 1976; "Bobby Rush Paves Way for Thompson," *Chicago Tribune*, October 27, 1976; "Bobby Rush Seeks Legislative Nod," *Chicago Tribune*, November 24, 1977; United Black Voters of Illinois, "Inner City Campaign Budget," 1976, box 138, folder 8, TB.

34. Cohen and Taylor, *American Pharaoh*, 554 (quote), 547–49, 551–53.

35. "Powerful, Meek Pay Last Respects to Mayor Daley," *Chicago Tribune*, December 23, 1976; "'For 21 Years, He Was the Boss, the Ultimate Clout,'" *New York Times*, December 22, 1976 (quotes). "Richard J. Daley," *Chicago Tribune*, December 21, 1976; "Daley: The First of a New Breed," *Chicago Tribune*, December 23, 1976; "Daley Ruled Chicago with Total Control," *New York Times*, December 21, 1976; "The Mayor," *New York Times*, December 22, 1976; "Daley: For the Glory of Chicago," *Los Angeles Times*, December 22, 1976.

36. Royko, *The Boss*, 8 (quote); "In the Wake of the News: Sox, Bears, Kids in the Park—Daley Loved Them All," *Chicago Tribune*, December 21, 1976; "Mayor Recalled for 'Little Things,'" *Chicago Tribune*, December 22, 1976; "Farewell to Mayor Daley," *Chicago Tribune*, December 23, 1976.

37. "Succession War May Be His Legacy," *Chicago Tribune*, December 20, 1976; Gus Savage interview, HMDA (quotes). "Wilson Frost: Loyalist—to a Point," *Chicago Tribune*, December 22, 1976; Travis, *Harold*, 95–96; Grimshaw, *Bitter Fruit*, 149; Savage, "Statement on behalf of Black Community Forum," December 23, 1976, box 11, folder 18, BHB; Gellman, "In the Driver's Seat," 72–73.

38. Grimshaw, *Bitter Fruit*, 143–44, 149–50; "Bilandic Chosen as Mayor," *Chicago Tribune*, December 29, 1976.

39. Travis, *Harold*, 101; Gus Savage and Wilson Frost interviews, HMDA (quotes). Grimshaw, *Bitter Fruit*, 149–50; "Frost Made Machine Hum for Blacks," "The Opportunity That Slipped Away," and "Bilandic Chosen as Mayor," *Chicago Tribune*, December 29, 1976.

40. Rivlin, *Fire on the Prairie*, 15; Fremon, *Chicago Politics Ward by Ward*, 85 (quotes). "Michael Bilandic" and "No Losers Please: How the Machine Will Prevail," *Chicago Tribune*, December 26, 1976; "Mayor Bilandic: Business as Usual," *Chicago Tribune*, December 30, 1976; Kleppner, *Chicago Divided*, 96.

41. Fremon, *Chicago Politics Ward by Ward*, 265–66; Kleppner, *Chicago Divided*, 96; "End Marches on Schools, Pucinski Asks," *Chicago Tribune*, July 29, 1965; "Pucinski Rips Racial Check on Employees," *Chicago Tribune*, December 16, 1969; "Ralph Nader's Report on Congressmen from Illinois," *Chicago Tribune*, October 23, 1972, "Policemen's Group Endorses Pucinski," *Chicago Tribune*, April 7, 1977; "An Interview with Roman Pucinski," *Chicago Reader*, April 8, 1977.

42. Rivlin, *Fire on the Prairie*, 37 (quote); Travis, *Harold*, 102–3; Rivlin, *Fire on the Prairie*, 36–37; Kleppner, *Chicago Divided*, 97; Carl, "Harold Washington and Chicago's Schools," 320–22; "Blacks Eye Sen. Washington for Mayor," *Chicago Sun-Times*, January 19, 1977; "A Metcalfe No on Washington," *Chicago Sun-Times*, January 22, 1977, box 11, folder 18, BHB.

43. "A Metcalfe No on Washington," *Chicago Sun-Times*, January 22, 1977 (quote); Kleppner, *Chicago Divided*, 97; Travis, *Harold*, 103–4; "Legislator Gets 40 Days in Jail," *Chicago Tribune*, March 28, 1972; "Loses Promised Support," *Chicago Tribune*, January 22, 1977; "Ralph Metcalfe Takes His Stand," *Chicago Tribune*, January 23, 1977; "Tucker Investing Plan Target of Suits," *Chicago Tribune*, February 6, 1977.

44. "Sen. Washington Enters Mayoral Race after 'Draft,'" *Chicago Tribune*, February 20, 1977; Gus Savage interview, HMDA; Washington campaign flier, box 11, folder 18, BHB (quotes). "An Interview with Harold Washington," *Chicago Reader*, March 4, 1977; "A Program for Stopping Arson—State Senator Harold Washington," "Washington Releases Spy File," "Statement of Full Employment and Affirmative Action by State Senator Harold Washington," box 11, folder 3, ISS; Travis, *Harold*, 108.

45. "An Interview with Harold Washington," *Chicago Reader*, March 4, 1977 (quotes); "IVI Unit Picks Washington in Dem Mayor Bid," *Chicago Tribune*, February 21, 1977; "IVI's Goal—Get City Blacks in Fold," *Chicago Tribune*, February 28, 1977; IVI endorsement, March 31, 1977, and press releases, April 7 and 18, 1977, box 11, folder 3, ISS.

46. Brenetta Howell Barrett interview (quote); Kleppner, *Chicago Divided*, 98.

47. Travis, *Harold*, 109–10; *Keep Strong*, July 1975 and March 1977 (quote); Helen Shiller and Brenetta Howell Barrett interviews.

48. "Pucinski Couples Concession with Future Challenge" and "Washington Doesn't

Talk Like a Loser," *Chicago Tribune*, April 20, 1977 (quotes); Chicago Democracy Project, "Election Results for 1977 Primary Election"; Grimshaw, *Bitter Fruit*, 151–53; Kleppner, *Chicago Divided*, 98–101.

49. Peter Knauss, "Is the Machine Sputtering?," *Chicago Reader*, September 27, 1974; *Chicago Tribune*, April 13, 1975 (quotes).

50. Francis-Fallon, *The Rise of the Latino Vote*, 53–131, 292–379; Krochmal, *Blue Texas*, 232–397.

## Chapter 4

1. Jesús "Chuy" García interview (quotes); "House Votes to Bar Illegal Aliens from Jobs," *Chicago Tribune*, April 7, 1997; "Illegal Alien Can Be Hired," *Chicago Tribune*, June 27, 1977; Illinois Legislative Investigating Commission, "Illegal Aliens," iii–vii, 33–35.

2. Walton and Salces, "Structural Origins of Urban Social Movements," 240–41; Belenchia, *Latinos and Chicago Politics*, 133–34; "Hispanic Chicago: A Growing Presence, a Desire for Betterment," *Chicago Tribune*, November 1, 1981.

3. "Vargas Llosa: Mexico Is the Perfect Dictatorship," *El País*, August 31, 1990 (quote); Jesús "Chuy" García and Linda Coronado interviews; Patiño, *Raza Sí, Migra No*, 214–15. Ten days before the opening of the 1968 Olympics in Mexico City, more than 300 students and other civilians protesting state suppression on campus were killed by security forces. See Poniatowska, *Massacre in Mexico*.

4. Belenchia, *Latinos and Chicago Politics*, 137; "They Help Dropouts to Drop In," *Chicago Tribune*, April 22, 1983; U.S. Census Bureau, "Poverty Status by Age, Race, and Hispanic Origin," and *Census Tracts*, "Poverty Status in 1979 of Spanish Origin Persons," P-1529.

5. Piña, "His Life," 49–50, 53–56; Fernández, *Brown in the Windy City*, 91–129; *UICC Illini* (student newspaper), October 1, 8, 22, 1973, and March 25 and April 22, 1974; Pallares, "The Chicago Context," 40.

6. Cruz, *City of Dreams*, 46.

7. "Pilsen Area Forms Committees to Push for New High School," *Chicago Tribune*, March 29, 1973.

8. "Pilsen Area Forms Committees to Push for New High School," *Chicago Tribune*, March 29, 1973; "Froebel: Frustrations at a Boiling Point," *Chicago Tribune*, June 10, 1973; Cruz, *City of Dreams*, 46; Alvarez, "A Community That Would Not Take 'No' for an Answer," 88–90.

9. Alvarez, "A Community That Would Not Take 'No' for an Answer," 89–92; Cruz, *City of Dreams*, 46–47; Walton and Salces, "Structural Origins of Urban Social Movements," 243–44; "Froebel Calm; 7 Teens Seized," *Chicago Tribune*, June 6, 1973; "Froebel: Frustrations at a Boiling Point," *Chicago Tribune*, June 10, 1973; "Board on Record for Pilsen School," *Chicago Tribune*, June 14, 1973, "Pilsen Leader Demands 'Disciplines Basics' in Education," *Chicago Tribune*, October 23, 1975.

10. Fernández, *Brown in the Windy City*, 210, 225–27, 243–60; Walton and Salces, "Structural Origins of Urban Social Movements," 245; Mora-Torres, "Pilsen," 5–6.

11. Gómez-Quiñones, *Mexican-American Labor*, 225 (quote); Piña, "His Life," 59; Linda Coronado interview; Fernández, *Brown in the Windy City*, 210; Amezcua, "A Machine in

the Barrio," 95–120, and *Making Mexican Chicago*, 149–52. For more on CASA's origins and evolution from a mutual aid society to a Marxist-Leninist organization, see Pulido, *Black, Brown, Yellow and Left*, 117–20; and Chávez, *¡Mi Raza Primero!*, 98–116. For more on La Raza Unida in Texas and elsewhere, see García, *United We Win*; Espinoza, "The Partido Belongs to Those Who Will Work for It."

12. "Our Illegal Aliens: Economic Scapegoats," *New York Times*, January 8, 1975 (quote); "Illegal Aliens Caught in Job Squeeze," *Washington Post*, August 17, 1975.

13. "Chicanos Contest Illegal Alien Hunt," *Chicago Tribune*, December 1, 1974.

14. "Chicanos Contest Illegal Alien Hunt," *Chicago Tribune*, December 1, 1974.

15. De los Ángeles Torres, "In Search of Meaningful Voice and Place," 89; "Aliens Take Million Jobs, Saxbe Charges," *Chicago Tribune*, October 31, 1974; "Illegal Entries Threaten Quality of U.S. Life," *Chicago Tribune*, November 24, 1974; "Chicanos Contest Illegal Alien Hunt," *Chicago Tribune*, December 1, 1974; "Illegal Aliens Should Go," *Chicago Tribune*, March 5, 1975, "Catholic Group Urges U.S. Amnesty for Illegal Aliens," *Chicago Tribune*, March 14, 1975; Jesús "Chuy" García, interview by John Betancur and Doug Gills, box 1, folder 3, RL; Piña, "His Life," 59–62.

16. Lozano, "Local Report: Campaign of Resistance and Unity," 1977, box 3, folder 22, RL (quote); "Change of Attitude toward Immigrants," *Washington Post*, May 22, 1977; "Questions and Answers about Alien Amnesty," *Chicago Tribune*, August 13, 1977; "U.S. Moves towards National I.D. Cards," *Keep Strong*, April 1977; "Attacks on Undocumented Workers Escalate," *Keep Strong*, May 1977; Gutiérrez, "Sin Fronteras?," 5; Francis-Fallon, *The Rise of the Latino Vote*, 325–43; Kazin, *What It Took To Win*, 261.

17. "Senate OKs House Slash of $1.8 Million for Abortion," *Chicago Tribune*, June 27, 1977.

18. Jesús "Chuy" García interview.

19. "House Votes to Bar Illegal Aliens from Jobs," *Chicago Tribune*, April 7, 1977; "U.S. Moves Towards National I.D. Cards," *Keep Strong*, April 1977; Illinois Legislative Investigating Commission, "Illegal Aliens," 1–4, 11–12, 15–17, 25–28, 33–36; Jesús "Chuy" García interview; Linda Coronado interview (quote).

20. The ILGWU, while known for organizing poor, working-class immigrants first in garments, and then other industries, had an almost all white, male, Jewish leadership, which increasingly could not fully represent the union rank and file. This was especially the case after Latinos became central to the industry. Tyler, *Look for the Union Label*.

21. Robert Starks, interview, in *Rudy Lozano*, 110.

22. Rudy Lozano, "Notes from Labor Workshops," 1978, box 3, folder 21, and "Report and Daily Analysis of Daily Activities," 1980, box 3, folder 20, RL; Piña, "His Life," 62–64; Linda Coronado interview; "'Larger in Death than in Life,'" *Chicago Tribune*, May 27, 1984; Gutiérrez, "Sin Fronteras?"; Fink, "Labor Joins La Marcha," 110–11.

23. "Power Once More Eludes Powerless," *Chicago Tribune*, July 25, 1975.

24. CASA, "Local Report: Campaign of Resistance and Unity," 1977, box 3, folder 22, and "Report and Daily Analysis of Daily Activities," 1979–80, box 3, folder 20, RL; "Jesse Charges Racism in Picking School Boss," *Chicago Tribune*, July 20, 1975; "A School Dilemma in Black and White," *Chicago Tribune*, July 23, 1975; "Blacks Upset by Selection of School Head," *Chicago Tribune*, July 24, 1975; "Hannon Must Be Fought 'School-by-School': Jesse," *Chicago Tribune*, July 27, 1975; "'Climatic' Effect on the Public Schools,"

*Chicago Tribune*, July 30, 1975; "Manford Byrd for School Superintendent," *Chicago Tribune*, December 1, 1980; Robert Starks, interview, in *Rudy Lozano*, 113–14.

25. "Power Elite Drafts City Master Plan," *Chicago Tribune*, May 21, 1973; Diamond, *Chicago on the Make*, 234–35; "Rehab Network Fights Housing Displacements," *Chicago Tribune*, December 6, 1979; Chicago Rehab Network, "Development without Displacement," 2–3, *Chicago Rehab Network Newsletter*, April 1981, 16–17; "The Company That Rules Chicago," *Keep Strong*, November 1977; Amezcua, *Making Mexican Chicago*, 172–74, 183–88.

26. Robert Giloth, "The Value of 'Networking,'" *Chicago Tribune*, February 11, 1981 (quote); Chicago Rehab Network, "Development without Displacement," 7, 20; *Chicago Rehab Network Newsletter*, April 1981, 10–11; "'The Company That Rules Chicago,'" *Keep Strong*, November 1977; Walton and Salces, "Structural Origins of Urban Social Movements," 243; Betancur and Gills, "The African American and Latino Coalition Experience in Chicago"; Brehm, "The City and the Neighborhoods," 243–44, n269.

27. "Activist No Longer an Outsider," *Chicago Tribune*, June 13, 1985; "Pastor Helping Immigrant [Arellano] Is a Longtime Driving Force [Rev. Walter Coleman]," *Chicago Sun-Times*, August 16, 2006; "Statement on the Seventh Anniversary of the ISC," *Keep Strong*, May 1977; "The People's Alderman," and "ISC Birthday Party," *Keep Strong*, July 1975; Helen Shiller interview.

28. *Keep Strong*, January, February, May, November, and December 1977. The great majority of underground and alternative newspapers, similar to the so-called activist businesses of the era, failed after just a few years, if that, often because they were run by a collective, on a shoestring budget, or could not adapt to changing customer interests. See McMillian, *Smoking Typewriters*; Davis, *From Head Shops to Whole Foods*.

29. Jorge Morales interview; "Humboldt Park: 'Community without Dreams,'" *Chicago Tribune*, June 4, 1978; Gottlieb, "Hoboken Is Burning."

30. Jorge Morales interview; "Latinos Demonstrate for Postal Jobs," *Chicago Tribune*, June 30, 1978; "Humboldt Park: 'Community without Dreams,'" *Chicago Tribune*, June 4, 1978; "Latinos Seek More Postal Jobs," *Chicago Tribune*, May 12, 1978; "Protesters Interrupt Sears Bank," *Chicago Tribune*, November 10, 1979.

31. Dick Simpson, "Press Statement," and Jorge Morales, "Press Statement," both October 24, 1978, UA 2010–03, box 1, folder 43, DS; "8 Latino Groups Sue City; Charge Job Bias," *Chicago Tribune*, October 25, 1978; "Too Few Latinos in U.S. Jobs: Study," *Chicago Tribune*, June 15, 1978; "Latino Postal Jobs Lag Here, Study Shows," *Chicago Tribune*, October 2, 1978; "Latino Employment," *Chicago Tribune*, November 23, 1978; "Humboldt Park: 'Community without Dreams,'" *Chicago Tribune*, June 4, 1978.

32. "Elections Ordered for Two Wards," *Chicago Tribune*, January 25, 1978; "I Will Take Our Community Struggles into the City Council," *Keep Strong*, March 1978; "Helen Shiller: Part of the New Opposition," *Keep Strong*, June–July 1978; Helen Shiller interview.

33. "For Alderman: Axelrod, Volini," *Chicago Tribune*, May 11, 1978.

34. "I Will Take Our Community Struggles into the City Council," *Keep Strong*, March 1978; "Helen Shiller: Part of the New Opposition," *Keep Strong*, June–July 1978, "An Interview with Helen Shiller," *Keep Strong*, Winter 1979; "Helen Shiller: She Terrified the Machine, Won the Hearts of Ordinary People," *Keep Strong*, June 1979; "Candidate Assails 'Machine' Tactics," *Chicago Tribune*, May 6, 1978; "Diverse Threesome Runs for 46th

Ward Alderman," *Chicago Tribune*, May 9, 1978; "Axelrod Elected in 46th Ward," *Chicago Tribune*, May 17, 1978; "Election Offices Damaged by Fire," *Chicago Tribune*, February 10, 1979, "Challenged in 46th Ward: Machine Making Last Stand on N. Side," *Chicago Tribune*, March 15, 1979; Helen Shiller interview; Fremon, *Chicago Politics Ward by Ward*, 305.

35. "A Gloomy Outlook for Independents," *Chicago Tribune*, April 2, 1978 (quote); Rivlin, *Fire on the Prairie*, 37.

36. "Mrs. Byrne's Handicap Race," *Chicago Tribune*, April 26, 1978; "Martyred Byrne No Joan of Arc," *Chicago Tribune*, April 28, 1978; "Byrne's Mayoral Run No Threat, Dems Say," *Chicago Tribune*, March 30, 1978; "See Jane Run, See Others Run," *Chicago Tribune*, May 3, 1978; "Jane Won for Women—By Not Trying To," *Chicago Tribune*, March 5, 1979; FitzGerald, *Brass*, 193–98; Granger and Granger, *Fighting Jane*, 202.

37. While racial analyses of this era of Chicago politics, especially the Black experience, are quite rich, few offer any kind of gender analysis—perhaps because Byrne did not run as a feminist. For instance, see Rivlin, *Fire on the Prairie*; Grimshaw, *Bitter Fruit*; Kleppner, *Chicago Divided*.

38. Other major cities had elected women as mayor in the late 1970s, especially in the South, including Raleigh, San Antonio, Austin, and Dallas.

39. FitzGerald, *Brass*, 152–79; Granger and Granger, *Fighting Jane*, 84–102, 136–49; "Two Are Identified in Food Bribe Probe," *Chicago Tribune*, April 22, 1965; "Probe State Meat Inspection," *Chicago Tribune*, October 13, 1965; Byrne, *My Chicago*, 215–18.

40. "Mayor 'Greased Way' for Taxi Hike: Byrne," *Chicago Tribune*, November 16, 1977; "Byrne Believes, But Do the Voters?," *Chicago Tribune*, July 16, 1978 (quotes). "Bilandic Fires Byrne; Says He Passed Lie Test," *Chicago Tribune*, November 22, 1977; "Full Text of Jane Byrne July 19 Taxi Memo," *Chicago Tribune*, November 17, 1977; "U.S. Halts Cab Probe, Finds No Wrongdoing," *Chicago Tribune*, January 23, 1979; Byrne, *My Chicago*, 255–68; Rivlin, *Fire on the Prairie*, 43–44; Cowie, *Stayin' Alive*, 299–300; Rossinow, *The Reagan Era*, 20–21.

41. "Byrne Revolt Is Already Over," *Chicago Tribune*, April 4, 1979; FitzGerald, *Brass*, 194–96; Dick Simpson, Helen Shiller, Linda Coronado, and Robert "Bob" Starks interviews; *Keep Strong*, Special Election Issue (1979); Tim Black letter to Jane Byrne, March 30, 1979, in box 9, folder 8, TB.

42. Coined by *Newsweek* in 1971, the phrase became a mantra for local media and city officials—to the point that it adorned the *Tribune* headline after Daley died in 1976. Diamond, *Chicago on the Make*, 231.

43. "Bilandic Likens Woes to Jesus' Crucifixion," *Chicago Tribune*, February 15, 1979; Granger and Granger, *Fighting Jane*, 214 (quotes). FitzGerald, *Brass*, 200–201; Rivlin, *Fire on the Prairie*, 44; "Jane Byrne Wins; Historic Upset in Big Turnout," *Chicago Tribune*, February 28, 1979; "A Slugfest in the Snow: Bilandic, the Incumbent," *Chicago Tribune*, February 25, 1979.

44. "The Byrne Revolt Is Already Over," *Chicago Tribune*, April 4, 1979 (quote); Byrne Transition Team, List of Members, 1979, and *Chicago Lawyer*, June 4, 1979, UA 83-7, box 1, folder 5, DS; Dick Simpson interview; "Byrne's Adviser Tells 'Easy' Condo Plan," *Chicago Tribune*, March 19, 1979; "City Transition Team Transits," *Chicago Tribune*, April 29, 1979; "How City Hall Fought to Suppress Secret Study of Chicago," *Chicago Tribune*, June 22, 1980; Preston, "Black Politics in the Post-Daley Era," 106.

45. Tim Black letter to Jane Byrne, 1979, box 9, folder 8, TB (quote); Rivlin, *Fire on the Prairie*, 46–48; Renault Robinson interview, HMDA.

46. "Don't Rejoice Yet, Hispanics," *Chicago Tribune*, December 4, 1981 (quote); Granger and Granger, *Fighting Jane*, 195, 197; FitzGerald, *Brass*, 205–6; Rivlin, *Fire on the Prairie*, 44–45; Belenchia, "Latinos and Chicago Politics," 140–41; Amezcua, "A Machine in the Barrio," 95–120, and *Making Mexican Chicago*, 209; Fremon, *Chicago Politics Ward by Ward*, 205; "Byrne, Latinos in Shouting Match," *Chicago Tribune*, March 24, 1979; "A Losing Strategy in School Battle," *Chicago Tribune*, January 11, 1981; "Alderman Says Blacks Will Fight Villalobos," *Chicago Tribune*, May 29, 1981; "One Step Forward," *Sin Fronteras*, June–July 1980, box 3, folder 22, RL. After Elena Martinez's firing, Byrne went on to tap Mary Gonzales to what turned out to be a strictly ceremonial transition team, removed Carmen Velasquez from the school board, and hired two Latino family friends, prompting charges of cronyism. Bolivian endocrinologist Hugo Muriel became the head of the city's Department of Health despite having no public health experience, while the first Latino on her administrative staff was one of her daughter's recently graduated college classmates and a native of El Salvador. "Unity Is Key at 2d Latino Action Talks," *Chicago Tribune*, November 22, 1979; "As 'Reformer,' Byrne Fails to Measure Up," *Chicago Tribune*, October 28, 1979; "Mayor Defends Her Latino Appointments," *Chicago Tribune*, November 22, 1979.

47. Reagan, "Address Accepting the Presidential Nomination"; "Remarks in New Orleans, Louisiana"; "Reagan Campaigns at Mississippi Fair," *New York Times*, August 4, 1980 (quotes).

48. "2 Chicago Blacks Boycott Reagan's Budget Meeting," *Chicago Tribune*, February 4, 1981 (quote); Rossinow, *The Reagan Era*, 8–9, 22–24, 59–60; Kazin, *What It Took To Win*, 260–66; David Adler, introduction to *African American Mayors*, 8; Matt Tyrnauer, dir., *The Reagans*; "How Chicago Fares in Reagan's Plan," *Chicago Tribune*, February 22, 1981; "Byrne Willing to Give Reagan Plan a Chance," *Chicago Tribune*, May 8, 1981; "U.S. Cuts May Cost Illinois a Half Billion," *Chicago Tribune*, May 10, 1981; "Reagan Cuts Hit Many City Services," *Chicago Tribune*, May 27, 1981; "Minority City Workers First to Go in Reagan Aid Cuts," *Chicago Tribune*, December 14, 1981.

49. Linda Coronado interview.

50. Jesús "Chuy" García, interview by Betancur and Gills, box 1, folder 3, RL.

51. Jorge Morales interview; Carlos Arango, interview, in *Rudy Lozano*, 122–23; United States, Department of Commerce, U.S. Bureau of Census, *The 1980 Census of Population*, 15–76; Jesús "Chuy" García, interview by Betancur and Gills, box 1, folder 3, and "To Achieve Unity, We Must Have Commitment," *Sin Fronteras*, September–October 1981, box 3, folder 25, RL; de los Ángeles Torres, "In Search of Meaningful Voice and Place," 87–91.

52. Fremon, *Chicago Politics Ward by Ward*, 9 (quote); *Ketchum v. City Council of Chicago*; Colman and Brody, "*Ketchum v. Byrne*."

53. "U.S. Acts to Block Chicago Ward Remap," *Chicago Tribune*, September 16, 1982 (quote); *Ketchum v. City Council of Chicago*; Colman and Brody, "*Ketchum v. Byrne*." In 1982, the three suits were consolidated into one and Mayor Byrne was dropped as a defendant, prompting the name change. See also "City Council OKs City Remap," *Chicago Tribune*, November 14, 1981; "U.S. Acts to Block Chicago Ward Remap," *Chicago Tribune*,

September 16, 1982; "New City Ward Remap Approved by Judge," *Chicago Tribune*, December 24, 1982; Fremon, *Chicago Politics Ward by Ward*, 8–9.

54. Linda Coronado interview (quotes); *El Sol de Pilsen*, January 1982, *La Opinión Latina*, 1982, *All Chicago City News*, January 12–25, 1982, Soliz campaign flier, and "Johnny Solo: A Latino in the Land of Opportunism," *Chicago Reader*, October 11, 1985, box 1, folder 2; *All Chicago City News*, February 4, 1982, *La Campaña*, February 1982, and *West Side Times*, February 4, 1982, box 4, folder 48, RL. *Chicago Tribune*, April 16 and 29, July 23, and October 19, 1981, February 16 and March 15, 1982; Robert Starks, interview, in *Rudy Lozano*, 113; de los Ángeles Torres, "In Search of Meaningful Voice and Place," 91.

## Chapter 5

1. Portions of this chapter appear as Mantler, "Rainbow Reformers."

2. CBUC flier, undated, box 24, folder 5, MC; Lutrelle "Lu" F. Palmer, II interview, HMDA (quotes). Lu Palmer interview, HH.

3. Lu Palmer interview, HMDA; Axelrod, *Believer*, 55 (quotes). Robert "Bob" Starks interview; "Washington, Burris Lead as Survey's Top Black Mayoral Choices," *Chicago Reporter*, August 1980; Rivlin, *Fire on the Prairie*, 26–27, 37–38, 40; Biles, *Mayor Harold Washington*, 60–61; Axelrod, *Believer*, 54; Kleppner, *Chicago Divided*, 144–45; Helgeson, *Crucibles of Black Empowerment*, 256–58.

4. Rivlin, who wrote the most narrative account on Harold Washington, more than anybody stresses Lu Palmer and his fellow conspirators. So do Grimshaw, *Bitter Fruit*; Alkalimat and Gills, "Chicago—Black Power vs. Racism"; and Kleppner, *Chicago Divided*, to a lesser extent.

5. Kleppner, *Chicago Divided*, 144 (quotes); "Byrne's Record on Race: Little Fire behind the Rhetoric," *Chicago Reporter*, September 1982; Brenetta Howell Barrett interview.

6. "Our Gutsy Mayor," *Chicago Tribune*, March 24, 1981; Byrne, *My Chicago*, 323; "Jane Byrne's Easter at Cabrini" (quotes). Rivlin, *Fire on the Prairie*, 46–47; Byrne, *My Chicago*, 312–23; Kleppner, *Chicago Divided*, 139; "Our Gutsy Mayor," *Chicago Tribune*, March 24, 1981; "No Hosannas for Gutsy Jane," *Chicago Tribune*, March 27, 1981; "Cabrini Protesters Call It 'Police State,'" *Chicago Tribune*, April 4, 1981; Moore, *The South Side*, 62–63. See also the "The U.S. Press on Jane Byrne," *Chicago Tribune*, March 29, 1981.

7. Kleppner, *Chicago Divided*, 136, 139, Baer, *Beyond the Usual Beating*, 87–88 (quotes); "Byrne's Record on Race: Little Fire behind the Rhetoric," *Chicago Reporter*, September 1982. See Baer, *Beyond the Usual Beating*, chap. 3.

8. "Byrne's Deliberate Insult to Blacks," *Chicago Tribune*, February 15, 1981 (quotes); Todd-Breland, *A Political Education*, 150–51, 152 (quote); Kleppner, *Chicago Divided*, 137–38, 140–41; "Byrne's Record on Race: Little Fire behind the Rhetoric," *Chicago Reporter*, September 1982.

9. "Will 17th Ward Be Heard?," *Chicago Tribune*, May 28, 1982; "Loner Robinson," *Chicago Tribune*, August 20, 1982 (quotes); Kleppner, *Chicago Divided*, 136–37, 141–43; Grimshaw, *Bitter Fruit*, 160–62; Fremon, *Chicago Politics Ward by Ward*, 120–21; "A Very Special Election," *Chicago Tribune*, May 28, 1982; "Byrne's Record on Race: Little Fire behind the Rhetoric," *Chicago Reporter*, September 1982; Kahrl, "The Short End of Both Sticks," 203–4; Gellman, "In the Driver's Seat," 74–75.

10. *Ketchum v. City Council of Chicago*; "U.S. Acts to Block Chicago Ward Remap,"

*Chicago Tribune*, September 16, 1982; "Hispanic Vote Emerges as New Battlefront in Council Wars," *Chicago Reporter*, September 1984.

11. "God Made Family, Marriage, Government," *Chicago Reporter*, January 1982 (quote); "Community Groups Look Beyond Back Yards in Push for Power," *Chicago Reporter*, April 1982; "West Town Fights Health Clinic Cutbacks," *Chicago Reporter*, February 1982; "Puerto Ricans Rap Alderman Appointment," *Chicago Tribune*, December 1, 1981; "Hispanic Leaders Blast Loss of Clout Due to City Redistricting," *Chicago Tribune*, April 29, 1982.

12. "The Life of the Party," *New Republic*, January 24, 1983; "Community Groups Look Beyond Back Yards in Push for Power," *Chicago Reporter*, April 1982 (quotes). This flies in the face of the kind of Alinsky-style neighborhood activism of the Back of the Yards Neighborhood Council and The Woodlawn Organization from a generation or two before.

13. ACORN became known for voter registration and other advocacy work for low- and middle-income families, starting in Little Rock, Arkansas, in 1972 and expanding to twenty-seven states by 1980. ACORN officially came to Chicago in 1983. Delgado, *Organizing the Movement*. See also "Black Ballot Revolt," *Chicago Defender*, February 1, 1975; and "CUL Launches Voter Registration Drive," *Chicago Crusader*, February 4, 1975, box II-215, folder 2123, CUL.

14. Frances Fox Piven and Richard Cloward argue that poor people could flood the system in any number of ways—in welfare offices, voter registration offices, and so on, to force change. The college-educated Coleman and Helen Shiller were both familiar with the argument. Fox Piven and Cloward, *Poor People's Movements*.

15. Walter "Slim" Coleman interview, HH; Travis, *Harold*, 144–45 (quotes). "Record Voter Sign-Up Here Relied on Blacks," *Chicago Tribune*, October 3, 1982; "City Report: Voter Sign-Ups May Hit Byrne," *Chicago Tribune*, October 7, 1982; "We Will Register 100,000!," *All Chicago City News*, August 21–September 4, 1982, in *Black Power in Chicago*; Coleman and Jenkins, *Fair Share*, 63–64; "Welfare Deal OKd; Checks on the Way," *Chicago Tribune*, May 15, 1982; *Power Organized for Welfare and Employment Rights v. Thompson*.

16. Rivlin, *Fire on the Prairie*, 50–51 (quote); "Black Picketing Predicted at Chicago-Fest," *Chicago Tribune*, July 30, 1982; Michaeli, *The Defender*, ix–x; Rutkoff and Scott, "Pinkster in Chicago"; Moore, *The South Side*, 88; West, "The Bud Billiken Parade."

17. Operation PUSH succeeded the Southern Christian Leadership Conference's Operation Breadbasket, which Jackson directed in Chicago until 1971. Deppe, *Operation Breadbasket*.

18. Kleppner, *Chicago Divided*, 145–46 (quote); Travis, *Harold*, 145–47; "A Boycott May Backfire," *Chicago Tribune*, August 1, 1982; "Jesse Jackson and Racial Politics," *Chicago Tribune*, August 13, 1982; "A Few Clouds Hang over ChicagoFest at the Close," *Chicago Tribune*, August 16, 1982.

19. Travis, *Harold*, 150–51, 148–49 (quotes); "One Man's Contribution," *Chicago Tribune*, October 13, 1982; Rivlin, *Fire on the Prairie*, 61–62.

20. Kleppner, *Chicago Divided*, 148–49; Grimshaw, *Bitter Fruit*, 163; "Voter Registration Drive Targets Hispanics," *All City Chicago News*, September 10, 1982, and "Catching Voter Fever," *Chicago Sun-Times*, September 9, 1982, in *Black Power in Chicago*. Voter registration numbers from this period vary widely from source to source, with some claims of

292 | Notes to Pages 128–31

upward of 230,000 new voters. A net total of 135,831 is the most reliable estimate for all voters, with about 125,000 African Americans.

21. "'How Much Time Do We Have? . . . No Time,'" *Chicago Tribune*, May 10, 1981 (quote); "Survey Pinpoints Why State Street Isn't That Great Anymore," *Chicago Tribune*, October 31, 1982; "State Unemployment Rate 12.5%," *Chicago Tribune*, October 9, 1982; Wilentz, *The Age of Reagan*, 147–49; Rossinow, *The Reagan Era*, 145–46; Moore, *The South Side*, 20–25.

22. Kleppner, *Chicago Divided*, 148–50; "Pollsters Are Only Clear Losers in Governor's Race," *Chicago Tribune*, November 4, 1982; "Revived Machine Facing Tough Tests," *Chicago Tribune*, November 7, 1982; "The Washington Strategy" and "Winter and Losers: Who Will House the Homeless?," *Chicago Reader*, November 26, 1982.

23. "A New Kind of Election," *Chicago Tribune*, November 18, 1982 (quotes).

24. "The Washington Strategy," *Chicago Reader*, November 26, 1982; "Washington in Race for Mayor," *Chicago Tribune*, November 11, 1982 (quotes). Jorge Morales interview; "The Washington Strategy," *Chicago Reader*, November 26, 1982; Steve Askin, "After the 1977 Election," box 1, folder 53, SA; Cambridge Survey Research, January 1983, box 42, folder 3, MC.

25. "Washington Earned Reputation as Liberal: How They Voted," *Chicago Tribune*, April 3, 1983; Rivlin, *Fire on the Prairie*, 37–38; Wilentz, *The Age of Reagan*, 141–44.

26. For the original sanctuary movement, see Lorentzen, *Women in the Sanctuary Movement*; Coutin, *The Culture of Protest*; Davidson, *Convictions of the Heart*.

27. María "Nena" de los Ángeles Torres interview; "A Frightening Wave of Racial Violence," *Chicago Tribune*, January 9, 1981 (quotes); Modesto Rivera interview; Jesús "Chuy" García, interview by Jeff Spitz; "Washington: A Thoughtful Legislator," *Washington Post*, February 24, 1983; "Hispanics Use New Voting Rights Act to Reshape Texas Politics," *Washington Post*, April 25, 1983; "Illegal-Alien Plan Includes ID System," *Chicago Tribune*, March 18, 1982; "U.S. Acts to Block Chicago Ward Remap," *Chicago Tribune*, September 16, 1982; "Benefits of Crackdown on Illegal Alien Worker Questioned," *Chicago Tribune*, November 5, 1982; *Ketchum v. Byrne*; U.S. Senate, *Voting Rights Act*, 1646–50.

28. Cambridge Survey Research, January 1983, box 42, folder 3, MC; "80% Solution," *Chicago Reader*, March 1983; Askin, "After the 1977 Election," box 1, folder 53, SA; Thompson, *Double Trouble*, 41, 138; Sonenshein, "Can Black Candidates Win Statewide Elections?"; Muñoz and Henry, "Coalition Politics in San Antonio and Denver." Political scientists characterize Bradley's campaigns as "deracialized" in contrast with Black mayors in cities with Black majorities. Austin and Middleton, "The Limitations of the Deracialization Concept."

29. Rivlin, *Fire on the Prairie*, 68–69, 90–91; "Byrne-Daley Race Narrows," *Chicago Tribune*, July 18, 1982; "The Son Also Rises: Richard M. Daley Steps Out from His Father's Shadow," *Chicago Tribune*, September 12, 1982; "Fast Eddie Bending Even His Own Rules," *Chicago Tribune*, October 24, 1982; "Byrne Insists Polls Don't Worry Her," *Chicago Sun-Times*, October 23, 1982; "Western Avenue," *Chicago Reporter*, March 1983; Koeneman, *First Son*, 56–59, 66–84; "Can You Find the Reformer in This Group?," *Chicago Reader*, February 18, 1983; "House of Screams," *Chicago Reader*, January 25, 1990.

30. Kahn, *The Political Consequences of Being a Woman*; Braden, *Women Politicians and the Media*.

31. "Will the Real Jane Stand Up?," *Chicago Tribune*, November 7, 1982 (quotes); "Picture It: Byrne Riding the Airwaves into Thick of Primary," *Chicago Tribune*, December 12, 1982. "Save Our City," *Chicago Reporter*, March 1983; Kleppner, *Chicago Divided*, 163–65; "An Opinionated Psychobiography of Mayor Jane Byrne," *Chicago Sun-Times*, February 9, 1983; Rivlin, *Fire on the Prairie*, 81; Byrne, *My Chicago*, 330. Melvin Holli and Paul Green argue that the male-dominated Chicago press corps and political establishment largely refrained from attacking her as a woman, ignoring the subtler standards to which she was often held. Holli and Green, *Bashing Chicago Traditions*, 5–7. More than thirty years later, in 2015, another combative incumbent mayor, Rahm Emanuel, donned a sweater and took to the airwaves to repackage himself in a kinder, gentler mode—an effort that worked well enough to win reelection.

32. Washington, "Crisis of Leadership in Chicago"; "It May Take All in Byrne's Power to Win Her a 2d Term," *Chicago Tribune*, July 28, 1982 (quotes). "Mayoral Politics and Polish," *Chicago Tribune*, November 24, 1982; "Race in the Race: The Candidates and Their Strategies," "Western Avenue," "Save Our City," and "Washington Forced Press to Grapple with Race in Campaign," all *Chicago Reporter*, March 1983; Rivlin, *Fire on the Prairie*, 82–83; Kleppner, *Chicago Divided*, 156–61.

33. Jacquelyne Grimshaw interview, HMDA; "Democrat Mayoral Trio Nears 1st Set of Hurdles," *Chicago Tribune*, November 28, 1982 (quotes). "The Activist," *Chicago Tribune*, April 17, 1983.

34. Askin, "After the 1977 Election," box 1, folder 53, SA (quote); Rivlin, *Fire on the Prairie*, 83–84; "The Activist," *Chicago Tribune*, April 17, 1983; Mantler, "'Organize the People,'" 9–11, 22.

35. "80% Solution," *Chicago Reporter*, March 1983 (quote). John Betancur and Doug Gills were first to identify these three distinct groups—an analysis that generally still holds up. Betancur and Gills, "The African American and Latino Coalition Experience in Chicago," 62.

36. "On the Cancellation: This Bitter Earth," n.d. (November 1982), box 24, folder 5, MC; Rivlin, *Fire on the Prairie*, 88 (quotes); "80% Solution," *Chicago Reporter*, March 1983; Kleppner, *Chicago Divided*, 154; Grimshaw, *Bitter Fruit*, 171–73; Biles, *Mayor Harold Washington*, 70–72.

37. Hal Baron memo to research committee, December 10, 1982, box 4, folder 15, MC (quotes); Mier and Moe, "Decentralized Development," 71–72; Biles, *Mayor Harold Washington*, 75.

38. Biles, *Mayor Harold Washington*, 76–78, 145–46; Kretzmann, "The Affirmative Information Policy," 206; Giloth, "Making Policy with Communities," 111. The "Washington Papers" can be found in box 23, folder 12, MC, and under "Transition materials," box 4, folder 49, RL.

39. "Neighborhoods Cry Foul over World's Fair," *Chicago Reader*, October 8, 1982; Third mayoral debate, January 1983 (quotes). "School Board Elections Aim of City 'Congress,'" *Chicago Tribune*, August 23, 1982; "Activist Groups Draft 'Platform' for City Races," *Chicago Tribune*, August 30, 1982; "Groups Seeking Clearer Signals on World's Fair," *Chicago Tribune*, September 17, 1982; "More Data Asked on World's Fair," *Chicago Tribune*, March 1, 1983; "Pilsen Coalition Says Fair Officials 'Shut Us Out,'" *Chicago Tribune*, April 23, 1983; "Community in Rebellion," *Keep Strong*, June–August 1982; Gills, "Chicago

Politics and Community Development"; Mier and Moe, "Decentralized Development," 44–49, 66–67, 69–70. See also de los Ángeles Torres, "The Commission on Latino Affairs," 178–79; 1985 minutes of the Mayor's Advisory Commission on Latino Affairs, Chicago History Museum.

40. Press statement by Community Workshop on Economic Development, n.d., box 30, folder 8, RM; Mier and Moe, "Decentralized Development," 70 (quotes). Betancur and Gills, "The African American and Latino Coalition Experience in Chicago," 65; "Draft Platform of the Community Workshop for Economic Development," box 8, folder 9, September 15, 1982, RM; "Enterprise Zones—Hope or Just Politics?," *Chicago Tribune*, December 28, 1982. CWED's board reflected the city's racial (although not gender) diversity of community activism, including Mexican American Vasquez; Puerto Ricans Jorge Morales and Peter Earle; African Americans Squire Lance, J. Archie Hargraves, and Bob Lucas; and whites Robert Mier and Robert Brehm. As for enterprise zones, in just fifteen years, between 1981 and 1996, they went from zero to an estimated 2,840 in forty states, with mixed success at best in reinvigorating employment and development in otherwise impoverished, mostly urban districts across the country. See Peters and Fisher, *State Enterprise Zone Programs*; Wilder and Rubin, "Rhetoric Versus Reality."

41. José "Cha-Cha" Jiménez interview, January 20, 2012; "Interview with Rev. Jorge Morales," *El Independiente*, March 25, 1983, box 21, RL (quotes). Jorge Morales interview; List of Latino Supporters, box 25, folder 17, MC; Gottlieb, "Hoboken Is Burning"; Ansfield, "The Crisis of Insurance and the Insuring of the Crisis."

42. Rudy Lozano for 22nd Ward alderman, flier, 1983, box 4, folder 43, RL; María "Nena" de los Ángeles Torres interview (quotes). Fremon, *Chicago Politics Ward by Ward*, 147–48, 165; "Latinos Give the Party a Chance as Independent Efforts Falter," *Chicago Reporter*, December 1982; "Save Our City," *Chicago Reporter*, March 1983; "CBUC Endorses Rudy Lozano," February 16, 1983, box 4, folder 46, Lozano campaign press release, February 16, 1983, box 4, folder 43, *Chicago Sun-Times*, May 10, 1985, box 4, folder 44, and Lozano, press statement—Harrison High closing, January 12, 1983, box 5, folder 50, RL; "The Trouble with Harrison High," *Chicago Reader*, May 20, 1983.

43. "Politics: Washington Is Mounting a Campaign of Confusion," *Chicago Tribune*, January 16, 1983 (quote); "Running with Washington," *Chicago Reader*, February 11, 1983.

44. "Byrne Wins Backing of CFL During Stormy Union Meeting," *Chicago Tribune*, February 2, 1983 (quote); Charles Hayes interview, HMDA; CBTU, "Report of the Executive Council," 1983, box 90, folder 10, TB; Kleppner, *Chicago Divided*, 121–24.

45. "Can You Find the Reformer in This Group?," *Chicago Reader*, February 18, 1983 (quotes); Jacky Grimshaw interview; Stewart-Winter, *Queer Clout*, 156–58; Todd-Breland, *A Political Education*, 157. Washington routinely discussed the feminization of poverty on the campaign trail. "Women's Rally Speech," January 19, 1983, box 45, folder 23, and "Position Paper on Women's Issues," n.d., box 5, folder 21, MC; "Washington Papers," box 23, folder 12, MC, and under "Transition materials," box 4, folder 49, RL, 34–38.

46. "Running with Washington," *Chicago Reader*, February 11, 1983; "Voters to Decide if Black Aldermen Are Power Brokers or Puppets," *Chicago Reporter*, December 1982; Rivlin, *Fire on the Prairie*, 76.

47. "Mondale's Choice Angers Jesse," *Chicago Tribune*, February 3, 1983 (quote); "Richard Daley for Mayor," *Chicago Sun-Times*, February 3, 1983; "The Tribune's Endorsements," *Chicago Tribune*, February 20, 1983; "Running with Washington," *Chicago*

*Reader*, February 11, 1983; "Washington Picks Up Support," *Chicago Defender*, January 13, 1983; "Voters to Decide if Black Aldermen Are Power Brokers or Puppets," *Chicago Reporter*, December 1982; Rivlin, *Fire on the Prairie*, 76.

48. "Dems Clash Over Taxes in Debate," *Chicago Tribune*, January 19, 1983 (quote); "3 Candidates for Chicago Mayor Clash in Debate on Finances," *New York Times*, January 19, 1983; "3 Winners Emerge from Mayor Debates," *Chicago Tribune*, February 2, 1983; Kleppner, *Chicago Divided*, 172–74; Grimshaw, *Bitter Fruit*, 174–75. Kleppner and Grimshaw argue that there were actually two debates—Washington versus Byrne and Daley versus Byrne. While Daley lost ground to Byrne, Washington gained on the mayor, according to polls Kleppner details.

49. "Washington Impresses Black Voters," *Chicago Tribune*, January 23, 1983 (quote); Kleppner, *Chicago Divided*, 174; Grimshaw, *Bitter Fruit*, 175. On the press, see "Washington Forced Press to Grapple with Race in Campaign," *Chicago Reporter*, March 1983; "The Press: Black and White and Red All Over," *Chicago Reader*, March 4, 1983; "The Press: Hysteria in the Making," *Chicago Reader*, April 22, 1983.

50. "Washington Assails Foes in Thunderous Rally," *Chicago Tribune*, February 7, 1983; Grimshaw, *Bitter Fruit*, 176 (quotes). "Blacks Show Faith in the Ballot Box," *Chicago Tribune*, February 9, 1983; Jacky Grimshaw, Helen Shiller, and Robert "Bob" Starks interviews; "Washington Rallying?," *Chicago Reader*, February 11, 1983. Every account of the UIC rally recognized its symbolic and psychological importance for the candidate and the campaign. Kleppner, *Chicago Divided*, 175–76; Rivlin, *Fire on the Prairie*, 99; Nolan, *Campaign!*, 129–30; Grimshaw, *Bitter Fruit*, 175–76.

51. Rivlin, *Fire on the Prairie*, 100 (quotes); "Dems Slugging in Last Round; Foes Trade Charges on Race Issue," *Chicago Tribune*, February 21, 1983; Axelrod, *Believer*; Biles, *Mayor Harold Washington*, 84–85; Kleppner, *Chicago Divided*, 177–78.

52. "Harold Washington: Interview with Jacky Grimshaw," *Streetwise*, April 17, 2013; Jacky Grimshaw interview.

53. Travis, *Harold*, 177; Rivlin, *Fire on the Prairie*, 101–2; "Just Another Election Day," *Chicago Reader*, February 25, 1983; "Washington Wins: Heavy Black Turnout Key to Victory," *Chicago Tribune*, February 23, 1983; "Election Coverage Shows Chicago's TV News Is Distant Runner-Up on Race," *Chicago Tribune*, February 24, 1983.

54. Biles, *Mayor Harold Washington*, 86–87; Kleppner, *Chicago Divided*, 181–85; Grimshaw, *Bitter Fruit*, 177–78; Alkalimat and Gills, *Harold Washington and the Crisis of Black Power*, 58–74; Fremon, *Chicago Politics Ward by Ward*, 20. A few writers have tried to overcredit so-called white Lakefront liberals on the North Side, starting with the *Sun-Times*. "Washington Key: Lakefront Votes," *Chicago Sun-Times*, February 24, 1983. See also Holli and Green, *Bashing Chicago Traditions*. The precise numbers for the 1983 primary are quite slippery, however. Perhaps not surprising for a municipal election in Chicago, there are numerous discrepancies even in the official canvassing sheets found at the Chicago Public Library. My numbers here come from Kleppner, *Chicago Divided*, 134, 165–67, and are slightly different from those of Alkalimat and Gills, *Harold Washington and the Crisis of Black Power*, and Fremon, *Chicago Politics Ward by Ward*. But all support the conclusion that Black voters provided the full plurality, if only barely.

55. "At Least 14 Runoffs for City Council Seats" and "The Aldermanic Results," *Chicago Tribune*, February 24, 1983.

56. Byrne, *My Chicago*, 338; Rivlin, *Fire on the Prairie*, 103 (quotes).

## Chapter 6

1. "Washington Moves to Defuse Race Issue," *Chicago Tribune*, February 25, 1983 (quote); "Dems Seek Peace with Washington," *Chicago Tribune*, February 24, 1983; Kleppner, *Chicago Divided*, 188–91.

2. For instance, see Grimshaw, *Bitter Fruit*; Rivlin, *Fire on the Prairie*; Kleppner, *Chicago Divided*; Biles, *Mayor Harold Washington*.

3. "Dems Seek Peace with Washington," *Chicago Tribune*, February 24, 1983; "Top Dems Shun Byrne," *Chicago Tribune*, March 17, 1983; "Dems Say Byrne to Seek Re-election as Write-In," *Chicago Tribune*, March 16, 1983 (quotes). "Jane Byrne Ends Her Write-In Bid to Stay in Office," *New York Times*, March 24, 1983; Rivlin, *Fire on the Prairie*, 112.

4. "Washington Moves to Defuse Race Issue," *Chicago Tribune*, February 25, 1983; "Epton: Dems 'Hide' Faces," *Chicago Tribune*, March 3, 1983; Byrne, *My Chicago*, 344; Alkalimat and Gills, *Harold Washington and the Crisis of Black Power in Chicago*, 83–85; Rivlin, *Fire on the Prairie*, 112; Travis, *Harold*, 182, 184; Holli and Green, *Bashing Chicago Traditions*, 10; Kleppner, *Chicago Divided*, 127–31.

5. "GOP's Epton Must Temper His Tantrums," *Chicago Tribune*, April 3, 1983; Kleppner, *Chicago Divided*, 201 (quotes). "Epton Accused of Attacks, Evasion," *Chicago Reader*, April 1, 1983; Biles, *Mayor Harold Washington*, 90–93; Rivlin, *Fire on the Prairie*, 107–9, 121–22; Kleppner, *Chicago Divided*, 197–201. Many observers, from David Axelrod to Abdul Alkalimat, began using the language of the Great White Hope during the general election.

6. On white stereotypes of Black criminality in Chicago and elsewhere, see Balto, *Occupied Territory*; Muhammad, *The Condemnation of Blackness*.

7. Rivlin, *Fire on the Prairie*, 114–15, 128; "Big Tax Boosts Needed to Shore Up City, Washington Says," *Chicago Tribune*, November 19, 1982 (quotes). Citizens for Epton, "Issues Papers," n.d., box 1, folder 3, "The Case against Harold Washington, 1967–1983," April 8, 1983, box 1, folder 11, and Zachary G. Fiala, "1983 Chicago Mayoral Race: Bernard Epton Campaign Strategy," March 1983, box 1, folder 8, BE; "Guide for the Perplexed," *Chicago Reader*, April 8, 1983; Whitehead, "The Chicago Story"; Kleppner, *Chicago Divided*, 204–7. Reagan won a resounding victory in 1980, partly thanks to registered Democrats, especially in the South. The role of "Reagan Democrats" has been overstated, however, in urban centers such as Chicago and Baltimore, where working-class whites more likely than not stayed home. Durr, *Behind the Backlash*.

8. Politically Concerned People, "Do Not Surrender Your Destiny!," "Dear Neighbor," March 1983, box 46, folder 16, and Anti-Washington fliers, box 46, folder 17, MC; Anonymous Supporters of Epton, Anti-Washington fliers, 1983, box 1, folder 9, BE; "A One-Issue Mayoral Race," *Chicago Tribune*, March 27, 1983; Kleppner, *Chicago Divided*, 211–13; Travis, *Harold*, 194; Grimshaw, *Bitter Fruit*, 181; Rivlin, *Fire on the Prairie*, 116; de los Ángeles Torres, "The Commission on Latino Affairs," 172. Other examples are in box 46, folders 16–17, MC. See also David Moberg, "Guide for the Perplexed," *Chicago Reader*, April 8, 1983.

9. "Washington Moves to Defuse Race Issue," *Chicago Tribune*, February 25, 1983; "The Constituency of Fear," *Chicago Tribune*, March 27, 1983; Kleppner, *Chicago Divided*, 211 (quotes). "Bernard Epton Mayoral Spots"; Hurwitz and Peffley, "Playing the Race Card in the Post–Willie Horton Era."

10. "'It's a Racial Thing, Don't Kid Yourself': An Oral History of Chicago's 1983 Mayoral Race," *New York* (magazine), April 2, 2019, "Chicago's Ugly Election," *Newsweek* April 11, 1983, (quotes). "St. Pascal's Makes News—Hard Way," *Chicago Tribune*, April 1, 1983; "Chicagoans Display No Signs of Unity," *New York Times*, March 29, 1983; "Mondale and Washington Booed by Angry Whites," *Washington Post*, March 28, 1983; Travis, *Harold*, 192–93; Kleppner, *Chicago Divided*, 208–9; Holli and Green, *Bashing Chicago's Traditions*, 11.

11. Kleppner, *Chicago Divided*, 188; Rivlin, *Fire on the Prairie*, 104–7.

12. "Washington Moves to Defuse Race Issue," *Chicago Tribune*, February 25, 1983 (quotes); "Jackson Didn't Steal the Show, but He Was a Big Part of It," *Chicago Tribune*, February 27, 1983; Rivlin, *Fire on the Prairie*, 109–11. Rivlin's account is particularly attuned to the energy spent managing Jackson's role during the campaign. As the city's most prominent and controversial Black leader, Jackson's influence can be overstated, but the disregard for him—even his absence—in other accounts seems odd. Alkalimat and Gills characterize the decision for Jackson to stay behind the scenes as more mutual than it might actually be. Alkalimat and Gills, *Harold Washington and the Crisis of Black Power in Chicago*, 75–76.

13. McDermott memo to Raby, undated, box 3, folder 6, MC; David Moberg, "Guide for the Perplexed," *Chicago Reader*, April 8, 1983 (quotes). Marilyn Norling memo to Maxine Leftwich, March 1, Joseph Gardner memo to Al Raby, March 28, and Earle memo to Washington, "Campaign Strategy in Latino Community," March 14, 1983, box 3, folder 4, Earle and Coronado memo to Al Raby and Ken Glover, March 1, Earle memo to Glover, March 4, and Earle memo to Washington and Raby, March 9, 1983, box 4, folder 11, MC; "It's Politics on Parade at St. Pat's," *Chicago Tribune*, March 18, 1983.

14. David Moberg, "Guide for the Perplexed," *Chicago Reader*, April 8, 1983; Whitehead, "The Chicago Story"; Rivlin, *Fire on the Prairie*, 121–22; Kleppner, *Chicago Divided*, 226–28.

15. Aida Giachello and Raúl Hinojosa, "Proposal for a City of Chicago Commission on Latino Affairs," March 28, 1983, box 21, folder 3, MC (quote); Edwin Claudio, "Harold Washington's program for Chicago's Latino Community," March 14, 1983, box 21, folder 3, MC.

16. Earle memo to Washington, March 14, 1983, box 3, folder 4, and Earle memo to Washington and Raby, March 7, 1983, box 4, folder 11, MC (quotes); John Betancur interview; "En la unidad está la fuerza," 1983, box 4, folder 40, List of Latino supporters, April 2, 1983, box 25, folder 17, MC; Amezcua, "A Machine in the Barrio."

17. Earle memo to Harold Washington, March 14, 1983, Elena Martinez and Maurice Everette memo to Al Raby, Project Positive, March 31, 1983, box 3, folder 4, Steven Carter memo to Al Raby and Ken Glover, March 20, 1983, box 4, folder 11, Congressman Washington's briefing notes (Latino events), February–April 1983, box 45, folder 54, MC; "As Others Roll Along in Race, Byrne Starts Over," *Chicago Tribune*, March 21, 1983; de los Ángeles Torres, "The Commission on Latino Affairs," 172; María "Nena" de los Ángeles Torres interview.

18. Gutiérrez, *Still Dreaming*, 13–16; Modesto Rivera, John Betancur, and Paul Siegel interviews (quotes); Mantler, "Rainbow Reformers," 227–28.

19. Damski columns, March 17 (quote) and March 10, 1983, *GayLife*, box 36, folder 22, MC; "Gays and Pols: The Constituents Woo Their Candidate," *Chicago Reader*, April 8, 1983; Stewart-Winter, *Queer Clout*, 156–61.

20. Chicago Democracy Project, "Election Results for 1983 General Election."

21. This framing is best represented in Grimshaw, *Bitter Fruit*; Helgeson, *Crucibles of Black Empowerment*; Kleppner, *Chicago Divided*; Rivlin, *Fire on the Prairie*.

22. Kleppner, *Chicago Divided*, 223 (quote), 217–22. Chicago Democracy Project, "Election Results for 1983 General Election"; Raby memo to Emergency Committee, March 28, 1983, box 3, folder 3, MC.

23. "Winner Takes Hispanic Bloc," *Chicago Tribune*, April 14, 1983; "It's Coalition Politics in Chicago," *Chicago Tribune*, April 16, 1983; "Washington's Victory: All Blacks, Most Latinos, 17% Whites," *Chicago Reader*, May 1983; "Black-Hispanic Alliance's Future Pondered," *Chicago Sun-Times*, April 15, 1983. Scholarly credit to Latinos includes Gills, "Chicago Politics and Community Development", 52; Betancur and Gills, "The African American and Latino Experience in Chicago," 59–87; Cordova, "Harold Washington and the Rise of Latino Electoral Politics," 31–57; Torres, "Latino Politics in Chicago," 248–53; Rivlin, *Fire on the Prairie*, 124–25; Mantler, "Rainbow Reformers." For whites, see Biles, *Mayor Harold Washington*; Stewart-Winter, *Queer Clout*; Holli and Green, *Bashing Chicago Traditions*.

24. "Election of Black Mayor in Philadelphia Reflects a Decade of Change in City," *New York Times*, November 10, 1983; "New Orleans Victor Credits White Votes," *New York Times*, November 14, 1977; Colburn and Adler, *African American Mayors*.

25. "Washington Wins, Dirtiest Election Is Over—Amen!," *Chicago Defender*, April 13, 1983; "4 Winners Give Council a New Look," *Chicago Tribune*, April 14, 1983; Jacky Grimshaw interview; "Washington Winner in Bitter Chicago Election for Mayor," *Washington Post*, April 13, 1983 (quotes); "Seven Incumbents Defeated in Aldermanic Runoffs" and "10,000 Backers Swell Hall," both in *Chicago Tribune*, April 13, 1983.

## Chapter 7

1. Washington inaugural address, Chicago City Council, *Journal of the Proceedings*, April 29, 1983, 7–11; "Mayor Comes in Firing," *Chicago Tribune*, April 30, 1983 (quotes). "Inaugural Surprises Some, Pleases Others," *Chicago Tribune*, April 30, 1983; "What Washington Inherited," *Chicago Tribune*, May 1, 1983; Rivlin, *Fire on the Prairie*, 144–45. In contrast, New York faced debts in the billions and nearly—and probably should have—declared bankruptcy in 1975. One reason was New York was more generous in its postwar social spending than Chicago. Phillips-Fein, *Fear City*.

2. "Gang Wars, Council Wars," *Chicago Tribune*, December 5, 1984 (quote); "Washington Calls Council Division 'War,'" *Chicago Tribune*, May 26, 1983; Rivlin, *Fire on the Prairie*, 147–50; Biles, *Mayor Harold Washington*, 116–21.

3. "Power Struggle or Racism, Voters Frown on Council's Feuding," *Chicago Tribune*, May 29, 1983; Rivlin, *Fire on the Prairie*, 144–45 (quotes).

4. Biles, *Mayor Harold Washington*, 107 (quote); Marable, *How Capitalism Underdeveloped Black America*, 31–34; Rossinow, *The Reagan Era*, 139–60. With some variation, Black and Latino mayors in Los Angeles, Atlanta, Gary, San Antonio, New York, New Orleans, and Washington, D.C., to name a few cities, faced similar internal and external challenges. See Thompson, *Double Trouble*; Kaufmann, "Black and Latino Voters in Denver"; Piliawsky, "The Impact of Black Mayors on the Black Community"; Biles, "Black

Mayors"; Colburn and Adler, *African American Mayors*; Katz, *Why Don't American Cities Burn?*

5. José "Cha-Cha" Jiménez interview, January 20, 2012.

6. Alkalimat and Gills, *Harold Washington and the Crisis of Black Power in Chicago*, 118, 137–39.

7. José "Cha-Cha" Jiménez interview, January 20, 2012, and Modesto Rivera interviews (quotes). "A Model of Resistance," *Keep Strong*, January 1976; "11 Indicted Here in FALN Blasts," *Chicago Tribune*, December 11, 1980; "100,000 on Hand as Puerto Rican Celebration Ends," *Chicago Tribune*, June 6, 1983; Mantler, "'Organize the People,'" 20–21.

8. "Black-Hispanic Alliance's Future Pondered," *Chicago Sun-Times*, April 15, 1983; Gary Rivlin, "Who Killed Rudy Lozano?," *Chicago Reader*, 1985 (quotes). "Lozano Widow OKs Citizen Group to Probe His Slaying," *Chicago Sun-Times*, July 19, 1983; "Lozano Myth Unfair to Lozano the Man," *Logan Square Free Press*, June 1986; Gary Rivlin, "Who Killed Rudy Lozano?," *Chicago Reader*, 1985, box 4, folder 37, RL.

9. Linda Coronado and María "Nena" de los Ángeles Torres interviews (quotes). De los Ángeles Torres, "Commission on Latino Affairs," 174–75; "Latino Group Critical of Washington," *Chicago Tribune*, October 5, 1983.

10. María "Nena" de los Ángeles Torres interview (quotes); de los Ángeles Torres, "Commission on Latino Affairs," 174–75; "Hispanics Named to Chicago Posts," *Chicago Tribune*, November 16, 1983; "Mayor Hires Few Women, Hispanics at Top," *Chicago Tribune*, December 4, 1983; MACLA minutes, November 22, 1983, and January 4, 1984, and Report to the Commissioner, December 14, 1983, box 1, folder 3, MACLA; Mayor's Advisory Committee on Asian American Affairs, 1984, box 5, folder 2, and Mayor's Advisory Commission on Women's Affairs, 1984, box 26, folder 43, CSS.

11. Linda Coronado interview; de los Ángeles Torres, "Commission on Latino Affairs," 176; "Benjamin Reyes: Surprise Choice to Fulfill Mayoral Vow," *Chicago Reporter*, April 1984 (quotes).

12. Montes letter to Harold Washington, April 14, 1983, box 5, folder 21, MC; Lanahan and Donahue letter to Washington, January 13, 1984, box 26, folder 40, CSS (quotes). WUBC meeting minutes, May 17 and July 5, 1983, box 26, folder 40, and "1984 Executive Summary Report of the Mayor's Advisory Commission on Women's Affairs," August 26, 1984, box 26, folder 43, CSS; "Mayor Cuts His Pay 20%," *Chicago Tribune*, May 1, 1983; "Mayor's Order Creates Women's Commission," *Chicago Tribune*, January 13, 1984.

13. Washington, "Statement on Women in City Government," 1987, box 26, folder 54, CSS; "200 Women Defend Mayor against Byrne," *Chicago Tribune*, January 22, 1987; Peggy Montes interview, HMDA; "Mayor's Staff: Outsiders Are In," *Chicago Sun-Times*, special reprint issue, 1986, box 42, folder 6, RM.

14. *Boletín* (MACLA's official publication), November 1984 and July 1985 (quotes) and February/March 1985, box 1, folder 4, MACLA; "Washington Reform Progress Burdened by Errors, Politics," *Chicago Reporter*, April 1985; de los Ángeles Torres, "Commission on Latino Affairs," 179–80; Biles, *Mayor Harold Washington*, 239–41.

15. "Mayor's Staff: Outsiders Are In," *Chicago Sun-Times*, special reprint issue, 1986, box 42, folder 6, RM; "Mayor's Mystery Man: Workhorse Who Covets Power," *Chicago Reporter*, February 1984; "Washington Reform Progress Burdened by Errors, Politics," *Chicago Reporter*, April 1985; "Mayor Hires Few Women, Hispanics at Top," *Chicago*

*Tribune*, December 4, 1983. From Maynard Jackson's Atlanta to Marion Barry's Washington, D.C., affirmative action policies tended to favor Black men in top positions more than anyone else.

16. "Everybody's Mayor," *Chicago Reader*, March 19, 1992; Biles, *Mayor Harold Washington*, 243–44 (quotes). Robert "Bob" Starks interview; Rivlin, *Fire on the Prairie*, 156–57; Gills, "Chicago Politics and Community Development," 53.

17. "Mr. Hayes' Victory," *Chicago Tribune*, July 28, 1983; Bob Starks interview, HMDA (quotes). "Palmer Win Would Be Good Sign," *Chicago Tribune*, July 22, 1983; "Hayes' Win Gives Mayor a Victory to Celebrate," *Chicago Tribune*, July 28, 1983; Robert "Bob" Starks interview; "Mayor's Mystery Man," *Chicago Reporter*, February 1984; "Everybody's Mayor," *Chicago Reader*, March 19, 1992.

18. Sandoval-Strausz, *Barrio America*, 121; Diamond, *Chicago on the Make*, 223–25. Maynard Jackson of Atlanta and Marion Barry of Washington, D.C., are just two examples of Black mayors elected during the economic decline of the 1970s who turned to aggressive affirmative action policies to reduce job losses. Bayor, "African American Mayors and Governance in Atlanta," 181–84; Myers Asch and Musgrove, *Chocolate City*, 394–95, 399.

19. "Washington Reform Progress Burdened by Errors, Politics," *Chicago Reporter*, February 1985 (quote); "Minorities New Force in City Contract Bidding," *Chicago Tribune*, July 29, 1984; "Oberman Proposes Board to OK Purchases," *Chicago Tribune*, August 14, 1984; "One Cheer for the Washington Administration," *Chicago Tribune*, April 27, 1986; "Affirmative Action Is Put on Trial in Dispute with City," *Chicago Tribune*, June 14, 1987. It should be noted that the *Tribune*'s coverage was routinely and philosophically critical of the administration's set-aside program.

20. "Mayor Briefs Allies on Selling Budget to Council," *Chicago Tribune*, November 16, 1983; "Satisfied Judge Signs Settlement in Shakman Case," *Chicago Tribune*, June 22, 1983 (quotes). "Patronage End Ordered: Judge Issues Steps to Prohibit Political Hiring," *Chicago Tribune*, April 5, 1983; *Michael L. Shakman and Paul M. Lurie et al., Plaintiffs, v. the Democratic Organization of Cook County, Defendants.*

21. "Ally of Washington Demands 'the Spoils,'" *Chicago Tribune*, July 30, 1983; "The First 100 Days," *Chicago Tribune*, August 7, 1983 (quotes). Dick Simpson interview; Jacquelyne Grimshaw interview, HMDA; Rivlin, *Fire on the Prairie*, 152; Biles, *Mayor Harold Washington*, 111.

22. Kretzmann, "The Affirmative Information Policy," 199, 201, 207, 215–16; Washington transition team, *Blueprint of Chicago Government: A Study for Mayor Harold Washington*, May 1983, executive summary, 2, box 179, folder 4, TB (quotes). "Just How Open Is the New Open Door Policy at City Hall?," *Chicago Tribune*, November 13, 1983; Ben Joravsky, "Where the Crimes Are: Neighborhood Groups and Police Cooperate on a Computerized Mapping Project," *Chicago Reader*, August 6, 1987. See also Schudson, *The Rise of the Right to Know.*

23. Helen Shiller interview; "Mayor Vetoes Budget Bill, Then Orders Own Changes," *Chicago Tribune*, October 12, 1983; "City's Rubber-Stamp Budget Era Finished," *Chicago Tribune*, November 13, 1983; "Budget Reflects Mayor's Style," *Chicago Tribune*, November 21, 1983; "City Council Passes $1.88 Billion Budget," *Chicago Tribune*, December 28, 1983; Washington, Budget Address, in *Journal of the Proceedings of the City of Chicago*, November 14, 1984; Rivlin, *Fire on the Prairie*, 162–63.

24. "City Hears Pilsen's Plan to Beat Gangs," *Chicago Sun-Times*, January 10, 1985; "Those Are Your Kids in Gangs, Parents Told," *Chicago Sun-Times*, January 28, 1985; "W. Siders Urge Ways to Thwart Gang Crime," *Chicago Sun-Times*, January 11, 1985; and "Tough Stance on Gangs Urged," *Lerner*, January 30, 1985, Newspaper clippings, box 8, folder 8, PSRS (quotes). "Tale of 2 Block Clubs," *Lerner*, January 29, 1985, Newspaper clippings, box 8, folder 8, PSRS; "New Upsurge in Street Gangs," *Chicago Tribune*, January 8, 1984. The *Tribune* ran a five-part series in January 1984 on the rise of gang crime and violence, but the series was quite light on the socioeconomic reasons for gang membership. For a better understanding of gang culture in Chicago, see Venkatesh, *Off the Books* and *Gang Leader for a Day*.

25. "Top Cop's Warning," *Chicago Tribune*, November 3, 1987 (quote); "Crime Commission Rips Chicago Police," *Chicago Tribune*, September 6, 1983; "The Summerdale Scandal and the Case of the Babbling Burglar," *Chicago Tribune*, July 7, 2013; Donner, *Protectors of Privilege*; Williams, *From the Bullet to the Ballot*, 167–90; Rossinow, *The Reagan Era*, 123–24, 149–51.

26. "Rice Now City's Third Most Important Cop," *Chicago Defender*, August 20, 1979; Losier, "The Public Does Not Believe the Police Can Police Themselves," 9; and Fred Rice Jr. interview, HMDA (quotes). "A Cop Who Cares—But Carefully," *Chicago Defender*, March 17, 1975; "Rice Likely Top Cop," *Chicago Tribune*, August 23, 1983; "New Police Chief Changes Strategy to Fight Crime," *Chicago Tribune*, August 28, 1983; "Cop Watch," *Chicago Reader*, July 16, 1992; Fred Rice, in Black, *Bridges of Memory*, 139–41.

27. Stewart-Winter, *Queer Clout*, 157–58; Troy, *Morning in America*, 288–89.

28. "Police Grow to Rely Less on Deadly Force," *Chicago Tribune*, June 23, 1986 (quote); "Rice Probing Officer's Slaying of Unarmed CHA Resident," *Chicago Tribune*, April 4, 1985; "Chicago Police Have Fewer Shootings, More Arrests," *Chicago Tribune*, April 16, 1990; Charles McNickle memo to Michael Holewinski, re: Gang Crime Statistics, October 16, 1985, box 8, folder 4, and David Fogel memo to Holewinski, re: Office of Professional Standards budget, January 27, 1986, PSRS; "Number of Blacks Shot, Abused, Cursed by Police Down under Supt. Rice," *Chicago Metro News*, September 12, 1987; Chicago Police Department, *Statistical Summary* and *Chicago Police Annual Report*; *Tennessee v. Garner*, 471 U.S. 1 (1985); Muhammad, *Condemnation of Blackness*; "The Truth about Chicago's Crime Rates," *Chicago* (magazine), May 2014.

29. "Deaf to the Screams," *Chicago Reader*, July 31, 2003; Baer, *Beyond the Usual Beating*, 6, 127 (quotes). "House of Screams," *Chicago Reader*, January 25, 1990; "The Shocking Truth," *Chicago Reader*, January 9, 1997; "Cop Watch," *Chicago Reader*, July 16, 1992; Ralph, *The Torture Letters*, 57–99; Taylor, *The Torture Machine*, 54, 149. For instance, the Atlanta child murders in 1981 exposed class rifts between Black mayor Maynard Jackson, his working-class constituencies, and the police, a situation he tried to smooth over by championing the conviction of Wayne Williams as the sole killer. Hobson, *The Legend of the Black Mecca*, 94–130. See also the Chicago Torture Archive, based at the University of Chicago: https://chicagotorturearchive.uchicago.edu/.

30. "The Shocking Truth," *Chicago Reader*, January 9, 1997 (quote); David Fogel memo to Holewinski, re: Office of Professional Standards budget, January 27, 1986, PSRS; "Policing Brutality," *Chicago Tribune*, June 20, 1984; "House of Screams," *Chicago Reader*, January 25, 1990; Chicago Police Department, *Annual Report*, 1984, 1985, 1986; Losier, "The Public Does Not Believe the Police Can Police Themselves," 9–11.

31. Susan Weed memo to Moe, Holewinski, and Vince Bakeman, September 14, 1986, box 26, folder 21, CSS; Forman, *Locking Up Our Own*, 119–84 (quotes). Holewinski memo to Mayor Washington, May 28, 1986, box 8, folder 4, and Gardner memo to Tony Gibbs, November 28, 1984, box 8, folder 6a, PSRS; "Crack Puts New Pop In Cocaine Market," *Chicago Tribune*, May 21, 1986; "Mayor's Antidrug Push Starts with an Internal Skirmish," *Chicago Tribune*, August 15, 1986; Murch, "Crack in Los Angeles," 163; Myers Asch and Musgrove, *Chocolate City*, 401–7; Chicago Police Department, *Annual Report*, 1986, 1987.

32. "U.S. May Cut Aid to CHA if Swibel Stays," *Chicago Tribune*, March 18, 1982; Hunt, *Blueprint for Disaster*, 261 (quotes). Rivlin, *Fire on the Prairie*, 47–48, 243–44; "Robinson Deserves Chance in CHA," *Chicago Tribune*, August 17, 1983; Moore, *The South Side*, 70–75; Austen, "The 1992 Horror Film." See also Fuerst, *When Public Housing Was Paradise*.

33. "Heavy CHA Burden Lifted from Mayor," *Chicago Tribune*, January 18, 1987; "CHA Record a Time Bomb That's Still Ticking for Washington," *Chicago Tribune*, February 17, 1987; "CHA Ignored Warnings," *Chicago Tribune*, April 26, 1987; "Black Leaders Rate Mayor's First Term Performance," *Chicago Reporter*, October 1987; Rivlin, *Fire on the Prairie*, 245–46; Biles, *Mayor Harold Washington*, 178–80, 259; Chicago Housing Authority materials, 1986, box 3, folders 30–31, CSS; Hunt, *Blueprint for Disaster*, 261–67.

34. Biles, *Mayor Harold Washington*, 283–84; Rossinow, *The Reagan Era*, 60–61.

35. "Infant Deaths Add Issue to Budget Battle," *Chicago Tribune*, March 27, 1985, "City Infant Mortality Continues Slide," *Chicago Tribune*, October 1, 1985; "$6 Million to Fight City's Infant Deaths," *Chicago Tribune*, July 10, 1986; "Dead Babies," *Chicago Reader*, August 15, 1986; Edwards letter to Turnock, July 16, 1986 (quote), and Turnock letter to Edwards, July 7, 1986, box 14, folder 13, Turnock letter to Edwards, July 18, 1986, box 14, folder 8, and María Torres letter to Edwards, January 16, 1986, box 16, folder 31, CSS; Biles, *Mayor Harold Washington*, 283; Copeland and Meier, "Gaining Ground," 254; Rossinow, *The Reagan Era*, 60–61, 94–95.

36. Edwards memo to Michael Holewinski, September 7, 1984, box 2, folder 11, and Edwards testimony to budget committee, October 21, 1986, box 2, folder 24, CSS; Stewart-Winter, *Queer Clout*, 199–200 (quotes). "City Health Commissioner to Quit March 1," *Chicago Tribune*, August 29, 1987; "The AIDS Dilemma," *Chicago Tribune*, September 6, 1987; Biles, *Mayor Harold Washington*, 284; Self, *All in the Family*, 388–89; Rossinow, *The Reagan Era*, 129–34; Brier, *Infectious Ideas*.

37. "Mayoral Hopefuls Court Gay Voters," *Chicago Tribune*, February 5, 1987; "City Health Commissioner to Quit March 1," *Chicago Tribune*, August 29, 1987; "Mayor Backs Gays, Draws Fire," *Chicago Sun-Times*, January 23, 1987; *Chicago Outlines*, July 2, 1987, and "Action Is Needed on the Silent Killer," June 15, 1987, box 11, folder 26, and Mayor's Commission on Gay and Lesbian Issues, "Gay and Lesbian Agenda," n.d. [1987], box 4, folder 38, CSS; "New Directions in Chicago," *Chicago Outlines*, December 10, 1987, box 66, folder 18, ESM; Charles Kelly memo to Mercedes Mallette, January 30, 1984, box 28, PEP; Stewart-Winter, *Queer Clout*, 165–67, 199–200; Biles, *Mayor Harold Washington*, 284. See Cohen, *Boundaries of Blackness*.

38. Troy, *Morning in America*, 135–36; "Mike Rokyo, the Voice of the Working Class, Dies at 64," *New York Times*, April 30, 1997 (quotes). Wilentz, *The Age of Reagan*, 168–70; Rossinow, *The Reagan Era*, 93–95, 134; Kruse and Zelizer, *Fault Lines*, 132; "Public's Approval of Reagan in Poll Rising but Limited," *New York Times*, July 3, 1983.

39. *Black Scholar* devoted an entire issue to the debate, featuring reprints of key essays in favor of a third party by activist-journalist Chuck Stone and political scientists Ronald Walters and Ron Daniels and those advocating the development of power and influence within the party by Gary mayor Richard Hatcher and Congressman John Conyers Jr. See Stone, "Black Politics: Third Force, Third Party or Third-Class Influence?" (1969), Walters, "Strategy for 1976: A Black Political Party" (1976), Daniels, "The National Black Political Assembly: Building Independent Black Politics in the 1980s" (1980), Hatcher, "Black Politics in the '70s" (1972), and Conyers, "Toward Black Political Empowerment: Can the System Be Transformed?" (1975), all in *Black Scholar* 15, no. 4 (July/August 1984): 2–44.

40. Rivlin, *Fire on the Prairie*, 188–90; "Black Presidential Bid Gains Support," *Washington Post*, May 1, 1983; John Conyers Jr., "Transforming Politics with a 'Coalition of the Rejected,'" *Washington Post*, July 23, 1983; "Group of Black Leaders Supports Idea of Bid by Black Presidency," *New York Times*, June 21, 1983.

41. "Group of Black Leaders Supports Idea of Bid by Black Presidency," *New York Times*, June 21, 1983, "A Black Presidential Candidacy Is Weighed for '84," *New York Times*, March 30, 1983; "Why the Chorus of Naysayers?," *Washington Post*, November 4, 1983 (quotes). Frady, *Jesse*, 308–10.

42. "Hispanics Wary of Jesse Jackson's 'Freedom Train,'" *Chicago Tribune*, October 17, 1983; "Ald. Davis to Battle Collins for Congress Seat," *Chicago Tribune*, November 2, 1983; "No Decision on Jackson, Mayor Says," *Chicago Tribune*, February 10, 1984; "Mayor Backs Jackson—For Now," *Chicago Tribune*, February 16, 1984; "Fractious Politics Widen Rift in City Race Relations," *Chicago Reporter*, August 1984; Rivlin, *Fire on the Prairie*, 192.

43. Rivlin, *Fire on the Prairie*, 194; Biles, *Mayor Harold Washington*, 157–58; "Fractious Politics Widen Rift in City Race Relations," *Chicago Reporter*, August 1984; "Trying to Win the Race," *Time*, July 2, 1984; "CBS News' Blunders at Convention," *Los Angeles Times*, July 20, 1984; "Washington Pulls Plug on CBS-TV Interview," *Chicago Tribune*, July 19, 1984; Barker and Walters, *Jesse Jackson's 1984 Presidential Campaign*.

44. "Simon Success Has 2 Fathers," *Chicago Tribune*, November 8, 1984; Kruse and Zelizer, *Fault Lines*, 131–32.

## Chapter 8

1. "Tears, Beers on Winning Side," *Chicago Tribune*, April 30, 1986; Gutiérrez, *Still Dreaming*, 226–27.

2. Gutiérrez, *Still Dreaming*, 204–17; Rivlin, *Fire on the Prairie*, 225–26; Fremon, *Chicago Politics Ward by Ward*, 172–73.

3. Modesto Rivera interview (quote); Gutiérrez, *Still Dreaming*, 218–27; Cordova, "Harold Washington and the Rise of Latino Electoral Politics," 42–44; Fremon, *Chicago Politics Ward by Ward*, 172–73; "26th Ward Mirrors State of City Politics," *Chicago Tribune*, March 12, 1986; "26th Ward Gangs Make Politics Their Turf," *Chicago Tribune*, April 27, 1986.

4. "Candidates Storm Election Offices," *Chicago Tribune*, January 18, 1986; "The Latin Vote," *Chicago Tribune*, February 9, 1986; "Mayor Backs 6 for Remap Aldermen," *Chicago Tribune*, March 2, 1986; "Hispanics Rejoice as 2 Enter City Hall 'Club,'" *Chicago Tribune*, March 26, 1986; Fremon, *Chicago Politics Ward by Ward*, 171–72.

5. "Hispanics in Chicago: Conclusion," *Chicago Reporter*, April 1985 (quote); "Hispanics in Chicago: The Cubans," *Chicago Reporter*, August 1984; "The Mexicans," *Chicago Reporter*, October 1984; "The Puerto Ricans," *Chicago Reporter*, December 1984; "Other Hispanics," *Chicago Reporter*, February 1985; "Hispanic Media Cash In on Swelling Market," *Chicago Reporter*, September 1985; "Hispanic Vote Emerges as the New Battlefront in Council Wars," *Chicago Reporter*, September 1984; "The Latin Vote," *Chicago Tribune*, February 9, 1986; "Picking Up Political Clout," *Hispanic Business*, April 1986, box 11, folder 10, and "Hispanic Ascendancy and What It Will Mean," *Crain's Chicago Business*, May 5, 1986, DSS.

6. "Interview with Rev. Jorge Morales," *El Independiente*, March 25, 1983, box 21, RL (quote); Jorge Morales, Nancy Jefferson and John McKnight, Report of the Neighborhoods Policy Task Force, August 22, 1983, box 2, folder 3, CH; MACLA, "The State of Chicago's Latinos: A Report to the Latino Community and Mayor-Elect Richard M. Daley," April 20, 1989, box 1, folder 6, MACLA.

7. Mier and Moe, "Decentralized Development," 66–69.

8. Blakely, "Ode to Rob Mier," 2; "Chicago's New Development Chief Stresses Jobs," *Chicago Tribune*, August 7, 1983; "Washington Reform Progress Burdened by Errors, Politics," *Chicago Reporter*, April 1985 (quotes). Mier and Moe, "Decentralized Development," 78–84; Biles, *Mayor Harold Washington*, 125–29; Helgeson, *Crucibles of Black Empowerment*, 262–63; Wiewel and Giloth, "Planning for Manufacturing"; Marchiel, *After Redlining*.

9. Mier and Moe, "Decentralized Development," 91 (quote); Wiewel and Giloth, "Planning for Manufacturing"; "City Official Rebuts *Tribune*'s Development Series," *Chicago Tribune*, October 16, 1988; Amezcua, *Making Mexican Chicago*, 224–29.

10. Giloth, "Playskool and Populism," 15, undated manuscript, box 39, folder 6, RM, and Mier memo to DED staff, March 13, 1985, box 1, RG (quotes). Helgeson, *Crucibles of Black Empowerment*, 262–63. Susan Rosenblum letter to Robert Mier, November 1, 1984; "Toy Firm Rapped on Move East," *Chicago Sun-Times*, October 16, 1984; "NW Side Seeks to Reverse Playskool Plant Shuttering," *Crain's Chicago Business*, November 5, 1984; "Neighbors Join Forces with City to Keep Playskool Plant from Closing," *Logan Square Free Press*, November 8, 1984; "After Playskool," *In These Times*, December 5–11, 1984, box 1, RG; Wiewel and Giloth, "Planning for Manufacturing."

11. "City Official Rebuts *Tribune*'s Development Series," *Chicago Tribune*, October 16, 1988 (quotes); Mier and Moe, "Decentralized Development," 85–91; Biles, *Mayor Harold Washington*, 131–33, 206–8, 212–14; Betancur et al., "The Chicago Rehab Network," 30–33.

12. "The Chicago 1992 World's Fair: Who Will Profit?," "Minority Firms Sing the Blues in New Orleans," and "$7 Million Spent while Minorities Await Contracts," *Chicago Reporter*, February 1985 (quote); Ganz, *The 1933 Chicago World's Fair*. Erik Larson's *The Devil in the White City*, a nonscholarly telling of a serial killer operating during the fair, introduced the 1893 exposition to a new generation.

13. "Latino Panel Urges Opposition to World's Fair," *Chicago Defender*, March 16, 1985, and MACLA, "The Proposed 1992 World's Fair: Consequences for Chicago's Latinos," 1985, box 1, folder 8 (quotes). *Commission on Latino Affairs / Comisión sobre Asuntos Latinos*, September 1984, and *Boletín*, November 1984 and April/May 1985, box 1, folder 4, MACLA; World's Fair Advisory Committee, "A Report to Mayor Harold Washington," October 1983, box 24, folder 2, "Fitch Continues Pushing World's Fair at Lake Cal," *Daily*

*Calumet*, September 17, 1983, and Association for Fair Alternatives, "The Lake Calumet World's Fair Alternative," October 3, 1983, box 23, folder 8, RM; "The Chicago 1992 World's Fair: Who Will Profit?," *Chicago Reporter*, February 1985.

14. "The Chicago 1992 World's Fair: Who Will Profit?," *Chicago Reporter*, February 1985 (quotes).

15. Gail Weisberg memo to Mier, August 23, 1983, box 23, folder 7, RM; Hollander, "The Department of Planning under Harold Washington," 132–33.

16. Matt 25:35 (quote); "Local Minister Defends Sanctuary Movement," *All Chicago City News*, January 31, 1985, box 22, RL; García, *Seeking Refuge*, 13–43; García, *Father Luis Olivares*; Davidson, *Convictions of the Heart*; Lorentzen, *Women in the Sanctuary Movement*; Harold Washington, "Testimony on Proposed Immigration Reform and Control Act of 1985," October 9, 1985, box 12, folder 40, and Randy Pauley memo to Kari Moe, August 18, 1986, box 12, folder 38, CSS. There were important differences between sanctuary activists in Tucson and Chicago over the degree of centralized action, the role of civil disobedience, and whether only war refugees or all victims of unequal structures should be helped.

17. Washington remarks, March 7, 1985, box 12, folder 25 (quote), and Executive Order 85-1, March 7, 1985, box 12, folder 39, CSS; "Immigration Agents Threaten Top City Official," *All Chicago City News*, February 15, 1985, box 22, RL; "City Deals Immigration Officials a Blow," *Chicago Tribune*, March 8, 1985; "Why the Census Asking about Citizenship Is Such a Problem," *HuffPost*, March 27, 2018.

18. Randy Pauley memo to Kari Moe, August 18, 1986, box 12, folder 38 (quote), "Operation Taxicab" internal notes, 1985, CSS; "The Mayor's Aid to Aliens," *Chicago Tribune*, March 14, 1985; "U.S. Investigates Cabbie License Fraud," *Chicago Tribune*, March 26, 1985; "Support for Mayor against INS," *Chicago Tribune*, April 1, 1985; "Raids Pull Cabbies Off Road," *Chicago Tribune*, December 18, 1985; "Cabdriver Test Doesn't Hack It," *Chicago Tribune*, December 19, 1985; "Chicago's History as a Sanctuary City," *All Chicago City News*, May 23, 2019.

19. Kari Moe memo to Ernest Barefield, April 27, 1987, box 5, folder 14 (quote), Washington remarks to Subcommittee on Immigration and Reform Policies of the U.S. Senate Judiciary Committee and the Subcommittee on Immigration, Refugees, and International Law of House of Representatives Judiciary Committee, October 9, 1985, box 12, folder 40, and Anita Zibton letter, August 19, 1986, in box 12, folder 38, CSS; "Chicago's History as a Sanctuary City," *Chicago Tribune*, April 30, 2020; Bohn, Freedman, and Owens, "The Criminal Justice Response to Policy Interventions," 214–19; Sandoval-Strausz, *Barrio America*, 237 (quote), 231–44.

20. Linda Coronado interview; "Quake Aid Offers Political Relief," *Chicago Tribune*, September 30, 1985; "The Toll in Mexico City" and "Relief Pipeline to Mexico City," *Chicago Tribune*, September 24, 1985 (quotes). "Quake Relief Efforts 'Snowball' as Money, Supplies Pour In," *Chicago Tribune*, September 26, 1985; "Mayor Gets Standing Ovation from City Council," *Chicago Tribune*, September 18, 1986; García, "Mexican Earthquake: People Make the Difference," *All Chicago City News*, October 1, 1985, box 34, PEP; Alton Miller memo to press corps, September 14, 1986, box 12, folder 25, DSS.

21. "Jesús 'Chuy' García's Journey from a Village to the Race against Mayor Emanuel," *Chicago Reader*, January 21, 2015; Gutiérrez, *Still Dreaming*, 173 (quotes). Jesús "Chuy" García interview; Fremon, *Chicago Politics Ward by Ward*, 148, 305.

22. Jesús "Chuy" García interview (quote); "Hispanic Candidates Say Voter Sign-Up Blocked," *Chicago Tribune*, February 25, 1984; "Hispanic Vote Emerges as New Battlefront in Council Wars," *Chicago Reporter*, August 1984; "Jesús 'Chuy' García's Journey from a Village to the Race against Mayor Emanuel," *Chicago Reader*, January 21, 2015.

23. "Pilsen Street Hustler Takes On Old Guard at City Hall," *Chicago Reporter*, November 1984 (quote); Tom Weinberg, "Vito Marzullo"; "New 25th Ward Rejoices," *Chicago Tribune*, February 23, 1986; Fremon, *Chicago Politics Ward by Ward*, 165.

24. "32d Ward David Wakes Up Goliath," *Chicago Tribune*, March 21, 1984 (quotes); Gutiérrez, *Still Dreaming*, 172–90; Fremon, *Chicago Politics Ward by Ward*, 215.

25. "Old-Fashioned Politics," *Washington Post*, March 26, 1986; "Hispanic Showdown Brews in Ward Race," *Chicago Tribune*, January 6, 1986 (quotes). "Party of Juan," *Chicago Reader*, April 23, 1987; "Hispanic Vote Emerges as New Battlefront in Council Wars," *Chicago Reporter*, September 1984; Fremon, *Chicago Politics Ward by Ward*, 166–67.

26. Jesús "Chuy" García interview; "Hispanic Vote Emerges as New Battlefront in Council Wars," *Chicago Reporter*, September 1984 (quotes). "Jesús 'Chuy' García's Journey from a Village to the Race against Mayor Emanuel," *Chicago Reader*, January 21, 2015; Fremon, *Chicago Politics Ward by Ward*, 148–49; Amezcua, "A Machine in the Barrio," 110–12.

27. "Why Gutierrez Scares Eddie," *Chicago Sun-Times*, April 5, 1986 (quote); Gutiérrez, *Still Dreaming*, 198–209; "Hispanic Hopefuls Scramble to Organize for Special Elections," *Chicago Reporter*, February 1986.

28. "Mayor Gets Way on Nominees," *Chicago Tribune*, May 10, 1986; "Mayor's Delayed Victory," *Chicago Tribune*, May 11, 1986; "Mayor Captures Committees," *Chicago Tribune*, June 7, 1986; "Court Win for Mayor on Council," *Chicago Tribune*, August 1, 1986.

29. Salamon, Lester, Pamela Holcomb, James C. Musselwhite Jr., and Kristen Gronbjerg, "Human Services Spending in Chicago: The Changing Roles of Government and Private Funders," 1987, box 13, folder 18, CSS (quote); Wilentz, *The Age of Reagan*, 209–44; "Chicago Hopes Congress Will Stanch Budget Cuts," *Chicago Tribune*, January 6, 1987.

30. "Mayor Hits Reagan for 'War' on Cities," *Chicago Tribune*, February 11, 1986; "Mayor Begins Fight in Congress to Preserve Federal Funding," *Chicago Tribune*, May 6, 1986 (quotes). "Mayor Returns to the Front," *Chicago Tribune*, June 25, 1986; Sharon Gist Gilliam, "President Reagan's Proposed 1987 Budget Impact on Chicago," February 18, 1986, box 23, folder 23, and "President Reagan's Proposed 1988 Proposed Budget Impact on Chicago," February 1987, box 23, folder 24, CSS; Biles, *Mayor Harold Washington*, 237–38.

31. "Property Tax Increase Passes," *Chicago Tribune*, September 25, 1986 (quote); "Mayor to Plead Case for $180 Million Plan," *Chicago Tribune*, October 13, 1986; Walker, "Reforming the Role of Human Services"; Brehm, "The City and the Neighborhoods," 238–69.

32. "Group Helping Tenants Take Landlords to Task over Repairs," *Chicago Tribune*, July 13, 1987; "State Bill Would Ravage Tenant Law, Aldermen Say," *Chicago Tribune*, May 19, 1987 (quotes). Rivlin, *Fire on the Prairie*, 227–28; "Tenants Rights Bill Passes City Council," *Chicago Tribune*, September 9, 1987; "Taxi Industry Reform Passes," *Chicago Tribune*, February 4, 1987; "Washington Wins Ethics Code Battle," *Chicago Tribune*, February 12, 1987; "Renters Still in the Dark about Rights," *Chicago Tribune*, April 27, 1987; *Journal of the Proceedings of the City Council of Chicago, Illinois*, September 8, 1986, and

February 3, 1987; Metropolitan Tenant Organization, "30th Anniversary of Chicago's Landmark Residential Landlord Tenant Ordinance."

33. "Byrne to Run Again," *Chicago Tribune*, April 14, 1985 (quote); "Byrne: They Tried to Pay Me Not to Run," *Chicago Tribune*, January 18, 1985; Rivlin, *Fire on the Prairie*, 230–31.

34. "A Better Way to Elect a Mayor," *Chicago Tribune*, July 29, 1986; "Daley Gets in the Game," *Chicago Tribune*, August 17, 1986; Biles, *Mayor Harold Washington*, 244–48; Rivlin, *Fire on the Prairie*, 227–28; Holli and Green, *Bashing Chicago Traditions*, 36–43.

35. While there are no less than ten books focusing on Washington's 1983 victory, just one—Melvin Holli and Paul Green's *Bashing Chicago Traditions*—offers an in-depth look at the 1987 reelection campaign.

36. "Many Powerful Unions to Skip Mayoral Support," *Chicago Sun-Times*, February 6, 1987; "Unions in New Political Role," *Chicago Sun-Times*, February 16, 1987; "Set-Aside Winners Giving Big to Mayor," *Chicago Tribune*, February 18, 1987; "Incumbency Big Plus for Washington," *Chicago Tribune*, February 22, 1987; "Contributions Cascade in for Washington," *Chicago Tribune*, February 24, 1987; "'87 Labor for Washington," n.d., box 35, and J. H. Jackson, "We Support Mayor Harold Washington," n.d., box 98, PEP; Holli and Green, *Bashing Chicago Traditions*, 67–89.

37. Holli and Green, *Bashing Chicago Traditions*.

38. Nick Rabkin memo to Robert Mier, January 15, 1987, box 2, RG (quote); "Byrne on Location for Kickoff Sequel," *Chicago Tribune*, July 18, 1985; Biles, *Mayor Harold Washington*, 136–37.

39. "Byrne Slipping in Campaign Geared to Avoid the Fray," *Chicago Tribune*, December 23, 1986; "Crime Statistics Figuring into Campaign," *Chicago Tribune*, February 16, 1987; Rivlin, *Fire on the Prairie*, 234; Biles, *Mayor Harold Washington*, 251–52.

40. Fremon, "Harold Washington: Getting Ready for a Second Term," January/February 1987, box 12, folder 8, CSS (quote); "Hispanics Receptive to Byrne's Advances," *Chicago Tribune*, January 6, 1987; "Courting Hispanics: Can They 'Swing' the Election?," *Chicago Tribune*, February 12, 1987; "Analysis of Hispanic Precincts Shows Mexican/Puerto Rican Split," *Chicago Reporter*, April 1987; Biles, *Mayor Harold Washington*, 248–49.

41. Fremon, "Harold Washington: Getting Ready for a Second Term," January/February 1987, box 12, folder 8, CSS; Achy Obejas memo to Ken Glover, January 21, 1987, box 98, PEP (quotes). Obejas, "Latino Press Briefing," n.d. [1987?], box 98, PEP; Washington campaign, "The Record on Hispanics," 1987, box 176, folder 6, ACW; "Analysis of Hispanic Precincts Shows Mexican/Puerto Rican Split," *Chicago Reporter*, April 1987; MVREP, "The Hispanic Vote," n.d., box 12, folder 27, DSS; "Poll Shows Clerk Race Wide Open," *Chicago Tribune*, February 16, 1987; *Boletín*, July 1985, box 15, folder 2, CSS.

42. Achy Obejas, interview by Tracy Baim, July 11, 2011, Chicago, https://www.chicagogayhistory.com/biography.html?id=490 (quote); "For Lesbians and Gay Men, the Choice Is Clear," March 1987, box 4, folder 38, CSS; "Gay-Rights Ordinance Fails," *Chicago Tribune*, July 30, 1986; "Mayor Backs Gays, Draws Fire," *Chicago Sun-Times*, January 23, 1987; Stewart-Winter, *Queer Clout*, 161–66; Holli and Green, *Bashing Chicago Traditions*, 183.

43. "Mayor Record on Women Praised," *Chicago Tribune*, December 22, 1986; Peggy Montes, "'Her Story': A Synopsis of the Women's Network," n.d., folder 4 (quotes), and meeting minutes, "Chicago Women's Network for Re-election of Harold Washington

in 1987," August 27, 1986, folder 3, box 176, folders 3–9, ACW; Chicago Commission on Human Relations, January 12, 1987, box 5, folder 12, "Asians Likely to be Next Key Political Bloc in City," Nadig Newspapers, June 10, 1987, box 24, folder 10, and L. Maglaya memo to Kari Moe and Jacky Grimshaw, "Filipino Concerns," March 11, 1987, box 11, folder 16, CSS; "Why Mayor Washington Is the Choice in '87," *Chicago Assyrian*, December 1986, box 28, PEP; "Asians Find Votes Speak Chicago's Language," *Chicago Tribune*, January 16, 1987; Rivlin, *Fire on the Prairie*, 239–40; Starks and Preston, "The Political Legacy of Harold Washington," 161–62.

44. "Byrne Slipping in Campaign Geared to Avoid the Fray," *Chicago Tribune*, December 23, 1986; "Analysis of Hispanic Precincts Shows Mexican/Puerto Rican Split," *Chicago Reporter*, April 1987; MVREP, "The Hispanic Vote," n.d., box 12, folder 27, DSS; Fremon, *Chicago Politics Ward by Ward*, 16, 20.

45. "Washington, Haider in the Primary," *Chicago Tribune*, February 8, 1987 (quote); "Washington Is Our Choice," *Chicago Defender*, February 14, 1987; Fremon, *Chicago Politics Ward by Ward*, 15–16; Biles, *Mayor Harold Washington*, 253–54; Holli and Green, *Bashing Chicago Traditions*, 77–78.

46. "Washington, Haider in the Primary," *Chicago Tribune*, February 8, 1987; "Campaign Erupts over Mob Story," *Chicago Tribune*, March 24, 1987; Fremon, *Chicago Politics Ward by Ward*, 17–18; Biles, *Mayor Harold Washington*, 258–63; Holli and Green, *Bashing Chicago Traditions*, 94–111; Karhl, "The Short End of Both Sticks," 208.

47. "Vrdolyak '87," 1987, box 35, PEP (quote); "Washington, Haider in the Primary," *Chicago Tribune*, February 8, 1987; "Campaign Erupts over Mob Story," *Chicago Tribune*, March 24, 1987; Fremon, *Chicago Politics Ward by Ward*, 17–18; Biles, *Mayor Harold Washington*, 258–63; Holli and Green, *Bashing Chicago Traditions*, 103–11.

48. Helen Shiller interview; "Byrne Supports Mayor," *Chicago Tribune*, March 1, 1987; "Mayor Washington Has Finally Decided to 'Go Negative,'" *Chicago Tribune*, February 4, 1987 (quotes). "Kennedy Sings the Mayor's Tune," *Chicago Tribune*, March 28, 1987; Jacky Grimshaw interview; Biles, *Mayor Harold Washington*, 262–63; Conrad Worrill memo to Washington, n.d. [1987?], box 98, PEP.

49. "Runoffs Give the Mayor a Tighter Grip on Council," *Chicago Tribune*, April 8, 1987; "City's Hispanics Strengthen Coalition with Blacks," *Chicago Tribune*, April 10, 1987; Fremon, *Chicago Politics Ward by Ward*, 207–8; "Analysis of Hispanic Precincts Shows Mexican/Puerto Rican Split," *Chicago Reporter*, April 1987; MVREP, "The Hispanic Vote," n.d., box 12, folder 27, DSS; Starks and Preston, "The Political Legacy of Harold Washington," 161–62; Chicago Democracy Project, "Election Results for 1987 General Election."

## Chapter 9

1. "Madhouse Inside and Outside," *Chicago Tribune*, December 2, 1987 (quote); "City Unites in Sorrow to Tell the Mayor Farewell," *Chicago Tribune*, November 28, 1987; "Seven Wretched Days," *Chicago Reader*, December 24, 1987.

2. "Madhouse Inside and Outside," *Chicago Tribune*, December 2, 1987 (quotes); "Council Elects Sawyer Mayor," *Chicago Tribune*, December 2, 1987; "Sawyer Is a Master at Playing the Game," *Chicago Tribune*, December 3, 1987; "Seven Wretched Days," *Chicago Reader*, December 24, 1987.

3. "Race Played Major Role in Mayoral Battle," *Chicago Reader*, January 1988; "The Day Harold Washington Died," *Chicago* (magazine), November 20, 2017 (quotes). "The Blacks and the Browns," *Chicago Reader*, November 5, 1987.

4. Diamond, *Chicago on the Make*; Green and Holli, *Restoration 1989*; Kleppner, "Mayoral Politics Chicago Style"; Rossinow, *The Reagan Era*, 149–50.

5. In 1993, "moderate" Republicans Rudy Giuliani and Richard Riordan used "law and order" to defeat Black incumbents and served two terms as mayors of New York City and Los Angeles, respectively. In 1991 in Philadelphia, centrist Democrat Ed Rendell succeeded that city's first Black mayor, Wilson Goode, while Arkansas governor Bill Clinton won the White House in 1992 as a middle-of-the-road "New Democrat."

6. "Slow Start for a Second-Term Mayor," *Chicago Tribune*, July 5, 1987 (quote); "Losing Luster," *Chicago Tribune*, August 23, 1987; "Mayor Has It His Way on Budget," *Chicago Tribune*, October 22, 1987; "Mayor Adding 1,000 City Jobs," *Chicago Tribune*, October 18, 1987; Helen Shiller and Robert "Bob" Starks interviews; "The Blacks and the Browns," *Chicago Reader*, November 5, 1987.

7. "Mayor Was Closing Gap with Business" (quote) and "Harold Washington and Chicago," *Chicago Tribune*, November 26, 1987; "One Year without Washington," *Chicago Reader*, November 24, 1988; "Mayor Draws Fire for N. Loop Tactics," *Crain's Chicago Business*, August 31, 1987; Diamond, *Chicago on the Make*, 258; Colburn and Adler, *African American Mayors*.

8. "Bears Stadium Proposal Splitting Up West Side," *Chicago Tribune*, April 16, 1987; "Community Talks Are Line of Scrimmage for Stadium," *Chicago Tribune*, April 26, 1987; Biles, *Mayor Harold Washington*, 210–12; "Field of Pain," *Chicago* (magazine), June 21, 2007.

9. "Republicans Hold Ground on O'Hare," *Chicago Tribune*, June 30, 1986; Brenetta Howell Barrett interview (quotes). "One Cheer for the Washington Administration," *Chicago Tribune*, April 27, 1986; "Lack of Licenses Will Rob Outdoor Cafes of Sun," *Chicago Tribune*, April 28, 1987; "City Facing More Probes," *Chicago Tribune*, December 27, 1987; "Cabbies Get Chance to Be Their Own Boss," *Chicago Tribune*, April 1, 1988; Rivlin, *Fire on the Prairie*, 249; Biles, *Mayor Harold Washington*, 291.

10. "The Blacks and the Browns," *Chicago Reader*, November 5, 1987 (quotes); Torres, "The Commission on Latino Affairs," 181–83; María "Nena" de los Ángeles Torres interview; MACLA, "The State of Chicago's Latinos: A Report to the Latino Community and Mayor-Elect Richard M. Daley," April 20, 1989, box 1, folder 6, MACLA; "A Nonbinding Vote Puts State on Guard," *Chicago Tribune*, March 14, 1988; "National Guard Battle Looms," *Chicago Tribune*, April 12, 1987.

11. María "Nena" de los Ángeles Torres interview; Torres, "The Commission on Latino Affairs," 185 (quotes). "The Blacks and the Browns," *Chicago Reader*, November 5, 1987; Luz Martinez, translation of editorial, *El Heraldo del Norte*, September 15, 1986, box 16, folder 32, CSS; Amezcua, *Making Mexican Chicago*.

12. "Chicago's Schools Hit as Worst," *Chicago Tribune*, November 7, 1987; "Mayor: We'll Clean Up Schools," *Chicago Tribune*, November 8, 1987 (quotes). "Bilingual Teachers Hit U.S. Education Boss," *Chicago Tribune*, April 3, 1986; National Commission on Excellence in Education, *A Nation at Risk*; Hal Baron and Kari Moe memo to Ernest Barefield, July 31, 1986, box 31, folder 18, CSS; "After All These Years of Waiting, Will Manford Byrd

Fly?," *Chicago Reporter*, March 1985; Todd-Breland, *A Political Education*, 159–61; Carl, "Harold Washington and Chicago's Schools," 329–31.

13. Hal Baron memo to Harold Washington, December 29, 1986, box 31, folder 2 (quote), Hal Baron and Kari Moe memo to Ernest Barefield, July 31, 1986, box 31, folder 18, and Hal Baron memo to Harold Washington, October 9, 1986, "Mayor's Education Summit," October 21, 1986, "Education Summit Participants," 1986, box 31, folder 4, CSS; Hal Baron interview; Todd-Breland, *A Political Education*, 160–63; Carl, "Harold Washington and Chicago's Schools," 332–34; "School Reform Gets Tepid Biz Response," *Crain's Chicago Business*, October 12, 1987.

14. National Commission on Excellence in Education, *A Nation at Risk* (quote); Kotlowitz, *There Are No Children Here*; Kozol, *Savage Inequalities*; Todd-Breland, *A Political Education*, 165.

15. Todd-Breland, *A Political Education*, 165 (quote), 159, 164–65; Carl, "Harold Washington and Chicago's Schools," 335–36.

16. "Forum Asks Local Power," *Chicago Tribune*, December 2, 1987; Hal Baron interview (quotes). "Strike's Wake Leaves Winners and Losers," *Chicago Tribune*, October 5, 1987; "A 1st Step to Reform in Schools," *Chicago Tribune*, October 12, 1987; "Teachers OK Pact Despite Heavy 'No' Vote," *Chicago Tribune*, October 17, 1987; Charles Payne interview; Carl, "Harold Washington and Chicago's Schools," 315–16, 336–39; Todd-Breland, *A Political Education*, 165–66.

17. "School Reform Pressure Continues; Competing Plans Vie for Support," *Chicago Reader*, January 1988; Toni Preckwinkle memo to Hal Baron and Kari Moe, April 26, 1986, box 31, folder 30, CSS; "Mayor: We'll Clean Up Schools," *Chicago Tribune*, November 8, 1987; Hal Baron interview (quotes). Todd-Breland, *A Political Education*, 167–68.

18. Todd-Breland, *A Political Education*, 172 (quote), 167–71, 181–82; Superville, "Chicago Local School Councils' Experiment," 14–15; Hal Baron interview.

19. Hal Baron interview (quote); Shipps, "The Invisible Hand," 73; Linda Coronado interview; Carl, "Harold Washington and Chicago's Schools," 340; Todd-Breland, *A Political Education*, 182–84; Superville, "Chicago Local School Councils' Experiment," 14.

20. "Welcome Aboard, Rev. Jackson," *Chicago Tribune*, September 11, 1987 (quote); "Can Jackson Get Elected President? Let's Stop Asking," *Chicago Tribune*, October 13, 1987; "Jesse Jackson's Campaign to Win the White House Is Taken Very Seriously the Second Time Around," *Wall Street Journal*, October 8, 1987; "Jackson Busy Courting Blacks in Office, and Converting Some," *New York Times*, September 25, 1987; "The Jesse Factor," *Afro-American*, August 5, 1987; "Schmoke, Other Politicians Face Endorsement Dilemma," *Baltimore Sun*, March 27, 1988; Rossinow, *The Reagan Era*, 243.

21. "Mayor Takes Practical Road to Jackson," *Chicago Tribune*, September 9, 1987 (quote); "GE Union Ponders Boycott as Cicero Plant Hopes Dim," *Chicago Tribune*, September 26, 1987; Biles, *Mayor Harold Washington*, 293–94; Frady, *Jesse*, 378–94, 399–401. Frady, in fact, argues that despite losing the state primary, Jesse Jackson and his presidential campaign in New York City primed the coalition that made David Dinkins that city's first Black mayor.

22. "Learning to Manage on Their Own," *Chicago Tribune*, June 30, 1986; Hunt, *Blueprint for Disaster*, 263 (quotes). "Dedicated CHA Dwellers Learn Persistence Pays," *Chicago Tribune*, August 25, 1987; "Black Leaders Rate Mayor's First-Term Performance,"

*Chicago Reporter*, October 1987; Jacquelyne Grimshaw interview, HMDA; Miller, *Harold Washington*, 306–15.

23. Miller, *Harold Washington,* 316; "Washington Leads Mayors' Campaign for Housing," *Chicago Tribune*, September 14, 1987 (quotes). "HUD's 'March on Chicago' Is Insulting," *Chicago Sun-Times*, August 28, 1987; "Mayor's Last Day—It's Business as Usual, and Then," *Chicago Sun-Times*, November 26, 1987; Hunt, *Blueprint for Disaster*, 265–66; Laurence Lynn and Kathryn M. Neckerman, "Poverty in Chicago," June 1986, box 23, folder 21, CSS; Miller, *Harold Washington*, 1–10; "Hindsight: After He Collapsed, Nothing Could Save the Mayor," *Chicago Tribune*, March 20, 1988; Venkatesh, *Off the Books*, 242–62.

24. "Hindsight: After He Collapsed, Nothing Could Save the Mayor," *Chicago Tribune*, March 20, 1988 (quote); "He Started the Day in Great Mood," *Chicago Tribune*, November 26, 1987; Michael James interview; Rivlin, *Fire on the Prairie*, 254–55.

25. "Seven Wretched Days," *Chicago Reader*, December 24, 1987 (quote).

26. "Is Tim Evans for Real?," *Chicago Reader*, March 16, 1989 (quotes); Fremon, *Chicago Politics Ward by Ward*, 41–42, 193–95; Jacquelyne Grimshaw interview, HMDA; "There's a Fire in the Kitchen and the Kitchen Is on the West Side," *Austin News Weekly*, December 14, 1987, box 66, ESM.

27. Eugene Sawyer interview, HMDA; "New Directions in Chicago," *Chicago Outlines*, December 10, 1987, box 66, folder 18, ESM (quotes). "Is Tim Evans for Real?," *Chicago Reader*, March 16, 1989; Stewart-Winter, *Queer Clout*, 176–77, 180–83; Sawyer press release, December 21, 1988, box 25, folder 9, ESM; "Council Passes Gay Rights Ordinance," *Chicago Tribune*, December 22, 1988.

28. "The Silent Mayoralty," *Chicago Tribune*, December 11, 1988 (quotes); "Council OKs Record Budget," *Chicago Tribune*, December 17, 1987; Brenetta Howell Barrett and Hal Baron interviews.

29. Dick Simpson et al., "The War of the Roses: The Unusual City Council Roll Call Votes from March 30–November 30, 1988," Chicago: Office of Social Science Research, UA 2999-38, box 2, folder 8, DS, 3–4; Kleppner, "Mayoral Politics Chicago Style," 177–78.

30. "Are Sawyer Advisers Friends or Foes?," *Chicago Tribune*, June 22, 1988; "The Silent Mayoralty," *Chicago Tribune*, December 11, 1988; "Jobs Chief Cerda Fired by Sawyer," *Chicago Tribune*, January 23, 1988 (quotes); "Hispanic Faction Split by a World of Differences," *Chicago Tribune*, January 31, 1988; "The Cokely Affair: A Crisis That Didn't Have to Happen," *Chicago Reporter*, June 1988; Kleppner, "Mayoral Politics Chicago Style," 178–79; Grimshaw, *Bitter Fruit*, 201–2.

31. "Keeping Current," *Chicago Reporter*, March 1988 (quote); "Year Nine: City's AIDS Office Continues to Struggle," *Chicago Reporter*, March 1989; "Gays' Role in Mayoral Campaign Linked to Rights Bill," *Chicago Tribune*, December 21, 1988; ACT-UP demands memo to Chicago Department of Health, undated, box 26, folder 5, ESM; Stewart-Winter, *Queer Clout*, 202; Grimshaw, *Bitter Fruit*, 203.

32. "Jackson Backing Mayor in Primary," *Chicago Tribune*, January 25, 1989; "Strategy in the Final Days Crucial to Race," *Chicago Tribune*, February 20, 1989 (quotes). "Labor May Sit Out Mayoral Primary," *Chicago Tribune*, December 15, 1988; "Davis Joins the Evans Camp as Ministers Support Sawyer," *Chicago Tribune*, December 16, 1988; "Sawyer Setting His Sights on Daley," *Chicago Tribune*, December 29, 1988; "Evans Refuses to Back Sawyer," *Chicago Tribune*, February 17, 1989; "1989 or 1991: It's a Question of Power,"

*Chicago Metro News*, April 9, 1988; "On the Stump with Sawyer," *Chicago Reader*, February 23, 1989; Grimshaw, *Bitter Fruit*, 205–6.

33. "Hispanic Vote," April 1988, and "Analysis of Hispanic Precincts Shows Mexican/Puerto Rican Split," *Chicago Reporter*, April 1987; "Jackson Backing Mayor in Primary," *Chicago Tribune*, January 25, 1989; "Mayor Sawyer's Accomplishments for Hispanics," undated, box 27, folder 6, ESM.

34. "Gutierrez's Turnabout Has Heads Spinning," *Chicago Tribune*, February 13, 1989 (quote); "Latinos Face Mayoral Race and 1990s with Uncertainty," *Chicago Reporter*, February 1989; "Nuestro apoyo a Richard M. Daley," *El Norte*, February 22, 1989, 1989 Election Campaign files, box 80, ESM; Gutiérrez, *Still Dreaming*, 264–67.

35. "Sawyer Says Prospect of White Mayor Prompted His Call for Succession Vote," *Chicago Reporter*, January 1988; "Black Voter Turnout Key to Mayor's Race," *Chicago Reporter*, February 1989 (quotes). "On the Stump with Sawyer," *Chicago Reader*, February 23, 1989; "Community Groups Worry They Will Be Left Out," *Chicago Reporter*, January 1988; "Registration Figures Give Daley a Lift," *Chicago Tribune*, February 10, 1989; "Strategy in the Final Days Crucial to Race," *Chicago Tribune*, February 20, 1989; "Labor May Sit Out Mayoral Primary," *Chicago Tribune*, December 15, 1988; Green and Holli, *Restoration 1989*, vii–xii; Kleppner, "Mayoral Politics Chicago Style," 177–78.

36. Green, "The 1989 Mayoral Primary Election"; Fremon, "Media Coverage," 139–58; "Is Rich Daley Ready for Reform?," *Chicago Reader*, February 9, 1989; "A Less Liberal Lakefront Likes Daley," *Chicago Tribune*, December 14, 1988; "Memories Bind Hispanics to Daley," *Chicago Tribune*, December 13, 1988; "Strategy in the Final Days Crucial to Race," *Chicago Tribune*, February 20, 1989.

37. "Is Rich Daley Ready for Reform?," *Chicago Reader*, February 9, 1989 (quote); Green and Holli, *Restoration 1989*, vii–xii, 164; Baer, *Reinventing Democrats*; Al From, interview by Russell Riley; Kazin, *What It Took To Win*, 272–77. Daley campaign aide David Wilhelm would go on to be instrumental in grassroots canvassing work for Bill Clinton's presidential campaign three years later. Of course, future Chicago mayor Rahm Emanuel also cut his political teeth as a Clinton campaign aide and White House chief of staff. "Think Local, Act Global," *Chicago Tribune*, November 20, 1992.

38. Casuso, "Hispanics," 73; "Richard Daley's Primary Victory" (quotes) and "Exuberant Daley," *Chicago Tribune*, March 1, 1989; Kleppner, "Mayoral Politics Chicago Style," 171–75.

39. Green, "The 1989 General Election"; Casuso, "Hispanics," 38, 73 (quotes). Kleppner, "Mayoral Politics Chicago Style," 174–76.

40. Kleppner, "Mayoral Politics Chicago Style," 172–76; Green, "The 1989 General Election," 33–51; Starks and Preston, "The Political Legacy of Harold Washington," 166–67.

41. Green, "The 1989 Mayoral Primary Election"; Hinz, "Lakefronters," 12, 74–80, 79 (quote); Kleppner, "Mayoral Politics Chicago Style," 176–76; Stewart-Winter, *Queer Clout*, 209.

## Epilogue

1. Stewart-Winter, *Queer Clout*, 207–13, quote 211; Grimshaw, *Bitter Fruit*, 206–9, 214–20; Amezcua, *Making Mexican Chicago*, 238–39.

2. "Democratic Form of Governance Began with the Neighborhoods," *Chicago Tribune*, May 4, 2003; "The Hack Who Pissed Off Harold," *Chicago Reader*, January 29, 2009 (quotes). Robert "Bob" Starks, Helen Shiller, Jesús "Chuy" García, Linda Coronado, and Dick Simpson interviews; Grimshaw, *Bitter Fruit*, 214–20; Todd-Breland, *A Political Education*, 187–88; Diamond, *Chicago on the Make*, 309–11.

3. "The TIF That Keeps on Taking," *Chicago Reader*, June 5, 2008; Jesús "Chuy" García interview (quotes). Stewart-Winter, *Queer Clout*, 217–19; Diamond, *Chicago on the Make*, 281–84; "Million Dollar Lies," *Chicago Reader*, August 11, 2006; "The Shadow Budget," *Chicago Reader*, October 22, 2009; Gordon, "Blighting the Way"; Kahrl, "The Short End of Both Sticks," 208–9; Dinces, *Bulls Markets*.

4. Spirou and Judd, *Building the City of Spectacle*; Taylor, *The Torture Machine*, 399 (quotes). "LeRoy Martin's Anti-rights Tirade No Mere Faux Pas," *Chicago Tribune*, July 16, 1991; "Daley, GOP Deal on Anti-crime Bill," *Chicago Tribune*, November 30, 1994; "How's He Doing: A Daley Report Card," *Chicago Reader*, February 21, 1991; Chicago Police Department, *Annual Reports*, 1991–97, https://home.chicagopolice.org/statistics-data/statistical-reports/annual-reports/; Alexander, *The New Jim Crow*, 54–57, 208–17; Klinenberg, *Heat Wave*, 1–13, 97–109, 147–57, 152 quote; Diamond, *Chicago on the Make*, 260–61, 366, n4; Forman, *Locking Up Our Own*.

5. Todd-Breland, *A Political Education*, 180–87, 220–22; "Why Chicago Teachers Hate Rahm," *Chicago Reader*, September 12, 2012; "Savior Stories," *Chicago Reader*, September 9, 2020.

6. "The Mystery of Mayor Daley," *Chicago* (magazine), August 16, 2008 (quote); "The Fuel of a New Machine," *Chicago Reader*, March 30, 1989; Krebs and Pelissero, "Fund-Raising Coalitions in Mayoral Campaigns"; Hogan and Simpson, "Campaign Contributions and Mayoral/Aldermanic Relationships."

7. Board of Election Commissioners for the City of Chicago, "2015 Municipal Runoffs—April 7, 2015," "2015 Municipal General—February 24, 2015," "2011 Municipal General—2/22/11," "2007 Municipal Runoffs—4/17/07," "2007 Municipal General - 2/27/07," "2003 Municipal Runoffs—4/1/03," "2003 Municipal General—2/25/03," chicagoelections.gov.

8. "A Black Woman Will Lead Chicago," *Chicago Reader*, March 22, 2019; "Lori Lightfoot Is Elected Chicago Mayor, Becoming First Black Woman to Lead City," *New York Times*, April 2, 2019; "Lori Lightfoot, Chicago's Incoming Mayor, Ran on Outsider Appeal," *New York Times*, April 3, 2019 (quotes). WBEZ, "You Created a Movement," April 2, 2019; "Chicago Makes History," *USA Today*, April 2, 2019.

9. "Lori Lightfoot Elected Mayor," *Chicago Tribune*, April 2, 2019 (quote); "Lori and Toni Were Missing in Action," *Chicago Reader*, March 29, 2019; "A Black Woman Will Lead Chicago," *Chicago Reader*, March 22, 2019; "Ald. Carrie Austin and Chief of Staff Indicted on Bribery Charges," *Chicago Tribune*, July 1, 2021.

10. "Racism Stains Chicago Police, a Report Finds," *New York Times*, April 14, 2016; "Chicago Will Be Run by a Black Woman. But Is It Ready for Reform?," *Washington Post*, February 28, 2019 (quotes). "Is Lori Lightfoot Really the Progressive Candidate?," *Chicago Reader*, January 17, 2019; "Lori and Toni Were Missing in Action," *Chicago Reader*, March 29, 2019; "A Black Woman Will Lead Chicago," *Chicago Reader*, March 22, 2019; "Lori Lightfoot Elected Mayor," *Chicago Tribune*, April 2, 2019.

11. Board of Election Commissioners for the City of Chicago, "2019 Municipal

General—2/26/19," chicagoelections.gov; Chicago Democracy Project, "How Did Chicago's Segregated Neighborhoods Vote in the Mayoral Election?"

12. "Over 6 Million in Illinois Cast Ballots," *Chicago Sun-Times*, December 4, 2020.

13. Huq and Ginsburg, "How to Lose a Constitutional Democracy"; Levitsky and Ziblatt, *How Democracies Die*; "How Far Are Republicans Willing to Go? They're Already Gone," *New York Times*, June 9, 2021.

# Bibliography

## Primary Sources

### Manuscript Collections

Chicago History Museum
    Robert Giloth Papers
    Mayor's Advisory Commission on Latino Affairs Records
    Robert Mier Papers
Chicago Public Library, Harold Washington Library Center, Harold Washington
  Archives and Collections
    Community Services Sub-cabinet Records
    Development Sub-cabinet Records
    Illinois State Senatorial Records
    Mayoral Campaign Records
    Political Education Project Records
    Pre-mayoral Photograph Collection
    Public Safety/Regulatory Sub-cabinet Records
Chicago Public Library, Harold Washington Library Center, Special Collections
    Steve Askin Papers
    Eugene Sawyer Mayoral Records
Chicago Public Library, Harold Washington Library Center, Municipal Reference
  Collection
    Government Publications
Chicago Public Library, Woodson Regional Library, Vivian Harsh Research Collection
    Brenetta Howell Barrett Papers
    Timuel D. Black Jr. Papers
    Charles A. Hayes Papers
    Rev. Addie Wyatt and Rev. Claude Wyatt Papers
DePaul University Special Collections and Archives, Chicago
    Young Lords Collection
Martin Luther King Jr. Center for Peace and Nonviolent Change, Atlanta
    Dr. Martin Luther King Jr. Papers
University of Illinois, Chicago, Daley Library, Special Collections
    Chicago Urban League Records
    Christopher Cohen Papers
    Bernard Epton Papers
    Rudy Lozano Papers
    Richard M. Daley Papers
    Dick Simpson Papers
Washington University Libraries, Film and Media Archive, St. Louis, Missouri
    Henry Hampton Collection

## Government Documents

Board of Election Commissioners for the City of Chicago. "2003 Municipal General—
2/25/03." chicagoelections.gov.
———. "2003 Municipal Runoffs—4/1/03." chicagoelections.gov.
———. "2007 Municipal General—2/27/07." chicagoelections.gov.
———. "2007 Municipal Runoffs—4/17/07." chicagoelections.gov.
———. "2011 Municipal General—2/22/11." chicagoelections.gov.
———. "2015 Municipal General—February 24, 2015." chicagoelections.gov.
———. "2015 Municipal Runoffs—April 7, 2015." chicagoelections.gov.
———. "2019 Municipal General—2/26/19." chicagoelections.gov.
Chicago Board of Election Commissioners' Canvassing Sheets, 2nd Ward Alderman,
February 23, 1971, and February 25, 1975. Municipal Reference Collection, Chicago
Public Library.
———, 5th Ward Alderman, February 23, 1971, and February 25, 1975. Municipal Reference Collection, Chicago Public Library.
———, 46th Ward Alderman, February 23, 1971, and February 25, 1975. Municipal Reference Collection, Chicago Public Library.
Chicago City Council. *Journal of the Proceedings of the City Council of Chicago, Illinois,
1983–1987.* https://www.chicityclerk.com/legislation-records/journals-and-reports
/journals-proceedings.
———. "Washington Inaugural Address." *Journal of the Proceedings* (Chicago), April 29,
1983.
Chicago Police Department. *Statistical Summary*, 1982–85. https://home.chicago
police.org/statistics-data/statistical-reports/annual-reports/.
———. *Chicago Police Annual Report*, 1986–97. https://home.chicagopolice.org
/statistics-data/statistical-reports/annual-reports/.
Illinois Legislative Investigating Commission. *Illegal Aliens—Joliet: A Report to the
Illinois General Assembly*, July 1978. https://www.ncjrs.gov/pdffiles1/Digitization
/51757NCJRS.pdf.
*Ketchum v. City Council of Chicago.* 630 F. Supp. 551, 1985 U.S. Dist.
*Michael L. Shakman and Paul M. Lurie et al., Plaintiffs, v. the Democratic Organization
of Cook County, Defendants.* 481 F. Supp. 1315, 1979 U.S. Dist. LEXIS 9610. United
States District Court for the Northern District of Illinois, Eastern Division, Septem-
ber 24, 1979.
National Advisory Commission on Civil Disorders. *Report of the National Advisory
Commission.* Washington, D.C.: U.S. Government Printing Office, 1968.
*Power Organized for Welfare and Employment Rights v. Thompson.* 559 F. Supp. 54; 1983
U.S. Dist. LEXIS 18325.
*Tennessee v. Garner.* 471 U.S. 1. 1985.
U.S. Census Bureau. *1970 Census of Population, Supplementary Report: Low Income
Neighborhoods in Large Cities, Chicago.* Washington, D.C.: U.S. Government Printing
Office, 1970.
———. *Census Tracts: Chicago, Ill.—1980 Census of Population and Housing.* Washing-
ton, D.C.: U.S. Government Printing Office, 1980.

U.S. Commission on Civil Rights. *Report of the United States Commission on Civil Rights.* Washington, D.C.: U.S. Government Printing Office, 1959.

U.S. Senate, Subcommittee on the Constitution, Committee on the Judiciary. *Voting Rights Act*, part 1. Washington, D.C., 1982.

### *Internet-Accessed Documents and Videos*

Austen, Ben. "The 1992 Horror Film That Made a Monster Out of a Chicago Housing Project." *Zócalo Public Square*, August 17, 2018. https://www.zocalopublicsquare.org/2018/08/17/1992-horror-film-made-monster-chicago-housing-project/ideas/essay/.

Ayers, Thomas G. "Summit Agreement." *Fulfilling the Dream*, August 1966. http://cfm40.middlebury.edu/node/48.

"Bernard Epton Mayoral Spots." March 1983. http://mediaburn.org/video/bernard-epton-mayoral-spots/.

Chicago Democracy Project. "Election Results for 1977 Primary Election and 1975 Primary Election, Mayor, Chicago, IL." Old site. http://chicagodemocracy.org/oldsite.jsp.

——. "Election Results for 1983 General Election, Mayor, Chicago, IL." Old site. http://chicagodemocracy.org/index.jsp.

——. "Election Results for 1987 General Election, Mayor, Chicago, IL." Old site. http://chicagodemocracy.org/oldsite.jsp.

——. "How Did Chicago's Segregated Neighborhoods Vote in the Mayoral Election?" March 11, 2019. https://sites.northwestern.edu/chicagodemocracy/2019/03/11/race-segregation-mayor-2019-general/.

"Jane Byrne's Easter at Cabrini." Media Burn independent video archive, April 1981. https://mediaburn.org/blog/chicago-mayor-jane-byrnes-easter-celebration-in-cabrini-green-1981/.

Janney, Albert. "The Chicago League of Negro Voters." Undated. http://fedora.dlib.indiana.edu/fedora/get/iudl:871676/OVERVIEW.

——. "To Increase the Power of Negro Voters—The Chicago Plan." June 1959. http://www.thekingcenter.org/archive/document/report-chicago-plan-chicago-league-negro-voters.

Méndez, Mervin. "A Community Fights Back: Recollections of the 1966 Division Street Riot." *Diálogo* 2 (1998). http://via.library.depaul.edu/cgi/viewcontent.cgi?article=1018&context=dialogo.

Metropolitan Tenant Organization. "30th Anniversary of Chicago's Landmark Residential Landlord Tenant Ordinance." September 7, 2016. https://www.tenants-rights.org/30th-anniversary-of-chicagos-landmark-residential-landlord-tenant-ordinance/.

National Commission on Excellence in Education. *A Nation at Risk: The Imperative for Educational Reform.* April 1983. https://www2.ed.gov/pubs/NatAtRisk/index.html.

Reagan, Ronald. "Address Accepting the Presidential Nomination at the Republican National Convention in Detroit." July 17, 1980. http://www.presidency.ucsb.edu/.

——. "Remarks in New Orleans, Louisiana, at the Annual Meeting of the

International Association of Chiefs of Police." September 28, 1981. http://www
.presidency.ucsb.edu/.

Rustin, Bayard. "From Protest to Politics: The Future of the Civil Rights Movement."
February 1965, box 1, folder 122, American Left Ephemera Collection, 1894–2008,
AIS.2007.11, Archives Service Center, University of Pittsburgh, http://digital.library
.pitt.edu/u/ulsmanuscripts/pdf/31735066227830.pdf.

Third mayoral debate. January 1983. https://www.pbs.org/video/chicago-tonight
-april-15-2013-web-extra-harold-washington-1983/.

U.S. Census Bureau. "Poverty Status by Age, Race, and Hispanic Origin." https://www
.census.gov/data/tables/time-series/demo/income-poverty/historical-poverty
-people.html.

"Vito Marzullo." Media Burn independent video archive, 1978. https://mediaburn.org
/video/vito-marzullo/.

Washington, Harold. "Crisis of Leadership in Chicago." University of Illinois, 1982.
http://eblackchicago.org/HAROLD/uofi82.htm.

WBEZ. "Can Chicago Brag about the Size of Its Polish Population?" October 26, 2015.
https://www.wbez.org/shows/curious-city/can-chicago-brag-about-the-size-of-its
-polish-population/ef8c74cd-8835-4eb7-8e81-11203e78fc2d.

## Periodicals

*Afro-American* (Baltimore)
*All Chicago City News*
*Amsterdam News*
*Baltimore Sun*
*Austin News Weekly*
*Boletín*
*The Booster*
*BPINS* (Chicago)
*Black Panther*
*Black Scholar*
*La Campaña*
*Chicago* (magazine)
*Chicago Assyrian*
*Chicago Crusader*
*Chicago Daily News*
*Chicago Defender*
*Chicago Lawyer*
*Chicago Metro News*
*Chicago Outlines*

*Chicago Reader*
*Chicago Rehab Network
  Newsletter*
*Chicago Reporter*
*Chicago Sun-Times*
*Chicago Tribune*
*Crain's Chicago Business*
*Daily Calumet* (Chicago)
*GayLife*
*El Heraldo del Norte*
*Hispanic Business*
*HuffPost*
*Hyde Park Herald*
*El Independiente*
*In These Times*
*Jet*
*Keep Strong* (Chicago)
*Lincoln Park–Lake View
  Booster*

*Logan Square Free Press*
*Los Angeles Times*
*Milwaukee Star*
*New Republic*
*New York* (magazine)
*New York Times*
*La Opinión Latina*
*El País* (Madrid)
*Rising Up Angry* (Chicago)
*El Sol de Pilsen*
*Streetwise*
*Time*
*UICC Illini* (Chicago)
*Uptown News* (Chicago)
*USA Today*
*Wall Street Journal*
*Washington Post*
*West Side Times*

## Oral Histories by Author (in Author's Possession)

Hal Baron, June 29, 2016, Chicago.
Brenetta Howell Barrett, July 1, 2016, Chicago.
John Betancur, August 6, 2013, telephone.
Linda Coronado, June 30, 2016, Chicago.

María "Nena" de los Ángeles Torres, June 27, 2012, Chicago.
Jesús "Chuy" García, June 23, 2016, Chicago.
Jacky Grimshaw, June 6, 2013, Chicago.
Michael James, June 5, 2013, Chicago.
José "Cha-Cha" Jiménez, December 19, 2011, telephone.
José "Cha-Cha" Jiménez, January 20, 2012, telephone.
Obed López Zacarías, July 11, 2006, telephone.
Jorge Morales, August 29, 2012, Chicago.
Charles Payne, June 1, 2016, Chicago.
Modesto Rivera, June 23, 2012, Chicago.
Helen Shiller, with Erik Gellman, June 8, 2016, Chicago.
Paul Siegel, June 7, 2013, Chicago.
Dick Simpson, June 27, 2016, Chicago.
Robert "Bob" Starks, June 21, 2016, Chicago.

### *Oral Histories from the HistoryMakers® Digital Archive and Others*

Larry Bullock (A2000.045), by Adele Hodge, July 20, 2000, Chicago, HMDA.
Walter "Slim" Coleman, by Blackside Inc., April 13, 1989, HH.
Al From, by Russell Riley, April 27, 2006, https://millercenter.org/the-presidency/presidential-oral-histories/al-oral-history-2006.
The Honorable Wilson Frost (A2003.227), by Larry Crowe, October 9, 2003, Chicago, HMDA.
Jacquelyne Grimshaw (A2003.001), by Larry Crowe, January 10, 2003, Chicago, HMDA.
The Honorable Charles Hayes (A1993.002), by Julieanna Richardson, January 1, 1993, Chicago, HMDA.
José "Cha-Cha" Jiménez, by Mervin Mendez, December 6, 1993, Chicago, YL.
Peggy Montes (A2001.050), by Julieanna Richardson, October 1, 2001, Chicago, HMDA.
Achy Obejas, by Tracy Baim, July 11, 2011, Chicago, https://www.chicagogayhistory.com/biography.html?id=490.
Edward "Buzz" Palmer (HM A2002.157), by Larry Crowe, July 26, 2002, Chicago, HMDA.
Lu Palmer, conducted by Blackside Inc., April 14, 1989, HH.
Lutrelle "Lu" F. Palmer II (HM A2002.087), by Larry Crowe, May 22, 2002, Chicago, HMDA.
Fred Rice Jr. (HM A1993.005), by Larry Crowe, June 27, 2002, Chicago, HMDA.
Renault Robinson (HM A2002.107), by Larry Crowe, July 7, 2002, Chicago, HMDA.
Bobby Rush, by Blackside Inc., October 20, 1988, HH.
Howard Saffold (HM A2002.091), by Larry Crowe, June 5, 2002, Chicago, HMDA.
The Honorable Gus Savage (HM A2001.068), by Julieanna Richardson, April 26, 2001, Washington, D.C., HMDA.
The Honorable Eugene Sawyer (HM A2003.024), by Larry Crowe, January 29, 2003, Chicago, HMDA.
Bob Starks (HM A2009.147), by Larry Crowe, December 15, 2009, Chicago, HMDA.

## Films

Alk, Howard, and Mike Gray, dirs. *The Murder of Fred Hampton*. Chicago Media Group, (1971) 2019.

Santisteban, Ray, dir. *The Rainbow Coalition*. Nantes Media, 2019.

Tyrnauer, Matt, dir. *The Reagans*. Altimeter Films, 2020.

Winston, Joe, dir. *Punch 9: The Election of Harold Washington*. Tallgrass Films, 2021.


## Secondary Sources

### Published Articles and Books

Alexander, Michelle. *The New Jim Crow: Mass Incarceration in the Age of Colorblindness*. New York: New Press, 2010.

Alkalimat, Abdul, and Doug Gills. "Chicago—Black Power vs. Racism: Harold Washington Becomes Mayor." In *The New Black Vote: Politics and Power in Four American Cities*, edited by Rod Bush, 53–179. San Francisco: Synthesis, 1984.

———. *Harold Washington and the Crisis of Black Power: Mass Protest*. Chicago: Twenty-First Century, 1989.

Alvarez, René Luis. "A Community That Would Not Take 'No' for an Answer: Mexican Americans, the Chicago Public Schools, and the Founding of Benito Juarez High School." *Journal of Illinois History* 17, no. 1 (2014): 78–98.

Amezcua, Mike. "A Machine in the Barrio: Chicago's Conservative Colonia and the Remaking of Latino Politics in the 1960s and 1970s." *The Sixties* 12, no. 1 (2019): 95–120.

———. *Making Mexican Chicago: From Postwar Settlement to the Age of Gentrification*. Chicago: University of Chicago Press, 2022.

Anderson, Alan B., and George W. Pickering. *Confronting the Color Line: The Broken Promise of the Civil Rights Movement in Chicago*. Athens: University of Georgia Press, 1986.

Año Nuevo de Kerr, Louise. "Chicano Settlements in Chicago: A Brief History." *Journal of Ethnic Studies* 2 (1975): 22–32.

———. "Mexican Chicago: Chicano Assimilation Aborted, 1939–1954." In *The Ethnic Frontier: Essays in the History of Group Survival in Chicago and the Midwest*, edited by Melvin G. Holli and Peter d'Alroy Jones, 293–328. Grand Rapids, Mich.: William B. Eerdmans, 1977.

Ansfield, Bench. "The Crisis of Insurance and the Insuring of the Crisis: Riot Reinsurance and Redlining in the Aftermath of the 1960s Uprisings." *Journal of American History* 107, no. 4 (March 2021): 899–921.

Araiza, Lauren. *To March for Others: The Black Freedom Struggle and the United Farm Workers*. Philadelphia: University of Pennsylvania Press, 2013.

Arrendondo, Gabriela F. *Mexican Chicago: Race, Identity and Nation, 1916–39*. Urbana: University of Illinois Press, 2008.

Austin, Curtis. *Up against the Wall: Violence in the Making and Unmaking of the Black Panther Party*. Fayetteville: University of Arkansas Press, 2006.

Austin, Sharon Wright, and Richard T. Middleton IV. "The Limitations of the

Deracialization Concept in the 2001 Los Angeles Mayoral Election." *Political Research Quarterly* 57, no. 2 (June 2004): 283–93.

Axelrod, David. *Believer: My Forty Years in Politics*. New York: Penguin, 2015.

Baer, Andrew S. *Beyond the Usual Beating: The Jon Burge Police Torture Scandal and Social Movements for Police Accountability in Chicago*. Chicago: University of Chicago Press, 2020.

Baer, Kenneth S. *Reinventing Democrats: The Politics of Liberalism from Reagan to Clinton*. Lincoln: University of Kansas Press, 2000.

Baldwin, Davarian. *Chicago's New Negroes: Modernity, the Great Migration, and Black Urban Life*. Chapel Hill: University of North Carolina Press, 2007.

Balto, Simon. *Occupied Territory: Policing Black Chicago from Red Summer to Black Power*. Chapel Hill: University of North Carolina Press, 2019.

Barker, Lucius Jefferson, and Ronald Walters. *Jesse Jackson's 1984 Presidential Campaign: Challenge and Change in American Politics*. Urbana: University of Illinois Press, 1989.

Bayor, Ronald H. "African American Mayors and Governance in Atlanta." In *African American Mayors: Race, Politics and the American City*, edited by David R. Colburn and Jeffrey S. Adler, 178–99. Urbana-Champaign: University of Illinois Press, 2005.

Behnken, Brian D. *Fighting Their Own Battles: Mexican Americans, African Americans, and the Struggle for Civil Rights in Texas*. Chapel Hill: University of North Carolina Press, 2011.

———, ed. *The Struggle in Black and Brown: African American and Mexican American Relations during the Civil Rights Era*. Lincoln: University of Nebraska Press, 2010.

———, ed. *Civil Rights and Beyond: African American and Latino/a Activism in the Twentieth-Century United States*. Athens: University of Georgia Press, 2016.

Beito, David T., and Linda Royster Beito. *Black Maverick: T. R. M. Howard's Fight for Civil Rights and Economic Power*. Urbana: University of Illinois Press, 2009.

Belenchia, Joanne M. *Latinos and Chicago Politics*. Chicago: Urban Affairs Center, 1978.

Berger, Dan. *Captive Nation: Black Prison Organizing in the Civil Rights Era*. Chapel Hill: University of North Carolina Press, 2014.

Bernstein, Shana. *Bridges of Reform: Interracial Civil Rights Activism in Twentieth-Century Los Angeles*. New York: Oxford University Press, 2010.

Betancur, John, and Douglas C. Gills. "The African American and Latino Coalition Experience in Chicago under Mayor Harold Washington." In *The Collaborative City: Opportunities and Struggles for Blacks and Latinos in U.S. Cities*, edited by John Betancur and Douglass C. Gills, 59–87. New York: Garland, 2000.

Betancur, John, Michael Leachman, Anne Miller, David Walker, and Patricia A. Wright. "The Chicago Rehab Network." Development without Displacement Task Force background paper. Chicago: UIC Nathalie P. Voorhees Center for Neighborhood and Community Improvement, 1995.

Biles, Roger. "Black Mayors: A Historical Assessment." *Journal of Negro History* 77 (1992): 109–25.

———. *Crusading Liberal: Paul H. Douglas of Illinois*. Dekalb: Northern Illinois University Press, 2002.

————. *Mayor Harold Washington: Champion of Race and Reform in Chicago*. Urbana: University of Illinois Press, 2018.

Black, Earl, and Merle Black. *The Rise of Southern Republicans*. New York: Belknap, 2002.

Black, Timuel D., Jr. *Bridges of Memory: Chicago's Second Generation of Black Migration*. Chicago: DuSable Museum of African American History, 2007.

Black, Timuel D., Jr. *Sacred Ground: The Chicago Streets of Timuel Black*. Evanston, Ill.: Northwestern University Press, 2019.

*Black Power in Chicago: A documentary survey of the 1983 mayoral democratic primary*. Chicago: People's College Press, 1983.

Blakely, Edward J. "Ode to Rob Mier: Planner of Our Time." *Journal of Planning Literature* 9, no. 4 (1995): 396-98.

Bohn, Sarah, Matthew Freedman, and Emily Owens. "The Criminal Justice Response to Policy Interventions: Evidence from Immigration Reform." *American Economic Review: Papers and Proceedings* 105, no. 5 (2015): 214–19.

Braden, Maria. *Women Politicians and the Media*. Lexington: University Press of Kentucky, 1996.

Bradley, James. "The University of Chicago, Urban Renewal, and the Black Community." *Black Perspectives*, April 12, 2021.

Branch, Taylor. *At Canaan's Edge: America in the King Years, 1965–1968*. New York: Simon & Schuster, 2007.

Brantley, Allyson. *Brewing a Boycott: How a Grassroots Coalition Fought Coors and Remade American Consumer Activism*. Chapel Hill: University of North Carolina Press, 2021.

Brehm, Robert. "The City and the Neighborhoods: Was It Really a Two-Way Street?" In *Harold Washington and the Neighborhoods*, edited by Pierre Clavel and Wim Wiewel, 238–69. New Brunswick, N.J.: Rutgers University Press, 1991.

Brier, Jennifer. *Infectious Ideas: U.S. Political Responses to the AIDS Crisis*. Chapel Hill: University of North Carolina Press, 2011.

Brilliant, Mark. *The Color of America Has Changed: How Racial Diversity Shaped Civil Rights Reform in California, 1941–1978*. Oxford University Press, 2010.

Byrne, Jane. *My Chicago*. Chicago: Northwestern University Press, 2003.

Carl, Jim. "Harold Washington and Chicago's Schools between Civil Rights and the Decline of the New Deal Consensus, 1955–1987." *History of Education Quarterly* 41, no. 3 (2001): 311–43.

Carson, Clayborne. *In Struggle: SNCC and the Black Awakening of the 1960s*. Cambridge, Mass.: Harvard University Press, 1981.

Casuso, Jorge. "Hispanics." In *Restoration 1989: Chicago Elects a New Daley*, edited by Paul Michael Green and Melvin G. Holli, 70–73. Chicago: Lyceum, 1991.

Chandler, Christopher. *Harold Washington and the Civil Rights Legacy*. Woodbury, Tenn.: Woodbury, 2014.

Chase, Robert. *We Are Not Slaves: State Violence, Coerced Labor, and Prisoners' Rights in Postwar America*. Chapel Hill: University of North Carolina Press, 2020.

Chávez, Ernesto. *Mi Raza Primero! Nationalism, Identity, and Insurgency in the Chicano Movement in Los Angeles, 1966–1978*. Berkeley: University of California Press, 2002.

"Chicago's First Hispanic Alderman: How William E. Rodriguez Broke Ethnic—and Political—Barriers." *Chicago* 30, no. 11 (November 1981): 144–47.

Clavel, Pierre. *Activists in City Hall: The Progressive Response to the Reagan Era in Boston and Chicago.* Ithaca, N.Y.: Cornell University Press, 2010.

Clavel, Pierre, and Wim Wiewel, eds. *Harold Washington and the Neighborhoods.* New Brunswick, N.J.: Rutgers University Press, 1991.

Clayson, William. *Freedom Is Not Enough: The War on Poverty and the Civil Rights Movement in Texas.* Austin: University of Texas Press, 2010.

Cohen, Adam, and Elizabeth Taylor. *American Pharaoh: Mayor Richard J. Daley—His Battle for Chicago and the Nation.* Boston: Little, Brown, 2000.

Cohen, Cathy J. *Boundaries of Blackness: AIDS and the Breakdown of Black Politics.* Chicago: University of Chicago Press, 1999.

Cohen, Lizabeth. *Making a New Deal: Industrial Workers in Chicago, 1919–1939.* New York: Cambridge University Press, 1990.

Colburn, David R., and Jeffrey S. Adler, eds. *African American Mayors: Race, Politics and the American City.* Urbana-Champaign: University of Illinois Press, 2005.

Coleman, Slim, and George Jenkins. *Fair Share: The Struggle for the Rights of the People.* Chicago: Justice Graphics, 1989.

Colman, Jeffrey D., and Michael T. Brody. "*Ketchum v. Byrne*: The Hard Lessons of Discriminatory Redistricting in Chicago." *64 Chicago-Kent Law Review* 497 (1988).

Connolly, N. D. B. *A World More Concrete: Real Estate and the Remaking of Jim Crow South Florida.* Chicago: University of Chicago Press, 2014.

Copeland, Gary, and Kenneth Meier. "Gaining Ground: The Impact of Medicaid and WIC on Infant Mortality." *American Politics Quarterly* 15, no. 2 (April 1987): 254–73.

Cordova, Teresa. "Harold Washington and the Rise of Latino Electoral Politics." In *Chicano Politics and Society in the Late Twentieth Century,* edited by David Montejano, 31–57. Austin: University of Texas, 1999.

Countryman, Matthew J. "'From Protest to Politics': Community Control and Black Independent Politics in Philadelphia, 1965–1984." *Journal of Urban History* 32 (2006): 813–61.

———. *Up South: Civil Rights and Black Power in Philadelphia.* Philadelphia: University of Pennsylvania Press, 2006.

Coutin, Susan Bibler. *The Culture of Protest: Religious Activism and the U.S. Sanctuary Movement.* Boulder, Colo.: Westview, 1993.

Cowie, Jefferson. *Stayin' Alive: The 1970s and the Last Days of the Working Class.* New York: New Press, 2010.

———. *The Great Exception: The New Deal and the Limits of American Politics.* Princeton, N.J.: Princeton University Press, 2016.

Cruz, Wilfredo. *City of Dreams: Latino Immigration to Chicago.* Lanham, Md.: University Press of America, 2007.

Danns, Dionne. *Something Better for Our Children: Black Organizing in Chicago Public Schools, 1963–1971.* New York: Routledge, 2003.

Davidson, Miriam. *Convictions of the Heart: Jim Corbett and the Sanctuary Movement.* Tucson: University of Arizona Press, 1988.

Davis, Joshua Clark. *From Head Shops to Whole Foods: The Rise and Fall of Activist Entrepreneurs.* New York: Columbia University Press, 2017.

Delgado, Gary. *Organizing the Movement: The Roots and Growth of ACORN.* Philadelphia: Temple University Press, 1986.

de los Ángeles Torres, María. "In Search of Meaningful Voice and Place: The IPO and Latino Community Empowerment in Chicago." In *La Causa: Civil Rights, Social Justice and the Struggle for Equality in the Midwest,* edited by Gilberto Cardenas, 81–106. Houston: Arte Público, 2004.

———. "Latino Politics in Chicago." In *Chicago's Future in a Time of Change,* edited by Dick Simpson, 248–253. Champaign, Ill.: Stipes Publishing, 1993.

———. "The Commission on Latino Affairs: A Case Study of Community Empowerment." In *Harold Washington and the Neighborhoods,* edited by Pierre Clavel and Wim Wiewel, 165–87. New Brunswick, N.J.: Rutgers University Press, 1991.

D'Emilio, John. *Lost Prophet: The Life and Times of Bayard Rustin.* New York: Free Press, 2003.

de Onís, Catalina M. "What's in an 'X'? An Exchange about the Politics of 'Latinx.'" *Chricú Journal: Latina/o Literatures, Arts, and Cultures* (2017): 78–91.

Deppe, Martin L. *Operation Breadbasket: An Untold Story of Civil Rights in Chicago, 1966–1971.* Athens: University of Georgia Press, 2017.

Despres, Leon, with Kenan Heise. *Challenging the Daley Machine: A Chicago Alderman's Memoir.* Evanston, Ill.: Northwestern University Press, 2005.

Diamond, Andrew J. *Mean Streets: Chicago Youths and the Everyday Struggle for Empowerment in the Multiracial City, 1908–1969.* Berkeley: University of California Press, 2009.

———. *Chicago on the Make: Power and Inequality in a Modern City.* Berkeley: University of California Press, 2017.

Dinces, Sean. *Bulls Markets: Chicago Basketball Business and the New Inequality.* Chicago: University of Chicago Press, 2018.

Dittmer, John. *Local People: The Struggle for Civil Rights in Mississippi.* Urbana: University of Illinois Press, 1994.

Donner, Frank. *Protectors of Privilege: Red Squads and Police Repression in Urban America.* Berkeley: University of California Press, 1992.

Drake, St. Clair, and Horace Cayton. *Black Metropolis: A Study of Negro Life in a Northern City.* Rev. ed. New York: Harper & Row, (1945) 1962.

Durr, Kenneth. *Behind the Backlash: White Working-Class Politics in Baltimore, 1940–1980.* Chapel Hill: University of North Carolina Press, 2003.

Ehrman, John. *The Eighties: America in the Age of Reagan.* New Haven, Conn.: Yale University Press, 2005.

Enck-Wanzer, Darrel. *The Young Lords: A Reader.* New York: New York University Press, 2010.

Espinoza, Dionne. "'The Partido Belongs to Those Who Will Work for It': Chicana Organizing and Leadership in the Texas Raza Unida Party, 1970–1980." *Aztlán* 36, no. 1 (2011): 191–210.

Fairclough, Adam. *To Redeem the Soul: The Southern Christian Leadership Conference and Martin Luther King Jr.* Athens: University of Georgia Press, 2001.

Felker-Kantor, Max. *Policing Los Angeles: Race, Resistance, and the Rise of the LAPD.* Chapel Hill: University of North Carolina Press, 2018.

Fernández, Johanna. "Between Social Service Reform and Revolutionary Politics: The Young Lords, Late Sixties Radicalism, and Community Organizing in New York City." In *Freedom North: Black Freedom Struggles Outside of the South,* edited by Jeanne Theoharis and Komozi Woodard, 255–86 New York: Palgrave Macmillan, 2002.

———. *The Young Lords: A Radical History.* Chapel Hill: University of North Carolina Press, 2020.

Fernández, Lilia. *Brown in the Windy City: Mexicans and Puerto Ricans in Postwar Chicago.* Chicago: University of Chicago Press, 2012.

Fink, Leon. "Labor Joins La Marcha: How New Immigrant Activists Restored the Meaning of May Day." In *¡Marcha! Latino Chicago and the New Immigrant Rights Movement,* edited by Amalia Pallares and Nilda Flores-González, 109–22. Springfield: University of Illinois Press, 2010.

Finley, Mary Lou, et al., eds. *The Chicago Freedom Movement.* Lexington: University of Kentucky Press, 2016.

FitzGerald, Kathleen Whalen. *Brass: Jane Byrne and the Pursuit of Power.* Chicago: Contemporary, 1981.

Flores, John H. *The Mexican Revolution in Chicago: Immigration Politics from the Early Twentieth Century to the Cold War.* Urbana: University of Illinois Press, 2018.

Flores-Rodríguez, Ángel G. "The Young Lords, Puerto Rican Liberation, and the Black Freedom Struggle: An Interview with José 'Cha-Cha' Jiménez." *OAH Magazine of History* 26, no. 1 (January 2012): 61–64.

Foley, Michael Stewart. *Front Porch Politics: The Forgotten Heyday of American Activism in the 1970s and 1980s.* New York: Hill & Wang, 2013.

Foley, Neil. "Becoming Hispanic: Mexican Americans and the Faustian Pact with Whiteness." In *Reflexiones: New Directions in Mexican American Studies,* edited by Neil Foley, 53–70. Austin: University of Texas Press, 1997.

———. "Partly Colored or Other White: Mexican Americans and Their Problem with the Color Line." In *Beyond Black and White: Race, Ethnicity, and Gender in the U.S. South and Southwest,* edited by Stephanie Cole, Stephanie, Laura F. Edwards, and Alison M. Parker, 123–44. College Station: Published for the University of Texas at Arlington by Texas A&M University Press, 2004.

———. "Straddling the Color Line: The Legal Construction of Hispanic Identity in Texas." In *Not Just Black and White: Historical and Contemporary Perspectives on Immigration, Race, and Ethnicity in the United States,* edited by Nancy Foner and George M. Fredrickson, 341–54. New York: Russell Sage Foundation, 2004.

———. *Quest for Equality: The Failed Promise of Black-Brown Solidarity.* Cambridge, Mass.: Harvard University Press, 2010.

Forman, James, Jr. *Locking Up Our Own: Crime and Punishment in Black America.* Farrar, Straus and Giroux, 2017.

Fox Piven, Frances, and Richard Cloward. *Poor People's Movements: Why They Succeed, How They Fail.* New York: Vintage, 1978.

Frady, Marshall. *Jesse: The Life and Pilgrimage of Jesse Jackson.* New York: Simon & Schuster, 2006.

Francis-Fallon, Benjamin. *The Rise of the Latino Vote: A History.* Cambridge, Mass.: Harvard University Press, 2019.

Fremon, David. *Chicago Politics Ward by Ward.* Bloomington: Indiana University Press, 1988.

———. "Media Coverage: Chicago Daley News." In *Restoration 1989: Chicago Elects a New Daley,* edited by Paul Michael Green and Melvin G. Holli, 139–58. Chicago: Lyceum, 1991.

Fuerst, J. S. *When Public Housing Was Paradise: Building Community in Chicago.* New York: Praeger, 2003.

Ganz, Cheryl. *The 1933 Chicago World's Fair: A Century of Progress.* Urbana: University of Illinois Press, 2008.

Garb, Margaret. *Freedom's Ballot: African American Political Struggles in Chicago from Abolition to the Great Migration.* Chicago: University of Chicago Press, 2014.

García, Ignacio M. *United We Win: The Rise and Fall of La Raza Unida Party.* Tucson: University of Arizona Press, 1989.

García, María Cristina. *Seeking Refuge: Central American Migration to Mexico, the United States, and Canada.* Berkeley: University of California Press, 2006.

García, Mario T. *Father Luis Olivares, a Biography: Faith Politics and the Origins of the Sanctuary Movement in Los Angeles.* Chapel Hill: University of North Carolina Press, 2018.

Garrow, David, ed. *Chicago 1966: Open Housing Marches, Summit Negotiations, and Operation Breadbasket.* Brooklyn, N.Y.: Carlson, 1989.

Gellman, Erik. "'Carthage Must Be Destroyed': Race, City Politics, and the Campaign to Integrate Chicago Transportation Work, 1929–1943." *Labor: Studies in Working-Class History of the Americas* 2, no. 2 (2005): 81–114.

———. "'The Stone Wall Behind': The Chicago Coalition for United Action and Labor's Overseers, 1968–1973." In *Black Power at Work: Community Control, Affirmative Action, and the Construction Industry,* edited by David Goldberg and Trevor Griffey, 112–33. Ithaca, N.Y.: ILR Press and Cornell University Press, 2010.

———. *Death Blow to Jim Crow: The National Negro Congress and the Rise of Militant Civil Rights.* Chapel Hill: University of North Carolina Press, 2012.

———. "In the Driver's Seat: Chicago's Bus Drivers and Labor Insurgency in the Era of Black Power." *Labor: Studies in Working-Class History of the Americas* 11, no. 3 (2014): 49–76.

———. *Troublemakers: Chicago Freedom Struggles through the Lens of Art Shay.* Chicago: University of Chicago Press, 2020.

Gills, Doug. "Chicago Politics and Community Development: A Social Movement Perspective." In *Harold Washington and the Neighborhoods,* edited by Pierre Clavel and Wim Wiewel, 34–63. New Brunswick, N.J.: Rutgers University Press, 1991.

Giloth, Robert. "Making Policy with Communities: Research and Development in the Department of Economic Development." In *Harold Washington and the Neighborhoods,* edited by Pierre Clavel and Wim Wiewel, 100–120. New Brunswick, N.J.: Rutgers University Press, 1991.

Gómez-Quiñones, Juan. *Mexican-American Labor, 1790–1990.* Albuquerque, N.M.: University of New Mexico Press, 1994.

Gordon, Colin. "Blighting the Way: Urban Renewal, Economic Development, and the Elusive Definition of Blight." *Fordham Urban Law Journal* 31, no. 2 (January 2004): 305–37.

Gottlieb, Dylan. "Hoboken Is Burning: Yuppies, Arson, and Displacement in the Postindustrial City." *Journal of American History* 106, no. 2 (September 2019): 390–416.

Granger, Bill, and Lori Granger. *Fighting Jane: Mayor Jane Byrne and the Chicago Machine.* New York: Dial, 1980.

Green, Adam. *Selling the Race: Culture, Community, and Black Chicago.* Chicago: University of Chicago Press, 2007.

Green, Paul Michael. "The 1989 General Election." In *Restoration 1989: Chicago Elects a New Daley,* edited by Paul Michael Green and Melvin G. Holli, 3–31. Chicago: Lyceum, 1991.

Green, Paul Michael, and Melvin G. Holli, eds. *Restoration 1989: Chicago Elects a New Daley.* Chicago: Lyceum, 1991.

Grimshaw, William J. *Bitter Fruit: Black Politics and the Chicago Machine, 1931–1991.* Chicago: University of Chicago Press, 1992.

Grossman, James R. *Land of Hope: Chicago, Black Southerners, and the Great Migration.* Chicago: University of Chicago Press, 1991.

Gutiérrez, David G. "Sin Fronteras? Chicanos, Mexican Americans, and the Emergence of the Contemporary Mexican." *Journal of American Ethnic History* 10, no. 4 (Summer 1991): 5–37.

Gutiérrez, Luis. *Still Dreaming: My Journey from the Barrio to Capitol Hill.* New York: W. W. Norton, 2013.

Guzmán, Joshua Javier. "Latino, the Word." *English Language Notes,* 2018, 143–45.

Haas, Jeffrey. *The Assassination of Fred Hampton: How the FBI and the Chicago Police Murdered a Black Panther.* Rev. ed. Chicago: Lawrence Hill, 2019.

Hall, Jacquelyn Dowd. "The Long Civil Rights Movement and the Political Uses of the Past." *Journal of American History* 91 (2005): 1233–63.

Hampton, Henry, and Steve Fayer, eds. *Voices of Freedom: An Oral History of the Civil Rights Movement from the 1950s through the 1980s.* New York: Bantam, 1991.

Hayward, Steven F. *The Age of Reagan: The Conservative Counterrevolution, 1980–1989.* New York: Crown Forum, 2009.

Helgeson, Jeffrey. *Crucibles of Black Empowerment: Chicago's Neighborhood Politics from the New Deal to Harold Washington.* Chicago: University of Chicago Press, 2014.

Hinojosa, Felipe. *Apostles of Change: Latino Radical Politics, Church Occupations, and the Fight to Save the Barrio.* Austin: University of Texas Press, 2021.

Hinton, Elizabeth. *America on Fire: The Untold History of Police Violence and Black Rebellion since the 1960s.* New York: Liveright, 2021.

Hinz, Greg. "Lakefronters." In *Restoration 1989: Chicago Elects a New Daley,* edited by Paul Michael Green and Melvin G. Holli, 74–80. Chicago: Lyceum, 1991.

Hirsch, Arnold R. *Making the Second Ghetto: Race and Housing in Chicago, 1940–1960.* Chicago: University of Chicago Press, 1998.

Hobson, Maurice. *The Legend of the Black Mecca: Politics and Class in the Making of Modern America.* Chapel Hill: University of North Carolina Press, 2017.

Hogan, Sean, and Dick Simpson. "Campaign Contributions and Mayoral/Aldermanic Relationships: Building on Krebs and Pelissero." *Urban Affairs Review* 37, no. 1 (2001): 85–95.

Hollander, Elizabeth. "The Department of Planning under Harold Washington." In *Harold Washington and the Neighborhoods*, edited by Pierre Clavel and Wim Wiewel, 121–45. New Brunswick, N.J.: Rutgers University Press, 1991.

Holli, Melvin G., and Paul M. Green, eds. *Bashing Chicago Traditions: Harold Washington's Last Campaign, Chicago, 1987*. Grand Rapids, Mich.: William B. Eerdmans, 1989.

———. *The Making of the Mayor: Chicago, 1983*. Grand Rapids, Mich.: William B. Eerdmans, 1984.

Hunt, D. Bradford. *Blueprint for Disaster: The Unraveling of Chicago Public Housing*. University of Chicago Press, 2009.

Huq, Aziz and Tom Ginsburg. "How to Lose a Constitutional Democracy." *UCLA Law Review* 65 (2018): 78-169.

Hurwitz, Jon, and Mark Peffley. "Playing the Race Card in the Post–Willie Horton Era." *Public Opinion Quarterly* 69, no. 1 (Spring 2005): 99–112.

Innis-Jiménez, Michael. *Steel Barrio: The Great Mexican Migration to South Chicago, 1915–1940*. New York: New York University Press, 2013.

Jeffries, Hasan Kwame. *Bloody Lowndes: Civil Rights and Black Power in Alabama's Black Belt*. New York: New York University Press, 2009.

Jenkins, Philip. *Decade of Nightmares: The End of the Sixties and the Making of Eighties America*. New York: Oxford University Press, 2005.

Johnson, Cedric. *Revolutionaries to Race Leaders: Black Power and the Making of African American Politics*. Minneapolis: University of Minnesota Press, 2007.

Jones, Patrick. *Selma of the North: Civil Rights Insurgency in Milwaukee*. Cambridge, Mass.: Harvard University Press, 2010.

Joseph, Peniel. *Waiting 'til the Midnight Hour: A Narrative History of Black Power in America*. New York: Henry Holt, 2006.

Judd, Dennis R., Dick Simpson, and Janet L. Abu-Lughod. *The City, Revisited: Urban Theory from Chicago, Los Angeles, and New York*. Minneapolis: University of Minnesota Press, 2011.

Kahn, Kim Fridkin. *The Political Consequences of Being a Woman: How Stereotypes Influence the Conduct and Consequences of Political Campaigns*. New York: Columbia University Press, 1996.

Kahrl, Andrew. "The Short End of Both Sticks: Property Assessments and Black Taxpayer Disadvantage in Urban America." In *Shaped by the State: Toward a New Political History of the Twentieth Century*, edited by Brent Cebul, Lily Geismer, and Mason B. Williams, 190–217. Chicago: University of Chicago Press, 2019.

Katz, Michael. "Why Aren't U.S. Cities Burning?" *Dissent*, Summer 2007. https://www.dissentmagazine.org/article/why-arent-u-s-cities-burning.

———. *Why Don't American Cities Burn?* Philadelphia: University of Pennsylvania Press, 2012.

Kaufmann, Karen. "Black and Latino Voters in Denver: Responses to Each Other's Political Leadership." *Political Science Quarterly* 118 (Spring 2003): 107–25.

Kazin, Michael. *What It Took To Win: A History of the Democratic Party*. New York: Farrar, Strauss and Giroux, 2022.

Kleppner, Paul. *Chicago Divided: The Making of a Black Mayor*. DeKalb: Northern Illinois University Press, 1985.

———. "Mayoral Politics Chicago Style: The Rise and Fall of a Multiethnic Coalition, 1983–1989." *National Political Science Review* 5 (1994): 152–80.

Klinenberg, Eric. *Heat Wave: A Social Autopsy of Disaster in Chicago*. Chicago: University of Chicago Press, 2002.

Koeneman, Keith. *First Son: The Biography of Richard M. Daley*. Chicago: University of Chicago Press, 2013.

Kotlowitz, Alex. *There Are No Children Here: The Story of Two Boys Growing Up in the Other America*. New York: Doubleday, 1992.

Kozol, Jonathan. *Savage Inequalities: Children in America's Schools*. Reprint. New York: Crown, 2012.

Krebs, Timothy, and John Pelissero. "Fund-Raising Coalitions in Mayoral Campaigns." *Urban Affairs Review* 37, no. 1 (2001): 67–84.

Kretzmann, John. "The Affirmative Information Policy: Opening Up a Closed City." In *Harold Washington and the Neighborhoods*, edited by Pierre Clavel and Wim Wiewel, 199–220. New Brunswick, N.J.: Rutgers University Press, 1991.

Krochmal, Max. *Blue Texas: The Making of a Multiracial Democratic Coalition in the Civil Rights Era*. Chapel Hill: University of North Carolina Press, 2016.

Kruse, Kevin M. and Julian E. Zelizer. *Fault Lines: A History of the United States Since 1974*. New York: W. W. Norton, 2019.

Larson, Erik. *The Devil in the White City*. New York: Vintage, 2004.

Lassiter, Matthew D. "Ten Propositions for the New Political History." In *Shaped by the State: Toward a New Political History of the Twentieth Century*, edited by Brent Cebul, Lily Geismer, and Mason B. Williams, 363–76. Chicago: University of Chicago Press, 2019.

Laws, Mike. "Why We Capitalize 'Black' (and Not 'White')." *Columbia Journalism Review*, June 16, 2020. https://www.cjr.org/analysis/capital-b-black-styleguide.php.

Lawson, Steven. *Running for Freedom: Civil Rights and Black Politics in America since 1941, Fourth Edition*. New York: Wiley-Blackwell, 2014.

Lee, Sonia Song-Ha. *Building a Latino Civil Rights Movement: Puerto Ricans, African Americans, and the Pursuit of Racial Justice in New York City*. Chapel Hill: University of Chicago Press, 2014.

Levinsohn, Florence Hamlish. *Harold Washington: A Political Biography*. Chicago: Chicago Review Press, 1983.

Levitsky, Steven and David Ziblatt. *How Democracies Die*. New York: Crown, 2018.

Lombardo, Timothy. *Blue-Collar Conservatism: Frank Rizzo's Philadelphia and Populist Politics*. Philadelphia: University of Pennsylvania Press, 2018.

López, Clara. "LADO: Latin American Defense Organization." *Diálogo* 1, no. 2 (1998): 22–27.

Lorentzen, Robin. *Women in the Sanctuary Movement*. Philadelphia: Temple University Press, 1991.

Losier, Toussaint. "'The Public Does Not Believe the Police Can Police Themselves': The Mayoral Administration of Harold Washington and the Problem of Police Impunity." *Journal of Urban History* 46, no. 5 (2017): 1050–65.

Luckingham, Bradford. *Minorities in Phoenix: A Profile of Mexican American, Chinese*

*American, and African American Communities, 1860–1992.* Tucson: University of
Arizona Press, 1994.

Manning, Christopher. *William L. Dawson and the Limits of Black Electoral Leadership.*
Dekalb: Northern Illinois University Press, 2009.

Mantler, Gordon K. *Power to the Poor: Black-Brown Coalition and the Fight for Economic
Justice, 1960–1974.* Chapel Hill: University of North Carolina Press, 2013.

———. "Rainbow Reformers: Black-Brown Activism and the Election of Harold
Washington." In *Civil Rights and Beyond: African American and Latino/a Activism
in the Twentieth-Century United States,* edited by Brian D. Behnken, 217–40. Athens:
University of Georgia Press, 2016.

———. "'Organize the People': The 1975 City Council Races in Multiracial Chicago."
*Journal of Civil and Human Rights* 3, no. 2 (Winter 2017): 1–29.

Marable, Manning J. *How Capitalism Underdeveloped Black America: Problems in Race,
Political Economy and Society.* Chicago: Haymarket, 2015.

———. *Race, Reform, and Rebellion: The Second Reconstruction in Black America,
1945–1990.* 2nd ed. Jackson: University Press of Mississippi, (1991) 2001.

Marable, Manning J., and Leith Mullings, eds. *Let Nobody Turn Us Around: An African
American Anthology.* 2nd ed. New York: Rowman and Littlefield, 2009.

Marchiel, Rebecca. *After Redlining: The Urban Reinvestment Movement in the Era of
Financial Deregulation.* Chicago: University of Chicago Press, 2020.

Mariscal, George. *Brown-Eyed Children of the Sun: Lessons from the Chicano Movement,
1965–1975.* Albuquerque: University of New Mexico Press, 2005.

Martin, Bradford. *The Other Eighties: A Secret History of America in the Age of Reagan.*
New York: Hill & Wang, 2011.

McMillian, John. *Smoking Typewriters: The Sixties Underground Press and the Rise of
Alternative Media in America.* New York: Oxford University Press, 2011.

McWilliams, Carey. *Brothers under the Skin.* New York: Little, Brown, 1944.

Michaeli, Ethan. *The Defender: How the Legendary Black Newspaper Changed America.*
New York: Houghton Mifflin Harcourt, 2016.

Mier, Robert, and Kari J. Moe. "Decentralized Development: From Theory to Practice."
In *Harold Washington and the Neighborhoods,* edited by Pierre Clavel and Wim
Wiewel, 64–99. New Brunswick, N.J.: Rutgers University Press, 1991.

Miller, Alton. *Harold Washington: The Mayor, the Man.* New York: Bonus, 1989.

Moore, Natalie. *The South Side: A Portrait of Chicago and American Segregation.* Reprint. London: Picador, 2019.

Mora-Torres, Juan. "Pilsen: A Mexican Global City in the Midwest." *Diálogo* 9, no. 1
(2005): 3–7.

Muhammad, Khalil Gibran. *The Condemnation of Blackness: Race, Crime, and the
Making of Modern Urban America.* Cambridge, Mass.: Harvard University Press,
2019.

Muñoz, Carlos, Jr., and Charles P. Henry. "Coalition Politics in San Antonio and
Denver: The Cisneros and Peña Mayoral Campaigns." In *Racial Politics in American
Cities,* 1st ed., edited by Rufus P. Browning, Dale Rogers Marshall, and David H.
Tabb, 179–90. New York: Longman, 1990.

Murch, Donna. "Crack in Los Angeles: Crisis, Militarization, and Black Response in the Late Twentieth-Century War on Drugs." *Journal of American History* 102, no. 1 (June 2015): 162–73.

Musgrove, George Derek. *Rumor, Repression, and Racial Politics: How the Harassment of Black Elected Officials Shaped Post–Civil Rights America*. Athens: University of Georgia Press, 2012.

Musgrove, George Derek, and Hasan Kwame Jeffries. "'The Community Don't Know What's Good for Them': Local Politics in the Alabama Black Belt during the Post–Civil Rights Era." In *Freedom Rights: New Perspectives on the Civil Rights Movement*, edited by Danielle L. McGuire and John Dittmer, 305–28. Lexington: University of Kentucky Press, 2011.

Myers Asch, Chris, and George Derek Musgrove. *Chocolate City: A History of Race and Democracy in the Nation's Capital*. Chapel Hill: University of North Carolina Press, 2019.

Navarro, Armando. *La Raza Unida Party: A Chicano Challenge to the U.S. Two-Party Dictatorship*. Philadelphia: Temple University Press, 2000.

Nolan, Peter. *Campaign! The 1983 Election That Rocked Chicago*. Chicago: Amika, 2012.

Novak, William J. "The Myth of the Weak American State." *American Historical Review* 113, no. 3 (June 2008): 752–72.

Ogbar, Jeffrey O. G. *Black Power: Radical Politics and African American Identity*. Updated ed. Baltimore: Johns Hopkins University Press, 2019.

Ortiz, Paul. *An African American and Latinx History of the United States*. New York: Beacon, 2018.

Pacyga, Dominic. *American Warsaw: The Rise, Fall, and Rebirth of Polish Chicago*. Chicago: University of Chicago Press, 2019.

Padilla, Felix M. *Latino Ethnic Consciousness: The Case of Mexican Americans and Puerto Ricans in Chicago*. South Bend, Ind.: University of Notre Dame Press, 1985.

———. *Puerto Rican Chicago*. South Bend, Ind.: University of Notre Dame Press, 1987.

Pallares, Amalia. "The Chicago Context." In *¡Marcha! Latino Chicago and the Immigrant Rights Movement*, edited by Amalia Pallares and Nilda Flores-González, 37–62. Springfield: University of Illinois Press, 2010.

Patiño, Jimmy. *Raza Sí, Migra No: Chicano Movement Struggle for Immigrant Rights in San Diego*. Chapel Hill: University of North Carolina Press, 2017.

Patterson, James T. *Restless Giant: The United States from Watergate to Bush v. Gore*. New York: Oxford University Press, 2005.

Perlstein, Rick. *Nixonland: The Rise of a President and the Fracturing of America*. New York: Scribner's, 2009.

Peters, Alan H., and Peter S. Fisher. *State Enterprise Zone Programs: Have They Worked?* Kalamazoo, Mich.: W. E. Upjohn Institute, 2002.

Phillips-Fein, Kim. *Fear City: New York's Fiscal Crisis and the Rise of Austerity*. New York: Metropolitan, 2017.

Piliawsky, Monte. "The Impact of Black Mayors on the Black Community: The Case of New Orleans' Ernest Morial." *Review of Black Political Economy* 13, no. 4 (Spring 1985): 5–23.

Piña, Francisco. "His Life." In *Rudy Lozano: His Life, His People*. Chicago: Taller de Estudios Comunitarios, 1991.

Podair, Jerald. *City of Dreams: Dodger Stadium and the Birth of Modern Los Angeles.* Princeton, N.J.: Princeton University Press, reprint, 2019.

Poniatowska, Elena. *Massacre in Mexico.* Translated by Helen R. Lane. New York: Viking, 1975.

Preston, Michael. "Black Politics in the Post-Daley Era." In *After Daley: Chicago Politics in Transition*, edited by Samuel K. Gove and Louis H. Masotti, 88–117. Chicago: University of Illinois Press, 1982.

Pulido, Laura. *Black, Brown, Yellow, and Left: Radical Activism in Los Angeles.* Berkeley: University of California Press, 2006.

Rakove, Milton. *Don't Make No Waves, Don't Back No Losers: An Insider's Analysis of the Daley Machine.* Bloomington: Indiana University Press, 1975.

———. *We Don't Want Nobody Nobody Sent: An Oral History of the Daley Years.* Bloomington: Indiana University Press, 1979.

Ralph, James. *Northern Protest: Martin Luther King Jr., Chicago, and the Civil Rights Movement.* Cambridge, Mass.: Harvard University Press, 1993.

Ralph, Laurence. *The Torture Letters: Reckoning with Police Violence.* University of Chicago Press, 2020.

Reed, Adolph. *Stirrings in the Jug: Black Politics in the Post-segregation Era.* Minneapolis: University of Minnesota Press, 1999.

Reynolds, Barbara. *Jesse Jackson: America's David.* Washington, D.C.: JFJ Associates, 1985.

Rice, Jon. "The World of Illinois Panthers." In *Freedom North: Black Freedom Struggles outside the South, 1940–1980*, edited by Jeanne Theoharis and Komozi Woodard, 41–64. New York: Palgrave Macmillan, 2003.

Rivera, Marisol, and Judson L. Jeffries. "From Radicalism to Representation: Jose 'Cha-Cha' Jimenez's Journey into Electoral Politics." *Journal of African American Studies* 23 (2019): 299–319.

Rivlin, Gary. *Fire on the Prairie: Harold Washington, Chicago Politics, and the Roots of the Obama Presidency.* Philadelphia: Temple University Press, (1992) 2013.

Rodriguez, Marc. *The Tejano Diaspora: Mexican Americanism and Ethnic Politics in Texas and Wisconsin.* Chapel Hill: William P. Clements Center for Southwest Studies, Southern Methodist University, and University of North Carolina Press, 2011.

Rose, Don. "The Rise of Independent Black Political Power in Chicago." In *The Chicago Freedom Movement: Martin Luther King Jr. and Civil Rights Activism in the North*, edited by Mary Lou Finley et al, 263-73. Lexington: University of Kentucky Press, 2016.

Rossinow, Doug. *The Reagan Era: A History of the 1980s.* New York: Columbia University Press, 2015.

Royko, Mike. *The Boss: Mayor Richard J. Daley of Chicago.* New York: Plume, 1971.

*Rudy Lozano: His Life, His People.* Chicago: Taller de Estudios Comunitarios, 1991.

Rury, John L. "Race, Space, and the Politics of Chicago's Public Schools: Benjamin Willis and the Tragedy of Urban Education." *History of Education Quarterly* 39, no. 2 (1999): 117–42.

Rutkoff, Peter, and William Scott. "Pinkster in Chicago: Bud Billiken and the Mayor of Bronzeville, 1930–1945." *Journal of African American History* 89, no. 4 (Fall 2004): 316–30.

Sandoval-Strausz, A. K. "Latino Landscapes: Postwar Cities and the Transnational Origins of a New Urban America." *Journal of American History* 101, no. 3 (December 2014): 804–31.

———. *Barrio America: How Latino Immigrants Saved the American City*. New York: Basic Books, 2019.

Satter, Beryl. *Family Properties: Race, Real Estate, and the Exploitation of Black Urban America*. New York: Metropolitan, 2009.

———. "Cops, Gangs, and Revolutionaries in 1960s Chicago." *Journal of Urban History* 42, no. 6 (November 2016): 110–34.

Schudson, Michael. *The Rise of the Right to Know: Politics and the Culture of Transparency, 1945–1975*. Cambridge, Mass.: Belknap, 2015.

Self, Robert O. *All in the Family: The Realignment of American Democracy Since the 1960s*. New York: Hill & Wang, 2012.

———. *American Babylon: Race and the Struggle for Postwar Oakland*. Princeton, N.J.: Princeton University Press, 2005.

Seligman, Amanda. *Block by Block: Neighborhoods and Public Policy on Chicago's West Side*. Chicago: University of Chicago Press, 2005.

———. "But Burn—No: The Rest of the Crowd in Three Civil Disorders in 1960s Chicago." *Journal of Urban History* 37, no. 2 (2011): 230–55.

Serrano, Darrel Wanzer. *The New York Young Lords and the Struggle for Liberation*. Philadelphia: Temple University Press, 2015.

Shipps, Dorothy. "The Invisible Hand: Big Business and Chicago School Reform." *Teachers College Record* 99, no. 1 (Fall 1997): 73–116.

Skerry, Peter. *Mexican Americans: The Ambivalent Minority*. New York: Free Press, 1993.

Sonenshein, Raphael J. "Can Black Candidates Win Statewide Elections?" *Political Science Quarterly* 105, no. 2 (Summer 1990): 219–41.

Spirou, Costas, and Dennis R. Judd. *Building the City of Spectacle: Mayor Richard M. Daley and the Remaking of Chicago*. Ithaca, N.Y.: Cornell University Press, 2016.

Starks, Robert T., and Michael B. Preston. "Harold Washington and the Politics of Reform in Chicago: 1983–1987." In *Racial Politics in American Cities*, edited by Rufus P. Browning, Dale Rogers Marshall, and David H. Tabb, 88–107. New York: Longman, 1990: 88–107.

———. "The Political Legacy of Harold Washington: 1983–1987." *National Political Science Review* 2 (1990): 161–68.

Stewart-Winter, Timothy. *Queer Clout: Chicago and the Rise of Gay Politics*. Philadelphia: University of Pennsylvania Press, 2016.

Sugrue, Thomas J. *The Origins of the Urban Crisis: Race and Inequality in Postwar Detroit*, revised ed. Philadelphia: University of Pennsylvania Press, 2005.

———. *Sweet Land of Liberty: The Forgotten Struggle for Civil Rights in the North*. New York: Random House, 2008.

Superville, Denisa. "Chicago Local School Councils' Experiment Endures 25 Years of Change." *Education Week*, October 7, 2014.

Taylor, Flint. *The Torture Machine, Racism and Police Violence in Chicago*. Chicago: Haymarket, 2019.

Theoharis, Jeanne. *A More Beautiful and Terrible History: The Uses and Misuses of Civil Rights History*. Boston: Beacon, 2018.

Thompson, Heather. *Blood in the Water: The Attica Prison Uprising of 1971 and Its Legacy*. New York: Pantheon, 2016.

Thompson, J. Phillip. *Double Trouble: Black Mayors, Black Communities and the Call for a Deep Democracy*. New York: Oxford University Press, 2005.

Todd-Breland, Elizabeth. "Barbara Sizemore and the Politics of Black Educational Achievement and Community Control, 1963–1975." *Journal of African American History* 100, no. 4 (2015): 636–62.

———. *A Political Education: Black Politics and Education Reform in Chicago since the 1960s*. Chapel Hill: University of North Carolina Press, 2018.

Toro-Morn, Maura I. "Boricuas en Chicago: Gender and Class in the Migration and Settlement of Puerto Ricans." In *The Puerto Rican Diaspora: Historical Perspectives*, edited by Carmen Teresa Whalen and Víctor Vázquez-Hernández, 128–50. Philadelphia: Temple University Press, 2005.

Travis, Dempsey. *Harold, the People's Mayor: An Authorized Biography of Mayor Harold Washington*. Chicago: Urban Research, 1988.

Troy, Gil. *Morning in America: How Ronald Reagan Invented the 1980s*. Princeton, N.J.: Princeton University Press, 2005.

Troy, Gil, and Vincent J. Cannato, eds. *Living in the Eighties*. New York: Oxford University Press, 2009.

Ture, Kwame (Stokely Carmichael), and Charles V. Hamilton. *Black Power: The Politics of Liberation*. New York: Vintage, (1967) 1992.

Tyler, Gus. *Look for the Union Label: History of the International Ladies' Garment Workers' Union*. New York: Routledge, 2016.

Tyson, Timothy B. *The Blood of Emmett Till*. New York: Simon & Schuster, 2017.

Vaca, Nick. *Presumed Alliance: The Unspoken Conflict between Latinos and Blacks and What It Means for America*. New York: Rayo, 2004.

Venkatesh, Sudhir. *Gang Leader for a Day: A Rogue Sociologist Takes to the Streets*. New York: Penguin, 2008.

———. *Off the Books: The Underground Economy of the Urban Poor*. Cambridge, Mass.: Harvard University Press, 2009.

Walker, Judith. "Reforming the Role of Human Services." In *Harold Washington and the Neighborhoods*, edited by Pierre Clavel and Wim Wiewel, 146–64. New Brunswick, N.J.: Rutgers University Press, 1991.

Walton, John, and Luis Salces. "Structural Origins of Urban Social Movements: The Case of Latinos in Chicago." *International Journal of Urban and Regional Research* 3, no. 2 (June 1979): 235–50.

West, E. James. "The Bud Billiken Parade." *Black Perspectives*, June 16, 2022.

Whitaker, Matthew C. *Race Work: The Rise of Civil Rights in the Urban West*. Lincoln: University of Nebraska Press, 2005.

White, Brian. "The Leadership Council for Metropolitan Open Communities: Chicago and Fair Housing." In *The Chicago Freedom Movement: Martin Luther King Jr. and Civil Rights Activism in the North*, edited by Mary Lou Finley et al, 131-53. Lexington: University of Kentucky Press, 2016.

Whitehead, Ralph, Jr. "The Chicago Story: Two Dailies, a Campaign—and an Earth-quake." *Columbia Journalism Review*, July/August 1983, 25–30.

Wiewel, Wim, and Robert Giloth. "Planning for Manufacturing: Chicago after 1983." *Journal of Planning History* 14, no. 1 (2015): 19–37.

Wilder, Margaret G., and Barry M. Rubin. "Rhetoric versus Reality: A Review of Studies of State Enterprise Zone Programs." *Journal of the American Planning Association* 42 (1996): 473–91.

Wilentz, Sean. *The Age of Reagan: A History, 1974–2008*. New York: Harper, 2008.

Wilkerson, Isabel. *The Warmth of Other Suns: The Epic Story of America's Great Migration*. New York: Vintage, 2011.

Wilkins, Roy, and Ramsey Clark. *Search and Destroy: A Report by the Commission of Inquiry into the Black Panthers and the Police*. Chicago: Metropolitan Research Center, 1973.

Williams, Jakobi. *From the Bullet to the Ballot: The Illinois Chapter of the Black Panther Party and Racial Coalition Politics in Chicago*. Chapel Hill: University of North Carolina Press, 2013.

Woodard, Komozi. *A Nation within a Nation: Amiri Baraka (LeRoi Jones) and Black Power Politics*. Chapel Hill: University of North Carolina Press, 1999.

# Index

*Page numbers in italics refer to illustrations.*

AAPL. *See* Afro-American Patrolmen's League (AAPL)
Abernathy, Ralph, 49, 53, 248
Acevedo, José, 44
ACT UP, 246
Adamowski, Benjamin, 28, 34
Addams, Jane, 43, 92
affirmative action, 103, 165, 176–77, 180, 202, 227, 230, 261, 300n15, 300n18; for African Americans, 120, 173–74, 242, 255; for Latinos, 111, 156, 167, 172, 218, 231; for women, 171–72
African American, as term, 9. *See also* Black freedom struggle; coalition-building, Black-Latino-white
Afro-American Patrolmen's League (AAPL), 33, 36–37, 41, 50, 53, 57, 85, 110, 133, 186
AIDS, 7, 166, 188–89, 242, 246, 248, 254
Aid to Families with Dependent Children. *See* welfare
Alatorre, Soledad, 94
aldermen. *See* Chicago City Council
Alexander, Michelle, 257
Alinsky, Saul, 92, 102–3, 291n12
Alliance to End Repression, 41, 50, 52
Altman, Robert, 101
Amalgamated Meatcutters, 83
American Civil Liberties Union, 53
American Friends Service Committee, 24
American Indians, 59, 73, 75
Amezcua, Mike, 111
Amigos for Daley, 44, 94
amnesty, for undocumented residents, 89, 96, 206

*Amsterdam News*, 56
Amtrak, 112
Anaya, Toney, 157
Anti-Crosstown Action Committee, 54
Anti-Drug Abuse Act, 185. *See also* crack cocaine; War on Drugs
Appalachia, 40, 48, 73, 75, 100–101
Aranda, Mario, 233
Arango, Carlos, 205
Armed Forces of National Liberation, 78, 167, 196
Arrendondo, Gabriela, 276n5
arson for hire, 91, 101, 103, 137
Asian Americans, 5, 73, 170, 221
Assembly to End Prejudice-Injustice-Poverty, 27
Association for Workers Rights, 46
Association of Community Organizations for Reform Now (ACORN), 124, 291n13
Assyrians, 221
Atlanta, 15, 53, 174, 191, 298n4, 300n15, 300n18, 301n29
Axelrod, David, 68, 118, 144, 149, 223, 232, 249, 280n10, 296n5
Axelrod, Ralph, 104–5

Back of the Yards, 24, 43, 291n12
Badillo, Herman, 157
Baer, Andrew, 183
Baltimore, Md., 65, 149, 176, 233, 296n7
Balto, Simon, 37
Baraka, Amiri, 5, 14, 56
Barefield, Ernest, 174, 188, 229, 245, 247
Barnett, Richard, 145
Barnett, William "Butch," 69–70, 72
Baron, Harold "Hal," 134, 233–36, 243, 262
Barrow, Willie, 233

Beitler, J. Paul, 259
Benedict, Tom, 103
Benito Juarez High School, 93
Bennett, William, 232
Bentley, Lemuel, 22–23
Bernardin, Joseph, 233
Betancur, John, 158
Bickerdike Redevelopment Corporation,
    214
Biden, Joe, 257
Bilandic, Michael: 1977 mayoral cam-
    paign of, 80–83, 86; 1979 mayoral cam-
    paign of, 109–11, 144, 214, 217; as mayor,
    103–8, 171, 222, 240
Biles, Roger, 134
Binga, Jesse, 17
Black, Timuel "Tim," 25, 32, 60, 78, 108–11,
    *109*, 117, 212
Black, Zenobia, 117
Black Crime Commission, 41
Black Disciples, 32, 51
Black freedom struggle, 5–6, 15–16, 30,
    63, 82, 98, 212, 271n15. *See also* Chicago
    Freedom Movement (CFM); King,
    Martin Luther, Jr.
Black mayors (nationally), 65, 130, 176,
    184, 192, 228, 292n28, 300n18
*Black Metropolis* (Cayton and Drake),
    18
Black nationalism, 13–14, 117, 133, 138,
    167, 174, 192, 245. *See also* Black Panther
    Party; Hampton, Fred; Palmer, Lutrelle
    "Lu"
*Black Panther* (newspaper), 46, 48
Black Panther Party, 4–5, 36, 38–39, 49,
    64, 69–72, 85, 93, 100–101, 180. *See also*
    Hampton, Fred; Lee, Bobby; Rainbow
    Coalition (1969); Rush, Bobby
*Black Scholar, The*, 191, 303n39
Blackstone Rangers, 32, 51
Black Taxpayers Federation, 123
Black Youth Project 100, 261
Bloom, Lawrence "Larry," 129, 140, 241
Boler, L. Roscoe, 164
Bonilla, Tony, 141, 192, 195

boycott: ChicagoFest, 125–26; economic,
    21, 63, 95; political, 156; schools, 16,
    23–24, 26, 93, 273n22
Boykin, Jack "Junebug," 48
*Bracero* program, 42
Bradley, Ed, 193
Bradley, Tom, 15, 130, 292n28
Brady, Frank, 197, 210
Brazier, Arthur, 24
Bridgeport, 10, 30, 66, 82, 84, 145
Briscoe, Tommy, 83–85
Bronzeville, 18, 69, 99, 117, 136, 203
Brooks, Deton, 29–30
Brown, Elaine, 71
Brown, Eloise, 98
Brown, Frank London, 22
Brown, Ron, 251
Brown Berets, 93
Bryant, Clory Lee, 25–26
Brzeczek, Richard, 121, 143, 181
Bua, Nicholas, 177
Bud Billiken parade, 125
building code enforcement, 136
Bullock, Larry, 72, 77
Burge, Jon, 121, 183–84
Burke, Edward "Ed," 81, 106, 110, 112, 123,
    219, 260; Eugene Sawyer and, 225–26,
    242; Harold Washington and, 149, 164,
    179, 212, 228
Burris, Roland, 259
Burroughs, Margaret, 212
Bush, Earl, 57
Bush, George H. W., 151, 249
Byrd, Manford, Jr., 98, 174, 232–34
Byrne, Jane: 1979 mayoral campaign of, 3,
    91, 104–6, 108–10, *109*, 258; 1983 mayoral
    campaign of, 130–32, 138–49, 155–58,
    181, 191, 295n48; 1987 mayoral cam-
    paign of, 211, 214–15, 217–24; adminis-
    tration of, 112, 114, 135, 163–64, 172–74,
    178–79, 182–83, 201–2, 213, 232, 240,
    256; African Americans and, 110–11,
    117–18, 121–27; background of, 106–7;
    Cabrini-Green episode and, 120–21,
    141; ChicagoFest and, 125–26, 217; gay

men and, 140, 158; Latinos and, 108, 111, 157, 289n46; sexism against, 106, 131–32, 146, 288n37; snow storm and, 108–9, 222

Caballeros de San Juan, 44
cab industry, 107, 205, 214, 228, 243
Cabrini-Green, 120–21, 141, 186
Caddell, Pat, 154
Caldwell, Lewis, 40
Camacho, Eduardo, 198
Campaign to Control High Rises, 54
*Candyman*, 120, 186
carceral state. *See* mass incarceration
Carey, Bernard, 52, 58, 78, 149
Carter, Jimmy, 78–79, 89, 96, 101, 112, 154
Carter, Marlene, 197, 210
Cartwright, Gene, 235
CASA-HGT. *See* Center for Autonomous Social Action-General Brotherhood of Workers (CASA-HGT)
Casa Aztlan, 93, 96, 113
Castillo, Leonel, 96
Casuso, Jorge, 198, 250–51
Cayton, Horace, 16, 18; *Black Metropolis*, 18
CBUC (Chicago Black United Communities), 117–18, 126, 133, 138
Center for Autonomous Social Action-General Brotherhood of Workers (CASA-HGT), 90, 94–95, 97–98, 113, 136, 138. *See also* García, Jesus "Chuy"; immigration; Lozano, Rudy
Center for Urban Affairs and Policy Research (Northwestern University), 178
Center for Urban Economic Development (University of Illinois Chicago), 199
Central Americans, 43, 138, 156
Cerda, Maria, 157, 205, 219, 245, 247
Cermak, Anton, 19
CFM. *See* Chicago Freedom Movement (CFM)
Chatham, 127
Chávez, Cesar, 71, 97
Chevere, Gloria, 219, 222, 231–32

Chew, Charles, 25, 32, 40
Chicago 21 Plan, 99
Chicago 1992 Committee, 136
Chicago Area Republican Gay Organization, 190
Chicago Association of Neighborhood Development Organizations, 136
Chicago Bears, 202, 229
Chicago Black United Communities (CBUC), 117–18, 126, 133, 138
Chicago Board of Education, 17, 93, 121–22, 234, 236. *See also* Chicago Public Schools
Chicago Cardinals, 202
Chicago City Council, 4, 21, 61, 73, 80, 82, 91, 115, 123, 260, 262–63; Budget Committee, 189; Jane Byrne and, 107, 111, 123–24; Finance Committee, 149; independents on, 52, 103, 105; Latinos and, 44, 74, 115, 130, 170, 209, 211; remapping by, 114, 197; Rules Committee, 23; Eugene Sawyer and, 241, 244; Harold Washington and, 154, 161, 179, 192, 212, 214, 224. *See also* Council Wars; Democratic machine (Chicago)
Chicago Committee on Urban Opportunity, 29
Chicago Cubs, 198
*Chicago Defender*, 27, 60, 66, 142, 150, 161, 189
Chicago Federation of Labor, 139, 216
ChicagoFest, 125–26, 156, 217
Chicago Freedom Movement (CFM), 4, 16, 25, 30–31, 33, 45–46, 58, 64, 67, 82, 133, 265, 274n26. *See also* King, Martin Luther, Jr.; Raby, Al
Chicago Gay Alliance, 5
Chicago Health Department, 180, 187–89, 246
Chicago Housing Authority (CHA): Jane Byrne and, 110, 120, 122, 125; Eugene Sawyer and, 244; Harold Washington and, 174, 180, 183, 186, 208, 222, 228, 238. *See also* Cabrini-Green; Robinson, Renault

*Chicago Lawyer*, 155

Chicago League of Negro Voters, 25, 33

*Chicago Metro News*, 71

Chicago Peace Council, 36, 49

Chicago Police Board, 52, 261

Chicago Police Department: activism against, 33–34, 36, 41, 50–52, 59, 137, 208, 223, 260–62; African Americans and, 18, 23, 37, 52, 54–56, 58–59, 70, 121, 253; Jane Byrne and, 110, 112, 121, 139, 143; corruption of, 28, 35, 55, 57, 78, 103; explicit politics by, 83; gay men and, 140, 159, 182; general violence by, 39–40, 44, 54, 68, 183, 257, 260–61, 275n24; Latinos and, 32, 44–48, 85, 91, 157, 283n29; Red Squad of, 35, 49, 53; riots by, 17, 35–38; torture by, 41, 121, 130, 183, 257; Harold Washington and, 172, 179–84, 217, 257. *See also* Afro-American Patrolmen's League (AAPL); Burge, Jon; Red Squad; Rice, Fred

Chicago Public Schools: activist critique of, 59, 65, 69–70, 137, 156, 182, 223, 232–33; Jane Byrne and, 121; Richard M. Daley and, 254–55, 257–58; inequality in, 8, 17, 20, 29, 34–35, 82–83, 199, 253; student boycotts of, 23, 93; teachers strike and, 232–36, 258; Harold Washington and, 199, 228, 233–36, 258

*Chicago Reader*, 66–67, 84, 87, 155, 184, 242, 260

Chicago Real Estate Board, 17

Chicago Rehab Network, 99

*Chicago Reporter*, 154, 176, 198

Chicago School Finance Authority, 122

*Chicago Sun-Times*, 68, 79–80, 104, 142, 183, 211

Chicago Teachers Union, 216, 231–32, 258

Chicago Transit Authority, 93, 110, 122–23, 212, 216

*Chicago Tribune*: endorsements by, 66, 68, 106, 142, 222, 279n3; other editorializing by, 45, 67, 94, 104, 126–28, 151, 153, 164, 228, 250; reporting by, 23, 34, 79–86, 103–5, 109, 120, 131, 172–73, 178, 198,

205, 239, 244, 270n6, 280n6, 300n19. *See also* Axelrod, David; Jarrett, Vernon

Chicago Urban League, 21, 23, 124, 154, 234

Chicago White Sox, 198, 202, 229–30

Chicago Women's Liberation Union, 5

Chicago Workshop on Economic Development (CWED), 136–37, 200, 294n40

Chicago Works Together, 135, 200

Chicano: activists, 14–15, 25, 89, 93–96, 98, 100, 157, 254; movement, 91; as term, 11

Chico, Gery, 259

Chinatown, 201, 203

Chisholm, Shirley, 56

Ciccone, Richard, 105

Cicero, 237

Ciezadlo, Francis, 151

Cincotta, Gale, *173*

Cioch, Lois, 155

Cisneros, Henry, 207

Citizens Alert, 41, 52, 184

City Club of Chicago, 36

civil rights movement. *See* Black freedom struggle

Clark, Mark, 39, 49, 51–52, 54, 58, 180

Clark, Ramsey, 39

Claudio, Edwin, 123

Clay, Nate, 127

Cleaver, Eldridge, 14, 71

Clinton, Bill, 249, 253, 257, 271n21, 309n5, 312n37

Cloward, Richard, 125, 291n14

coalition-building, Black-Latino-white: about crime, 52, 55; CASA-HGT and, 98; challenge to redistricting, 123; contingency of, 4, 169, 225–28, 241–42, 247–49, 252; electoral, 25, 61, 65–66, 71, 75–77, 90–91, 103, 120; "fairness" and, 133, 136, 156, 174; Jesse Jackson and, 203–4, 237; Bayard Rustin and, 13–15; Harold Washington and, 1, 3–4, 6, 145–46, 152, 160, 189–90, 195, 210, 217, 222, 224, 263. *See also* Rainbow Coalition (1969); Rainbow Coalition (1984)

Coalition for the Election of Black Independent Aldermanic Candidates, 71
Coalition for United Community Action (CUCA), 51
Coalition of Black Trade Unionists, 54, 59, 139
Coalition of Labor Union Women, 98
Coalition to Stop Chicago 21, 99
Cohen, Christopher "Chris," 73, 75–78, 104, 283n29
Cohen, Curly, 124
Cohen, Lizabeth, 7
Cohen, Wilbur, 73
COINTELPRO (Counter Intelligence Program), 49
Cokely, Steve, 245
Coleman, Walter "Slim": Intercommunal Survival Committee and, 75, 77, 85–86, 100–101, 169, 196, 211, 262, 291n14; voter registration and, 124–25; Harold Washington and, 129, 221, 224
Commission on Gay and Lesbian Issues, 190, 243. See also gay men and lesbians; human rights ordinance
Commission on Human Relations, 45, 170
Committee for a Black Mayor, 59–61, 83–84
committeemen. See Cook County Democratic Committee
Commonwealth Edison, 229
Community Development Block Grants, 135, 200
Community for Creative Non-violence, 239
Community Renewal Society, 103, 198
Comprehensive Employment and Training Act (CETA), 99
Compton, James, 203
Concerned Citizens for Police Reform, 41, 55
condominium conversion, 67
Congressional Black Caucus, 54, 71, 143, 191
Congressional Quarterly, 129
Congress of Racial Equality, 14
"conservative colonia," 111, 157, 170

Conservative Vice Lords, 32
Consumers Tire & Supply Co., 176
Conyers, John, 191, 303n39
Cook County Board of Commissioners, 107, 155, 262
Cook County Board of Election Commissioners, 115, 125
Cook County Democratic Committee, 26, 54, 78, 80–81, 104, 107, 122, 132; committeeman's duties, 19–20; Harold Washington and, 147–49, 158, 177, 197, 207–10, 226, 240, 246. See also Democratic machine (Chicago)
Cook County Hospital, 127, 187
Coordinating Council of Community Organizations (CCCO), 24–25, 29–30, 64. See also Chicago Freedom Movement (CFM); Raby, Al
Corbett, Jim, 204
Corona, Bert, 94
Coronado, Linda, 262; CASA-HGT and, 89–90, 93, 95, 97; Independent Political Organization and, 113, 115, 138; MACLA and, 170, 207, 219, 220; Harold Washington and, 156–57, 167, 169
corruption, 130, 180; in housing, 110, 230; by machine, 28, 35, 78, 260, 263; in Mexico, 90; by police, 121, 182–84. See also Chicago Police Department; Democratic machine (Chicago)
Council Wars, 163–66, 169, 172, 193, 198, 208, 249, 251
Cousins, William "Bill," 35, 57, 59–60, 67
COVID-19 pandemic, 9
crack cocaine, 185, 217–18. See also War on Drugs
Cranston, Alan, 141, 143, 191
Creamer, Robert, 155
crime: Jane Byrne and, 120, 127, 217; in Chicago, 69–71, 74, 91, 140, 221–23, 234–35, 238; Richard J. Daley and, 51, 66; Richard M. Daley and, 130, 132, 252–53; nationally, 119, 250, 257; in popular culture, 65; Harold Washington and, 155, 164, 166, 179–85

Crisis Intervention Network, 185, 214

Crosstown Expressway, 54, 69, 99

Cruz, Arcelis, 44. *See also* Division Street uprising (1966)

Cuban Americans, 10, 108, 138, 151, 160, 198, 232, 254

Cullerton, Thomas, 164

Currie, Barbara Flynn, 129, 140

Daley, Bill, 259

Daley, Richard J., 95, 202, 272n22; 1919 riots, 17, 43; 1955 mayoral campaign of, 15, 21, 28, 86; 1963 mayoral campaign of, 28–29, 181; 1971 mayoral campaign of, 50–52, 191; 1975 mayoral campaign of, 65–66; African Americans and, 21, 51–52; Jane Byrne and, 106; crime and, 35–36; William Dawson and, 21; death of, 3, 79, 270n6; Ralph Metcalfe and, 54–55, *55*; as party kingmaker, 15, 19–20, 57–58, 205, 227; urban renewal and, 43, 199

Daley, Richard M., 8, 82, 223, *255*; 1983 mayoral campaign of, 119, 128, 130–32, 138–39, 141–42, 145–46, 191; 1989 mayoral campaign of, 211, 215, 244–47; African Americans and, 132, 254–55; Democratic machine and, 215, 226–27, 253–60; Latinos and, 254; as legislator, 130–31; as mayor, 227, 253–60; neoliberalism and, 249–50, 253–54; as state's attorney, 183–84

Damato, Frank, 210

Damski, Jon-Henri, 158

Dávila, Orlando, 46

Davis, Angela, *27*

Davis, Danny: as activist, 59, 103, 108; as alderman, 113–15, 140, 156, 169, 192, 214, 240, 246, 248; as congressman, 262; as mayoral candidate, 256, 259

Davis, Fania, *27*

Davis, Graciela Martinez, 157

Davis, Milton, 164

Davis, Sammy, Jr., 68

Dawson, William, 32, 35, 54, 64, 69, 273n12; Black submachine of, 19–22,

26, 118; Richard J. Daley and, 15, 21, 28, 40, 254

Deanes, James, 235

Dearborn Park. *See* Chicago 21 Plan

De Avila, Frank, 206

debates, 69, 142–43, 145–46, 196, 222–23, 283n29, 295n48

deindustrialization, 2, 6–7, 24, 66, 90, 119, 151, 166, 176, 179, 200, 233

Del Rey (tortilla factory), 98

del Valle, Miguel, 170, 203, 218–19, 247

Democratic Leadership Council (DLC), 249–50

Democratic machine (Chicago), 8, 18–20, 34, 49, 64, 78, 90, 106, 117, 128, 149, 260, 270n6. *See also* Burke, Edward "Ed"; Byrne, Jane; Cook County Democratic Committee; Daley, Richard J.; Daley, Richard M.; Vrdolyak, Edward "Ed"

Democratic National Convention (DNC), 14, 35–37, 40, 54, 57, 65, 180, 192–93

Department of Consumer Affairs, 172, 230, 243

Department of Consumer Sales, 106–7

Department of Economic Development, 199, 204, 217, 221

Deppe, Martin, 50

DePriest, Oscar, 18–19, 69

Despres, Leon, 23, 52, 64, 67–68, 110, 165, 241

Detroit, 5, 14–16, 44, 56, 65, 71, 122, 127, 142, 149, 151

Devine-Reed, Pat, 47

Dickerson, Earl, 21, *27*, 273n12

Dickson, Pat, 113

Diggs, Charles, 5, 14, 56–57

Division of Human Services, 174, 179

Division Street uprising (1966), 41, 44–45, 48, 89, 99, 276n10

Dobbins, Lucille, 172

Domico, Marco, 115, 208–10

Donahue, Gloria, 171

Douglas, Paul, 34

Douglass, Frederick, 59

Drake, St. Clair, 18, 22; *Black Metropolis*, 18

drugs. *See* War on Drugs
Dukakis, Michael, 237, 247, 249
Duncan, Arne, 258
Dunne, George, 107, 155

Earle, Peter, 123, 156–57, 170, 294n40
earthquake, in Mexico City, 199, 206
economic development, 136, 165, 179,
    199–200, 202, 204, 213, 217, 228, 255–56,
    259
Economic Research and Action Project,
    24
Edgewater, 115, 180
education summit, 233–35, 275n37. *See
    also* local school councils (LSCs)
Edwards, Lonnie, 174, 187–90, 246
Eighteenth Street Development Corpora-
    tion, 100, 198
electoral politics, 1–2, 5–6, 9, 21, 23, 32, 48,
    73–74, 207, 226; Blacks and, 14–16, 41,
    59–61, 68, 73, 89, 91; Latinos and, 41, 44,
    63, 95, 104. *See also* coalition-building,
    Black-Latino-white
Elrod, Richard, 105
Emanuel, Rahm, 2, 8, 258–62, 293n31
enterprise zones, 128, 136–37, 200, 294n40
environmental justice, 7, 263
Epton, Bernard "Bernie," 149–61, 164, 219
Equality Illinois, 254
Equal Rights Amendment (ERA), 60, 83,
    149
Evans, Tim, 72, 140, 212, 226, 240, *241*,
    246–48, 250–52, 259–60
Ewell, Raymond, 40

Farmer, James, 14
Fernández, Lilia, 43, 46
Ferré, Maurice, 177, 179
Fesperman, Bill "Preacherman," 48, 50, 74
Figueroa, Arcelis, 123
Figueroa, Raymond, 224
Finney, Leon, 234
Fletcher, Arthur, *27*
Flores, Claudio, 45
Floyd, George, 9
Fogel, David, 184

Foley, Michael, 271n20
Foner, Henry, 94
Ford, Gerald, 79
Forman, James, Jr., 257
fracturing. *See* gerrymandering
Fraga, Teresa, 92–93
France, Ervin, 55, 245
Franklin, Aretha, 86
Freedom of Information (FOI), 178–79
Freeman, Aaron, 163
Freeman, Charles, 33
Froebel Elementary School, 92
Frontenay, Hilda, 123
Frost, Wilson, 60, 80–81, 83, 108

Gage Park, 32, 127
Gaines, Brenda, 172
gangs, 4, 8; African Americans and, 40,
    51; Chicago Freedom Movement and,
    31–32; crime and, 120, 164, 179–80, 185,
    211, 217, 257; Latinos and, 44, 46, 92,
    168, 208; politics and, 75, 151, 196; white
    ethnics and, 17, 43, 48. *See also* Young
    Lords Organization
Garcia, Rick, 254
García, Jesus "Chuy," 202, 262; 1984
    committeeman campaign of, 208;
    1986 aldermanic campaign of, 197, 210;
    2015 mayoral campaign of, 2, 256, 259;
    background of, 207–8; CASA-HGT
    and, 89–91, 95–96, 108; Tim Evans and,
    247–48, 251; Independent Political
    Organization and, 113, 138; Harold
    Washington and, 146, 168–69, *197*, 210,
    219, 231, 240
Gardner, Ed, 126–27
Gardner, Joe, 185
Gary, Ind., 14, 41, 56, 71, 151, 298n4
gay men and lesbians, 4, 259; activism by,
    158, 182, 188–90, 246; Jane Byrne and,
    140, 158; Richard M. Daley and, 248,
    250, 254; Harold Washington and, 5,
    154, 158–60, 166, 170, 182–83, 188–90,
    219–20, 230–31, 242. *See also* human
    rights ordinance
Geary, Chuck, 75

Gellman, Erik, 30

gentrification, 5, 7, 24, 99, 136, 201, 252, 256

Gephardt, Dick, 223

gerrymandering, 90, 114

Giachello, Aida, 156

Giles, Percy, 197

Gill, Joseph, 207

Gilliam, Sharon Gist, 172, 213, 243–44

Giloth, Robert "Bob," 100, 201

Glenn, John, 191

Gold Coast, 26, 120, 150

Goldwater, Barry, 34

Gonzales, Mary, 93, 289n46

Goode, Wilson, 192, 309n5

*Good Times*, 120, 186

Gorbachev, Mikhail, 210

Gore, Al, 250

Great Depression, 119, 190, 203

Great Migration, 16

Green, Adam, 18, 273n22

Green, Paul, 3, 149, 216, 293n31

Gregory, Dick, 30, 34, 86

Grimshaw, Jacky, 133, 144, 161, 172, 223, 232, 245, 262

Grimshaw, William, 35, 66, 68

Gutiérrez, Luis, 262; 1984 committeeman campaign of, 158, 209; 1986 aldermanic campaign of, 195–97, 209–12; background of, 209; Richard M. Daley and, 247–48, 250, 252, 254; Eugene Sawyer and, 244–45; Harold Washington and, 157, *211*, 211–12, 231

Haggard, Merle, 101

Haider, Don, 222

Halpin, John, 222

Hamburg Club, 17, 43

Hampton, Fred: aftermath of death, 39–41, 49–52, 54, 58; assassination of, 38–39, 180; background of, 47; Black Panther Party and, 4, 47, 69–70, 271n16; political philosophy of, 40–41, 100, 281n16; Rainbow Coalition (1969) and, 38, 48, 71, 86

Hanrahan, Edward, 41, 52, 58, 66–67, 100

Hansbrough, Mac, 66

Hansen, Bernard, 223

*Harlan County, USA*, 101

Harold Washington Party, 246, 250

Harrison High School, 92, 98, 138

Hart, Gary, 191

Hasbro/Playskool factory, 201

Hatcher, Richard, 5, 14, 56, 191, 303n39

Hayes, Charles, 59–60, 8, 85, 98, 139, 175

Head Start, 30

Heart of Uptown Coalition, 100, 124, 143–44, 158, 169, 196, 211. *See also* Coleman, Walter "Slim"; Intercommunal Survival Committee (ISC)

Henry, Bill, 242

Hill, John, 52

Hinojosa, Raúl, 156

Hirsch, Arnold, 26

Hispanic, as term, 10

Hispanic Democratic Organization, 254

Holewinski, Michael, 105, 179–80, 184

Holli, Melvin, 3, 149, 216, 293n31

Holman, Claude, 25

*Hoop Dreams*, 120

Hoover, J. Edgar, 49

Horowitz, Michael, 105

Horton, Willie, 151, 249

Horwitz, Izzy, 26

Houlihan, James, 105

housing, 14; activism, 26, 54, 74, 99–100, 140, 200–201, 231, 236; affordable, 67, 91, 98, 135, 156, 211, 214, 260, 262–63; deteriorating, 16–17, 43–45, 119, 123, 136, 238; as electoral issue, 25, 28, 34; open, 19, 21, 32, 82; segregation, 15, 23, 35, 43. *See also* Chicago Housing Authority (CHA); gentrification; urban renewal

Houston, 5, 15, 100

Howard, T. R. M., 22

Howell Barrett, Brenetta, 27, 262; activism of, 78, 83; as department head, 230, 243; 1964 congressional campaign of, 13; Protest at the Polls and, 13, 26; Harold Washington and, 85, 167, 172

Howlett, Michael, 78
Hulett, John, 14
Hull House, 43, 92
human rights ordinance, 228, 242
Humboldt Park, 111, 198–99, 227; activism
    in, 123; arson in, 137; Division Street
    uprising in, 32, 41, 45; Luis Gutiérrez in,
    195–96, 209; Puerto Rican migration
    to, 44, 114; Harold Washington cam-
    paign in, 154, 156, 218, 224
Humes, Marian, 140, 175
Hunt, D. Bradford, 238
Hyde, Henry, 159
Hyde Park, 67–69, 77, 127–28, 140, 149, 160,
    175, 202, 280n10
Hynes, Thomas, 215, 222

Illinois Bell, 134
Illinois Gay and Lesbian Task Force, 189
Illinois General Assembly, 89–91, 95, 136,
    155, 209, 230, 235
Illinois Public Action Council, 155
immigration: African, 206; Central
    American, 156, 204–5; as electoral
    issue, 166, 219; European, 42–43, 93,
    286n20; Mexican, 90, 94–97; opposi-
    tion to, 138, 205–6; reform, 96, 129, 192,
    206
Immigration and Naturalization Service
    (INS), 94, 205
Immigration Reform and Control Act of
    1986 (IRCA), 206. See also Simpson-
    Mazzoli Act
independent movement. See Chicago
    League of Negro Voters; Protest at the
    Polls
Independent Political Organization of
    the Near West Side (IPO), 91, 98, 113–15,
    123, 136, 138, 144, 169, 203, 208, 211
Independent Precinct Organization
    (IPO), 65, 75, 113
Independent Voters of Illinois (IVI), 65,
    71, 85, 113, 130, 177
infant mortality, 137, 188, 231
Innis-Jiménez, Michael, 42

Institutional Revolutionary Party (PRI),
    90
Intercommunal Survival Committee
    (ISC), 5, 75–77, 85–86, 102, 104. See
    also Coleman, Walter "Slim"; Heart of
    Uptown Coalition; Keep Strong (maga-
    zine); Shiller, Helen
Interfaith Organizing Project, 229
International Ladies Garment Workers
    Union (ILGWU), 97–98, 138, 286n20
Iran-Contra Affair, 213, 237

Jackson, Jesse: 1971 mayoral campaign,
    50, 191; 1984 presidential campaign, 7,
    47, 141, 191–93; 1988 presidential cam-
    paign, 7, 47, 237–39, 247; ChicagoFest
    and, 125–26; National Black Political
    Convention, 14, 56–57; Operation
    Breadbasket and, 32, 50, 53; Operation
    PUSH, 53, 72, 74, 114; other activism
    and, 49, 51, 57, 59, 65, 68, 98, 241, 246;
    Harold Washington and, 129, 141, 146,
    151, 153–54, 192, 297n12. See also Rain-
    bow Coalition (1984)
Jackson, J. H., 216
Jackson, Johnnie, 98
Jackson, Maynard, 191, 301n29
Jackson Park, 202
James, Mike, 239
Janney, Albert, 22
January 6 insurrection, 263
Jarrett, Vernon, 57, 68, 98, 106, 108–10,
    121–22, 143, 211
Jefferson, Nancy, 59, 83, 110, 124, 140, 171,
    180, 181, 229, 246
Jiménez, José "Cha-Cha," 78; background
    of, 46; 1975 aldermanic campaign,
    63–64, 67, 73–77, 91, 101, 104, 283n29;
    Rainbow Coalition (1969) and, 47;
    Harold Washington and, 85, 90, 137,
    139, 144, 158, 167–68; Young Lords and,
    44, 46–47, 76, 252. See also Lake View;
    Lincoln Park; Rainbow Coalition
    (1969); urban renewal; Young Lords
    Organization

jobs. *See* affirmative action;
  unemployment
Johnson, Bennett, 22–23, 26, 33
Johnson, Cedric, 4
Johnson, Irene, 238
Johnson, Lyndon Baines, 13, 29–30, 34, 73,
  82, 276n11
Jones, Carter, 23, 25–26
Jones, Robert, 180
Joravsky, Ben, 255

Kass, John, 239
Katz, Michael, 5
Keane, Tom, 57, 78, 114
*Keep Strong* (magazine), 77, 86, 101–2,
  104–5, 108
Kellam, Robert, 197, 209
Kelley, Clifford, 140
Kelly, Ed (mayor), 19
Kelly, Ed (parks superintendent), 149, 212
Kennedy, Edward "Ted," 79, 112, 141, 148,
  157, 190–91, 223
Kennedy, Eugene, 131–32
Kennedy, John F., 106, 276n11
Kennedy, Robert F., 36, 276n11
Kennelly, Martin, 21, 28, 154
Kenwood-Oakland Community Organi-
  zation, 99, 239
*Ketchum v. Byrne*, 123, 130, 197–99, 209
*Ketchum v. City Council of Chicago*, 123,
  130, 197–99, 209
King, Coretta Scott, 191
King, Martin Luther, Jr., 6, 13, 51, 67;
  Chicago Freedom Movement and, 4,
  30–33, *31*, 54; death of, 36, 47; Al Raby
  and, 25, 45, 68. *See also* Jackson, Jesse;
  Raby, Al
Kissinger, Clark, 36
Kleppner, Paul, 126, 159, 250, 280n5
Klinenberg, Eric, 257
Knauss, Peter, 87
Knoxville, Tenn., 203
Kool and the Gang, 126
Kotlowitz, Alex, 234
Kozol, Jonathan, 234

Kozubowski, Walter, 81, 219
Kretzmann, John, 178–79

labor unions, 24, 54, 83, 90, 98, 190, 237,
  258; African Americans and, 21–22, 98,
  123, 139, 182, 232, 235, 258; Democratic
  machine and, 64, 87, 90, 139, 176; elec-
  toral politics, 13, 27, 54, 59; Latinos and,
  94, 97, 286n20; Harold Washington
  and, 123, 139, 216, 232
Ladky, Ann, 140
Lake Calumet, 204
Lakefront liberals, 65, 154, 160, 295n54.
  *See also* gay men and lesbians; Singer,
  William "Bill"
Lake View, 44, 73–74, 76, 137, 202, 205, 252
Lanahan, Kathy, 171
Lane, Vincent, 244
Langford, Anna, 59, 67, 78, 161, 251
La Raza Unida party, 15, 94
Laroche, Gwendolyn, 234
Latin American Defense Organization
  (LADO), 46, 54
Latin American Recruitment Program,
  92
Latino, as term, 10
Latino Institute, 46, 203, 233
Latinos for Political Progress (LPP), 123
Latinx, as term, 10
Lathrop, Ross, 68–69, 77, 280n9
LaVelle, Avis, 249
Leadership Council for Metropolitan
  Open Communities, 32
League of United Latin American Citi-
  zens (LULAC), 142, 192, 195
Learning Works Compact, 233
LeClaire Courts, 113, 238
Lee, Bobby, 38, 47–48, 50
Legal Assistance Foundation, 115
Lesbian/Gay Progressive Democratic
  Organization, 242
Levin, Ellis, 104–5
Levison, Stanley, 32
Lewis, Ben, 26
Lightfoot, Lori, 3, 8–9, 259–61

Lincoln Park, 42, 44, 46–48, 136, 252

Little Village (South Lawndale), 41, 43, 94, 98, 113–15, 138, 154, 156, 160, 168, 197, 201, 218

local school councils (LSCs), 235–36, 243, 254, 258

Logan Square, 44, 48, 126, 154

Loop, 11, 16, 43, 46, 69, 73, 99, 127, 133, 135, 199–200, 255–56

López Zacarías, Obed, 46

Los Angeles, 5, 16, 43, 157, 209; Black mayor in, 15, 71, 130, 298n4; Chicanos and, 93–94; police violence in, 183, 185; white mayor in, 228, 309n5

Love, Ruth, 122

Lowndes County Freedom Organization, 14

Lozano, Emma, 168, 247, 262

Lozano, Guadalupe "Lupe," 212, 224, 247

Lozano, Rudy, 89, 108, 247, 262; background of, 91–92; CASA-HGT and, 93–94, *95*, 96; death of, 168–69; Independent Political Organization and, 91, 113–15, 123; labor movement and, 97–98, 113; 1983 aldermanic campaign of, 115, 138–39, 207; Harold Washington and, 116, 129, 138, *139*, 140, 146, 154, 156–57

*Lu's Notebook*, 134

machine. *See* Democratic machine (Chicago)

MACLA. *See* Mayor's Advisory Commission on Latino Affairs (MACLA)

Majerczyk, Aloysius, 149

Malcolm X, 13, 46

Mann, Bob, 129

Martin, LeRoy, 243–44, 257

Martinez, Elena, 108, 111, 157, 289n46

Martinez, Joseph, 111–12, 123–24

Marzullo, Vito, 110, 115, 138, 147, 149, 208–10

Masotti, Louis, 110

mass incarceration, 186, 217, 257

Mattachine Society, 52

Mayer, Jane, 221

Mayor's Advisory Commission on Women's Affairs, 171, *173*

Mayor's Advisory Commission on Latino Affairs (MACLA), 129, 169–70, 172–73, 188, 203–4, 219, 231

Mayor's Policy Advisory Cabinet, 172

McBride, Art, 115

McCarthy, Gerry, 259

McClain, Clarence, 178

McCormick Place, 161, 243

McCormick Theological Seminary, 47, 99

McDermott, John, 154

McDonald, Laquan, 261–62, 278n27

McFerren, Coretta, 235

McGovern, George, 57, 65, 79

McMillen, Thomas, 114

McNeil, E. Duke, 59

Medicaid, 90, 112, 188

Medical Committee on Human Rights, 54

Merton, Thomas, 46

Metcalfe, Ralph, 103, 146, 254, 262; background of, 20, 54; Democratic machine and, 21, 35, 39–40, *55*, 57, 59–61, 64; police violence and, 40–41, 54–56; Harold Washington and, 33, 83–84

Mexican Independence Day Parade, 197–98

Mexican Revolution, 42, 90

Mexico City, 199, 206, 285n3

Midway Airport, 205–6, 230

Midway Plaisance, 202

Midwest Coalition for the Defense of Immigrants, 95, 115, 205

Midwest Community Council, 124, 171, 229

Midwest Voter Registration Project, 127

Mier, Robert "Rob," 137, 167, 199–202, 204, 217, 221, 243, 256, 294n40

Millennium Park, 256

Miller, Alton, 240

Milwaukee, 101, 176

Mississippi, 14, 16, 22, 25, 30–31, 65, 82, 112, 271n16

Mississippi Freedom Democratic Party, 14, 65
Mitchell, Arthur, 19–20
Model Cities, 75, 282n27
Moe, Kari, 137, 172, 201, 206, *243*, 262
Mojica, David, 167
Mondale, Walter, 141, 152, 157, 190–93, 236
Montes, Peggy, 171, *173*, 175
Montgomery, James, 174
Moore, Joe, 259
Morales, Jorge: activism of, 102–3, 108, 111, 123–24, 294n40; background of, 101–2; Harold Washington and, 129, 137, 156, 170, 199
Morrow, Richard, 233
Moyers, Bill, 29
Mujeres Latinas en Acción, 93, 96
Muñoz, Marcos, 75
Munyon, Thomas, 44
Mustin, Ronnell, 113, 208

Nash, Pat, 19
*Nashville*, 101
Natarus, Burton, 213–14
National Association for the Advancement of Colored People (NAACP), 24, 26, 39–40, 47
National Black Political Convention (1972), 5, 14, 41, 56, 71, 191
National Black United Front, 226, 248
National Hispanic Leadership Conference, 192
National Negro Congress, 20
National Organization for Women (NOW), 140
Native Americans, 59, 73, 75
Navarro, Javier, 75
Navy Pier, 202, 217
Neal, Steve, 251
Negro Labor Relations League, 20
neighborhoods: African American, 16–18, 23–24, 93, 98, 126, 256, 260; Latino, 45–46, 111, 137–38, 154, 156, 199, 260; middle class, 252; white, 42, 151; working class, 72, 74, 84, 127, 212, 221, 258

"neighborhoods first" rhetoric, 11, 104, 135–37, 180, 199–203, 204, 214, 227, 229
Neighborhoods Task Force, 199
Neistein, Bernie, 26
neoliberalism, 166, 253, 260. *See also* Daley, Richard M.
Netsch, Dawn Clark, 96, 140
Newark, 5, 14, 71
New Deal, 6–7, 19
Newhouse, Richard, 32, 57, 59, 60–61, 66, 84, 123, 146
New Orleans, 160, 203, 298n4
Newton, Huey, 71
New York City, 14, 43, 47, 50, 101, 157, 163, 183, 186, 309n5, 310n21
Nixon, Richard, 37, 52, 56–58, 65, 122, 149
Nolan, Sam, 121
Norgle, Charles, 197
Northwest Hispanic Democratic Coalition, 156
North Lawndale, 31, *113*
nuclear freeze movement, 7

Oakland, Calif., 71, 101, 122, 271n16, 282n27
Obama, Barack, 2, 3, 8, 216, 232, 258–59
Obejas, Achy, 219–20, 242
Oberman, Marty, 140
O'Brien, Thomas, 26
Odom, Herbert, 55
Office for Professional Standards (OPS), 182–84
O'Hare International Airport, 108, 176, 205, 230
Old Town, 46, 182
O'Neill, Tip, 124
Operation Bootstrap, 42
Operation Breadbasket, 32, 50, 53, 102, 291n17
Operation PUSH, 72, 84, 114, 125, 127, 233, 246, 291n17
Orange, James, 45
Ordower, Sid, 171
Orr, David, 140, 214, 226, 240, 251, 262

Padilla, Felix, 45

Palmer, Edward "Buzz," 36–37

Palmer, Jorja, 117, 119

Palmer, Lutrelle "Lu," 58, 273n12, 290n4; activism of, 117–19, 124, 127, 138, 204; Jane Byrne and, 120–21; Jesse Jackson and, 192; Eugene Sawyer and, 245; Harold Washington and, *119*, 124, 129, 133–34, 149, 167, 174–75, 177, 219, 231. *See also* Chicago Black United Communities (CBUC)

Parent Community Council (PCC), 234–35

Parent Teacher Association (PTA), 24, 26

Parker, Charles Mack, 25

Partnership for Education Progress, 233

Pauley, Randy, 206

Peace and Freedom Party, 14, 71

People's Church, *76*

People's Coalition for Education Reform, 235

People's Coalition to Boycott Chicago-Fest, 126

People's Movement for Voter Registration, 124. *See also* voter registration

People's Organization for Welfare Economic Reform (POWER), 124–25, 127

Percy, Charles, 34, 82

Philadelphia, 5, 30, 65, 148, 160, 185, 192, 228, 309n5

Pilsen, 97, 111, 168, 180; activism in, 91–96, 98–99, 113–14, 207–8; electoral politics in, 115, 138, 154, 156, 160; Mexican migration to, 41, 43; Harold Washington, 198–99, 218, 227; World's Fair and, 138, 200–201, 203–4

Pilsen Neighbors Community Council, 93, 96, 98, 103, 204

Pincham, Eugene, 218

"pinstripe patronage," 8, 259

Piven, Frances Fox, 125, 291n14

Plank, Betty, 52

Police Accountability Task Force, 261

police violence, 5–7, 32, 39–41, 44–45, 51, 54, 68, 121, 130, 137, 183–84, 211, 257, 260–62. *See also* Chicago Police Department

Political Action Organization (PAO), 123

political classes. *See* Chicago Black United Communities (CBUC); Palmer, Lutrelle "Lu"

Political Education Project (PEP), 185

Poor People's Coalition of Lincoln Park, 47

Preckwinkle, Toni, 3, 235, 259–60, 262

Prieto, Jorge, 157

Proposition 13, 107

Protest at the Polls, 26–27, 33, 58, 63, 120

Public Action, 155

public health, 2, 8, 187–88, 289n46

Pucinski, Roman, 64, 82–83, 86

Puerto Rican Defense Committee, 78, 167

Puerto Rican People's Day Parade and Festival, 198

Quinley, Darrell, 77

Raby, Al: Chicago Freedom Movement and, 24–25; Martin Luther King Jr. and, 25, 30–32, *31*; 1975 aldermanic campaign of, 64, 67–69, 71–72, 74, 77, 86, 280n9; Harold Washington and, 133–34, 146, 152–54, 174–75, 265. *See also* Coordinating Council of Community Organizations (CCCO)

Rainbow Coalition (1969), 4, 40–41, 47–50, 54, 58, 64–65, 71–73, 86, 277n16. *See also* Black Panther Party; Hampton, Fred; Young Lords Organization; Young Patriots

Rainbow Coalition (1984), 192, 237

Rakove, Milton, 19

Ralph, Laurence, 183

Ramos, Manuel, 47

Raspberry, William, 191–92

Rayner, A. A. "Sammy," 26, 35–36, 75

Raza Unida, La, 15, 94

Reagan, Ronald, 1–2, 249, 253; 1980 presidential campaign of, 112, 149–50, 296n7;

Reagan, Ronald (*continued*)
1984 presidential campaign of, 141, 190–91, 193; Age of Reagan, as term, 6–7, 271n18; AIDS policy and, 189; Cold War and, 205–6, 210; federal budget and, 7, 112, 186–88, 213, 237–38; as governor, 34, 107; immigration and, 205–6; Iran-Contra and, 213; race and, 7, 112–14, 123, 129, 166–67, 216, 271n21; War on Drugs and, 181, 185; Harold Washington and, 7–8, 129, 143, 148, 165, 232
Red Lion, 239
Red Squad, 35, 40, 49, 52–53, 181, 217, 278n24
Reed, Adolph, 6
Regional Council of Negro Leadership, 22
Regional Transit Authority, 101
Republican Party (Chicago), 17, 56, 78, 150, 177. *See also* Reagan, Ronald; Thompson, James "Big Jim"
*Return of the Jedi*, 163
Reyes, Benjamin, 170–72, 231
Reynolds, Barbara, 63
Rice, Fred, 174, 180–85, 217
riots, 16–18, 40, 45, 276n11. *See also* uprisings
*Rising Up Angry* (newspaper), 63, 74, 101
Rising Up Angry (organization), 48, 54
Rivera, Modesto "Mo," 158, 167–68, 196, 266
Rivlin, Gary, 33, 107, 125, 146, 270n6, 275n44, 290n4, 297n12
Rizzo, Frank, 65
Robert Taylor Homes, 72, 121, 145, 186
Robinson, Renault, 129, 151; Afro-American Patrolmen's League and, 33, 36–37, 85; Chicago Housing Authority and, 110, 120, 122, 174, 186–87; as Washington campaign manager, 133
Rockefeller, Nelson, 79
Rodriguez, William Emilio, 44, 73
Roeser, Tom, 243
Rogers Park, 214, 239, 259

Roman Catholics, 17, 24, 44, 52, 54, 79, 82, 106, 112, 151–52, 154, 160, 233
Roosevelt, Franklin, 19
Roosevelt University, 22, 70
*Roots*, 101
Rose, Don, 33, 87, 108, 140, 260
Rosen, Frank, 115
Rostenkowski, Dan, 149, 158, 209, 215, 247
Royko, Mike, 80, 150, 153, 190
Rush, Bobby, 262; 1975 aldermanic campaign of, 64–65, 67, 69–72, 75; 1983 aldermanic campaign of, 161; 1999 mayoral campaign of, 253, 259; Black Panther Party and, 47, 50, 51, 57, 70, 74, 281n16; other independent politics, 78, 246
Rush University Medical Center, 229
Rustin, Bayard, 13–16, 272n2, 272n4

Sable, Ron, 189
Sain, Kevin, 109
Sampson, Al, 117
San Antonio, Tex., 130, 207, 288n38, 292n28, 298n4
Sanchez, Alfred, 223
sanctuary movement, 7, 129, 156, 199, 204–6, 219, 262
Santiago, Miguel, 170, 197, 199, 209
Satter, Beryl, 35
Savage, Gus, 1, 22, 26, 33, 80–81, 83–84
Save Our Neighborhoods, 221
Sawyer, David, 131–32
Sawyer, Eugene: as acting mayor, 227, 235, 240, 241, 242–44, 258; becoming acting mayor, 8, 225–26; gay rights and, 242–44; lack of leadership skills of, 226, 235, 242, 244–46; 1989 mayoral campaign of, 245–52, 254; Harold Washington and, 140, 225, 240
Saxbe, William, 94
schools. *See* boycott; Chicago Board of Education; Chicago Public Schools; education summit
Schulter, Eugene, 223
Seale, Bobby, 71, 271n16

segregation, 15, 17–18, 23, 29–30, 48, 82, 122, 257. *See also* Chicago Housing Authority (CHA); Chicago Public Schools; housing

Sellers, Cleveland, 14

Shakman, Michael, 177

Shakman decree, 177–78, 254

Shaw, Robert, 148, 244–45

Sherman, Niles, 177

Shiller, Helen: 1978 aldermanic campaign of, *102*, 104–5; 1979 aldermanic campaign of, 105, 108; 1987 aldermanic campaign of, 224; activism of, 77, 85, 100–101, 169, 291n14; as alderman, 240, 251, 262; background of, 101; Harold Washington and, 143–44, 146, 179, 223, 228, 254. *See also* Intercommunal Survival Committee (ISC); *Keep Strong* (magazine)

Shuttlesworth, Fred, 25

Siegel, Paul, 75–76, 78, 101, 140, 146, 158

Simon, Paul, 193, 247

Simpson, Dick, 52, 67, 74–75, 103, 108, 110, 140, 178, 205, 244, 260, 262

Simpson, Rosie, 24

Simpson-Mazzoli Act, 129, 192. *See also* Immigration Reform and Control Act of 1986 (IRCA)

Singer, William "Bill," 57, 60–61, 65–67, 84, 104–5, 110, 252, 279n3

Sive-Tomashefsky, Rebecca, 140, 212

Sloan, Norm, 242

Smith, Ed, 192

Smith, Zirl, 187

Snyder, Mitch, 239

Socialist Workers Party, 148

Soft Sheen Products, 126–27

Solidarity Party, 223

Soliz, Juan: 1982 legislative campaign of, 91, 114–16, 138; 1986 aldermanic campaign of, 196, 209–10, 215; Harold Washington and, *139*

South Africa, 7, 206, 231

South Armour Square, 202

South Chicago, 43, 156–57

Southern Christian Leadership Conference (SCLC), 30–32, 45, 49, 53, 64, 248, 291n17. *See also* Chicago Freedom Movement (CFM); King, Martin Luther, Jr.

South Shore, 67, 164

Spanish Coalition for Housing, 46, 99–100

Spanish Coalition for Jobs, 46, 99, 103

Springfield. *See* Illinois General Assembly

St. Louis, 202, 238

Stamps, Marion, 121, 124, 140, *141*, 251

Starks, Robert (priest), 97–98

Starks, Robert (professor), 108, 117–18, 163, 174–75, 224, 228, 254, 262

State of the Black Economy Symposium, 27

Stemberk, Frank, 138, 207–8, 210

Stevenson, Adlai, III, 125, 128, 141

Stevenson, Lynward, 29–30

Stewart-Winter, Timothy, 182

Stone, Chuck, 63, 303n39

Strategic Defense Initiative, 190

Streeter, Allan, 114, 122, 192

Student Nonviolent Coordinating Committee, 6, 13, 47, 271n16

Students for a Democratic Society, 24, 30

Summerdale police scandal, 28, 181

Summit Agreement (1966), 32, 275n37. *See also* Chicago Freedom Movement (CFM)

Super Bowl, 229

Swibel, Charles, 110, 186–87. *See also* Chicago Housing Authority (CHA)

Task Force for Black Empowerment, 124, 134, 144, 154, 174–75, 224, 246

Task Force for Youth Crime Prevention, 179

Taste of Chicago. *See* ChicagoFest

taxes, 28, 79, 83, 94, 127, 136–38, 149, 256, 260, 271n20; Ronald Reagan and, 107, 112, 188, 190, 253; Harold Washington and, 122–23, 142, 150, 158, 161, 179, 213–14, 221–24, 228–30, 252 tax-increment financing (TIF), 229, 256, 268

Taylor, Flint, 184

Taylor, James, 96–97

teachers strike, 234, 257–58. *See also* Chicago Teachers Union

*Tennessee v. Garner*, 183

Terkel, Studs, 79

Terry, Peggy, 71, 272n3

The Woodlawn Organization (TWO), 24, 29, 234, 291n12

Thomas, John, 223

Thompson, James "Big Jim," 78, 127–28, 213, 215

Thompson, William "Big Bill," 17–18, 147, 179

Thurman, Hy, 48

Tijerina, Reies López, 14, 272n3

Till, Emmett, 22

Tillman, Dorothy, 218, 231

Tlatelolco Massacre, 90

Todd-Breland, Elizabeth, 122, 236

Torres, Manny, 195–97, 211

Torres, Maria Los Angeles "Nena," 129, 138, 156–57, 169–72, 175, 188, *220*, 225, 231–32, 254, 262. *See also* Mayor's Advisory Commission on Latino Affairs (MACLA)

torture, 41, 121, 130, 181, 183–84, 227, 257. *See also* Burge, Jon; Chicago Police Department; police violence

Town Meeting, 189–90

Travis, Dempsey, 239

Tucker, Robert, 84

Turner, Art, 115, 169

Turnock, Bernard, 188

UIC (University of Illinois Chicago), 92, 94, 98, 103, 199, 207–8, 222, 229, 251, 295n50

Underground Railroad, 205

unemployment, 13, 24, 94, 125, 127, 132, 190, 238; among African Americans, 45, 48, 178, 199, 233; among Latinos, 42, 74, 85, 102–3, 137, 199, 233

United Black Voters of Illinois (UBVI), 78

United Center, 256

United Electricians, 115

United Farm Workers, 75, 97

United Packinghouse Workers, 24, 59

United Presbyterian Church, 47

United Steel Workers of America, 24

University of Chicago, 24, 64, 67–68, 149

University of Illinois Chicago (UIC), 92, 94, 98, 103, 199, 207–8, 222, 229, 251, 295n50

uprisings, 31, 36, 41, 44–45, 48, 89, 99, 102

Uptown, 24, 48, 71, 73–75, 179, 224, 262; activist coalition in, 85, 100–102, 124, 126, 143–44, 158, 169, 196, 211

Urban Institute, 213

urban renewal, 5, 24, 29, 43, 47, 54, 59, 67, 74, 77, 85; as political issue, 91–92, 137, 229, 256; Young Lords and, 46–48, 77. *See also* Jiménez, José "Cha-Cha"; University of Illinois Chicago (UIC)

U.S. Civil Rights Commission, 23

U.S. Department of Housing and Urban Development, 186

U.S. Office of Education, 25

Vallas, Paul, 259

Van Dyke, Jason, 261, 278n27

Vargas Llosa, Mario, 90

Vasquez, Arturo, 113, 136, 200, 207, 245, 294n40

Vaughn, Jacqueline, 235

Velasquez, Carmen, 289n46

Velasquez, Juan, 140, 146, 169–70, 197, 208–10

Vietnam War, 13, 30, 34, 36–37, 57, 71, 82

Villalobos, Raul, 111

Vivian, C. T., 51

voter registration, 32, 242, 248, 271n16; in 1975 campaigns, 64, 68, 74–75, 77; in 1983 campaigns, 104, 113, 124–27, 129, 134, 136, 138, 291n14, 291n20; by ACORN, 124, 291n13

Voting Rights Act of 1965, 14, 33, 114, 129–30, 199

Vrdolyak, Edward "Ed": 1987 mayoral campaign of, 215–16, 222–24; 1989 mayoral campaign of, 250–51; appeals to racism, 144, 148, 151, 166, 222–23, 249; as Jane Byrne ally, 110, 128, 131, 138, 144, 149; Council Wars and, 164, *165*, 166, 193, 210; Bernard Epton and, 147–49; Eugene Sawyer and, 225–26; Harold Washington and, 157, 172, 193, 196, 211–12, 260; as Young Turk, 81
"Vrdolyak Twenty-Nine," 164. *See also* Council Wars

Walker, Dan, 67–69, 78
Walls, Bill, 219
Ware, Flo, 272n3
Ware, William "Bill," 154, 169–70, 174
War on Drugs, 181, 185, 206, 271n21
War on Poverty, 29–30, 73
Warren, Ed, 148
Washington, D.C., 150, 170, 185, 193, 209, 298n4, 300n15, 300n18
Washington, Harold: 1977 mayoral campaign of, 64, 82–86, 106; 1983 mayoral primary campaign of, 1–4, 9, 118–20, 123–46 passim; 1983 mayoral general campaign of, 147–61 passim; 1987 mayoral primary campaign of, 217–22; 1987 mayoral general campaign of, 222–24; AIDS policy and, 187–89; announces historic mayoral run, 128–29; background of, 22, 33, 54; budget and, 163, 179, 213; charisma of, 3, 33, 146, 226, 244, 248; as congressman, 129–30; crime and, 155, 164, 166, 179–85; death of, 240; Democratic machine and, 84–85, 104–5; education and, 232–36; Jesus "Chuy" García and, 146, 168–69, *197*, 210, 219, 231, 240; gay rights and, 166, 188–89, *243*; health of, 239–40; housing and, 174, 186–87, 238–39; immigration and, 204–7; Jesse Jackson and, 153–54, 190–92, 236–37; José "Cha-Cha" Jiménez and, 85, 90, 137, 139, 144, 158, 167–68; Latinos and, 78, 96–97, 113, 115, 137–38, 156–58, 167–71, 195–210 passim, *211*, 218–19, 231–32; legacy of, 254–57, 262–63; Rudy Lozano and, 116, 129, 138, *139*, 140, 146, 154, 156–57; in mayoral debate, 142; Ralph Metcalfe and, 33, 54, 60, 83–84; neighborhoods and, 11, 104, 135–37, 180, 199–203, 204, 214, 227, 229; police department and, 180–86; Ronald Reagan and, 7–8, 129–30, 190–92; Helen Shiller and, 143–44, 146, 179, 223, 228, 254; as state legislator, 33, 40, 49, 139; target of racism, 144, 151–52, 164, 223; at University of Illinois Chicago rally, 143; voting rights and, 130; Ed Vrdolyak and, 144, 164, *165*, 223–24; whites and, 144, 151–52, 221; women and, 139, *141*, 171–73, *181*, 221
Washington, Roy, 20
"Washington Papers," 134–35
Waste Management, 176
Watergate, 65, 79
Watts, Los Angeles, 44
Webb, Dan, 114
W. E. B. Du Bois Club, 30
Weed, Susan, 185
welfare, 24, 27, 166, 249, 253; activism around, 46, 53–54, 69, 77, 100–101, 112, 125, 291n14
Wellington Avenue United Church of Christ, 205
Westside Coalition for Unity and Political Action, 164
West Side Jobs Retention Network, 201
West Town, 44, 99, 114, 156–57, 199, 214
Westtown Concerned Citizens Coalition (WCCC), 100–101, 111
White City, 203, 304n12
Wigoda, Paul, 57
Wilhelm, David, 249, 312n37
Wilkins, Roy, 39
Williams, Eugene, 17
Williams, Sidney, 68
Williams, Wayne, 301n29
Willis, Benjamin "Ben," 23–24, 27
Willmott, Peter, 233

Wilson, Ben, 179

Wilson, Joan, 164

Women Embarrassed by Byrne, 221

Women's Network for Washington, 139, 171, *181*

Women Strike for Peace, 24

Women United for a Better Chicago (WUBC), 171

Wonder, Stevie, 126

World's Columbian Exposition (1893), 202–3

World's Fair (1933, 1982, 1984), 203

World's Fair (1992), 135–36, 200, 202–4, 214, 260, 266

Worrill, Conrad, 117, 192, 224, 226, 248

Wrigley Field, 202

Wrigleyville, 202, 252

Wyatt, Addie, 83, 110, 171–72, 212, 221, 224, 246

Wyatt, Claude, 246

Young, Andrew, *31*, 68, 191

Young, Coleman, 56–57, 192

Young, Quentin, 54

Young Lords Organization, 5, 49, *76*, 78, 167, 277n16; background of, 40, 44, 46; Rainbow Coalition (1969), 47–48, 73; urban renewal and, 47, 99, 252. *See also* Jiménez, José "Cha-Cha"

Young Patriots, 5, 40, 48, 74

Zimmerman, Bill, 152